MANAGING MULTIVENDOR NETWORKS

MANAGING MULTIVENDOR NETWORKS

Written by John Enck and Dan W. Blacharski

Managing Multivendor Networks

Library of Congress Catalog No.: 97-65030

ISBN: 0-7897-1179-6

99 98 97   6 5 4 3 2 1

Interpretation of the printing code: the rightmost double-digit number is the year of the book's printing; the rightmost single-digit number, the number of the book's printing. For example, a printing code of 97-1 shows that the first printing of the book occurred in 1997.

Screen reproductions in this book were created using Collage Plus from Inner Media, Inc., Hollis, NH.

Credits

PRESIDENT
Roland Elgey

PUBLISHING DIRECTOR
Brad R. Koch

EDITORIAL SERVICES DIRECTOR
Elizabeth Keaffaber

MANAGING EDITOR
Michael Cunningham

DIRECTOR OF MARKETING
Lynn E. Zingraf

ACQUISITIONS MANAGER
Elizabeth A. South

PRODUCT DEVELOPMENT MANAGER
Lisa Wagner

PRODUCT DIRECTOR
Carolyn L. Kiefer

PRODUCT DEVELOPMENT SPECIALIST
Kevin Kloss

PRODUCTION EDITOR
Brian Sweany

EDITORS
Lisa M. Gebken
Rebecca M. Mounts

ASSISTANT PRODUCT MARKETING MANAGERS
Karen Hagen
Christy M. Miller

TECHNICAL EDITORS
Robert Bogue
Bob Chronister
Bradley Lindaas

TECHNICAL SUPPORT SPECIALIST
Nadeem Muhammed

ACQUISITIONS COORDINATOR
Tracy Williams

OPERATIONS COORDINATOR
Susan Gallagher

EDITORIAL ASSISTANT
Virginia Stoller

BOOK DESIGNER
Ruth Harvey

COVER DESIGNER
Barbara Kordesh

PRODUCTION TEAM
Tammy Ahrens
Lissa Auciello
Kathleen Caulfield
Jerry Cole
Michelle Croninger
Sean Decker
Dave Faust
Stephanie Hammett
Joy Dean Lee
John L. Ley
Kevin J. MacDonald
Candi McCreary
Angel Perez
Heather Pope

INDEXER
Chris Barrick

Composed in *Century Old Style* and *ITC Franklin Gothic* by Que Corporation.

To my wife, Marlene, my children, Leanne and Sean, and my best pal, Astro.

John Enck

To my wife, Lotus, my son, Shanti, my parents, and to my cousin Marian for keeping me company over the Internet all the way from Sweden.

Dan W. Blacharski

About the Authors

John Enck is a computer and networking professional with over 18 years of field experience in multivendor environments. He is the author of numerous books and articles in this field and is currently the Managing Technical Editor for *Windows NT Magazine* and a Senior Technical Editor for *NEWS/400*.

Dan W. Blacharski is a technology and business writer, novelist, and satirist with several years experience. He has written several articles and books, and currently works out of his home in Santa Cruz, California.

Acknowledgments

The authors wish to thank Elizabeth South of Que, who made this book possible; Laura Derr of Cardinal Media, who was responsible for getting the authors together in the first place; and IBM Corp., Digital Equipment Corp., Hewlett-Packard Corp., Sun Microsystems, and Fore Systems for all the information they provided.

We'd Like to Hear from You!

As part of our continuing effort to produce books of the highest possible quality, Que would like to hear your comments. To stay competitive, we *really* want you, as a computer book reader and user, to let us know what you like or dislike most about this book or other Que products.

You can mail comments, ideas, or suggestions for improving future editions to the address below, or send us a fax at (317) 581-4663. For the online inclined, Macmillan Computer Publishing has a forum on CompuServe (type **GO QUEBOOKS** at any prompt) through which our staff and authors are available for questions and comments. The address of our Internet site is **http://www.mcp.com** (World Wide Web).

In addition to exploring our forum, please feel free to contact me personally to discuss your opinions of this book: I'm **104521,2411** on CompuServe and **ckiefer@que.mcp.com** on the Internet.

Thanks in advance—your comments will help us to continue publishing the best books available on computer topics in today's market.

Carolyn Kiefer
Product Development Specialist
Que Corporation
201 W. 103rd Street
Indianapolis, Indiana 46290
USA

Contents at a Glance

Contents

Preface

The New Edition

A lot has happened in the computer world since John Enck wrote the first edition of this book in 1990. The Internet has become wildly popular, which has led to the supremacy of TCP/IP; the mainframe is being slowly replaced (or at least augmented) by a distributed, client/server architecture; and high-speed technologies, such as ATM and FDDI, have significantly enhanced the very nature of networking.

John had three goals in writing this book:

- *To introduce and define the fundamental network architectures of four key computer manufacturers.* This information gives executive management a sufficient understanding of the basics for making informed, intelligent decisions about networks and networking strategies.

- *To help technical management and systems personnel begin the cross-training process.* By covering each vendor's systems and networking architectures using the same orientation and organization, this book gives you a common level of understanding and facilitates this horizontal training.

- *To explore standards and technologies that greatly affect the world of multivendor networking and data communications.* Many of these developments result from third-party efforts and serve to define a middle ground on which to build multivendor solutions.

In this edition, I have endeavored to supplant Mr. Enck's comprehensive work with information on some of the latest technologies and to cover some of the changes that have taken place in the networking industry during the past six years.

Representations Used in this Book

In order to make the text easier to understand, this book adopts several graphical representations. The following section includes examples of these representations to help you distinguish among the different elements.

ON THE WEB

This icon and format signal URL addresses for the Internet and World Wide Web of places that have related products or information, such as the Que home page at:

http:\\www.quecorp.com

N O T E Notes offer advice or general information related to the current topic. ▪

CAUTION

This paragraph format warns the reader of hazardous procedures (for example, using file transfer to move entire databases).

What About Sidebars?

Sidebars supplement the material in the chapter. Rather than provide specific technological information that can impact a network's manageability, sidebars offer, for example, updates on future technology and side discussions of a particular product's impact on the marketplace.

Introduction

Overview

Multivendor networks and a plate of liver and onions have a lot in common: they are both undeniably real; they both provide sustenance; and both of them are repulsive to a lot of people.

Unfortunately, multivendor networks get a bad rap from computer manufacturers who want to keep customers in their folds. The promotion of connections to other manufacturers' computers and networks is cloaked in a shadow of mystery and intrigue.

"Sure," says the sales rep, "you can connect their equipment to ours as long as you choose applications and interfaces that conform to the ISO's seven-layer standard. As you probably know, we are committed to providing solutions that conform to the OSI Reference Model."

The customer replies, "Can you be more specific? I want to implement one LAN to accommodate both types of systems."

"Well," the rep responds, "we support the IEEE 802.3 LAN using the IEEE 802.2 discipline. Of course, you might need to implement TCP to accommodate both systems until our upper-layer OSI products become available. And you might need to implement some type of LAN bridge if the other system doesn't accommodate the combined 802.2 and 802.3 frame formats."

In defense of the manufacturers, however, the question of connecting two systems rarely can be answered with a simple yes or no. Yet, the issues involved in connecting networks are often made more complex than they need to be. So, rather than looking to manufacturers to provide multivendor solutions, many customers turn to independent standards organizations such as the International Standards Organization (ISO), the Institute of Electrical and Electronics Engineers (IEEE), and the American National Standards Institute (ANSI). These organizations are discussed in Chapter 6, "Standards."

In theory, these organizations provide standards that can, and often should, be adopted by computer manufacturers to provide interoperability between systems. Unfortunately, standards organizations, which define standards on paper, are normally far ahead of the manufacturers, which must invent and produce the products. Thus, the ISO might recommend the perfect solution to a specific problem, but providing products that conform to that standard is a long-term goal or, even worse, not scheduled at all.

Nonetheless, adopting third-party standards remains a feasible approach for customers formulating long-range plans. This customer backing is extremely important to the standards organizations. After all, these organizations rarely have a stick big enough to beat any of the manufacturers into compliance; it is the pressure applied by customers that compels manufacturers to adopt standards.

Because of this chasm between standards and products, another set of solutions comes into play: those implemented by third-party companies or independent organizations to address specific or general data communications and networking products. Third-party solutions include the following:

- *File transfer products.* Specialized software and/or hardware that performs file transfers between two specific types of systems, as well as general products like Kermit (which was developed by Columbia University in New York City) and XMODEM.

- *Terminal access products.* Emulation software and/or hardware that enables one type of terminal to look like another type of terminal, specialized terminals that might have built-in emulation that enables them to look like two completely different types of terminals, or a "universal" terminal standard that might be layered onto two different manufacturers' networks.

- *Personal computer (PC) local area network (LAN) software.* Products like Novell Inc.'s NetWare and Banyan System's VINES allow the sharing of files, printers, and other resources in a LAN. Although they can work in conjunction with existing standards, they are not yet standards themselves.

- *Transmission Control Protocol/Internet Protocol (TCP/IP).* The suite of TCP/IP protocols and services provides basic interoperability (file transfer, terminal access and mail exchange) between diverse systems. Furthermore, TCP/IP is positioned as both an alternative to the Open Systems Interconnect (OSI) standards and a possible contender for the mantle of OSI upper-layer compliance. The growth of the Internet, which depends on TCP/IP, has led to widespread acceptance of this protocol suite and a decreased reliance on OSI standards.

- *Middleware.* A vaguely defined software product that typically sits between the client and server and forms a third tier in the client/server network. Middleware is a sort of go-between that attempts to translate between different types of systems. However, middleware is no universal translator: it is often limited to products conforming to a specific API.

There are other categories of products that fall under this umbrella. What role, if any, will these products play when the manufacturers adopt more international standards? In many cases the answer is none, because these products are short-term solutions that fill an immediate need. In other cases, the products might be adopted by the standards organizations and thus become standards in their own right.

Multivendor Network Scenarios

Just why you might require a multivendor networking solution is no great mystery or surprise. Some of the more prevalent reasons include the following:

- *Merger/acquisition.* When two companies or organizations merge and each entity uses a different manufacturer for its data processing equipment, there is a need for some type of connectivity. This requirement can be as simple as posting accounting data from one system to the other, or as complex as enabling the combined set of users to access both types of systems.

- *Large organizations.* In a large organization (or government), smaller agencies or operating departments frequently have unique computing equipment. Yet because these departments are all part of a larger entity, they must pass information upward (and possibly sideways) for the common good. Although this situation is similar to the merger scenario, it normally occurs less abruptly because the requirement for cross-connectivity can be seen well in advance.

- *Conversions.* This tends to be the least pleasant environment, primarily because the outgoing vendor does not have a burning desire to solve the communications problems of its soon-to-be ex-customer. Furthermore, many conversions require parallel processing between two dissimilar systems sharing a common set of users.

- *New applications.* When new applications are implemented on new computer systems, the multivendor network must interface existing users with the new application or combine the new application's data with data derived from another application on a different system.

- *No-growth position, increased demand.* Sometimes the demand for end-user access to a certain application can dramatically increase even though the data processing budget does not also increase. Here, the multivendor network must pool resources so more people can access the information.

■ *Information management.* Because many computer systems have highly specialized software and hardware components, they are often used to address specific technical requirements. In a medical environment, for example, one type of hardware might oversee and monitor laboratory instruments, another might run the patient tracking system, and yet another might run the general administration and accounting systems. Although these systems function properly without interacting, the need to cross-reference this information might arise.

■ *Legacy connectivity.* Organizations migrating from a mainframe to a distributed client/server environment do not always merely unplug the mainframe and sell it for scrap iron. Millions of lines of legacy code can be involved, and it is often wise to leverage that investment. Consequently, the mainframe might be pressed into use as a server in the client/server network or as a repository of data. This, of course, creates a need for a whole new class of connectivity products to join the legacy environment to the new environment.

Network Tools and Services

To solve the problems or answer the needs described in the previous scenarios, you might use the following network tools:

■ *Common terminal access.* In many cases, the issue is simply to get a larger set of users to access an existing, or even new, application. In a multivendor environment, the issue is how to access the application from a terminal that is foreign to the program.

■ *Resource sharing.* Often, the sharing of printers, tapes, and disk space not only saves money, but actually expands an application's usefulness by enabling it to use these new resources.

■ *File transfer.* The most common way to share information between systems is to place the information in a separate file and then transfer it from one system to another. If the information is integrated with an application program on either end, special processing is typically required to write or read the information from these transfer files.

■ *Program-to-program communications.* In many cases, program-to-program communications are used to exchange information between systems in real time. They can be implemented as an alternative to file transfer, or they might be used to tie together online databases operating on different systems.

Furthermore, from a broader perspective, two additional tools can be part of a networking solution:

■ *Electronic mail.* In a multivendor network, electronic mail can be used in two ways. First, a single system can be the central electronic mail system that all users should access, regardless of the system in which their primary application resides. Second, if several systems are being connected and each system has its own electronic mail system, a means of integrating these separate mail systems might be required. Electronic mail access has taken on even greater importance, as it is now used to facilitate the flow of business documents and electronic forms.

- *Network management.* When multivendor networks are connected, it is desirable (but difficult) to manage the combined networks as one unified entity. Unfortunately, each system's local network is usually unaware of its neighboring networks; therefore, the management and maintenance of multiple logical networks is necessary.

Each of these tools and applications is covered in more detail in the following sections.

Common Terminal Access

Being able to access any application from any terminal can solve a great number of problems, but it is not a simple technical task. In most cases, this function is provided by enabling one type of terminal to emulate another type of terminal when accessing a particular system, as shown in Figure 1.1. For example, Digital Equipment Corp. (DEC) terminals would emulate International Business Machines (IBM) terminals when they access IBM systems, and IBM terminals emulate DEC terminals when they access DEC systems.

FIG. 1.1
Common Terminal
Access

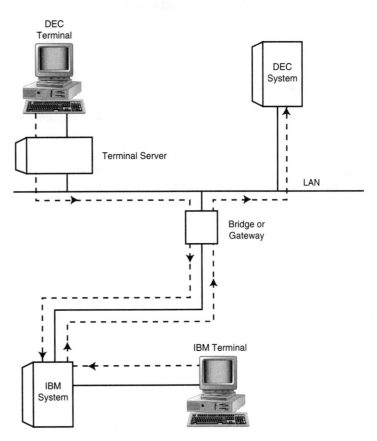

The beauty of this approach is that the application program is totally isolated and unaware that the terminal it is communicating with is a foreign device. Because the emulation is handling the translation of terminal functions, no changes are required to the application program(s). With common terminal access, adding support for foreign terminals is conceptually (and sometimes literally) no different from adding support for additional native terminals.

This emulation process is not without sacrifices and difficulties. To begin with, having one type of terminal emulate another uses processing overhead. Taking the data stream of one terminal and transforming it into the data stream of another terminal involves intensive central processing unit (CPU), character-by-character processing. If this processing is performed on the system that the terminal is physically attached to or is accessing, the emulation process will, by default, consume application resources. For this reason, emulation is often performed in a separate box or dedicated computer.

Another problem arises when more than two types of systems are involved. Though it is one thing to have two types of terminals that emulate each other, it is entirely another matter to have three types of terminals, each terminal emulating the other two. In this three-terminal scenario, six separate emulation products are employed (two for each terminal), and the chances of finding six such products are slim.

In terms of the emulation process itself, it can be broken into several technical tasks:

- *Keyboard mapping.* Different types of terminals sport very different keyboards and key usage. For example, an IBM terminal might have 24 function keys while a DEC terminal might only have four. Enabling each type of terminal to simulate the keyboard of the other is a difficult task, but it is mandated by the emulation process. A user must be able to generate the key sequences of the native terminal through the emulation process.

- *Screen presentation.* Although most terminals support video attributes (for example, bright, reversed, or underlined text) and commands to position the cursor at points on the screen, these attributes and positioning commands differ from terminal to terminal. At the same time, translating these sequences exactly between terminal types is critical to successful emulation. The bottom line is that the screen must appear the same (or very similar) on all types of terminals.

- *Transmission characteristics.* IBM terminals are block-oriented—that is, they transmit the information typed onto the screen only when the Enter key is pressed. Conversely, DEC terminals are character oriented—they transmit when each key is pressed. Therefore, when a character terminal is emulating a block terminal, the emulation process must buffer the characters typed until the equivalent of an Enter key is pressed. Conversely, when a block terminal is emulating a character terminal, it must take the full buffer and feed it to the application on a character-at-a-time basis. This is among the most difficult tasks of emulation processing.

Because of these technical difficulties and considerations, it would be advantageous to introduce a common type of terminal to which all applications conform. Historically, this has not been done successfully on a large scale. In modern times, however, X Window Systems terminals (multisession graphics devices developed by Massachusetts Institute of Technology) have come to play a significant role in defining universal standards.

Putting the technical issues aside, implementing universal terminal access can offer simple, straightforward solutions to many different problems. Some of these solutions include the following:

- *Centralizing electronic mail.* Because every terminal user can access a common system, a single electronic mail product that addresses the total user population could be implemented on one system.

- *Increasing user access without increasing the number of terminals or line costs.* Common access eliminates the need to place two or more terminals at the work spaces of users who require access to multiple systems. It also eliminates the steep costs of duplicating data communications lines to these work spaces.

- *Standardizing on one type of terminal.* Because any terminal can access the application pool, a single type or style of terminal can be used for end-user applications, regardless of who manufactures the terminal and who manufactures the system hosting the applications.

- *Choosing applications without regard for the system they run on.* Implementing terminal emulation can provide freedom of choice on future applications. Rather then being restricted to certain systems for future applications, possible future applications can be reviewed on their own merit.

Before the availability of emulation products, many office workers had problems finding a place to set down their morning coffee because their desks had to hold both a dumb terminal and a PC. 5250 emulation has advanced significantly over the years, and now includes mouse and hot spot support, and the capability to run multiple sessions. Some 5250 emulators, such as Walker Richer & Quinn's (Seattle, Washington) Reflection software, are programmable, so end users are able to add functionality. Reflection comes with its own implementation of Visual Basic, called Reflection Basic, and a separate API for controlling terminal sessions from applications. IBM's own Client Access software offers an alternate method for connecting PCs to the AS/400. Client Access replaces the older PC Support product, which was widely panned as sluggish and suffering from an awkward interface. Client Access, on the other hand, has an attractive, graphical interface, and as a native Windows product, offers significantly better performance.

Resource Sharing

In addition to terminals, other resources in a network are normally controlled by the system or manufacturer. By distributing these resources, you can often avoid duplication of expensive devices. The three resources that are primary candidates for sharing are printers, disk drives, and tape drives or other storage media (see Figure 1.2).

Moreover, although each of these resources can be shared in the context of a particular LAN implementation (for example, DEC's DECnet or Novell's NetWare), the same resources might not be shared among different implementations. For example, a LAN-attached printer might be used by any DEC system in a network but be unavailable to any Hewlett-Packard system or PC in the same LAN.

FIG. 1.2

An Example of Resource Sharing

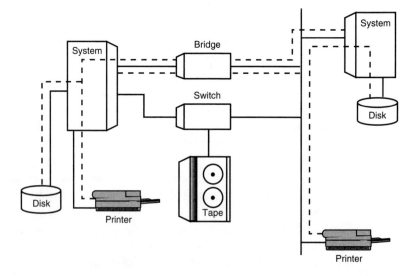

Finally, each type of resource has its own considerations, which are explored in the following sections.

Printers

Sharing a printing device among multiple users is commonplace. One system handles all output to a given printer and queues (or spools) the output to the printer. Therefore, in multivendor environments, the issue is rarely interfacing directly with the printer but interfacing with the spooling process.

In many ways, printer handling is a variation of file transfer processing. However, in addition to performing standard character code translations—translating American Standard Code for Information Interchange (ASCII) to Extended Binary Coded Decimal Interchange Code (EBCDIC) or vice versa—the printer sharing process must also deal with printer-specific directives that might differ from system to system. For example, the directive to issue a form feed might be different for specific IBM and DEC printers. This level of conversion is required because the process creating the output thinks it is writing to a native printer, so it uses native printer codes.

In addition to printer-specific code conversions, the print-sharing process must read and write these specialized queue files. On most systems, these files are stored in special locations using cryptic names, so the task of finding a print file to reroute to another printer might not be trivial. After the source print file is found, it is then written into a specialized queue file on the system handling the printer (see Figure 1.3).

FIG. 1.3
Printer Sharing

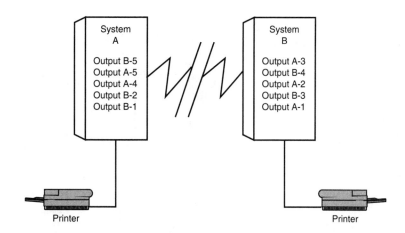

When sophisticated multivendor printer sharing is implemented, it is normally invisible to the user. The users simply initiate their output without thinking about the process that gets the file to the printer.

Disk Drives

Given the nature of minicomputers and mainframes, sharing raw storage space in multivendor networks is a rarity. For one thing, each system has its own operating system (typically a proprietary implementation) that interacts directly with disk devices in an optimized and nonsharable manner.

For PC LANs and their interfaces with minicomputers and mainframes, however, specific products have been engineered that enable PCs to access a larger computer's disk space as if it were local disk space. A portion of the larger computer's disk is transformed into a virtual PC hard disk or diskette (see Figure 1.4). Through the magic of the LAN, the PCs can read and write files and programs on these virtual disks as if they were native network disks. Of course, the load must be balanced appropriately; files should be distributed closest to where they are needed most. Otherwise, the server will be overburdened with file requests.

Although this strategy does address PC access to minicomputer and mainframe disk space, it does not do much for the computer host. The sponsoring computer, in fact, might not get similar access to the PC resources, so this style of implementation might be somewhat one-sided in terms of benefits.

At a higher level, some products allow a program on one system to read and write records in a file that resides on another system—for example, IBM's Distributed Data Management (DDM) implementation. Although IBM's implementation is, of course, specific to IBM systems, other companies have developed similar techniques to enable this level of access between dissimilar systems. Of these implementations, Sun Microsystem's Network File System (NFS) is widely implemented and has, in fact, been adopted as a network file access methodology by many of the leading computer manufacturers, including IBM and DEC.

FIG. 1.4
Virtual Network Files

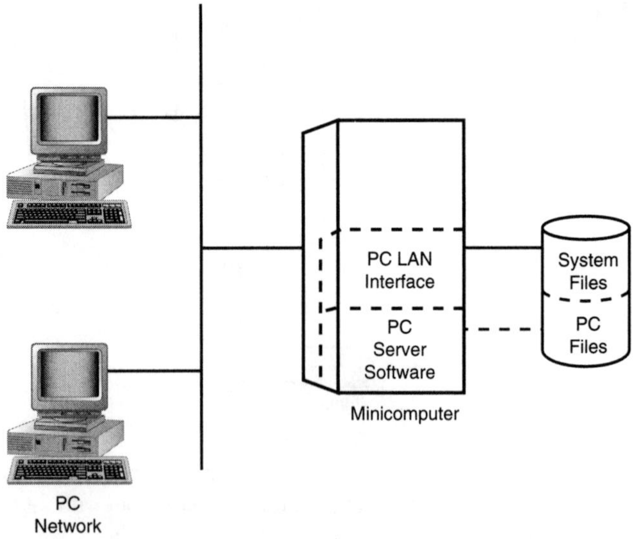

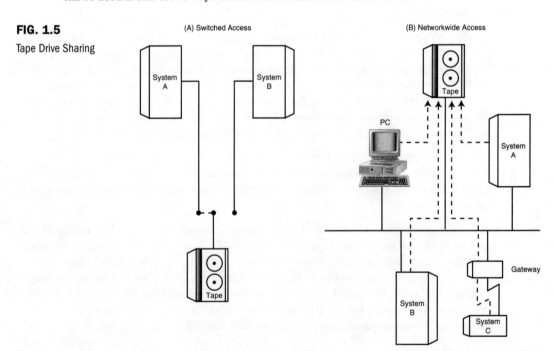

Storage Media

Although tape drives are rarely viewed as network-level devices, the minimal expense of this media makes sharing attractive (see Figure 1.5). In a multivendor network, a shared tape drive can be used in one of two ways: *switched access* and *networkwide access*.

FIG. 1.5
Tape Drive Sharing

In switched-access mode, the tape drive can be shared between multiple systems, but only one system can use it at a time. The advantage of this approach over transferring files from other systems to the system that controls the tape is that if the tape is switched for direct access for different systems, each system can read and write to the tape in its native format. The switch, in this case, might be hardware, software, or more likely a combination of the two.

If the tape drive is controlled by a single network function available networkwide, files distributed throughout the multivendor network can be merged on a single tape. This is similar to how tape servers function in PC LANs. Although this is an efficient way of providing networkwide backup, it does not necessarily provide portability from system to system.

An effective enterprise storage management system goes beyond network backup—it provides for the best use of resources, and makes sure that end users can access data when it is needed. An issue in storage management is establishing a way to access data stored on multiple devices and environments, and automating storage and retrieval of the data. Data classification establishes policies for different classes of data so that managers can decide on the best type of storage media for each type of data. For example, non-critical reports can be stored on less expensive media, while customer information might need to be stored so that it is immediately available. Hierarchical storage management (HSM) tools are available to automate the process of data classification, and subsequently migrate the data to the most appropriate type of storage.

Managing storage and backup can be done from either a UNIX perspective, which offers an open architecture and less-expensive products, or with the older, highly reliable IBM DFSMS product family. Although many tape and disk storage products for storing critical data are available, mainframe-class storage devices still offer the best reliability and performance. The availability of high-speed tape-mounting robots can yield an impressive data transfer rate, nearly approaching that of DASD. Still, other solutions must be considered. Remote distance unlimited DASD, for example, is sometimes used to provide for the availability of urgent, critical data. Redundant Arrays of Inexpensive Disks (RAID) technology has also become standard in many large enterprises, while CD-ROM jukeboxes and other optical storage solutions are becoming more efficient and affordable.

File Transfer

Of all multivendor services, file transfer is probably the best understood and most sought after. Files were being moved from one type of system to another long before LANs became popular. In the first implementations, files were moved via such common storage media as magnetic tape, punched card, or paper tape. As data communications and networking developed, these media-based transports were replaced by communications-based methods that emulated such products as the IBM 2780 and 3780 Remote Job Entry (RJE) stations. One computer would emulate a card punch, for example, while the other would emulate a card reader.

As data processing grew in size and in scope, these approaches became too limited to satisfy the variety of needs and demands for moving data. For example, nontechnical (or semi-technical) users often want to control the "when" and "what" of file transfers. In many cases, they even want to initiate the transfer themselves. This level of involvement by nontechnical personnel is simply not possible when using magnetic tape or RJE transport—both approaches require too much hands-on knowledge of hardware and/or the operating system.

Typical file transfer solutions have a relatively simple user interface to accommodate all levels of personnel (see Figure 1.6). A file transfer product can perform functions such as enabling the accounting department to transfer a file from the administration department to verify payroll or facilitating the exchange of documents and spreadsheets between users on dissimilar systems (as long as the actual word processing and spreadsheet packages can understand each other's information). And if the file transfer product is simple enough to use, these transactions can occur under the management of the people responsible for the information—no big brother from data processing required.

However, an easy-to-use interface does not diminish the potential power for file transfer. The same product can also be used to address some complex, application-oriented problems. It can extract information from one database, transfer the information to another system, and then update another database with that information. Therefore, in a dual (or multiple) database environment, file transfer is often used to move subsets of information from one system to another.

> **CAUTION**
>
> File transfer is not a good solution for moving an entire database from one system to the other because the information must be specifically extracted from the database and put into another format for the transfer.

Many file transfer products accommodate time-fired transfers. These transfers enable one system to collect information and transfer it to another system at predefined times. For example, a bank could transmit the day's transactions at the close of business, or a retail operation could send the cash registers data at the end of the day.

In addition to time firing, some transfer products provide event-firing mechanisms. These mechanisms perform such functions as transferring a file as soon as it becomes available or after two other files are transferred. By combining time firing and event firing, you can create extremely sophisticated transfer scenarios.

Behind the end-user interface and application aids are significant technical issues regarding file transfer and implementation. Some of the technical issues that affect the movement of information from one system to another include:

- *How information is encoded.* Information is normally stored in one of three formats: ASCII, EBCDIC or binary code. ASCII and EBCDIC are incompatible codes for information storage; computer systems normally use one or the other, but rarely both. DEC minicomputers, for example, use ASCII, while IBM mainframes use EBCDIC. Binary information, on the other hand, is common to all systems.

- *How codes are translated.* Any reasonable file transfer product can translate between ASCII and EBCDIC standards. This is important because a document written on an ASCII computer and then transferred to an EBCDIC computer must be translated to be read on the second system.

FIG. 1.6

File Transfer Among
Dissimilar Systems

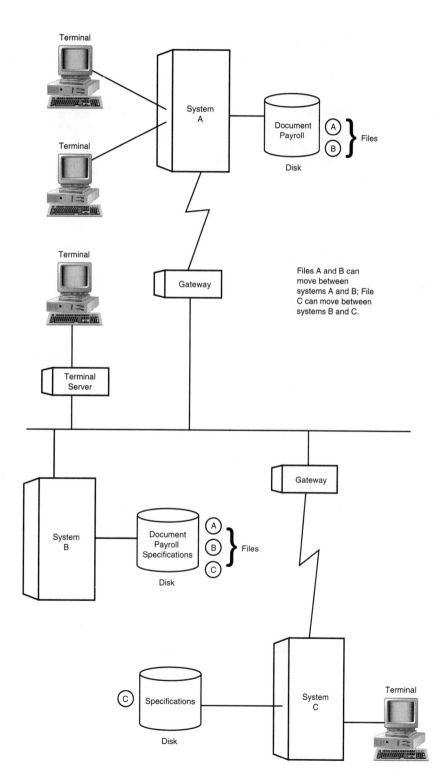

- *How information is structured in a file.* Files being transferred must preserve their structure. For example, if a file contains records of names and addresses, then the same record structure must be created on the other machine.

- *How fields are converted.* Within records, individual fields (or items) might have unique storage and translation requirements. If the information is financial, for example, numbers might be stored as whole numbers, numbers with fractional values, positive numbers, negative numbers, or combinations of these. When information is stored in unusual formats, translating the data between machines is often beyond the capability of even the best file transfer products, so a separate conversion might be required before the information can be transferred.

Encapsulation, one of the primary attributes of object-oriented technology, affords a new approach to data transfer. An object is a self-enclosed body of data, functions, and services, in which the system invoking the object is shielded from its internal workings. Techniques such as OpenDoc, CORBA, and Microsoft's OLE, which permit formatted data from one application to be brought into another application unchanged, are based on this technology.

Another factor that greatly contributes to the effectiveness (or ineffectiveness) of file transfer is how the product is structured. For the purpose of simplification, this structure can be broken into two parts:

- *Communication links.* At best, a file transfer product can move information between two systems only as fast as the communications link operates. If the product uses a 56 Kbps link, it can theoretically move up to 57,244 bits per second. Compared with a LAN connection operating at 10 Mbps, this is quite slow. Similarly, products that use even higher-speed channel attachments obtain an even higher data transfer rate.

- *Relationship to the applications.* If a file transfer product is based on software that resides on one (or both) computer systems, the software will compete with the application programs in the computers. Therefore, if the application programs demand a lot of the computer's attention, the performance of the file transfer will suffer. Similarly, if the file transfer consumes its fair share of the computer, the applications will suffer. An alternative approach is to implement the bulk of transfer processing in a third computer. This independent device then handles the CPU-intensive chore of data conversion and reformatting.

In both cases, there is a direct association between performance and price. The higher the performance…well, you know. Choosing the file transfer product that offers the best price/performance ratio is often as difficult as the transfer process itself.

Program-to-Program Communications

Whereas file transfer is the easiest multivendor networking tool to understand, program-to-program communications is the most difficult. For one, the user community usually can't see which programs manage what information. Without this knowledge, it is difficult to understand the reasons for implementing program-to-program communications.

Despite this difficulty, the flexibility of program-to-program communications enables it to address many situations for which common terminal access or file transfer products are inadequate. Examples of these situations include:

- *Control remote access.* Often, allowing users the freedom that goes with common terminal access and many file transfer products is inappropriate. When a high degree of control and security is required, a program-to-program solution can be implemented to control and monitor the files that a user can transfer between systems or to force a user accessing a remote system to use a predefined sign-on sequence. This prevents the user from accessing the remote system with a higher level of authorization than he or she needs.

- *Hide remote access.* Because program-to-program communications can accomplish many multivendor networking functions (common terminal access, file transfer, and so on), the end user can be completely isolated from the multivendor environment. This scenario is similar to controlling remote access except that program-to-program communications is used to accomplish all required multivendor functions; the end-user never sees any remote activity.

- *Provide coordination of real-time events.* Because program-to-program communications can pass along information as it is created, previously separate events can become interconnected. For example, in a manufacturing process in which the beginning of one event must wait for the conclusion of another event, program-to-program functions can automate the notification process. In a medical environment, information collected by a laboratory computer can be updated in a patient's medical history database and in billing records. Workflow software can implement program-to-program communications in this manner, and is in fact often used to automate business processes, allow simultaneous access to data, and avoid the "lag time" involved in handing off the process from one desk to the next.

- *Implement distributed databases.* Sometimes the total information requirement of an application is so large that it spans multiple computer systems. In this distributed environment, program-to-program communications can enable each system to access the other systems' information.

- *Implement a central database.* Rather than implement a distributed database, you can centralize information in a single computer system. If application programs running on other systems need access to any of the central data, they can use program-to-program services to obtain the information.

Program-to-program communications can be implemented in two ways. One implementation enables one program to appear to a remote system as though it were a terminal (see Figure 1.7). In this approach, the program logs on to the remote computer, accesses the program it wants, and interacts with it by simulating a user sitting at a terminal. Although this approach requires the overhead of emulating an end user, it requires custom programming on only one of the systems; the other program remains the same.

FIG. 1.7
Program-to-Program
Communications

Program A appears as another terminal to Program B.

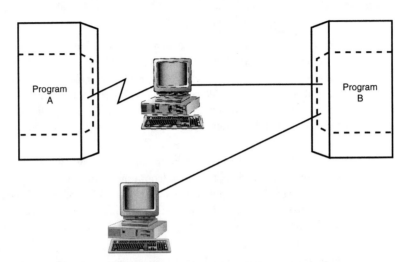

The second type of implementation enables two or more programs to communicate directly with each other. In most cases, both programs use a common set of access routines that let them establish a link with one another and transfer information. In large IBM networks, this is accomplished through the SNA LU 6.2 interface. For LANs, the implementation is usually unique to the networking service (for example, DECnet's task-to-task communications, HP's InterProcess Communications, and Sun's Remote Procedure Calls).

Although the tools to implement program-to-program communication are well-defined, the applications for it are wide open. Like most programming tools, the uses of program-to-program communications are highly dependent on their environment, applications, and programmers.

Electronic Mail

Electronic mail, or e-mail, can enable a network of people to communicate interactively. The backbone of every mail system is its capability to send notes and replies between its users (see Figure 1.8). This facility is faster (theoretically) than issuing memos and more convenient than tracking someone down via telephone.

Besides providing basic electronic communications, many e-mail packages also include, or are bundled with, software for automating common desktop and office functions, or facilitating the flow of documents throughout the enterprise. These functions include time management (appointment scheduling and to-do list maintenance) and information management. Many products provide special scripting languages so they can be customized for more specific functions (companywide bulletin boards, structured training, help guides, and so on).

FIG. 1.8
Sample Electronic Mail
System

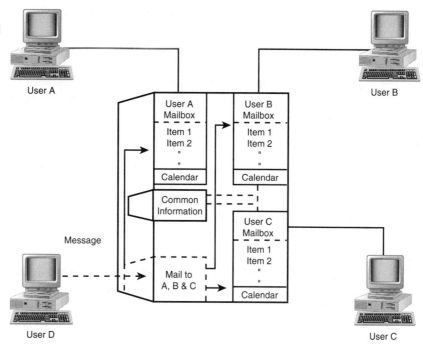

Implementing an e-mail package in a multivendor network can be done in a centralized or distributed manner. When implementing a centralized solution, one system can be designated the e-mail host. In this case, each terminal, regardless of manufacturer, must have access to that common system. As previously discussed, common terminal access is an appropriate means of accommodating this need.

In a distributed implementation, two or more systems serve as hosts to an e-mail solution. Although there are obvious benefits to running the same e-mail software throughout the enterprise (simplified training, better licensing deals, and universal access to vendor-specific features), different vendors' e-mail systems can still interoperate. Most modern systems comply with the SMTP standard, which allows for at least a basic level of interoperability. In this case, you must only ensure that the physical and logical links between the systems are compatible with the product's requirements.

Electronic mail differs significantly from file transfer. Some of the unique attributes of e-mail exchange include:

■ *Distribution lists.* To send or receive mail, a user must be defined as a participant within the e-mail system. When multiple systems are used, this list of users must be cross-referenced to track which users belong to which systems. If cross-referencing is not practical because of too many users or incompatible products, you must find a way to enable one system to distribute information to another system without knowing what users are where.

■ *Format of mail messages.* In many cases, you can use the system's native word processor to generate the contents of a message. However, because different manufacturers' word processing systems are usually incompatible with one another, you usually must implement a means of identifying the originating format and converting it into a more acceptable format.

Workflow Systems

Much has been made of the trend towards Business Process Reengineering (BPR). BPR is an extremely arduous procedure in which all business processes are examined, rethought, and reworked from the ground up. There is often a lot of resistance to BPR, especially on the part of end users, because of the disruption that affects people's comfortable routines. However, if effectively carried out, BPR can significantly enhance productivity.

BPR is often associated with workflow documentation, and in fact, the first step of a BPR analysis is often to document workflow. Looking at the flow of work throughout a department, or indeed the entire enterprise, lends itself to redesigning the very operations being documented. Oftentimes, a certain task that was done for years might prove irrelevant after it is documented. BPR has led to new technologies, including collaborative computing, document management, and automated workflow systems. Besides merely automating the flow of work and documents throughout the business unit, these tools can also significantly transform and redesign the way the work is done.

Workflow dispatches electronic documents or forms throughout a queue, routing the document to the next person based on pre-set business rules or a defined access list. It can be used to automate business processes, route projects throughout a business unit, and track the status of a project. Workflow software, when built on top of a client/server architecture, permits business tasks to be performed in rapid succession or even simultaneously by different workers. If the documents are presented in a traditional paper format, then only one person can use it at a time and it must be physically transferred to the next person in the workflow line. The electronic presentation of documents greatly speeds up the process.

Until recently, there was no way to connect messaging systems and workflow engines. Microsoft addressed this situation by adding extensions to its Messaging Application Programming Interface (MAPI), which permits the linking of messaging and workflow systems. In addition, a workflow consortium, of which Microsoft is a member, is also planning to publish an API to define how front-end applications can access multiple workflow systems. Microsoft's MAPI Workflow Framework defines a set of extensions for routing work from desktop applications to workflow systems in the form of MAPI messages. Under the Microsoft framework, a MAPI-based e-mail system can now trigger a workflow procedure.

Similar to the workflow model is groupware, a type of solution that permits groups of individuals to work collaboratively on a project. This also is built on an e-mail framework, and provides many of the same capabilities as workflow products. One of the most prominent groupware products is Lotus Development's Notes, a fully programmable tool that can highly automate tasks, facilitate communications, and streamline access to data. To scale to the enterprise level, however, groupware products must be able to integrate with existing network management tools. To accommodate this need, Lotus released SNMP agents for OpenView, which permits event messages to be sent from a Notes server to an SNMP management console. IBM, Lotus' parent, also has plans to integrate Notes with network managers from Sun and IBM.

Network Management

Network management in a multivendor network is a technical task rarely seen by end users. However, end users do often notice the effectiveness of a network's management when they experience network changes and problems.

The problems involved with managing multivendor networks are numerous and complex. In some cases, networks are geographically separate and linked through bridging and gateway devices. In others, various manufacturers share the same physical network, but each runs its information over that network independently. Sometimes, information runs over the same physical and logical network.

Therefore, when a component in a network ceases to operate correctly, there are many potential causes for the failure. Furthermore, given the increasing use of WANs, the geographical size of the network can be huge. For example, a DEC LAN in California might connect to an IBM network in Texas that might connect to a HP network in New York. Even worse, the group responsible for managing the network might be located only in New York, thus increasing the difficulty of diagnosing the Texas and California networks, even though they are linked together.

The primary job of network management is to monitor and report on the status of the whole network. A network management solution tracks the status of every component in the network, regardless of who the manufacturer is or what type of network it is operating on (see Figure 1.9).

As already mentioned, network management products are often invisible to the end users. But the use of such a product in conjunction with the overall networking strategy is an important aspect of maintaining any large single-vendor or multivendor network.

FIG. 1.9
Network Management
System

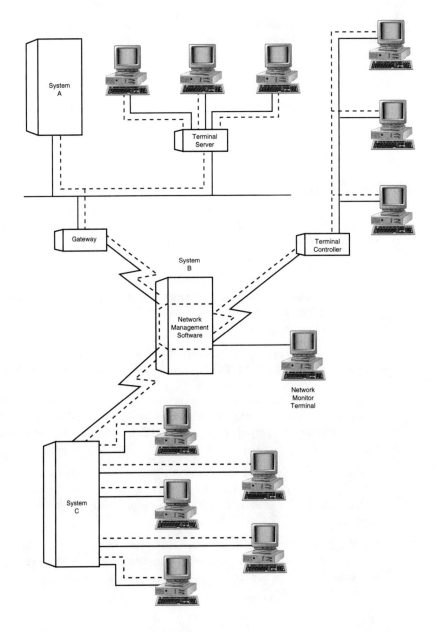

The Bottom Line

Examining networking and application needs to find the best solution is a complex task. It is important to understand networking issues and some underlying networking considerations. For example, to understand the difficulties in implementing a combined IBM and DEC network, it is important to understand how each network operates on its own. Similarly, to shop for multivendor solutions, you need to understand the application and range of available options.

The rest of this book is organized with these considerations in mind. Chapters 2 through 5 deal with the products and native networking architectures of Digital Equipment Corporation, Hewlett-Packard, IBM, and Sun Microsystems. Chapters 6 through 13 address multivendor networking issues, standards, product approaches, and network management. Finally, a glossary defines the terms and acronyms used in this book and throughout the data communications and networking industry. ●

CHAPTER 2

Digital Equipment Corporation

Company Background

Digital Equipment Corporation (DEC) was founded in 1957 by three graduates of Massachusetts Institute of Technology (MIT) operating out of an old mill in Maynard, Massachusetts. One of the original three founders, Ken Olsen, went on to lead the corporation and has been the most significant person to shape Digital. The fact that the corporate headquarters remains in Maynard is representative of the company's paradoxical commitment to both innovation and tradition.

During its early years, Digital produced specialized logic modules. Although it operated in a data processing world dominated by large, mainframe-style computers, Digital had the vision to pioneer minicomputers by introducing the PDP-1 in 1960. The revolutionary aspect of the PDP-1 was its interactive video terminal capability— the first such implementation of this now commonplace technology.

In 1970, Digital released the PDP-11, a 16-bit machine that became the most popular design of the PDP series. Used most often in manufacturing and technical environments for process and instrument control, the PDP-11 family remained in demand until it was discontinued in 1991. Following the growth of the PDP-11 market, Digital released a networking architecture in 1976 called the *Digital Network Architecture (DNA)*. The set of products and services defined by DNA is more commonly known as *DECnet*.

The PDP-11 design also served as the launching platform for another product: Digital's general-purpose, 32-bit Virtual Address Extension (VAX) computer. Introduced in 1977, the VAX gradually became Digital's premiere product—a building block for other products offering performance and disk capacity similar to that of mainframes. Among these products are VAX clusters, a computing environment released in 1983 and based on multiple VAX computers sharing a common repository of disk space; and the mainframe-level VAX 9000 Series, announced in 1989. In 1992, Digital released the Alpha AXP architecture, based on 64-bit RISC microprocessors. Today, the Alpha runs on all Digital machines, from PCs to high-end symmetric multiprocessing and clustered servers. Digital also offers a line of high-end Pentium Pro products, including the four-processor Prioris server and Celebris workstation.

Product Line Overview

Digital maintains a comprehensive manufacturing operation that designs and builds most of its products. Having paved the way for the so-called midrange computer market, Digital has expanded its product line up into the mainframe domain and down to the PC playground. In support of these offerings, Digital produces a complete line of terminals, printers, and assorted networking devices.

Digital's VAX family of computers ranged from the MicroVAX desktop system, all the way up to high-end symmetric multi-processing (SMP) servers. Every member of the VAX family supported the same operating systems and applications. The VAX family was based on CMOS V technology and was highly scalable, up to symmetric multiprocessing and clustering configurations. A number of different clustering options were possible under the VAX architecture, including clustering in a single office, or clustering systems that were geographically separated. However, the 32-bit nature of the VAX architecture was quickly hitting the wall, primarily because of address limitations.

In 1988, Digital formed a task force to explore ways to preserve its existing VAX VMS customer base through the coming decade, and in 1992, released the Alpha AXP architecture. The Alpha AXP architecture retains many of the VAX's attributes while offering significantly more power. The 32-bit VAX architecture was based on complex instruction set computing (CISC), whereas the 64-bit Alpha AXP architecture was reduced instruction set computer (RISC)-based. Digital subsequently ported its OpenVMS operating system to the Alpha AXP architecture to enable OpenVMS applications to take advantage of RISC's performance advantages.

The Alpha AXP architecture was designed for high-performance computing. In fact, OpenVMS AXP applications outperform OpenVMS VAX applications by a factor of 3.59 to 1. Digital built easy migration capabilities to enable customers to move from the VAX to the Alpha AXP architecture without significant recoding of their applications. Digital's Alpha AXP processors run multiple operating systems and have the ability to run native programs translated from VAX and MIPS architectures, thereby preserving their customers' existing VAX and MIPS investments.

Digital's goals in developing the Alpha AXP architecture were to provide:

- High performance
- Longevity
- The ability to run both VMS and UNIX operating systems
- Easy migration from VAX and MIPS architectures

To operate OpenVMS AXP, DEC OSF/1 AXP, and Microsoft Windows NT operating systems, Digital adopted some technology from their PRISM design. Under this model, a set of sub-routines (PALcodes) with controlled entry points were established for each operating system. For running VAX and MIPS binary images, Digital uses binary translation.

The Alpha AXP architecture is based on a shared-memory model. The first implementation was the DECchip 21064 microprocessor. At the time of its release in 1992, it was the world's fastest single-chip microprocessor—even listed in the *Guinness Book of Records* as such. The latest implementation, the 21164 Alpha microprocessor, runs at a blazingly fast 300MHz, and power can be increased further through symmetric multiprocessing or clustering. The Alpha AXP chip is capable of running multiple operating systems, and can run native programs translated from VAX and MIPS architectures.

The Alpha AXP architecture is now used throughout Digital's product line. The Alpha AXP's 64-bit architecture is designed with an eye towards high performance, and continues Digital's focus on multiple processors. The powerful 64-bit Alpha architecture is capable of bringing high-end features to smaller systems. The Alpha systems can run Digital UNIX, OpenVMS, and Windows NT; for sophisticated functions such as data warehousing, they can address massive files greater than 2G in size.

Digital released a 64-bit version of its Digital UNIX operating system in March, 1996. Digital UNIX 4.0 integrates the now pervasive *Common Desktop Environment (CDE) GUI,* which establishes a common look and feel between all major UNIX implementations. Digital UNIX 4.0 supports POSIX threads, real-time standards, and X11R6. Additionally, it conforms fully to the Single UNIX Specification (Spec1170) administered by the X/Open organization. The 64-bit nature of version 4.0 now enables Digital UNIX to run high-end applications such as data warehousing.

Digital Equipment Terminals

The Digital line of terminals is perhaps the most widely emulated line of character-oriented displays. The reasons are straightforward:

- Digital does an excellent job of providing ANSI compatibility, which enables Digital terminals to be used in environments that might not include Digital computer systems.
- The widespread use of the Digital PDP and VAX computer systems has enabled the Digital terminal line to penetrate deep into both the technical and end-user communities.

Ch
2

The following generations of products compose the fundamental line of Digital video terminal (VT) devices:

- *VT50 Family.* This is the father of the VT line. Although not as capable as today's products, the VT52 implementation in particular is still widely emulated by PCs and terminals that require character-oriented access. Its sibling, the VT55, offered support for combined on-screen text and graphics.

- *VT100 Family.* Introduced in 1978, the VT100 line offered improved speed and function over the initial VT50 models. Of significance was the VT100 line's support for both ANSI and VT52 compatabilities. The original VT100 sired the following models:
  - *VT101.* Became the new low-end product.
  - *VT102.* Offers advanced video options, including support for 132 columns by 24 lines.
  - *VT131.* Supports both conversational (character-oriented) and block mode (full-screen) transmission modes.
  - *VT125.* Combines text with bitmapped graphics capabilities. The VT125 includes implementation of Digital's Remote Graphics Instruction Set (ReGIS).

- *VT200 Family.* One of the most important features of the VT200 family is the keyboard layout. While the VT100 had a separate (right-hand) numeric keypad, the VT200 added another keypad for editing (located between the typewriter keys and the numeric keypad). Another significant change from the VT100 family was the introduction of a user-friendly on-screen menu to define the various set-up options (in contrast to the cryptic on-screen sequence used by the VT100). The VT200 family is composed of three major models:
  - *VT220.* A standard monochrome text-only video terminal.
  - *VT240.* Supports text and ReGIS monochrome graphics. It is composed of a keyboard, monitor, and a system unit box.
  - *VT241.* A color implementation of the VT240.

- *VT300 Family.* The VT300 line offersincreased performance and ergonomics (reduced glare and tilt/swivel base) over the VT200 line. The VT300 line includes:
  - *VT320.* The entry-level monochrome text video terminal.
  - *VT330.* The monochrome graphics (ReGIS) replacement for the VT240. The design of the VT330 eliminated the need for a separate system unit. Also noteworthy is the VT330's dual-session (dual-port) capability and improved graphics resolution. An improved, higher performance model of the VT330 was released as the VT330+.
  - *VT340.* A color implementation of the VT330. A high-performance version of the VT340 was released as the VT340+.

- *VT400 Family.* The VT400 family was introduced in 1990 as the planned replacement for the three-year-old VT300 line. The VT400 line includes improved resident fonts that enable it to display 24, 36, or 48 lines of text per display screen. The VT400 line was introduced with one model, the VT420—a monochrome text terminal. The VT420 supports dual ports (for dual sessions) and provides split-screen and cut-and-paste functions for managing both sessions.

■ *VT1000 Family.* The VT1000 is a specialized graphics workstation supporting icons and multiple windows in accordance with the X Window standard. The highly intelligent VT1000 also provides VT320 terminal emulation and support for both the Local Area Transport (LAT) protocol, Transmission Control Protocol/Internet Protocol (TCP/IP), and the standard X Window System protocol.

In most cases, Digital terminals transmit characters as they are pressed on the keyboard. Issues such as buffering and transmission optimization are handled by the computer system or by the devices between the terminal and the computer system. These considerations will be discussed later in this chapter.

Ch
2

PCs

The terms *personal computer* and *Digital Equipment Corporation* are not as synonymous as one might expect. It is not that Digital has been unable to apply its innovative talents in this arena, or that the resulting products did not come to market. The real problem rests with timing. Before IBM's release of the first PC, Digital had also been working on a small, personal microcomputer. At that time there was no single dominant hardware architecture or dominant operating system on the market (although the Control Program/Microprocessor [CP/M] was doing well at that time).

When IBM released the first PC in 1981 (and subsequently set the standards for today's market), Digital redoubled its efforts to get its own products to market. Digital produced not one but three possible contenders for the low-end market. Each had its own distinct advantages and disadvantages, and each was given an opportunity to prove itself.

The three products that resulted were the DEC Rainbow, the DECmate, and the Professional 300. Of these three, the DEC Rainbow was the only product that came close to being a clone of the IBM PC; the Rainbow ran Microsoft's MS-DOS operating system but did not feature the Basic Input/Output System (BIOS) and hardware-level compatibility with the IBM machines.

In contrast, the DECmate and the Professional 300 lines were corporate-oriented computers. For example, the DECmate featured sophisticated word-processing capabilities and could be networked easily with Digital's larger machines. The Professional 300, on the other hand, was intended to be a desktop version of the Digital's PDP computer.

None of these three products have any inherent, glaring faults, but all three were released in the shadow of the IBM PC (and the emerging clone market), which fell on them like a wet wool blanket. Although it is certainly unfair to call any of the products a market failure, none achieved the celebrity status earned by the IBM PC. Digital's resigned mindset was further evidenced by the release of the VAXmate, a follow-up product to the IBM PC/AT. Based on the same Intel 80286 microprocessor chip as the IBM AT, the VAXmate had limited expansion capabilities and was marketed only to existing Digital customers.

At the end of the 1980s, Digital was ready to take another chance on the IBM PC-compatible market. This time, however, it turned to Tandy Corporation (Radio Shack; Fort Worth, Texas) to manufacture a line of PC-compatible products for Digital. The resulting products were the DECstation 200, DECstation 300, and DECstation 400 lines—based on the Intel 80286, 80386, and 80486 processors, respectively. Although Digital downplayed the fact that it had out-sourced the product to Tandy, this fact was not lost on the market.

Finally, in 1990, Digital released the applicationDEC 433MP, a multi-user UNIX system based on the Intel 80486 microprocessor. This product was targeted at the small-business market and features support for multiple 486 processors and connectivity for up to 96 concurrent users. Its roots in PC and Personal System/2 (PS/2) technology are evident by its support for either the Extended Industry Standard Architecture (EISA) or Micro Channel Architecture (MCA) bus. If nothing else, the 433MP represents an interesting convergence of PC, engineering worksta-tion, and minicomputer technologies.

Digital's latest innovation, the Digital Personal Workstation, is designed around a processor-independent architecture, and offers the user a choice between Pentium, Pentium Pro, or Alpha processors. Users can move from Intel to Alpha with the change of a single card. Both processors are optimized to run Windows NT, and can be used to run many of the high-end applications, such as CAD or GIS, that had been limited to higher-end workstation products. It offers PCI or ISA Ethernet or token ring options for networking. The Celebris XL is based on Intel technology and features either single 100, 120, or 133 MHz; or dual 100 or 133 MHz Pentium processors. The Alpha XL runs 233 MHz and 266 MHz implementations of the Alpha 21064 processor. Several native Windows NT applications have been ported to the Alpha sys-tem as a result of an alliance between Digital and Microsoft.

Engineering Workstations

Digital's original response to the engineering workstation market was to couple high-resolution displays with various VAX processors. Capable of running either the VMS operating system or ULTRIX (Digital's implementation of UNIX), the product line was termed the *VAXstation.*

In general, as the capabilities of the mainstream VAX models grew, so did those of the VAX-stations. The VAXstation 100/500 line introduced in the early 1980s was replaced by the VAXstation II in 1985, a line that included a model with an independent graphics coprocessor. On the heels of the VAXstation II came the VAXstation 2000–7000, released in 1987 and 1988.

The VAX 7000 was designed as a high-performance system, suitable for high-volume transac-tions or distributed networks. Many mainframe-based applications could run on the VAX 7000, making it usable as a backbone platform for supporting business-critical applications. The VAX 7000, which was expandable to six CPUs, was built on Digital's CMOS technology and ran the OpenVMS operating system.

In 1989, Digital revamped its product line and stirred some new ingredients into the mix. The first ingredient was the use of a RISC architecture for some of the machines. Another was that the basic RISC processor used by Digital was, in fact, manufactured by MIPS Computer Systems, a third party supplier. Finally, these new RISC-oriented machines could run only ULTRIX (and thus were shunned from the VAX community).

Presumably to reduce confusion between the VAX-based and RISC-based products, Digital named the new line *DECstations* (a named shared by Digital's MS-DOS computers). Digital targeted this new lineup as a sweeping, low-end desktop blitz and paraded it in front of the public.

The product lineups consisted of the VAXstation 3000 Series (based on Digital complementary metal oxide conductor, or *CMOS,* VAX processor technology); the DECstation 5000 Series (based on the MIPS RISC architecture); and the DECstation 200, 300, and 400 Series (based on the Intel 80286, 80386, and 80486 microprocessors). While the low-end, PC-oriented DECstations were not presented as heirs to the engineering workstation throne, the association (by name alone) of the DECstation 3000 Series with these units raised both eyebrows and confusion.

The AlphaStation 255 and 500 families of UNIX and Windows NT workstations are the latest additions to Digital's line of midrange workstations. Digital's AlphaStations support Digital's new 64-bit operating systems (Digital UNIX and OpenVMS), as well as Windows NT.

The 500 supports dual-fast and wide SCSI-2 channels, Ethernet and Fast Ethernet, and can accommodate up to 512M of RAM. All products in the AlphaStation line include multimedia capabilities.

The PowerStorm PCI-based workstation graphics option is available for all Digital workstations. PowerStorm delivers superior graphics performance, using the common OpenGL API. PowerStorm was designed for 2-D and advanced 3-D applications that require high performance, such as motion and texture mapping.

Digital's RISC-based AlphaStations offer superior performance for applications such as modeling, imaging, animation or videoconferencing. The new 64-bit architecture can directly address up to 1G of real memory, making it easier to handle very large files without disk-swapping. The newest AlphaStations run the 64-bit RISC Alpha 21164 microprocessor, at speeds up to 300 MHz. Like the other Digital products running Alpha technology, it can run UNIX, OpenVMS or Windows NT.

The AlphaStation 250 is well-suited to mechanical or electrical CAD applications, and also offers collaborative computing facilities. The 200 is a somewhat lower-cost, entry-level product, but also offers the 64-bit computing environment, at speeds up to 233 MHz. On the high end are the AlphaStation 600 systems, which are the fastest and most ideal for high-end scientific research projects that involve complex visualization and calculation.

The AlphaStation 500 (see Figure 2.1) is well-suited for higher-end CAD applications or memory-intensive and CPU-intensive multimedia projects. The system runs the Alpha 21164 processor at 333, 400, or 500 MHz.

Midrange Offerings

The PDP-11 line, until it was discontinued, filled the lower end of the spectrum, if for no other reason than by virtue of being a 16-bit machine. The 32-bit VAX, on the other hand, was offered in a broad range of models, starting from the diminutive MicroVAX extending to the mainframe-oriented VAX 9000.

Ch
2

FIG. 2.1

Digital Equipment Alpha
500 Workstation

Photo courtesy of Digital Equipment Corporation

Both lines shared the dubious honor of using multiple bus designs. The three most common bus architectures are as follows:

- *UNIBUS.* The architecture used in the original PDP-11 and VAX-11 and at the high end of other VAX and PDP offerings.

- *Q-Bus.* Used in the lower end of both the PDP-11 and VAX lines.

- *VAXBI.* Unlike the Q-bus and Unibus architectures that were open to third-party vendors for the development of controllers and peripherals, the VAXBI is a closed architecture. Although this bus structure is specific to the higher end of the VAX line, it also supports the older Unibus design. Other buses, including the MASSBUS and the XMI and industry-standard VME bus, have also been used by Digital. Presently, Digital offers a PCI-VME Adapter for OpenVMS, for workstations and servers running OpenVMS Alpha but have the PCI I/O bus. This device bridges Alpha environments to the VME bus environment. Of special note is the XMI bus developed for the VAX 9000 and briefly discussed in the next section.

Because of its roots as an interactive multiprocessing system, the PDP-11 supported a variety of operating systems. The RSX line (RSX-11M, RSX-11M-PLUS, and RSX-11s) provided multiprocessing capabilities under priority-driven and/or real-time constraints. In contrast, RT-11 was at the low end, offering multiprocessing in a single-user environment.

While the PDP-11 maintained a respectable position at Digital until it was discontinued, the favorite offspring is still the VAX. The first VAX offering was the VAX-11 line, released in 1977. Whereas the PDP-11 was oriented more to the technical market, the VAX was suited better for the commercial and business markets. The primary operating system, VMS (Virtual Memory System), is a multiprocessing, interactive environment well suited to multi-user business applications. The secondary operating system, ULTRIX, is Digital's implementation of UNIX for the VAX. A real-time operating system, VAXELN, is also available (primarily as a migration tool for PDP-11 users).

Ch
2

The VAX product line contains two segments: the Q-Bus MicroVAX line and the VAXBI line. The MicroVAX line starts with the relatively old MicroVAX I and progresses to the MicroVAX 2000 (which, unlike other MicroVAX systems, uses its own bus structure); the MicroVAX II and the MicroVAX 3300, 3400, 3800, and MicroVAX 3900. These machines are targeted to smaller businesses and departments and are also a bridge from PDP to VAX technology.

With an eye to replacing the MicroVAX name and line, Digital introduced the VAX 4000 Series in 1990. These machines are positioned between the MicroVAX line and the low end of the VAX line, and functioned as uniprocessing departmental servers or high-end CAD workstations. From a performance perspective, the VAX 4000 Series offers a price/performance ratio that is significantly better than the high end of the MicroVAX line, while providing performance similar to the low end of the VAX series. This overlap is part of Digital's strategy to reposition the low end of its product line with its higher performance offerings.

In the big leagues, VAXBI systems start with the VAX 8200 Series, and then advance into the 8300, 8500, 8600, 8700, 8800, and 8900 Series. In recent years, Digital introduced the VAX 6200, 6300, and 6400 Series as the de facto replacements for the low end of the 8000 Series (the 8200 and 8300). In fact, the 6000 Series was designed to accommodate the multithreading of online transaction processing (OLTP). Additional requirements for OLTP are addressed by the VAXft 3000, a fault-tolerant system based on dual-processor MicroVAX 3000 technology.

At the top of the VAXBI line are the VAX 8600, 8700, 8800, and 8900 Series; the 9000 Series; and VAXclusters. While the high-end models of the older 8000 Series approached mainframe capabilities, they had some difficulty maintaining fast access to large capacities of memory and disk storage. These deficiencies were corrected in the VAX 9000.

Most of the VAX series are upgradable to the newer Alpha AXP architecture, and capable of running the OpenVMS or Digital UNIX operating systems. The Alpha AXP architecture afforded a new 64-bit architecture that can directly address up to 1G of real memory.

The AlphaServer 2000 series (see Figure 2.2), based on Digital's new 64-bit RISC technology, offers highly compact SMP servers with up to four processors; they are used primarily as departmental or LAN servers. The 2000 series runs the DECchip 21064 CPU at 150MHz, and supports DEC OSF/1 AXP, OpenVMS AXP, and Windows NT. The 3000 Series, running the 21064 CPU at 175MHz, offer extensive memory and storage capabilities, and is an excellent choice as a server for X Window terminals.

FIG. 2.2
Digital Equipment
AlphaServer Family

Photo courtesy of Digital Equipment Corporation

The 64-bit design of the Alpha AXP architecture provides much more power to the midrange, as well as added networking capacity and more file storage.

Top-End Offerings

Announced in 1989, the 64-bit VAX 9000 Series is Digital's best performing system, offering mainframe-level performance. Using a combination of CISC and RISC technology, the new processor and bus design (XMI) gave the 9000 a significant increase in data processing speed. To achieve compatibility with the mainstream midrange machines, the VAX 9000 also supports the VAXBI bus interface.

In addition to the main CISC/RISC system processor, the VAX 9000 supports specialized vector processors for parallel operations. The Star Coupler CI interface was enhanced for direct support of the XMI bus, and the resulting interface, termed *CIXCD,* brings higher throughput and new configuration options to VAXclusters. In the most general sense, the VAX 9000 was designed with one eye on compatibility between VMS and the existing VAX line, while the other eye focused on optimization and mainframe-class performance.

The RISC-based AlphaServer 8000 line has the ability to run up to 12 300-MHz 21164 Alpha processors, and combines the benefits of the mainframe with those of an open, client/server system. It can accommodate a 10-terabyte cluster storage, and is usable as a high-availability database server or OLTP server. This line includes the 8200, which is scalable up to six 300 MHz processors, and can run both Digital UNIX and OpenVMS. The 8200 and 8400 are the high end of the 8000 line, and are the first of the AlphaServer 8000 series which Digital plans to extend through three generations of products.

In designing the 8000 series, Digital had several goals, including support for legacy I/O subsystems and DEC 7000/10000 AXP compatibility. The 8000 series doubles the performance of the 7000/10000 AXP server line while providing a viable and fairly straightforward upgrade path. In designing the 8000, Digital's design team conducted a thorough analysis and performance study of the 7000/10000 systems. After the analysis, Digital decided that system data bandwidth and memory read latency goals were critical to their new design.

Read latency is the amount of time required for a CPU to read a piece of data into a register in response to a load instruction. *Cache memory* is a common way to minimize read latency. Latency tends to degrade as the number of processors is increased, and latency will improve as the amount of available bandwidth is increased. Comparable systems from HP and IBM do not stress low-memory latency in the design of the RISC System/6000 or the PA-8000 SMP systems. Although the older 7000/10000 AXP systems were comparable to the RS/6000 and PA-8000 in terms of latency, the AlphaServer 8000 was developed with an emphasis on low-memory read latency. The 7000/1000s had a latency of 560 nanoseconds, comparable to the ratings of the RS/6000 and PA-8000. On the 8000 platform, however, Digital achieved a read latency of 200 nanoseconds. In its design of the 8000 series, Digital pinpointed low latency as a major factor in high system performance.

Symmetric Multiprocessing and VMSclustering

Previously known as VAXclustering, *VMSclustering* is executed with Digital's OpenVMS Cluster Software. The software establishes an integrated OpenVMS environment, which can be distributed over multiple Alpha and VAX CPUs. VMSclusters can include both VAX and Alpha CPUs in the same cluster system.

To obtain high performance and greater computing capacity, Digital engineered two optional processing configurations: *symmetric multiprocessing* (SMP) and *clustering*. Both offer significant processing improvements.

SMP uses multiple processors sharing resources within a single VAX or Alpha AXP system. The SMP architecture enables the system to break up functions and process them independently. Thus, a disk access can be handled by one of the processors while another performs a CPU-intensive calculation. The number of processors available depends on the base model (note that not all models are capable of being used in SMP mode).

Although SMP does provide some benefits based on its architecture alone, applications must be specifically written (rewritten, or *DEComposed* as Digital calls it) for the SMP environment. One final advantage of the SMP approach is that it makes the system more fault-tolerant; if one processor malfunctions, the system can be restarted and instructed to ignore the faulty processor. While this is far from an online recovery operation, it sure beats being down until the hardware engineer arrives.

In contrast to SMP, clusters enable multiple systems to share disk storage in a highly optimized manner. Clusters use a common piece of hardware, called a *Star Coupler,* to provide a physically common point of contact between the multiple VAXs or Alpha AXPs and the disk subsystem (see Figure 2.3). A VMScluster system can contain an unlimited number of star couplers; the number of star couplers connected to a CPU is limited only by the number of adapters provided by the CPU. A single Star Coupler can interface multiple systems to one or more Hierarchical Storage Controllers (HSC) which, in turn, control multiple physical disk drives. The interface between the computers and the Star Coupler is referred to as the *interconnect,* a high-speed link designed for fault tolerance. If there is an interconnect failure, the VMScluster software will automatically resort to an alternate interconnect. The VMScluster software will support any combination of these interconnects:

FIG. 2.3

Sample VAXcluster

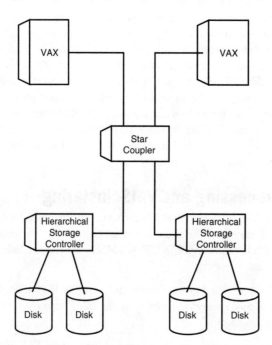

- Computer Interconnect (CI)
- Digital Storage Systems Interconnect (DSSI)
- Small Computer Storage Interconnect (SCSI)
- Fiber Distributed Data Interface (FDDI)
- Ethernet

CI and DSSI are special-purpose interconnects, designed for CPUs and subsystems in the VMSclusters. A maximum of 16 CPUs can be connected to a star coupler; a maximum of four CPUs can be connected to a DSSI. The SCSI bus is not used for CPU-to-CPU communications; therefore, CPUs connected to a multihost SCSI bus also require another interconnect to provide this capability. The purpose of the SCSI bus is to provide multihost access to SCSI storage devices.

Every aspect of a clustered system has built-in redundancy. And, the hardware-level design can be enhanced further by doubling (or tripling in some cases) the number of computers or amount of disk storage required. Overall, this makes for a highly efficient, highly fault-tolerant hardware architecture. The cluster design provides a self-contained backup system as well, and is an ideal solution to gradual expansion because the cluster can be built one system at a time.

However, no degree of hardware tolerance can salvage the data damaged by an application crashing or running amuck. And because the purpose of a cluster is to provide concurrent access to a large pool of information, the integrity of that information is of paramount importance—after all, there is no point in sharing a pool of garbage (unless you're a goat).

To preserve the integrity of information, clusters can (and usually do) implement the following safeguards:

- *Resource locking.* This allows various levels of locking on a clusterwide basis. It allows file-level, record-level, and even field-level locking.
- *Disaster rollback.* After a disaster, this restores information to a previous point at which it was known to be good. This feature usually works with recovery processing, as described next.
- *Recovery processing.* After information has been restored to a known good state, this feature reapplies the updates that occurred after that point and before the disaster. For example, if an application inadvertently corrupted the information at 12:05, the disk could be rolled back and then have the updates that occurred before 12:00 reapplied.
- *Security.* Maintaining an audit trail of what program applied what update at what time is often a critical part of preventing a disaster from repeating. An audit trail can find the offending program so it can be corrected.

On a much broader level, another technique to help maintain a high degree of data integrity and availability is disk shadowing. With this technique, you attach two disks to at least one (but preferably two) hierarchical storage controllers in a cluster so identical information is maintained on both disk drives. Please note, however, that you should use shadowing with the above recovery mechanisms to handle situations in which the application corrupts both copies of the information.

As previously discussed, VAXclusters initially were developed to help Digital compete in the higher end of the market. The advent of high-end systems from Digital, however, will not make the cluster obsolete. Instead, systems like the Alpha 8000 Series will be used in clusters to maximize and even increase their high performance.

To sum up the salient difference between SMP and clusters, SMP is an architecture that enables multiple applications within a computer to run in parallel (to a degree), sharing common memory and disk resources. Clusters, on the other hand, enable multiple applications on separate computers to share the same information stored on disk. With clusters, there is no need to redesign or DECompose programs to take advantage of the shared disk facility. Finally, SMP can be implemented within a cluster to achieve maximum performance (provided the computers in the cluster support multiple processors).

Strategy for Connectivity

Digital Equipment Corporation's strategy for connectivity is built upon DECnet. *DECnet* is a set of products and services designed and implemented based on the Digital Network Architecture (DNA). DECnet was originally implemented using proprietary protocols, but in the early 1990s, Digital shifted DECnet into the open network environment by incorporating support for both OSI protocols and for TCP/IP.

The shift toward open networking was the fifth major "phase" (revision) in the DECnet specifications. The original DECnet phase (Phase I) was introduced in 1976, and provided simple services for file transfer and program-to-program communication between PDP-11 machines running the RSX-11M operating system. At the time, this was fairly revolutionary, as software portability was almost non-existent. The subsequent phases added more networking and interoperability services, bringing DECnet up to the level of where it is today.

Phase II was released in 1978, and brought the capabilities of Phase I to all major operating systems (including VMS). Additional features included remote file access, network management tools, and support for point-to-point network configurations. Phase III, released in 1980, introduced a dynamic adaptive routing algorithm, which automatically calculated the best route to a message's destination. Under Phase II, a direct connection had to be created between systems. Phase III also offered support for X.25 packet switching networks as a method to connect systems, record-level access over the network, and downline loading. A Phase III network could include up to 255 nodes.

Introduced in 1982, Phase IV was a major jump in technology. Under this phase, Digital came to support ethernet, large LANs and WANs, virtual terminal services, and various communications servers and gateways.

Digital's Phase IV approach to combining DNA with Ethernet (resulting in DECnet) was the most revolutionary and sweeping networking architecture since IBM's Systems Network Architecture (SNA). Ethernet, the result of a collaboration among Digital Equipment, Intel Corporation, and Xerox Corporation, defines a physical interface that supports a data rate of 10 million bps over a shielded coaxial cable. Up to 1,024 nodes (addressable attachments) are supported. One of the major benefits of Phase IV was conformance with Open Systems Interconnect (OSI) standards.

The second important aspect of Ethernet is the collision-detection mechanism. Because any node on the network could transmit at any time, a regulation mechanism had to be created to recover from the inevitable collisions (which result in garbled information). The technique Digital and Xerox put in place was termed the Carrier Sense Multiple Access with Collision Detection (CSMA/CD).

Using the CSMA/CD technique, a node with information to transmit first listens to the network. If no one else is transmitting, that node goes ahead and sends. If, however, another node is transmitting on the network, that node waits for a predetermined length of time before attempting to transmit again. If two nodes transmit simultaneously, the collision is detected and both nodes wait for a random time period before attempting to retransmit.

The CSMA/CD technique is also used in the IEEE 802.3 network implementation. In fact, Ethernet and IEEE 802.3 are similar enough that nodes of both types can coexist on the same physical network (although the two implementations are also different enough that one type of node can't "understand" the other type's information).

Phase V was made available in 1991. It made significant changes to accommodate TCP/IP as an alternative to OSI standards for open networking. Digital had three goals in releasing Phase V: to permit a network to grow up to a million systems, to incorporate both OSI and TCP/IP standard protocol suites to provide for a higher level of system integration, and to support a distributed mode of operation. Although a Phase IV network could accommodate up to 64,000 nodes, the industry's move towards distributed, client/server computing soon limited Phase IV's viability. Phase V introduced a new routing algorithm, which can potentially support millions of nodes. This algorithm has since been adopted as a routing standard for both OSI and TCP/IP networks. Phase V also set out to provide a distributed networkwide naming service, and to permit nodes to generate their own addresses and register themselves automatically.

The Digital Distributed Name Service (DECdns) provides the following features: distribution (so naming information does not have to be stored in a single location), replication, dynamic updating, automatic updating, and a hierarchical naming structure. Adding a new node to a Digital Equipment network is remarkably simple when using DECnet with DECdns. The combination of these two products permit full autoconfiguration. Where DECdns assigns names to computer systems, X.500 names extend to naming individuals within a naming framework.

DECnet can be implemented on a LAN using Ethernet or over a WAN using a variety of routers and/or gateways to bridge the distant LANs. Technicalities notwithstanding, the primary function of DECnet is to deliver the following capabilities:

- *Task-to-task communications.* The capability of two programs (possibly running on dissimilar systems or written in dissimilar languages) to exchange information.
- *Remote file access.* The capability to transfer files to and from remote locations and to perform read and write (record-level) operations to a remote file.
- *Network terminal access.* The capability of terminals to access a remote system and run programs on that system as if they were locally attached terminals.
- *Network management.* The capability to locate and isolate network problems without bringing the whole network down.

Ch
2

■ *Downline loading.* The capability to load a program or task from one system onto another and run it on that system.

■ *Upline dumping.* The capability of a system during abnormal termination to send pertinent system information to an adjacent system. When the failed node has been restored, this information can then be downloaded to help it resume its normal operations.

Understanding the importance of DECnet is the key to understanding Digital's approach to data processing. It is much rarer to find a single, isolated, non-networked VAX than to find two or more Digital nodes communicating via ethernet.

Digital uses an X.500-based Directory Service, a general-purpose distributed directory similar to Banyan's StreetTalk and Novell's NetWare Distributed Services. Digital goes further than these two products in making the service accessible from any Web browser or messaging system. Digital's service can be used to hold any information that an organization wants to make public; sensitive data can be restricted. The directory can be divided between multiple directory servers, with each server having the ability to pass directory tasks to other servers that possess the relevant data. Digital X.500 Directory Service supports Internet and X.400-based networks, and can function as a superset of other directory services to form a global directory for messaging and other applications. The service is integrated with Digital's MAILbus 400 backbone, which acts as a bridge between SMTP and other enterprise mail systems. Developers can write applications to access the directory using the industry standard X/Open XDS API. With the Digital X.500 Directory Synchronizer, directory information can be exchanged and synchronized in a multivendor environment. Directories from many popular e-mail products can be synchronized, and it can also support legacy e-mail, Internet mail, and custom systems.

Messaging

Digital accommodates enterprisewide messaging in a multivendor environment with a range of products that adhere to industry standards. Digital's messaging strategy comprises a three-tier, client/server architecture, consisting of the enterprise backbone, departmental system, and the desktop.

The messaging infrastructure lives at the Enterprise Backbone Server tier, and provides mission-critical transport and directory services for heterogeneous mail environments, as well as management of the messaging network. Connectivity to X.400 and the Internet is also achieved at this level.

At the Departmental Server tier, a mail or groupware server is deployed, and access to the enterprise directory is achieved through a variety of servers, including MailWorks (a client/server messaging system for LAN mail connectivity), Microsoft Exchange Server, and ALL-IN-1. At the Desktop tier. E-mail clients can select from various products such as Microsoft Mail, Lotus cc:Mail, TeamLinks, and Windows 95.

The Digital and Microsoft Alliance

Recently, Digital entered into a messaging alliance with Microsoft to develop a joint enterprise mail infrastructure. The result of this alliance will be the eventual integration of ALL-IN-1 and MailWorks, with the Microsoft Exchange Server through MAILbus 400 and Digital X.500 Directory Service. *MAILbus 400* is a store-and-forward message transfer agent (MTA) that connects with other systems and services. MAILbus is based on the X.400 standard, and can therefore connect to a wide variety of other X.400 MTAs. DEC EDI (Electronic Data Interchange) provides connectivity between a company and its customers or suppliers.

Digital and Microsoft's alliance further ensures the interoperability of all Digital and Microsoft products. The Microsoft Exchange Server mail technology will be integrated with Digital's ALL-IN-1 and MailWorks products, and Digital's mail backbone will support Exchange Server. Digital will also support Microsoft's Windows Open Systems Architecture (WOSA) API in OpenVMS, which will permit application developers to write to both operating environments more easily. The alliance will contribute significantly to the integration of Windows NT into the enterprise.

Ch 2

Application/User Relationship

Although Digital offers a variety of different operating systems and hardware architectures, this section focuses on the most popular combination—the OpenVMS operating system on Alpha AXP.

OpenVMS is an interactive operating system, originally developed for the VAX, that gives each user the illusion that he or she is the only user on the computer. Each user can run programs and access files independently of other users. If shared services are required for access to a common data base, for example, the services are handled at a system level, invisible to the user. After a user is logged onto a given computer in the system, the further interaction between that user and the computer is termed a *session.*

Within a session, the interaction between the user and the application is typically character-oriented. Although Digital terminals and programs do support block-oriented transmission formats for data entry, the application usually reads single (or small groups of) characters from the keyboard as they are being typed.

For more sophisticated applications such as word processing, this reading method enables the terminal and the application to interact as a PC keyboard interacts with a PC—each key pressed can be interpreted as appropriate for that context. (This similarity is one of the reasons that PC software vendors migrate toward DEC equipment. Conceptually, they are very similar in intent and implementation.)

Although many other computer systems use a character-oriented, interactive interface (for example, the HP 3000 under its MultiProgramming Executive, or MPE), Digital has so refined this interface that it has become an integral part of Digital's applications development strategy.

Digital has also developed its own graphical interface for terminals and PCs. This interface, termed *DECwindows,* provides an alternative interface between the user and the applications. As X Window graphic terminals become more available, this method will become the preferred alternative to the traditional character-oriented interface. DECwindows can be used with the OpenVMS, ULTRIX, and MS-DOS operating systems.

Terminal Attachment Philosophy

Terminals can attach physically to the network through one of the following two devices:

- *A host.* In this case, the terminal attaches directly to a Digital Equipment host via an asynchronous link.

- *A terminal server (DECserver).* The terminal attaches (via an asynchronous link) to a specialized device that manages the interface between the physical network (ethernet) and the terminal.

The simplest connection consists of a terminal directly connected to a Digital host via a simple, asynchronous line (see Figure 2.4). With this attachment, the host responds directly to the terminal's activities without using any complicated protocol. By necessity, the terminal must activate a session on the attached host to access any local or remote application. The relationship between the terminal and host is a simple one-to-one connection (one terminal connecting to one host port).

FIG. 2.4

Direct Attached
Terminal

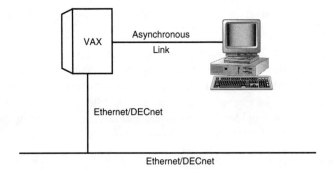

In the more normal case, however, terminals connect to terminal servers called *DECservers* (see Figure 2.5). Although the interaction between the terminal and its server is identical to the interaction between the terminal and a directly connected host (specifically, no complicated protocol is required), the interactions between the terminal server and the computers are quite different.

Terminal servers talk to Digital host computers using the LAT protocol. LAT operates independently from other DECnet protocols and provides two significant benefits:

- *Group transmission.* Under LAT, the terminal server collects characters from a terminal and sends them to the host as a group, rather than as individual transmissions. LAT transmission is often less disruptive for the computer hosting the application and therefore can improve performance.

FIG. 2.5
Terminal Server
Connection

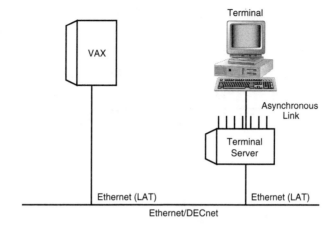

- *Multiple hosts.* Because LAT is not associated with any particular host, the terminals attached to the terminal server can connect to any of the hosts on the same ethernet LAN. In many cases, terminal servers provide a means for a single terminal to invoke different sessions on multiple hosts and switch back and forth between them.

More complicated are the cases in which a terminal directly connected to a host wants to access another host, or when a terminal on a terminal server wants to access a host that is not locally attached to the ethernet network but is attached to the wide area Digital network. In both instances, another protocol, *CTERM (Command Terminal)*, comes into play. A DECnet host uses the CTERM to shuttle information between a terminal and another host (see Figure 2.6). The drawback to this technique, however, is that it consumes resources in the host sponsoring the remote link (that is, the one initiating the connection).

Regardless of the type of connection, the terminal normally uses the XON/XOFF mechanism to control the flow of data. With this technique, the terminal sends an XOFF character to the host when it wants the host to stop transmitting and then sends an XON character when it is ready for the host to resume transmitting.

Peer-to-Peer Relationships

DECnet, by its very design and intent, promotes peer-to-peer relationships among its computing nodes. This peer-oriented relationship is at the core of the DNA that underlies products like the VAXcluster and even DECnet; to obtain true distributed processing, a network of peer processes (and therefore processors) must be established.

You can see how peer-to-peer relationships contribute to peer-to-peer processing and communications by looking at remote file handling and task-to-task communications. Regarding network file access, the entity requesting the remote file could be an application program, the Network File Transfer (NFT) utility, or just a standard copy command. In the case of an application program requesting a remote file, Digital supplies a set of routines called the *Network File Access Routines (NFARs)* to assist the program by performing some of the lower levels of the exchange. In the case of user commands, the interface is handled via *Record Management Services (RMS)*.

FIG. 2.6
LAT and CTERM

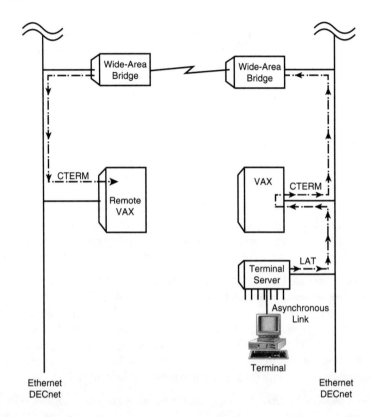

On the other side of the equation (that is, the computing node with the file to be accessed), resides a utility called the *File Access Listener (FAL)*. FAL listens for network requests for files on its node and translates the network request into a local operation. FAL communicates with the requesting entity via the *Data Access Protocol (DAP)*, which is part of the DNA. In truth, DAP actually handles most of the file transfer, another sign of how deep the peer-to-peer relationship is embedded in DECnet.

The issue of task-to-task communications is, however, a bit more complex. A task might have to communicate with another task that might not be running; or maybe it is running, but is unable to respond. Therefore, programs performing this type of network communications must follow some basic rules.

These rules, or *task-to-task communications,* begin with one program requesting a logical link to another program and identifying the location (node) and name of the target program. If the program is not known on the remote node or if the program is not able to receive communications, the network will reject the link request. If, on the other hand, the program is available and ready, then the link request will be delivered to the program, and then the program will accept or reject the request.

After the link has been requested and accepted, the programs can exchange data. Information can be sent one or both ways—it is a function of the application, not the network. When the communications are complete, one of the programs requests a termination of the link, and that logical link is disassembled.

In 1990, Digital refined the marketing of its peer-to-peer relationships with the introduction of Network Application Support (NAS). Targeted to compete against IBM's Systems Application Architecture (SAA), NAS is offered as a set of software products for developing and implementing distributed processing systems or client/server applications. Behind the marketing hype is Digital's solid peer-to-peer technology.

Ch
2

PC Integration Strategy

Although Digital Equipment's PC product line has some shaky history, there is nothing shaky about its PC integration strategy. Because Digital has such a strong LAN foundation with its DECnet strategy, the integration of PCs is simply a matter of interfacing them with the existing network. Furthermore, because of the wide presence of Digital midrange computers in the general marketplace, PC LAN vendors such as Novell have developed special products that enable Digital machines to participate in their third-party network architectures.

Digital Equipment provides two approaches to integration (see Figure 2.7).

FIG. 27
PC-DECnet Integration with DECnet-DOS and PCSA

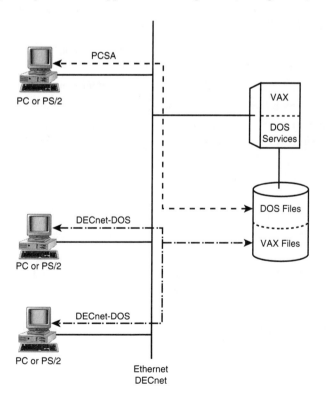

To integrate PCs into the standard DECnet architecture, Digital provides *DECnet-DOS,* which enables a PC to function as a DECnet computing node. DECnet-DOS offers the following fundamental capabilities:

■ *Task-to-task communication.* PC-based programs can use standard DECnet task-to-task communications.

■ *Remote file access.* The PC can initiate file exchanges with other DECnet computing nodes using the NFT utility.

■ *VT220 terminal emulation.* The PC can act as a terminal to access DECnet applications using the SETHOST utility. This utility makes the PC appear as if it were a terminal, physically attached to the target system. SETHOST also provides full local printer support with Digital printers.

■ *Use of disk space.* The PC can use disk space on a remote DECnet node as if it were local.

A DECnet-DOS node can be connected to the network with an Ethernet or asynchronous DECnet connection, using the PC's COM port as a physical link. The system to which the PC is attached must be a DECnet Phase IV, full-function node, supporting asynchronous DDCMP. For read-only operations, multiple DECnet-DOS nodes can simultaneously access the same network disk.

The other approach is Digital's Pathworks, formerly Personal Computing Systems Architecture (PCSA), which is a set of services that includes DECnet-DOS. Its benefits (in addition to those already listed for DECnet-DOS) are as follows:

■ Support for a variety of PC client workstations, including DOS, Windows, OS/2, Macintosh, Windows NT, NetWare, LAN Manager, and Windows for Workgroups.

■ Data sharing with UNIX and OpenVMS workstations, and VT or 3270 terminals.

■ Support for a variety of servers, including UNIX, Windows NT, OpenVMS, and OS/2.

■ Support for most network protocols, including TCP/IP, DECnet, IPX/SPX, NetBEUI, AppleTalk, and LAT. Access to gateways is also provided for SNA and X.25 networks.

■ The option to boot from the network so that PCs without hard disk drives can be configured to load their operating system and programs from a VAX-based virtual disk.

■ Print server capabilities whereby the networked PCs can use the print resources of the VAX server (in other words, the VAX running the Pathworks service software).

■ File services that enable files to be shared between MS-DOS and VMS.

Both of Digital's approaches work for any PC-compatible device (in other words, the solutions do not run only on Digital PCs). Also, both approaches require an Ethernet interface card (from any of a variety of vendors) in the PC.

Pathworks permit PC users to run non-PC applications and access data beyond the PC LAN. Pathworks' Network Connect interface permits PC users to access multivendor file and print services. Further host connectivity is offered with services that include terminal emulation, an X Window System server, and e-mail.

Several third-party PC LAN companies have been attracted to Digital's market. This attraction, coupled with Digital's impressive installed base and the relative ease with which software can be ported from the PC to Alpha, has spawned some interesting products, such as Windows NT versions of OpenVMS and Polycenter Manager.

Office Automation

Digital's offering in this area is the VAX/OpenVMS resident product ALL-IN-1. *ALL-IN-1* is a menu-driven system that, in its most basic form, provides electronic mail, calendar functions, and general information management functions. Furthermore, ALL-IN-1 can be enhanced to include sophisticated word processing and spreadsheet functions.

The basic package provides mail distribution and retrieval services to all participating ALL-IN-1 users. The calendar functions provide for individual (or group, in some cases) scheduling as well as general time-management functions. The information functions, however, are quite sophisticated and include forms-management tools to make data look attractive. Information entered into the facility can be used to create an online reference facility, a public notice facility, or any other file-oriented application.

More often than not, ALL-IN-1's electronic mail function is tied to the advanced word process-ing offered by the optional *WPS-PLUS* (usually pronounced "WIPS-PLUS"). WPS-PLUS is a word processor that uses the advanced capabilities of the standard VT200-style keyboard to provide word processing features similar to those found on dedicated word processors or PCs running high-end word processing software. These capabilities include word wrap, cut and paste, find and replace, headers, footers, multiple font types, and so on. To add even more sophistication, WPS-PLUS supports optional modules for spell and grammar checking.

Another option to the basic ALL-IN-1 package is *20/20,* a VAX-based spreadsheet from Access Technology Inc. (Indianapolis, Indiana). Conceptually similar to the well-known Lotus 1-2-3 spreadsheet, 20/20 offers a range of spreadsheet functions and the capability to display busi-ness graphics. Some of the more advanced features of 20/20 include project management (scheduling and tracking), as well as file interchange with Lotus 1-2-3 (via a conversion utility).

Besides ALL-IN-1, Digital's Alpha machines come equipped with the following:

- POLYCENTER systems management and data center automation for networked systems and clusters
- PATHWORKS for supporting Windows, DOS, OS/2, and Mac users
- LinkWorks for networking PCs, Macs, and Motif-based workstations and permitting them to share data and applications
- ACCESSWORKS middleware for desktop access to distributed information

Ch 2

Network Architecture

Any DECnet LAN of reasonable size begins with a *backbone*. Individual connections or tributaries of connections are dropped from the backbone, providing a relatively understandable network topology that is simple to change or grow.

The backbone can be either a *baseband* (for computer data only) or a *broadband* (for combined voice, video and data) medium. If a broadband medium is used, a converter extracts the information from the broadband medium and converts it into the more readily used baseband facility. The Ethernet baseband medium conforms to the IEEE 10BASE5 standard.

Connections to the baseband cable are made through transceivers (see Figure 2.8). *Transceivers* convert between the baseband medium and the ThinWire coaxial medium and/or a 15-wire medium. The most common transceivers are the H4000 series manufactured by Digital.

FIG. 2.8

Sample DECnet LAN

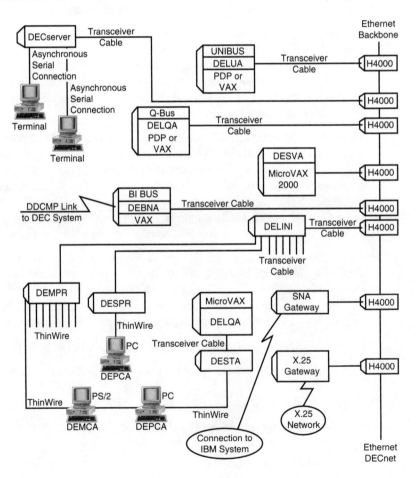

The cabling from the transceiver normally connects directly to an interface card within a system or to another type of network device. The type of interface card used depends on the bus of the host system. Some common interfaces that support connection via transceiver and their matching buses include DELUA for Unibus (PDP/VAX) systems, DELQA for Q-Bus (PDP/VAX) systems, DEBNA for VAXBI (VAX) systems, and DESVA for the MicroVAX 2000.

Another common network device that connects to a transceiver is the *Digital Ethernet Local Network Interconnect (DELNI)*. DELNI connects up to eight devices (via transceiver cables) to form a small LAN. DELNI can also connect to a baseband Ethernet cable (via an H4000 transceiver) to turn the other connected devices into tributaries of the backbone. (In smaller networks, DELNI is used alone or with other DELNIs to form a LAN that has no backbone.)

To connect PCs, IBM PS/2s, or other devices that operate in locations (or in numbers) that make standard transceiver connections difficult, Digital Equipment supports the use of a ThinWire medium. *ThinWire* is a thin coaxial medium that conforms to the IEEE 10BASE2 standard. ThinWire devices are linked on the coaxial cable via a T-shaped connector for each attached device. Common thin-wire devices include the following:

- *Digital ThinWire Ethernet Multi-Port Repeater (DEMPR)*. The DEMPR provides up to eight ThinWire segments. A DEMPR can be connected to a transceiver (or DELNI), or it can be used by itself or with other DEMPRs to create a stand-alone, ThinWire network.
- *Digital ThinWire Ethernet Single-Port Repeater (DESPR)*. A DESPR connects to a transceiver (or DELNI) on one side and provides a ThinWire segment on the other side.
- *Digital ThinWire Ethernet Station Adapter (DESTA)*. If a standard transceiver device is present in the middle of a ThinWire network, the DESTA can translate the ThinWire back into the standard transceiver interface. In a sense, the DESTA is the opposite of a DESPR (which connects a ThinWire device to a transceiver).
- *DEPCA*. An Ethernet ThinWire adapter for a standard PC/XT or PC/AT (8-bit) slot.
- *DEMCA*. An Ethernet ThinWire adapter for a PS/2 Micro Channel slot.

Terminals normally connect through terminal servers. Terminal servers can connect to the backbone via a transceiver or DELNI and interface to terminals via standard RS-232C asynchronous connections that can operate up to 19.2Kbps. Almost all terminal servers use the LAT protocol for terminals accessing computing nodes.

In addition to providing connectivity for terminals, terminal servers also allow connectivity to serial printers and modems. Two Digital terminal servers are:

- The DECserver 200. Allows the connection of up to eight serial devices. Multiple DECserver 200s can be implemented through multiple transceivers.
- The DECserver 550. A rack-mounted terminal server that supports a range of optional cards to provide additional connectivity or special-case connectivity (for example, connection of IBM 3270 terminals). A DECserver 550 connects via transceiver and can support 16–128 serial devices (through the use of optional cards).

Bridges, routers, and gateways can attach to Ethernet via transceivers. These highly specialized devices (normally computers in their own right) are used to implement WANs or to

Ch
2

provide interfaces with IBM equipment. Refer to Chapter 7, "LANs and WANs," for more information on these devices.

Also, a *Digital Data Communications Message Protocol (DDCMP) link* can connect Digital systems together over traditional telephone or serial links. DDCMP is an integral part of DECnet that is often essential in implementing networks that are low cost or non-PSDN (packet-switching public data networks). In a nutshell, DDCMP is a system-to-system communications method.

Finally, because most of the components offered by Digital conform to the IEEE 802.3 standards as well as the Ethernet standards, a functional, mixed-vendor network can be constructed with them. Such a network could use Digital Equipment systems and networking devices but run alternative network software such as TCP/IP. (In fact, because the equipment conforms to both standards, such alternative networking software as TCP/IP and HP's NS can run concurrently with DECnet on the same physical network.)

Digital is the leader in *Fiber Distributed Data Interface (FDDI)* switching, with its GigaSwitch product. FDDI is a high-speed fiber optic networking technology, often used as a backbone for joining together servers or multiple LANs. *GigaSwitch* is an FDDI switch that can significantly extend the useful lifetime of a LAN by increasing the amount of effective bandwidth available.

Digital is embracing virtual LAN (VLAN) technology with its enVISN architecture (for more information on virtual LANS, see the section "VLAN Technology" in Chapter 11, "Network Management"). Under *enVISN,* policy agents are created to ensure that the physical switch carries out quality of service, security, and membership policies relative to the VLAN architecture. Quality of Service features permit certain types of traffic to receive higher priority than others. For example, a system with quality of service features might grant the highest priority to transaction processing, and the lowest to file transfers. ●

CHAPTER 3

Hewlett-Packard

Company Background

From a modest start in 1939, Bill Hewlett and Dave Packard developed HP into a company that specialized in instruments and instrument control, marketing their products through independent sales organizations. Ten years later, in 1949, HP had sales in excess of $2 million and more than 100 employees. Throughout the 1950s and into the 1960s, HP continued to grow conservatively. In 1966, Hewlett-Packard released the first product that could be legitimately called a computer, the HP2116A. The HP2116A did not, however, mark the beginning of explosive growth in computer manufacturing—it merely signaled the start of HP's computer-line development.

In 1971, HP released its first hand-held scientific calculator. Unexpectedly, this product caused a tidal wave of demand that led HP to expand and refine its calculator products into a variety of specialized markets. The 1970s also saw HP define and refine its computer product line. Between the mid-70s and mid-80s, its computer offerings evolved into three basic lines: the HP 1000 real-time technical computer, the HP 3000 general business computer, and the HP 9000 engineering workstation.

Yet, HP was not widely regarded as a leading edge technology company. To be sure, HP had an excellent reputation for innovation in instrumentation, but this innovation was never seen in its computer line. In the late 1980s, however, HP gambled—and gambled big—by introducing a reduced instruction set computer (RISC) design in the HP 3000, its general business computer.

HP stayed in the spotlight with the acquisition of Apollo Computer in 1989. A seemingly dramatic departure from HP's normally conservative management style, this acquisition strengthened HP's overall position in the engineering workstation and workstation server market.

Product Line Overview

As a full-line manufacturer, Hewlett-Packard produces a range of products, from basic terminals to the high end of the midrange market. Although HP often positions itself against the low end of the IBM-based mainframe market, it does so more because of overlaps between IBM's own product lines than true mainframe-class power and performance in an HP computer.

The latest member of the PA-RISC processor family, the PA-7200, extends the previous single chip superscalar PA-7100 design with a number of design improvements. The PA-7200 permits higher clock frequencies and has an on-chip assist cache that combines with a hardware prefetch mechanism, which can significantly speed up many analytic and high-end applications. The prefetch algorithm permits instructions to be prefetched from memory on cache misses, and can offer significant performance improvements in a transaction processing environment.

HP Terminals

HP terminals are unique in that they can operate in several different modes, and actually switch in and out of these modes as directed by applications. From a data communications point of view, this approach offers efficiency—the application minimizes transmission between the terminal and itself without sacrificing ease of data entry. On the other hand, first-time HP programmers are often confused by this multipersonality technology.

In many ways, the HP terminal represents the crossbreeding of the character-oriented DEC VT terminal with the block orientation of the IBM 3270 and 5250 terminal families. Some of the terminal's more familiar, character-oriented operations include the following:

- *Character mode.* In this mode, individual characters are transmitted to the host as they are typed at the keyboard. This mode is similar to the way that DEC terminals operate normally.
- *Character/forms mode.* In this mode, specific areas of the screen are designated for data entry (termed unprotected fields) and the rest of the display is protected from alteration.

When an HP terminal is in character mode, the end of transmission is normally signaled when the operator presses the Return key. In block-mode operation, the operator must trigger transmission by hitting a separate Enter key.

Furthermore, HP terminals make a critical distinction between block mode and forms mode (HP actually refers to the latter as *format mode*). In block-mode operations, the terminal enters data locally; therefore, the user may edit data before pressing the Enter key to transmit the data. Forms mode, on the other hand, defines the rules for establishing protected, unprotected, and transmit-only fields on the terminal screen.

Forms mode does not require block mode, nor does block mode require forms mode. These modes are further complicated by a line setting that defines the size of the transmission. The functional capabilities that result from these seemingly unholy marriages include the following:

- *Block/line mode.* When the Enter key is pressed, the current line is transmitted to the host computer.
- *Block/line/forms mode.* This causes transmission of multiple fields on a single line.
- *Block/page mode.* This is the opposite of block/line mode. In this setting, the screen (or page) is transmitted when the Enter key is pressed.
- *Block/page/forms mode.* This mode is similar to the way 3270-type terminals operate in that all fields on the screen (or page) are transmitted to the host computer when the Enter key is pressed.

HP's X terminals are designed to accommodate the desktop computer's increasing role in corporate computing. HP's X terminal product line provides high-performance graphics and maximizes access to information and multivendor resources across the enterprise. HP has two lines of RISC-based X terminals—the low-end Entria Plus and the higher-end Envizex. Both run the Intel i960 RISC processor.

HP's Envizex color X station appears to the end user as a full-fledged workstation. The terminal's superb multimedia support provides full-motion MPEG video. The machine is the only X terminal to provide access to high-speed networks through 100VG-AnyLAN networking, and is also one of the only X terminals to include an optional internal floppy drive. The Envizex also builds in ThickLAN, ThinLAN, and standard twisted-pair network connectors, as well as optional Token Ring support.

The lower-end Entria X terminal is an excellent choice to upgrade from character-based ASCII or 3270 terminals. Mainframe access can be achieved through a transparent terminal emulation program and you will enjoy a color GUI-based X station, which can function as a plug-and-play HP 9000 server console. You can easily switch between console operations and system management applications on the same desktop. The Entria includes built-in support for ThinLAN and 10BaseT networking.

The HP Entria Plus line provides access to UNIX, Windows, Internet, and legacy applications—all from a single X station. The Entria and Envizex are referred to as *thin clients,* which make use of the network's infrastructure and devices as opposed to providing processing and storage for each desktop. HP's approach to X terminals provides a number of advantages, including auto-configuration and centralized maintenance of TCP/IP environments through Dynamic Host Configuration Protocol (DHCP). All of HP's X stations are also tightly integrated with HP's OpenView systems management software, which permits all of an enterprise's X stations to be centrally managed. OpenView offers a broad range of management features and is capable of managing any SNMP-compliant device.

The Entria Plus can function as an HP 9000 graphics server console, eliminating the need for multiple desktops. Both Entria Plus and Envizex come with HP's line of software, which includes the following:

Ch
3

- *HP Enware X Station Software.* One site copy is required to run HP X stations.
- *HP Enware X Terminal Manager.* Simplifies the administration of large groups of X terminals and permits an IP address to be assigned automatically through DHCP.
- *HP Enware CDE.* Provides a standard GUI for UNIX users.
- *HP Enware 3270.* A motif-based 3270 emulator for legacy mainframe or SNA connectivity.

In terms of network connectivity, both models can run on a standard Ethernet network; the Envizex can also be connected to a Token Ring or 100VG-AnyLAN infrastructure. Both models use standard 10Base-T and ThinLAN connectors. The included SharedX and SharedWhiteboard features permit multiple users linked with any X Window system and standard phone line to work cooperatively on a document.

PCs

Until the late 1980s, HP chose to follow the de facto standards set by the original IBM PC. The early machines were, in fact, Intel processors running MS-DOS software, but HP added its own enhancements to the product.

In an effort to overcome the cumbersome interface offered by standard MS-DOS (or PC-DOS), HP developed an alternative command processor that could be used in place of the standard COMMAND.COM processor. Good intentions notwithstanding, HP called this interface the Personal Applications Menu (PAM).

The PAM approach gave the end user an applications menu for selecting and running applications in a point-and-shoot fashion. It also provided a front-end to some of the more unfriendly DOS processes, such as formatting diskettes. However, PAM was not performance-oriented, so many veteran users simply abandoned PAM in favor of the standard command processor.

While it is neither important (nor fair) to review the entire history of HP's PC products, some of the more interesting innovations included the HP 125 dual terminal/computer, the HP 150 touchscreen terminal/computer and the HP Portable and Portable Plus. The HP 125 and HP 150 systems' built-in terminal functions made them popular alternatives to dedicated terminals. The HP Portable and Portable Plus were among the first of the MS-DOS transportable, quasi-laptop computers.

With the introduction of the HP Vectra in the mid-1980s, however, HP became a serious manufacturer of high-performance, IBM-compatible PCs. The Vectra is one of the original high-performance clones produced by a reputable manufacturer and offering performance in excess of the equivalent IBM models. Furthermore, in 1989 the 486 Vectra became the first PC on the market to offer the Extended Industry Standard Architecture (EISA) bus, an alternative to IBM's closed Micro Channel Architecture (MCA) for its PS/2 line.

Since the introduction of the Vectra line, HP has demonstrated a strong commitment to releasing network-ready PCs. A network-ready PC, as opposed to a PC designed for freestanding use, focuses on easy integration into an existing networking environment. HP addresses the issue of networkability in the Vectra line in several ways. The Vectra line supports several networking environments, industry-standard management is included, and the PCs offer remotely manageable security features. In addition, the higher-end Vectras are ready to attach to the network "out of the box."

The Vectra includes several technologies to maximize LAN performance, including an integrated PCI LAN adapter, PCI bus mastering, and parallel transfer technology. The presence of an integrated LAN adapter minimizes CPU usage, as compared to the alternative of placing a 16-bit ISA LAN adapter in a non-network-ready PC.

In addition, the HP Vectra XM Series 3 uses a parallel transferring driver. Typically, a LAN adapter is unable to transfer a frame to the CPU before the frame has been completely received from the network. The parallel transferring driver permits the transfer to the CPU to start in a parallel fashion, instead of sequentially. This model significantly improves throughput performance of the LAN interface.

The Vectra PCs are Desktop Management Interface (DMI)-enabled and include client-side DMI software. The DMI is a product of the Desktop Management Task Force (DMTF), of which HP is a founding member. DMI is a vendor-independent system that provides management information about the PC. Interestingly, the Vectra is one of the most network-ready PCs on the market. It can be turned on remotely from anywhere on an Ethernet LAN, and includes both local and remote support for HP's OpenView management platform.

The PC's Medium Access Control (MAC) address, which is accessible through remote DMI or the PC Setup program, is a unique address required to identify each Ethernet LAN adapter on a network. The availability of the MAC address through remote DMI eliminates both the need to physically discover the address by removing the case and the need to use a separate operating system utility.

HP is a leader in multiprocessing technology, first implementing the technology in its minicomputers and workstations in the 1980s. Multiprocessing at the PC level, however, is very new, and HP is one of the first vendors to implement Intel's Multiprocessor Specification (MPS) for dual processing on desktop PCs.

Engineering Workstations

Until the acquisition of Apollo Computer in 1989, the HP 9000 line of technical computers was HP's entry into this computation- and graphics-intensive, UNIX-hungry market. Designed to compete head-to-head in the engineering workstation market with Sun, DEC, IBM and others, the HP 9000 is now divided into the C Class and J Class categories. HP's workstation product line is largely based on the PA-7200 processor and provides a migration path to the innovative next-generation PA-8000 microprocessor. The workstations run the HP-UX UNIX operating system and sport the HP VUE user interface. Before the C Class and J Class machines, HP's workstations were divided into three basic categories: the 700/800 (RISC) Series; its predecessors, the 200/300/500 Series; and the HP Apollo 9000 Series 400, the first collaboration of the combined HP and Apollo divisions.

The HP 9000 Series 200, 300, and 500 computers were based on the Motorola MC68000 line of CPUs, although some configurations did include an Intel processor. These low-end units could optionally run one of three operating systems: BASIC, Pascal and HP-UX. While the BASIC and Pascal operating systems are HP proprietary (although somewhat portable because they are based on the programming languages of the same name), the HP-UX operating system is Hewlett-Packard's implementation of AT&T's UNIX.

On the high end, the HP 9000 Series 800 was HP's first technical venture into RISC architecture. RISC stands for Reduced Instruction Set Computer and is an alternative architecture to the standard Complex (or Complete) Instruction Set Computing (CISC). Under RISC architecture, computer hardware is optimized for absolute maximum performance and is streamlined so the software at some level (typically the compiler) has to handle the translation of complex activities into simple, high-speed hardware operations. In contrast, the CISC architecture uses specialized hardware and firmware to handle complex activities. Here, the software is streamlined, so the hardware has to compensate.

The demands for engineering workstation functions lie heavily in the areas of hardware performance. Real-time graphics displays (of extremely high resolution) driven by computation-intensive modeling programs are not trivial to produce. HP accommodates the need for real-time graphics with the inclusion of its VISUALIZE graphics accelerator in all of its workstation products. VISUALIZE combines the fast, RISC-based CPUs with an on-board RISC-based geometry accelerator.

Some of the newer designs also seek to optimize performance by having concurrent tasks handled by multiple CPUs. Under this multiprocessing model, a sophisticated CPU—independent of the main CPU—can handle the display.

Like its predecessors, the HP 9000 Series 800 runs the HP-UX operating system. But here, there are no esoteric options to run the BASIC or Pascal operating systems. HP's positioning of the Series 800 in the strict UNIX market, however, was very much in line with the market, which was moving away from proprietary (closed) operating systems to UNIX and its many derivatives. This position was further fortified by the introduction of the HP 9000 Series 700 in 1991. Hailed as the highest-performance workstation at the time of its introduction, the HP 9000 Series 700 also uses RISC technology to sponsor the HP-UX operating system.

HP's acquisition of Apollo in 1989 greatly changed the complexion of its engineering workstation offerings and also enhanced its overall position in that market. Although the Apollo line was also based on the Motorola MC68000 series of processors, it offered more synergy than compatibility when combined with the HP line. In many respects, this was the desired result.

Originally established in 1980 by former employees of DEC and Prime, Apollo had been a small but successful player in the workstation market, like its primary competitor, Sun Microsystems. Apollo offered a range of workstations that ran Apollo's proprietary Domain operating system. But it was in the area of networking that Apollo earned a great deal of attention.

Apollo adopted the philosophy that programmatic network access should be an integral but open part of the operating system. Toward this goal, Apollo introduced the Network Computer System (NCS), a methodology for allowing applications to exchange information with one another as well as access shared network resources. NCS has since become a standard of such interest that it has been licensed by other major manufacturers.

The fusion of Apollo's NCS with the HP approach to networking, as well as the fit of the Apollo product line with the HP 9000 line, have made the joining of Apollo with HP a very noteworthy union. The first offspring of this union was the HP Apollo Series 400 line. Like the Series 300, the Series 400 was based on the Motorola MC68000 line of microprocessors. Capable of running either the HP-UX or Apollo Domain operating system, the Series 400 was the first tangible result of HP's long-term plan to integrate the HP and Apollo workstation lines.

The C-class workstation family is well-suited to graphical applications such as electronic design automation (EDA), computational analysis, and other compute-intensive processing applications. The C class is available in two configurations: the C100, running a 100 MHz PA-7200 CPU, and the C120, running at 120 MHz. The C-class supports IEEE 802.3/Ethernet networking connections.

The high-performance HP 9000 J-class Workstations (see Figure 3.1) are available in two configurations, the J200 and J210. The workstations use HP's 2-D and 3-D graphics, and are appropriate for computational analysis, CAD, and 3-D design work. Like the C-class, the J-class workstations run the PA7200 processor and are upgradable to the PA8000. A second CPU module can be added to increase performance. Like the C-class, the J-class also supports IEEE 802.3/Ethernet network connections.

Midrange Offerings

The HP 1000 midrange line was quite popular, and enjoyed a long and successful life. However, it has largely been replaced with the HP 9000. The HP 1000 was found mainly in technical environments—on the shop floor or in medical labs controlling sophisticated instruments. A backplane-oriented, interrupt-driven machine that is vaguely reminiscent of 1960s technology, the HP 1000 was a real-time machine with interfaces to a variety of instruments. The machine was highly reliable and had a published mean time between failure (MTBF) of nine years. HP has since positioned the HP 9000 Series 700/800 computers as a replacement for the HP 1000 line.

The operating system for the HP 1000, Real Time Executive (RTE), is ideal for handling real-time operations. But, from a human interface perspective, it is appealing only to those who have long memories for short and cryptic commands.

The HP 3000, on the other hand, is a general business computer that marked HP's entry into the midrange market. In discussing the HP 3000 line, however, it is important to distinguish the old technology models from the new ones.

The first HP 3000 was introduced in 1972 as a general-purpose, 16-bit business minicomputer. This represented a significant departure for HP, which had previously stayed in more specialized markets. The operating system for the HP 3000 was termed MultiProgramming Executive (MPE). MPE was created by a group of engineers who had previously designed the Burroughs Corporation Master Control Program (MCP) operating system. A head-to-head comparison of MPE to MCP, however, would reveal far more differences than similarities.

FIG. 3.1

HP 9000 J-Class
Workstation

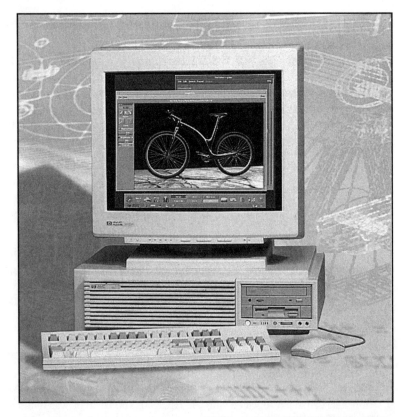

Photo courtesy of Hewlett-Packard Corp.

Unlike its relatives, the HP 9000 and the HP 1000, the HP 3000 was not designed to run special interfaces or highly complex, concurrent hardware activities. The HP 3000 is a general-purpose business machine designed to accommodate concurrent users working at administrative and business applications. Each user has a session environment from which he or she works independently of other users.

Taking a RISC

The introduction of RISC architecture really shook up the HP 3000 product line and its market. Inside HP, this project was known as "Spectrum." As previously discussed, HP had incorporated the RISC architecture into the HP 9000 earlier in the 1980s under the terminology HP Precision Architecture (HP-PA). Introducing RISC to the HP 9000 line, however, was not a great risk (no pun intended) because of the specialized hardware used in engineering workstations. After all, the more unique a workstation's hardware, the more likely the technical market will notice and accept it.

This same philosophy of "newer is better," however, is not prevalent in the general business computer market. End users are not interested in the possibilities of running the financial affairs of their companies on some new and not widely accepted computer architecture. Thus, crossing RISC into the HP 3000 was risky. Certainly, it did not require a massive hardware reengineering effort (the HP

9000 and HP 3000 RISC machines are built from the same base hardware components). HP was taking chances in two areas: customer acceptance of the new design, and reengineering MPE to function on a new hardware platform dramatically different from the old HP 3000 models.

When the HP 3000 RISC machines were introduced as the 900 Series, they were released with MPE-XL. This RISC-specific version of the operating system is capable of running in MPE compatibility mode to provide migration. Programs running in this compatibility mode do not achieve the same performance benefits as those programs running in native mode MPE, but portability was critical to the success of the product.

The release of the 900 Series did not bury the older, 16-bit CISC models of the HP 3000. In fact, HP continued to offer a low-end line (the MICRO 3000LX, 3000GX and 3000XE) as well as the midrange HP 3000 Series 70. These machines, renamed the Classic 3000 line, were released with support for the then current MPE-V operating system.

The HP 3000 continues to be widely respected as a strong and reliable general-purpose midrange system. However, there are very few new sales of the HP 3000 line, as new projects are more often based on UNIX Relational Database Management Systems (RDBMS) and applications. However, HP continues to support existing HP 3000 customers, the majority of whom plan to continue using their HP 3000s for many years. Although there are few new sales of HP 3000s, the existing customer base remains loyal. HP plans to continue offering enhancements to the HP 3000's integrated systems software, operating environment, and network database. For those HP 3000 users that require connectivity to UNIX-based RDBMS products, HP provides the means to interoperability.

The HP 3000 was never intended to be a platform for portable, third-party RDBMS products. The HP 9000, on the other hand, is HP's leading product for running RDBMS products from companies such as Oracle, Informix and Sybase. The hardware is basically the same in the HP 3000 and HP 9000; the different operating systems provide different personalities for the two environments. The HP 3000 offers tight integration between its MPE/iX operating system and the IMAGE/SQL network database, ALLBASE/SQL relational database, and other software components. In addition, HP has added POSIX APIs to MPE/iX and SQL access to IMAGE/SQL, which makes it easier for independent software vendors to port their applications to the HP 3000 platform.

The HP 9000 K-Class Symmetric Multiprocessing Server is a powerful midrange performer, based on the PA-7200 RISC processor and featuring a 64-bit design. The K-class is designed for high-speed networking, and includes optional high-speed FDDI, ATM and Fibre Channel networking capabilities, in addition to standard IEEE 802.3. The K-class expands up to four-way symmetric multiprocessing and supports the HP-UX UNIX operating system.

Top-end Offerings

HP's latest plan involves moving its largest customers to parallel processing. The HP 9000 EPS20 Enterprise Parallel Server (see Figure 3.2) is suitable for data warehousing and online transaction processing applications, or compute-intensive applications such as simulation or scientific visualization. HP offers two migration paths. The first combines multiple existing HP

9000 SMP servers into parallel clusters and the other solution deploys multiple HP 9000 T-class or K-class SMP servers as nodes, connected with a Fibre Channel link. Because this design allows sites to use their existing systems, moving to parallel clustering is fairly straightforward. Clusters can be created without new hardware, unlike massively parallel processing (MPP) systems, which require new hardware to be purchased.

FIG. 3.2
HP 9000 Model EPS20

Photo courtesy of Hewlett-Packard Corp.

The HP 9000 EPS20's parallel architecture differs from traditional parallel architectures, which often use loosely coupled uniprocessor nodes. By tightly coupling CPUs in an SMP infrastructure, a higher level of performance can be achieved. Additional SMP modules can be added as needed, and scaling is almost linear in most cases. The EPS can be seamlessly integrated into an existing multivendor environment and runs HP-UX, enabling it to support the thousands of existing commercial applications available for that platform.

Bundled with the EPS is HP's MC/System Environment (MCSE) administration software, which includes several system management tools and provides a centralized point of control for a variety of administrative tasks. MCSE includes the following:

■ *HP TaskBroker.* An X/Motif job scheduler and load balancer for distributed batch processing.

■ *Parallel Virtual Machine (PVM).* A library of parallel development tools for developing parallel applications.

■ *System Monitor Station.* An X/Motif interface application for system monitoring tasks.

■ *System Instant Ignition.* Used for automating system configuration, network integration, boot-up, and shut-down.

■ *HP-UX System Administration Manager Utility.* An enhancement for performing administrative tasks on a multi-computer EPS server.

The 64-bit EPS has a maximum external storage capacity of 8.3 terabytes. It has a maximum of four processors per node, up to eight modules, for a total of 32 120-MHz PA-7200 processors. The board can be upgraded to the PA-8000. The PA8000 design will offer nearly double the performance of a PA-7200 machine, going from 240 Peak MFLOPS (Millions of Floating Point Operations per Second) with the PA-7200 to 700 Peak MFLOPS (with the PA-8000).

HP's 64-bit, PA-8000 microprocessor uses a four-way superscalar design. The chip was designed for commercial data processing and compute-intensive applications, where data sets would otherwise be too large to fit into an on-chip cache. HP's design is unique in that it leaves primary instruction and data caches off-chip, thereby permitting them to be quite large.

Strategy for Connectivity

Hewlett-Packard's transition from CISC to RISC pales in comparison to the changes it has made in its overall network architecture. Specifically, HP entered into the 1980s with a simple strategy for the attachment of devices to host computers, with the most technically interesting interface at that time being HP-IB—HP's implementation of the IEEE-488 general-purpose interface for high-speed devices (disks, tapes, and so forth). By the end of the 1980s, however, HP had laid the groundwork for a comprehensive networking architecture that included LANs, WANs, and sophisticated graphics-based user interfaces.

HP chose to base its networking products on the IEEE 802.3 standard. The 802.3 implementation closely resembles the Ethernet II implementation used by DEC and others. In fact, they are so close that both types of networks can coexist on the same physical network (although they cannot communicate). For HP, the 802.3 implementation enables many prospective customers to plug HP gear into their existing Digital Ethernet networks.

With the issue of the physical topology of the network resolved, HP then went on to define the networking services (and software) that it would implement on its network. HP will unofficially acknowledge (and officially too, under the right circumstances) that it based its networking services design on the TCP/IP model.

However, in creating its Networking Services (NS) product line, HP sufficiently deviated from the TCP/IP standard to introduce levels of incompatibility with existing, competitive TCP/IP products.

Application/User Relationship

HP's approach to interfacing the human with the program uses a session philosophy in the multi-user environment. Specifically, the user logs on to the system, providing a proper user name and optional password, and can then access files or run programs that he or she has been given authority to read, write, or execute. This approach holds for the MPE (HP 3000), RTE (HP 1000), and the HP-UX (HP 9000) operating systems.

In this session environment, as far as the user can easily tell, he or she is the only person accessing that particular program at that time. The interaction between the user and the program can take on any of the terminal's characteristics (as discussed earlier in the section "HP Terminals"): the interaction can be free-form conversational entry, rigid and unforgiving template-based data entry, or virtually any structure in between. Again, this is one of the difficulties in learning HP—the wide range of choices can leave you hungering for rigid standards.

From the application's perspective, the program also recognizes only one user when it is running. In the simplest of applications, each user might have a copy of the program running out of the user's portion of the system's memory. From a programmer's perspective, this can ease the pain of program development because there is no need to take into consideration the complications caused by multi-user, multithreaded access (multiple users accessing the same program at the same time but at a different logical point in the program).

But reality dictates that large multi-user computers cannot truly give each user program and memory space. At a minimum, there must be a standard or interface that allows multiple programs to share data in a file. (After all, if everyone lived in their own little world and never needed to share or integrate information, they might as well each have stand-alone PCs and throw away the minicomputers and mainframes.)

To address these real-world, multi-user interfaces, HP uses layers of programs and provides central, shared resources to back them up. For example, while each user might have a copy of the portion of the program that is processing the screen, each copy of this program might in turn pass the data to another common program that coordinates all the input and output from all of the user programs. This arrangement ensures that Person A does not obliterate the information Person B is working on.

While it is probably unreasonable to go into further detail regarding how application programs are layered within the system, the availability and function of the central application resources are noteworthy. One of the key functions of any computer system is the database. To address this key area, HP provides a product called TurboIMAGE—a proprietary database package for its entire computer line (HP 1000, 3000, and 9000).

TurboIMAGE enables multiple programs to access and retrieve information based on a wide variety of selection criteria. It supports its own interface with programs and the Structured Query Language (SQL) interface. But TurboIMAGE is unique because it is one of the few databases developed by a computer manufacturer. Although end users do not see TurboIMAGE directly, the way that TurboIMAGE stores and retrieves information significantly controls what the users do see.

In contrast to TurboIMAGE's transparency is the physical appearance of the operating system. Until the late 1980s and early 1990s, the user saw a character-based (nongraphical) interface that prompted for action and then read back the typed response. In the late 1980s, HP adopted a graphics-based interface it termed NewWave. Although initially implemented on PCs with Microsoft Windows, NewWave was intended to also serve as an interface for graphics-based terminals. Furthermore, HP's experience developing NewWave greatly influenced its role in the development of the OSF/Motif graphic interface.

Following NewWave was HP-VUE, which ultimately formed the basis of the Common Desktop Environment (CDE), a standard GUI for all UNIX and X-based systems. CDE, a joint project led by HP and other prominent vendors, establishes a common look and feel for all UNIX systems, including workstations, X terminals and PCs, and provides for easier portability between UNIX-based operating systems. CDE does not actually represent any new technology, but instead incorporates existing technology from several vendors into a single, common standard. CDE includes HP's Visual User Environment (VUE), and is available on HP-UX and several other UNIX operating systems. Besides HP-VUE, CDE also includes elements of IBM's Common User Access Model.

In many respects, HP's approach to the user/application interface combines the best of both worlds. The user and the program appear to have a relatively simple one-to-one relationship while, in reality, these seemingly separate tasks are being centrally coordinated. The downside of this approach is the overhead and resources used to maintain the separate user identities and work areas.

Ch
3

Terminal Attachment Philosophy

Before HP's pervasive changes in its networking strategy, the relationship between an HP terminal and a computer was so straightforward that it bordered on boring. In the majority of installations, HP terminals were directly attached to the main computer via simple asynchronous connections. One terminal was attached to one port on the computer using one line.

These attachments generally used standard RS-232C connections (although options for RS-422 were also supported). Of the 25 supported RS-232C leads, direct-connected terminals can be configured to only three required lines: reference ground (7), transmit (2), and receive (3). An optional fourth line for frame ground (1) was more often ignored than used. Remote (modem) connections followed the more-or-less standard RS-232C asynchronous signals (pins 2–7, 20, and 22).

With this limited number of signals, the flow of data between the terminal and the computer is controlled through software—specifically, HP's proprietary, point-to-point terminal control protocol. Like the HP terminals and their multifaceted capabilities, the terminal protocol is also multilayered. Essentially, the flow control options can be lumped into the following groups:

- *DC1 handshaking.* This option, which regulates when the terminal can transmit data to the computer, has two different (and mutually exclusive) implementations. DC1 trigger is the simpler option; it specifies that the terminal can transmit after receipt of a DC1 control character. With the other option, DC1/DC2 handshake, the computer sends a

DC1 character, the terminal responds with a DC2 acknowledgment, the computer sends a second DC1, and then the terminal can transmit.

- *ENQ/ACK pacing.* This option ensures that the data is received correctly by the terminal and gives the terminal sufficient time to keep up with the computer. When ENQ/ACK is enabled, the computer breaks up a large transmission into small groups and terminates each group with the ENQ control character. When the terminal sees the ENQ, it responds to the computer with an ACK, thereby indicating it is ready for the next block of data.

- *XON/XOFF pacing.* XON/XOFF pacing also ensures that the side receiving the data is keeping up with the side transmitting the data. The XON and XOFF signals are the DC1 and DC3 control characters. XON/XOFF pacing has two implementations:

  - *XOFF transmitted by the terminal.* This implementation enables the terminal to terminate transmission, giving it time to process the data in its local buffer. When the terminal has caught up with the computer, it sends an XON, signaling the computer to resume transmission. (Also note that the user can perform this function by pressing Ctrl+S for XOFF and Ctrl+Q for XON, providing an opportunity to pause and review lengthy displays.)

  - *XOFF transmitted by the computer.* Here the perspective is reversed. The computer sends an XOFF to pause a transmission from the terminal and then sends an XON to resume it. Because the XON and XOFF characters are DC1 and DC3, this option cannot be used if either of the DC1 handshakes is enabled.

Of course, to make life complicated, any of these options can be used alone or, more likely, in a combination. Like the functional capabilities of the terminals, the flexibility of the data communications options can be overwhelming.

Even when HP made a major commitment to redevelop its LAN architecture along the lines of IEEE 802.3, terminal computer communications were not affected. Not until the introduction of the RISC-based HP 3000 Series 900 did HP change the way that terminals connected to computers; and even then, HP's changes affected only the HP 3000 RISC machines.

Given the general nature of IEEE 802.3 as a relatively high-speed (10 Mbps) coaxial-type of LAN, HP borrowed a page from the book of Digital Equipment and developed its own type of terminal servers, Distributed Terminal Controllers (DTCs). These DTCs took the place of asynchronous ports; in fact, each DTC interfaced up to 48 lines (terminals) to the IEEE 802.3 network, and consequently into the computer (see Figure 3.3).

While the DTCs introduced some new functions to HP's networking architecture (such as the ability for one terminal to connect to different hosts—a tough trick when they are hard-wired), the basic data communications flow between the terminal and the computer remained (for the most part) unchanged.

Peer-to-Peer Relationships

In HP's pre-NS days, establishing communications paths between programs (or even systems) was not a pretty sight. Within a machine, HP offered memory- and disk-based mailboxes to facilitate interprocess communications. This technique, however, required a great deal of standardization and cooperation from the programmers developing such applications.

FIG. 3.3
HP 3000 Series 900
Attachments

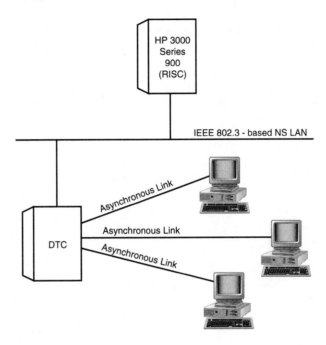

On a larger scale, the Data Services (DS) family of products provided system-to-system communications. The physical communications between systems was typically HP's implementation of a High-Level Data Link Control (HDLC) protocol, although support for X.25 connectivity was also permitted. Essentially, DS allowed terminals on one system to log onto other systems, files to be exchanged, and programs to open and access remote databases. But in comparison to NS, DS was a dinosaur waiting for a comet.

Because NS was modeled in many ways after the TCP/IP standard, its interprocess communications (IPC) methodology also follows the TCP/IP IPC standards. Much like Digital's task-to-task programmatic access, HP's NetIPC interface allows programs on the HP NS system to exchange information without requiring the programming gyrations necessary under the mailbox approach.

Furthermore, HP's acquisition of Apollo greatly enhanced its offering in this area. Apollo's own implementation of program-to-program communications—here, Apollo used the term remote procedure calls (RPCs)—was part of its overall Network Computing System (NCS). Apollo's approach to the matter became a subject of great interest to the computer industry as a whole, and the marriage of the two represented a new and significant standard to peer-to-peer processing.

PC Integration Strategy

Having chosen the IEEE 802.3 standard to implement its systemwide communications, HP borrowed its PC networking strategy from AT&T's StarLAN network. Integration of this separate network strategy with the backbone 802.3 computer system is handled through the use of a bridge.

With HP StarLAN, each PC is connected to a central hub using 1 Mbps thin wire (or optional twisted pair) cables (see Figure 3.4). Such systems as the HP 3000 can be connected directly to the same hub, or a node on the hub can be connected to an HP bridge that connects that hub to the backbone of the main 802.3 network.

A high-performance version of this basic network architecture is also available in the form of HP's StarLAN-10. StarLAN-10 differs from the original StarLAN in that it is based on a 10 Mbps coaxial medium and does not require a bridge to link with the main backbone (see Figure 3.5). Also note that either HP StarLAN or StarLAN-10 can be implemented as a stand-alone PC network—larger systems (HP 3000) need not be connected.

FIG. 3.4

HP StarLAN Network

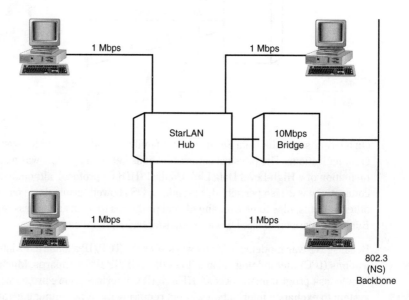

Although this PC networking strategy might seem somewhat less than awe inspiring, HP's advances in the area of user interfaces are noteworthy. Specifically, HP's NewWave, a graphical user interface for the PC environment, and the subsequent HP-VUE interface, provide an alternative to the IBM Presentation Manager (note that the release of NewWave preceded the final release of Presentation Manager).

NewWave, working with Microsoft Windows, provided a graphical interface that enables the user to select from programs and applications, regardless of where the applications reside or the information is located. VUE continued this functionality, and with the establishment of CDE, provided a single set of interfaces for HP-UX, IBM AIX, Solaris, UnixWare, and other

FIG. 3.5
HP StarLAN-10
Architecture

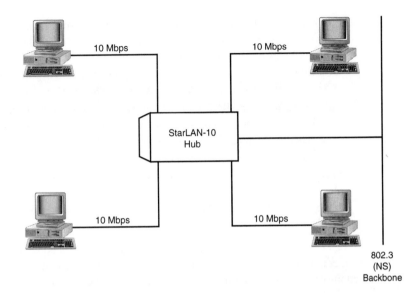

UNIX platforms. This enabled users to access data and applications from anywhere in the network, regardless of physical location or hardware platform.

NewWave, although it was a significant development, was also important in that it paved the road for other developments, including VUE and CDE. Within a year of NewWave's formal release, HP released NewWave Office. Whereas NewWave focused on bringing a better, graphical interface to the PC, NewWave Office is the first application implemented under the NewWave architecture. Under NewWave Office, the PC user selects an application whose core service (HP DeskManager) resides on an HP 3000 under the MPE operating system.

The HP implementation of CDE supports a variety of capabilities, including session management, window management, object/folder management, a full set of productivity tools and network services, and a set of GUI toolkits. CDE provides a set of policies and protocols for exchanging data between applications, and a file manager for manipulating objects.

Beyond improving the basic PC interface, HP's VUE pushes into the more traditional area of terminal interfaces. Here, by combining the graphical capabilities of X Terminals with its own implementation of X Window, VUE lays the foundation for a distributed computing environment that supports multiple systems and graphics terminals. Therefore, given the graphical, client/server foundation of VUE, HP's PC integration approach moves from a novel PC integration strategy to a networkwide standard for user/application interfaces.

Office Automation

The core product in HP's office automation package is HP Open DeskManager, which resides on an HP 3000 and uses HP's TurboIMAGE database system to maintain its structure and information. HP Open DeskManager provides office automation functions over a wide area encompassing different processing nodes (systems) and nonlocal users. HP Open DeskManager offers these features:

- *Electronic mail.* HP Open DeskManager provides a strong client/server-based electronic messaging system that integrates several commonly-used clients (such as Microsoft Mail and Lotus cc:Mail) into an HP 3000 messaging backbone. The system includes its own text editor, supports the native HP 3000 line editor, and can import or export files created by HP Word or any other program that can process standard text files.

- *Calendar/scheduling.* HP Open DeskManager provides an electronic calendar that includes to-do list processing and schedules meetings with other users. (This scheduling capability also includes finding common free times for all target participants). Users can also choose to deploy Microsoft's Schedule+ calendaring package as a front end.

- *Filing.* HP Open DeskManager can organize files or documents into folders that are placed in filing cabinets. This capability accommodates a range of functions, such as setting up an information database or simply filing inbound and outbound mail in a highly organized fashion.

HP Open DeskManager's unique interpretive language, combined with its capability of altering screen contents, enables customization of the product at almost any level. New commands and functions can be implemented to expand (or redefine) the role of the product.

Although HP Open DeskManager is a stand-alone product, it is also part of HP's NewWave Office strategy. As part of the bigger picture, Open DeskManager provides a core set of services on an HP 3000 computer that can be joined by other services such as HP Resource Sharing and HP Networked PC Management.

HP Open DeskManager can be used to provide electronic mail services to terminal users, while still allowing for future growth to PC clients and an electronic mail server backbone. The HP 3000-based messaging backbone is often more robust and easier to manage than PC-LAN-based e-mail systems, especially in a larger environment. Open DeskManager can be used to migrate to this enterprise messaging environment, while retaining an existing investment in PC messaging applications. The latest release can support both HP and non-HP user interfaces. Clients supported include Lotus cc:Mail, Microsoft Mail, HP NewWave Mail, and HP Advance Mail; these clients are all included in the basic package. HP is also planning to add support for additional Windows and Macintosh clients. Connectivity with other e-mail systems, including X.400, the Internet, EDI network, and products such as Digital's ALL-IN-ONE and IBM's PROFS, is provided through available gateways. PC users access the system through either terminal emulation or one of the aforementioned front-end clients.

Network Architecture

Because the HP line of computers does not yet share a common set of connectivity guidelines, the networking architecture of HP machines is quite diverse. This is not to say that the computers have no common ground for connectivity (in fact, they have several); rather, each line must be analyzed for its own relative merits. HP calls its network architecture AdvanceNet (see Figure 3.6).

FIG. 3.6

Sample HP AdvanceNet
Network

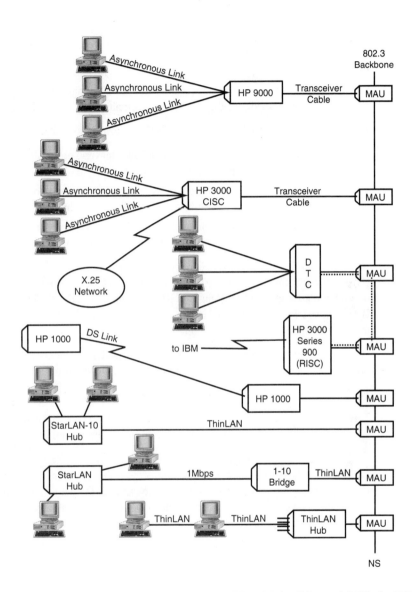

For example, while the HP 3000 Series 900 requires an IEEE 802.3 (or Ethernet) LAN, the HP 1000, HP 9000, and HP 3000 CISC computers support the IEEE 802.3 LAN as an option. In supporting the IEEE 802.3 standard, HP can use a ThickLAN backbone (conforming to the IEEE 10BASE5 standard) while also supporting ThinLAN (IEEE 10BASE2) coaxial segments. This implementation is compatible with Digital's Ethernet backbone and ThinWire coaxial segments. In HP terminology, however, attachments to the LAN are made via Medium Attachment Units (MAUs) instead of transceivers.

When all of the various models are connected to a common LAN, they can communicate with one another using either HP's Networking Services products (NS/1000, NS/3000, or NS/9000) or via TCP/IP (TCP/IP products are available from HP and from third-party companies).

Although the IEEE 802.3 LAN is the preferred methodology for system-to-system networking (with or without the use of third-party bridges to address WANs), an older product—Distributed Services (DS)—is often used with HP 1000 computers. In a nutshell, DS provides HDLC-type point-to-point links between HP 3000 and the older HP 1000 systems. Although DS is no longer an option for the HP 3000s, it remains available on HP 1000s.

To integrate PCs into the mainstream LAN, HP provides several different PC strategies:

- *HP StarLAN.* This is the traditional 1-Mbps star-topology LAN. In this case, a bridge interfaces the star's hub with the ThickLAN (via a MAU).

- *HP StarLAN-10.* An improved and faster (10 Mbps) version of the StarLAN. In this implementation, the star's hub can attach directly to the ThickLAN (via a MAU).

- *ThinLAN hub.* A similar product to Digital's ThinWire repeaters. The ThinLAN hub attaches to the ThickLAN (via a MAU) and provides multiple ThinWire segments.

HP uses two solutions to provide connectivity to IBM and Digital. For IBM connectivity, HP provides combined hardware/software products for its computer lines to implement bisynchronous and SNA SDLC links to IBM systems. For Digital Equipment connectivity, HP provides DEC-resident software that implements HP's NS within a VAX. In this scenario, the HP equipment and Digital equipment must reside on the same physical LAN.

HP also produces a variety of X.25 interface devices. The majority of these devices implement bridges between asynchronous connections (to computers or terminals) and the X.25 network.

To connect terminals to the system, HP employs several approaches (see Figure 3.7).

Terminals attach directly to HP 1000, HP 9000 and HP 3000 CISC machines via asynchronous serial links to ports (of varying levels of intelligence) integrated into the main system hardware.

For the HP 3000 Series 900, terminals connect to DTCs via asynchronous serial links, and the DTC, in turn, connects to the IEEE 802.3 LAN. Each DTC can support up to 48 direct-connect lines. This approach is remarkably similar to Digital's terminal server approach, with these exceptions:

- A DTC provides access to the HP 3000 Series 900 only. If a DTC-attached terminal must access a different type of HP computer, it must use some form of networking service or be used with a TS8 (as explained later).

- For a DTC to be fully functional (for example, for one terminal be able to access multiple Series 900s), it must be controlled by an OpenView DTC Manager (a PC attached to the LAN and running the HP management software).

The TS8 terminal server is used for terminal access to LAN-based HP computers. The TS8 provides asynchronous attachment for up to eight terminals (or printers) using the TCP/IP TELNET protocol. The value of a TS8 is directly related to the types of hosts in the network and the networking services that are available:

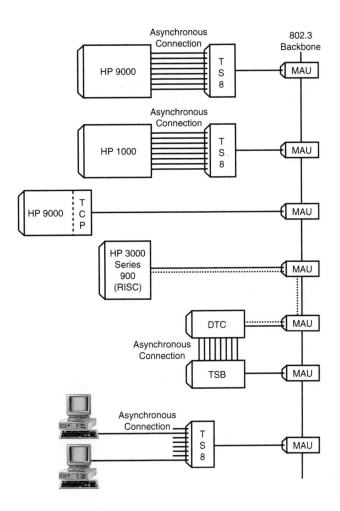

FIG. 3.7

HP Terminal Server Connections

- For the HP 9000 running TCP/IP, terminals attached to the TS8 can directly access that computer.
- For the HP 3000 Series 900, an additional TS8 (or multiple TS8s) must be attached to DTCs. The terminal attached to the first TS8 is routed through the second TS8 into the DTC and then into the Series 900 host.
- For all other cases, the HP host must also have one or more TS8s attached directly to its asynchronous ports. A terminal directly attached to a TS8 then is routed to a host-based TS8 that converts the traffic back to an asynchronous serial connection. ●

International Business Machines

Company Background

IBM's origin is rooted in a company that incorporated in 1911 as the Computing-Tabulating-Recording Company. Tom Watson acquired this company in 1914. Ten years later, in 1924, Watson opened a new chapter in the history of corporate America when he changed the name of his business automation company to International Business Machines (IBM) Corporation.

During its early years (1920 through the 1940s), the company produced and marketed a variety of office automation equipment such as punch-card tabulators and electric typewriters. In 1964, IBM released a computer that was destined to become the definition of a mainframe system—the IBM System/360. The System/360 was actually a third-generation computer, and the hardware/software design that enabled it to handle multiple tasks (programs) concurrently set new standards in the emerging computer industry.

IBM released the System/370 computer in 1970 as a follow-up to the System/360. Improvements in the memory and storage devices, coupled with a multiprocessing hardware architecture, enabled the System/370 to offer substantial performance improvements over its predecessor. The System/370's popularity continued where the System/360 left off, spawning two additional lines: the 9370, a scaled-down System/370 released in 1986; and the System/390, the ultramodern mainframe architecture released in 1990.

Even though IBM achieved market dominance on the high (mainframe) end of the market, it continued to expand its overall computer line to provide midrange and low-end solutions. In the midrange, small business market, IBM offered a series of computers, with the best known models of this era being the System/38 (released in 1978) and the System/36 (released in 1983). Then, in 1988, IBM released its Application System/400 (AS/400) computer.

In the low-end of the market, IBM set most of the standards for today's PCs. The success of the PC led IBM to develop and release the PC/XT (short for Extended Technology) in 1983 and the PC/AT (short for Advanced Technology) in 1984. These models, in turn, were replaced with the Personal System/2 (PS/2) line (introduced in 1987) and the Personal System/1 (PS/1) line (released in 1990).

Product Line Overview

IBM manufactures its own products in various plants around the globe and also has agreements with other companies to produce products for them. IBM is the largest U.S. computer manufacturer, measured by both sales and output. It not only produces computers, but also designs and manufactures terminals, printers, disk drives and more.

PowerPC

The RISC-based PowerPC platform is deployed throughout the IBM product family, from laptops to parallel processing supercomputers. PowerPC, an open standard, is the result of an alliance between Apple, IBM, and Motorola, and is not tied to any single operating system or hardware configuration. The PowerPC family contains multiple execution units for symmetrical superscalar operation, cache memory, and a multiprocessing interface.

The PowerPC architecture is based on reduced instruction set computing (RISC) technology. RISC differs substantially from complex instruction set computing (CISC), which is typically used in lower-end machines. In releasing its PowerPC product line, however, IBM is one of the first vendors to offer RISC-based PCs. The difference between CISC and RISC is that CISC processors contain several instructions to handle a variety of processing tasks; RISC processors contain only those instructions that are used most often, and when a complex instruction is required, the RISC processor will build it from a combination of its basic instructions.

IBM has also introduced its new line of PC 300 Pentium Pro systems, running at speeds of up to 200 MHz. The availability of the PC 330 and PC 350 might actually reflect an eventual shift away from the PowerPC platform. The systems can run Microsoftís Windows 95 or IBMís own Warp Connect operating system, and are well-suited for power-hungry multimedia applications.

Before the PowerPC architecture was designed, RISC designs were used only in high-end engineering workstations and servers. IBM and the PowerPC Alliance, however, hold the view that RISC technology is the next step in personal computing.

The alliance designed the first four members of the PowerPC family simultaneously. These four processors include the following:

- *PowerPC 601.* A 32-bit implementation that provides high performance for computer systems.
- *PowerPC 602.* A lower-power implementation of the PowerPC architecture, meant for use in home entertainment or commercial business devices.
- *PowerPC 603 and 603e.* Also low-power implementations, used in desktop computers and entry-level systems.
- *PowerPC 604 and 604e.* 32-bit implementations used in high-end workstations and SMP computer systems. The 604 and 604e are software- and bus-compatible with the 601 and 603 and 603e microprocessors.

The PowerPC Platform (PowerPC Microprocessor Common Hardware Reference Platform) is a set of specifications that defines a unified personal computer, combining the advantages of the Power Macintosh and the PC environment. Computers made to this open standard can run operating systems from either Apple, Microsoft, Novell, or SunSoft. The PowerPC Platform is an open reference architecture that is publicly available.

IBM Terminals

IBM has two mainstream terminal lines—one for the mainframe (System/390-architecture) computers and one for the midrange (System/3X-related) computers. The mainframe terminal line comprises the 3270 family of devices. The midrange computers, on the other hand, normally use the 5250 line of terminals.

Both terminals share a block orientation that lets the operator enter information into fields and correct the data at the terminal before transmitting it to the mainframe. Both terminals have models that support wide text (132 columns) and graphics displays. They also share a general connectivity philosophy that supports the attachment of multiple terminals to a computer using one or more lines (the connectivity aspect of IBM terminals will be addressed later in this chapter).

The 3270 family of terminals includes the 3178, 3270 PC, 3276, 3277, 3278, and 3279 color terminal. The 3270 family supports two types of function keys. One type is referred to as the Program Attention (PA) keys, and the other is the more standard Program Function (PF) keys. The 3270 family supports up to four PA keys (PA1 through PA4) and up to 24 PF keys (PF1 through PF24). Please note, however, that a variety of keyboards are available for each 3270 model, and some do not contain all 24 function keys.

The 5250 family is the terminal of choice for the System/36, System/38 and AS/400 systems (although they also have special provisions for supporting 3270 terminals). The modern 5250 family is composed of the 5251, 5291, 5292 (color), 3197 (color), 3180, and the 3196 terminals.

In contrast to the 3270's support of PA and PF keys, the 5250 family supports up to 24 Command Function (CF) keys. Please note, however, that different keyboards for the different 5250 models might not contain all 24 CF keys.

Ch
4

Like the hosting computers, the two families of terminals are oriented toward their respective markets. The 3270 is a more generalized workstation, suitable for a wide variety of applications. The 5250, on the other hand, is tailored for the menu orientation of the midrange systems and is better suited for general business applications (although the issue is certainly arguable).

Some fundamental operational differences between the 5250 family and the 3270 family are the following:

- In certain configurations, the 5250 has special capabilities that work with midrange software to perform such advanced word processing functions as word wrap and dual cursor operations. This feature is most notable under the AS/400 Office system.
- The 5250 has three special field operation keys:
  - The field exit key clears the contents of an alphanumeric field to the right of the cursor and then advances to the next field.
  - The field + and field exit keys are used to right-justify numbers in a numeric field, adding the appropriate sign (blank for positive or "-" for negative) at the right side of the number.
- The 5250 supports roll-up and roll-down keys that enable the terminal to scroll through multipage screens offered by the host.

The first position of a 5250 display (line 1, column 1) is reserved in most operations.

Most of these differences are minor, and simply serve to illustrate how each line of terminal is oriented toward a specific host line (mainframe or midrange). To a certain extent, this is one of the most unique features of the IBM terminal line—IBM is one of the few full-line manufacturers that does not offer a single line of terminals applicable across the entire computer line (like DEC's VT offerings or HP's terminal line).

Personal Computers

Having stayed out the personal computer market for so long, when IBM decided to jump, it decided to go in headfirst—and in a real hurry. Certainly its product, the Personal Computer (PC), was no technological powerhouse.

Before IBM's entry in 1981, the personal computer market was loaded with products from every manufacturer even remotely involved with electronics. Virtually every watchmaker, TV manufacturer, or major chip vendor had a product offering in this area. Most of these forgettable products used the CP/M operating system, and those that did not favored proprietary operating systems that have not seen the light of day since. The industry sadly lacked microcomputer standards.

Rumor has it that when IBM went shopping for an operating system, it first turned to Digital Research. Digital Research, however, was sitting happily on what it believed to be the top of the microcomputer heap, so it did not agree to the terms IBM offered. Much to its surprise, IBM then went to Bill Gates at Microsoft Corporation. Mr. Gates, in turn, went out and purchased ownership of another company's operating system. Thus, PC-DOS—and MS-DOS—was born.

The IBM PC included up to 640K (kilobytes) of memory, which was ten times the memory offered by most of the 64K CP/M machines. For storage, it featured a 5.25-inch floppy disk drive and the inevitable interface to a cassette tape recorder. To hurry the product to the market, IBM even turned to the Far East to supply some of the components. To increase the availability of applications, IBM appealed to key software companies to develop or port their products to the IBM PC.

IBM followed up on its original PC design with the PC/XT (Extended Technology) in 1983. The PC/XT introduced some relatively minor design changes in the original PC board but served to bring hard disk technology to the PC through the inclusion of a full-height (but slow at 85 ms) 10M hard disk drive. In the same year IBM released the scaled-down version of its the PC, called the PCjr.

In 1984, IBM released the IBM PC/AT (Advanced Technology). While the changes between the original PC and PC/XT were relatively small, the changes between the PC/XT and PC/AT were relatively large. First and foremost, the IBM PC/AT used the Intel 80286 processor instead of the PC/XT's 8088 processor. Second, the input/output bus (used for such option boards as the display adapter and disk controller) was improved to contain both 8-bit and 16-bit slots (the PC and PC/XT contained only 8-bit slots).

By 1987, the PC market had grown to unbelievable proportions, and IBM was quickly losing market share. IBM's market was being eroded by American manufacturers such as Compaq Computer Corp. and AT&T; by a massive number of off-shore (Taiwanese and Korean) manufacturers marketing through large companies, such as Leading Edge Hardware Products Inc.; and by small, garage-type operations. IBM sought to retrench its position by redesigning the architecture of the PCs, using a closed architecture that would force other manufacturers to sign license agreements with IBM if they wanted to use the same technology.

Ch
4

The result of IBM's research was announced in 1987 as the Micro Channel Architecture of IBM's Personal System/2 (PS/2) line—the replacement to the PC line. Shortly after the announcement of the PS/2 series, IBM discontinued the PC/XT and PC/AT models. Despite this discontinuation, the ISA Bus, (based on the AT bus) is still the most common PC bus design. The Micro Channel Architecture offers many advantages over the ISA Bus design. It provides for a large channel bandwidth, and includes an arbitration mechanism to prevent a single adapter from taking over the system. Other features of the Micro Channel Architecture include automatic configuration and a streaming technique that allows an address line to be used as an additional data line, effectively doubling channel throughput.

In addition to the change in hardware architecture, the PS/2 also served as the launching platform for a new multitasking operating system, Operating System/2 (OS/2). Despite the announcement of OS/2, however, IBM has continued to offer the popular PC-DOS operating system. In fact, when IBM introduced the PS/1 home computer in 1990, PC-DOS was the only operating system option.

There are two families of PCs now offered by IBM—the 300 and the 700 family. The high-end systems have a Pentium or Pentium Pro processor, PCI busmaster device controller, 6X CD-ROM, and 4M of Video memory. Networkable with optional Ethernet and Token Ring cards, the 700 provides networking and communications features and enhanced graphics.

Engineering Workstations

Engineering workstations are the weakest area of the IBM product line. IBM's initial RISC-based offering, the RT-System, was introduced in 1986 in the wake of IBM's sweeping success in the PC market. To a certain extent, IBM was hoping that the RT would ride on the coattails of the PC and become a success by association. The RT's alignment with the PC family is evident in its capability to use PC/AT adapter cards. As with many other engineering workstations, a co-processor option enables the RT to run PC-DOS concurrently with its native operating system, AIX. Unfortunately, the RT-System lacked sufficient innovation or price/performance advantage to rise to the top of the heap, and it never became a commercial success.

The RT line used a RISC architecture. As noted, the entire line ran the AIX operating system, IBM's version of UNIX. IBM's enhancements to AIX include support for up to one terabyte (one trillion bytes) of virtual memory and up to 16M of real memory. IBM has also addressed connectivity of the RT to other systems by including the SNA Logical Unit 6.2 (LU 6.2) interface and support for both IBM Token Ring and TCP/IP over Ethernet.

In early 1990, IBM totally revamped its engineering workstation line with the introduction of the RISC System/6000 (RS/6000) family of workstations and servers. Modern developments in RISC technology enabled the RS/6000 line to offer a dramatic performance increase over the older RT technology. The RS/6000 family runs the AIX operating system and is divided into two lines: Powerstation and Powerserver models. Powerstation models are targeted at individual workstation users, while the Powerserver models are intended to serve multiple users.

The Future of the RS/6000

New offerings in the RS/6000 line include a PowerPC-based workgroup and Internet server, and the introduction of multiple operating system options. Other new announcements include a multimedia software offering, which delivers multiple audio and video streams from the RS/6000 server to a variety of desktop clients over LANs and internetworks. IBM is also planning to incorporate Sun Microsystems' Java technology with the AIX operating system, so Java applets can be sent to clients across the corporate intranet or the public Internet. Another new feature will provide access to tape devices, and consolidate tape operations across a network of RS/6000 workstations. This creates a pool of tape resources, and facilitates centralized tape management.

The RS/6000 family runs from low-end ThinkPads, to workstations, to the high-end symmetric multiprocessor and parallel processing computers (all running the same version of AIX), making it one of the most scalable lines of RISC-based systems available. The RS/6000 supports multiple operating systems, including IBM AIX, Windows NT, and SunSoft Solaris. At the high end, the RS/6000 can function as an application or data server, and can be optimized for transaction-oriented applications; or for graphics-intensive workstation usage such as CAD or scientific visualization. It may also be applied to OnLine Transaction Processing (OLTP) applications, which process transactions in real time as they are received by the system.

Midrange Offerings

If you liked the television series M*A*S*H, then you'll love the AS/400—or so thought IBM when they used Alan Alda in prime-time commercials and high-visibility print ads as they brought the AS/400 to market. The early and overt commercialization of the AS/400 shows clearly that IBM is targeting the product toward the general business community. The emphasis is on multi-user business solutions and upward growth (or the perception of it, anyway).

Understanding this orientation is significant when you evaluate IBM's midrange offerings against Digital's and HP's. While HP and Digital offer products focused toward the technical environment, IBM offers products focused on the business environment. Given the scale of these types of systems, it is not at all unusual to find an IBM midrange processor in the front office and a DEC VAX in the lab, even in smaller businesses. Of course, the coexistence of VAX computers with IBM mainframes is commonplace in larger businesses.

In those dinosaur days before the AS/400, IBM offered two lines of midrange systems—the System/36 and the System/38. The System/36 ran an operating system called System Support Program (SSP) that featured, among other things, a menu-driven user interface that was simple and straightforward to use. Additionally, the System/36 featured connectivity options specifically geared toward the integration of PC networks with the System/36.

The System/38, on the other hand, was more upscale. It ran the Control Program Facility (CPF) operating system, which featured an extensive programming environment and an integrated relational database. The System/38 was geared for connectivity to mainframe systems.

All things considered, the two offerings were very similar in many categories, but not similar enough overall. For example, although IBM offered migration provisions to facilitate a move from a System/36 to a System/38, this migration was just painful enough to be avoided. To make the jump, you had to modify and recompile programs; and worse, the two systems' databases were not totally compatible. These differences formed a chasm wide enough to keep both product lines on the market simultaneously (much to IBM's chagrin).

The AS/400 was created to provide easy migration for all midrange users. The AS/400 borrowed more from the System/38 design than it did from the System/36, although many areas (like connectivity) are supersets of both capabilities. In a nutshell, the AS/400 combines the easy-to-use menu-orientation of the System/36 with the programming and database environment of the System/38.

Programs from the System/38 can run as is on the AS/400 (again attesting to the closeness between the AS/400 and System/38). IBM implemented improved migration aides for the operating system, OS/400, to enable System/36 programs to move to the AS/400 but, at a minimum, the programs have to be recompiled (and in some cases, rewritten) first. To further garner support for the AS/400, IBM offered third-party software developers AS/400 access and technical assistance to move their programs to the AS/400 before its official release. As a result of this effort, the 1988 AS/400 announcement included support for thousands of ready-to-run business applications.

The new AS/400 Advanced 36 (See Figure 4.1) offers a gradual migration path for S/36 users by enabling up to three System/36 configurations to run with an AS/400. Under this configuration, System/36 users can use their existing applications while still accessing the advanced features of the AS/400 operating system.

Ch
4

FIG. 4.1
IBM AS/400
Advanced 36

Photo courtesy of IBM Corporation

After a seemingly successful two-and-one-half years with the AS/400, IBM revamped the product line and made the first major version change in the OS/400 operating system. Announced in April 1991, the D-series AS/400 models offer dramatic improvements in price/performance ratios, and high-end D-series models cross over into the domain of mainframe computing power. Beyond the feature content, IBM's marketing program behind this new lineup clearly was oriented at moving any remaining System/36 and System/38 users over to the AS/400 architecture, as well as extending the AS/400's reach into other midrange environments.

The System/3X products and the AS/400 support the 5250 terminal family as the preferred workstation line. However, the System/36, System/38 and AS/400 all have special provisions built into their operating systems to handle 3270-type terminals.

The newest incarnation of the AS/400, the AS/400 Advanced System, supports high-speed communications and includes support for wireless LANs and an Integrated Fax Adapter. The Advanced System now runs the powerful 64-bit RISC PowerPC AS microprocessor. Existing applications can run unchanged on the Advanced System. The AS/400 includes IBM's AnyNet architecture, which permits communications over several public and private networks. It supports SNA, TCP/IP, IPX, Token ring, Ethernet, and other protocols. Some other additions include:

- *Web connection for OS/400.* Permits the AS/400 to function as a Web server on the Internet, and function as a repository for images and other data.
- *Support for high-speed communications.* Includes network adapters for 16/4 Mbps token ring Ethernet II or IEEE 802.3, FDDI, and Shielded Twisted Pair Distributed Data Interface. In addition, the High Speed Communications Adapter can support T1/J1 or E1 communication over Frame Relay, or point-to-point SDLC lines.

There are a number of models in the Advanced Series, including:

- *Model 300, 310, and 320.* These models include the System Power Control Network (SPCN) and Redundant Array of Inexpensive Disks (RAID-5) storage capability. All three have multiple processor options and modular designs.
- *Model 400.* This high-performance machine boasts 32M of main storage and 1.96G of DASD (Direct Access Storage Device) in the base configuration.
- *Models 500, 510, and 530.* These models support higher main storage and DASD, and can accommodate up to 200 communications lines.
- *Models 20S and 30S, 40S, 50S, 53S.* These are used primarily as departmental servers. Under the client/server strategy, the processing is shared between the AS/400 and intelligent clients. With Client Access/400 (formerly PC Support), client/server and traditional AS/400 applications can run side by side. The AS/400 is easy to install in an existing SNA or TCP/IP network, and can be used to manage a distributed client/server network. Supports a LAN Server/400 option for high-performance file serving to connected PCs. Since this service is tied to the operating system, one administrator can manage multiple LAN services from a central location. When deployed on a client/server network, it can be an application server, database, communications, print, or network management server for OS/2, Windows, DOS, UNIX, AIX, and Macintosh workstations.
- *Model P03.* This 22 pound, entry-level system has connections for up to 16 workstations. It is available for Token Ring or Ethernet LAN configurations supporting 16 workstations, or twinax configurations supporting 14 workstations.

Top-end Offerings

IBM's mainframe history began with the System/360 line; the success of the System/360 line led to the development and release of the System/370 in 1970. The System/370 introduced virtual storage to the IBM mainframe lineup. Its architecture became the foundation for the high-end 3030, 3080, and 3090 lines, as well as the lower-end 4300 and 9370 lines.

Ch
4

The 20-year dynasty of the System/370 architecture ended in 1990 when IBM introduced its System/390 architecture. The System/390 offered dramatic improvements in performance from improved processor technology and the use of fiber optic links for high-speed channel communications. At the same time it made the introduction, IBM unveiled a new family of mainframes under the name ES/9000. The ES/9000 is a broad line targeted to replace the older 9370, 4300 and 3090 lines. When IBM released the ES/9000 line in 1990, the initial models did not feature the improved processor technology but did offer fiber optic channels.

IBM shipped more large system processors in 1995 than ever before, primarily due to a surge in S/390 shipments. IBM was the first to adopt complementary metal oxide semiconductor (CMOS) technology for its large commercial computers. CMOS-based machines are less expensive to make and more efficient than the older bipolar mainframe technology. It requires less system cooling and takes up about 75 percent less floor space compared to the bipolar technology. The S/390's Coupling Facility can link two or more CMOS servers to form an IBM Parallel Sysplex environment, a large system image that can combine up to 32 servers, each running 10 CMOS microprocessors.

The OS/390 operating system includes products for systems management and distributed computing. The integration of VTAM, AnyNet and TCP/IP provide added flexibility, and enable the S/390 server to manage information across a multivendor network. OS/390 has an optional Security Server to prevent unauthorized access and ensure data integrity.

Multiple S/390 processors can be coupled as a single system, with data sharing and workload balancing. This method ensures a high uptime because there is no single point of failure.

Efficient backup is facilitated through its massive data storage capability, and users can dynamically add storage and processing without having to shut down the server. Print jobs can be distributed from NetWare LANs to S/390 printers, so the host system can access attached LAN printer resources.

IBM first started experimenting with CMOS in its laboratory in Germany in 1983 and first deployed it in its S/370 air-cooled mainframes in 1986. In 1990, CMOS technology broke into the ES/9000 line. In 1994, IBM introduced its Parallel Enterprise Servers, Parallel Transaction Servers, and Parallel Query Servers—all based on the CMOS technology. Initially, CMOS technology complemented bipolar technology in the entry-level and midrange arena, and it later moved to the high-end mainframe market. The older bipolar technology had been used for more than 25 years; CMOS can either replace or coexist with bipolar technology. CMOS uses far fewer parts than bipolar technology, which lowers the cost of computing. The S/390 CMOS microprocessors are compatible with existing systems and use up to 97 percent less energy—about the amount of electricity used by a household refrigerator. CMOS is more reliable than bipolar—the S/390 Parallel Enterprise Server, for example, has a failure rate of less than once every 20 years. Also, unlike the older machines, no raised floors are required, and it uses significantly less floor space.

The three operating systems most prevalent on the IBM mainframes are the following:

■ *Virtual Storage Extended (DOS/VSE)*. The oldest of the three operating systems, DOS/VSE is most often found on 4300 Series machines. DOS/VSE supports a suite of subsystems similar to those of MVS.

- *Multiple Virtual Storage (MVS)*. Usually found in business environments at the top end of the line. MVS is a direct descendent of the OS/VS2 originally released with the System/370. The popularity of MVS stems primarily from its suitability for running business applications.
- *Virtual Machine (VM)*. VM is unique in its capability to host other operating systems (thus, MVS can run underneath VM).

Each operating system has, in turn, its own set of variations. For example, MVS/Extended System Architecture (MVS/ESA) is different from MVS/Extended Architecture (MVS/XA) and both are, in turn, quite different from MVS/System Products (MVS/SP). The differences in the versions rest in the capacities of the virtual storage environments they can manage and therefore the size and number of programs they can run. The bottom line is that two machines running MVS might not be equivalent.

Both VSE and MVS share the same basic operating philosophy and architecture (see Figure 4.2).

FIG. 4.2

Traditional IBM O/S Environment

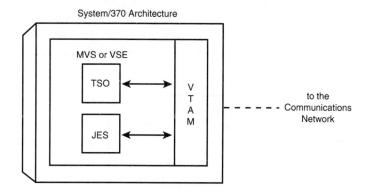

Running underneath the operating system are the following major subsystems:

- *Virtual Telecommunications Access Method (VTAM)*. VTAM controls the flow of information from the terminal network to the programs. It also plays a major role in sites that use IBM's Systems Network Architecture (SNA). The packages that existed before VTAM and provided similar functions include Basic Telecommunications Access Method (BTAM), Remote Telecommunications Access Method (RTAM) and Telecommunications Access Method (TCAM). IBM is planning to add TCP/IP features to VTAM, enabling it to control multivendor traffic.
- *Job Entry System (JES)*. JES is responsible for the batch environment of the mainframe. It processes jobs submitted from local terminals or Remote Job Entry (RJE) workstations (specialized devices that have their own input and output capabilities). For example, JES can be used to receive the day's transactions from a remote bank, update the information on the central files, and then send a printed report of the activities back to the remote bank. In MVS environments, JES might be known as JES2 or JES3 (for Releases 2 and 3). Under VSE, the job environment is handled by Priority Output Writers, Executions

Processors and Input Readers (POWER). Other memorable implementations of job-handling packages include Attached Support Processor (ASP) and Houston Automatic Spooling Program (HASP).

■ *Time Sharing Option (TSO)*. TSO provides an interface to terminals to enable program development and data file management. TSO is one of the most widely recognized ways of interfacing with a mainframe. Furthermore, within TSO is a menu-oriented utility named Interactive System Productivity Facility (ISPF) that provides a simple and easy-to-understand way of accessing TSO functions. Also note that TSO is capable of submitting jobs to the JES and monitoring their progress.

■ *Customer Information Control System (CICS)*. CICS implements transaction-based routing between the terminal network and the application programs. Essentially, CICS receives input from terminal users and then decides which application program is responsible for processing each user's transaction. Once determined, CICS delivers the transaction to the program. A program must be written specifically to run under CICS. CICS has become a de facto industry standard, and because several vendors write applications to CICS, it can be used to share information with non-IBM systems.

The VM operating system, on the other hand, carves the mainframe into multiple, virtual machines. Each user sees his or her own virtual machine and, more important, virtual machines can support other operating systems, such as VSE and MVS (see Figure 4.3).

FIG. 4.3
IBM VM Environment

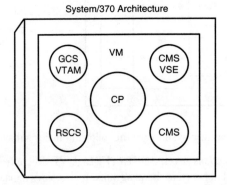

System/370 Architecture

The subsystems that work under VM include:

■ *Control Program (CP)*. CP is a central management facility for system resources.

■ *Conversational Monitor System (CMS)*. CMS provides the communications between the user and CP. CMS is responsible for managing a user's virtual machine (or hosting another operating system). Multiple copies of CMS facilitate multiple virtual machines.

■ *Group Control System (GCS)*. GCS is similar to CMS in that it is a virtual machine supervisor. GCS is used normally to host SNA-oriented subsystems, such as the Advanced Communications Function for VTAM (ACF/VTAM). This is the preferred methodology for implementing SNA in VM environments.

■ *Remote Spooling Communications System (RSCS)*. This is VM's job entry facility. RSCS runs in conjunction with the GCS.

In terms of terminal support, all of these mainframe systems are normally used with the IBM 3270 line of terminals.

Strategy for Connectivity

IBM unleashed its Systems Network Architecture (SNA) on the public in 1974. Before this occasion, the IBM world of data communications was filled with byte-oriented, synchronous protocols, such as the now-classic bisynchronous 3270-terminal protocol and the bisynchronous 2780 and 3780 RJE protocols. With the introduction of SNA, however, IBM replaced these protocols with bit-oriented Synchronous Data Link Control (SDLC) protocol variations, and the relationships between the various communications devices became more strict and formal.

In terms of topology, SNA was originally a networking architecture that featured a central host as the control point. It was continually refined and expanded in subsequent releases to support networks with multiple hosts and to facilitate host-to-host communications. Under SNA, each participating device is given a physical unit (PU) definition that establishes its role in the hierarchical relationship between the terminal and the host (see Figure 4.4).

The PU definitions are as follows:

- *Physical Unit Type 2.* PU 2 defines a device that controls workstations. This includes the traditional IBM cluster controllers (for example, 3274 and 3174) as well as the System/3X and AS/400 midrange systems.
- *Physical Unit Type 2.1.* PU 2.1 is a refinement to SNA that was added to enable peer-to-peer communications between intelligent PU 2 devices, such as midrange systems, PCs and PS/2s. This is an integral part of the Advanced Peer-to-Peer Networking (APPN) aspect of SNA.
- *Physical Unit Type 4.* A PU 4 device is a communications controller or front-end processor (for example, 3705 and 3725). This is a mainframe-oriented device that interfaces with the PU 2 and PU 2.1 devices which, in turn, interface with the actual terminals and workstations.
- *Physical Unit Type 5.* A PU 5 device is a host (mainframe) processor that provides global services to the SNA network. These devices sponsor the System Services Control Points (SSCPs).

NOTE Physical Unit Type 1 and Physical Unit Type 3 have no validity in the modern SNA architecture.

While PUs describe network devices that provide physical services, SNA logical units (LUs) define the contents of the data stream (information flow) between the PUs. LU definitions include the following:

- *Logical Unit Type 0.* LU 0 is used for unregulated, direct-link communications between two entities in the network (typically two programs). Any two programs using the LU 0 information flow must be programmed to define and use the same format for the information.

■ *Logical Unit Type 1.* LU 1 refers to the format of data sent to and received from specialized data processing workstations (such as RJE stations).

FIG. 4.4

SNA Physical Units

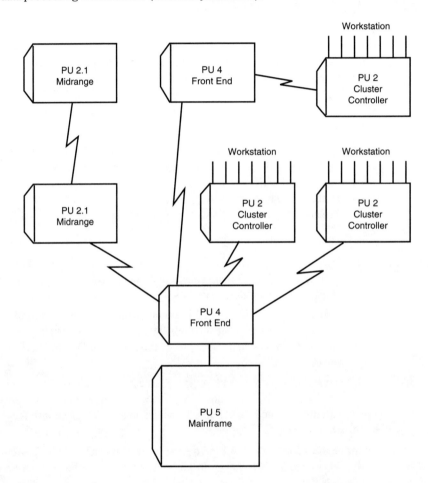

■ *Logical Unit Type 2.* LU 2 defines the format of data sent to and received from the 3270 family of workstations.

■ *Logical Unit Type 3.* LU 3 describes the format of data sent to the 3270 family of printers.

■ *Logical Unit Type 4.* LU 4 refers to the format of data sent to and received from dedicated word processing workstations.

■ *Logical Unit Type 6.1.* LU 6.1 is for program-to-program communications using one of the following SNA data formats: character string, 3270 workstation, logical message services, or user-defined.

- *Logical Unit Type 6.2.* LU 6.2 is also for program-to-program communications. Programs using the LU 6.2 definition can use either an SNA general data format or can define and use their own data format.

- *Logical Unit Type 7.* LU 7 defines the format of data sent to and received from the 5250 family of workstations.

N O T E The Logical Unit Type 6.2 is often used with Physical Unit Type 2.1 for Advanced Program-to-Program Communications (APPC). Under this approach, the PU 2.1 devices establish a peer-to-peer connection and then a program running on each device initiates an LU 6.2 conversation. In support of this, IBM supplies a library of LU 6.2 calls to facilitate programming the LU 6.2 interface. ▦

Beyond the introduction of many new concepts and terminology, the biggest immediate change that SNA posed to IBM customers was the switch from the well-understood, byte-oriented protocols to the bit-oriented Synchronous Data Link Control (SDLC) protocol and its variations.

Under the older bisynchronous formats, the information physically transmitted and received was relatively easy to understand because at its core was the actual data being transferred in its native character format. Surrounding that basic data were additional control characters that signaled the start of data, start of field, the field attributes, end of field, end of data, and so on. By sitting at a simple line monitor, a technician could see and identify the data itself.

Unfortunately, this approach has severe limitations. For example, if the information being sent is binary, it might turn into control characters when it is prepared for transmission. Because it is inappropriate to have an end-of-data control character in the middle of the data, additional structures and control characters must be inserted to handle these special cases. This need for special processing often greatly increases the amount of data transmitted and also requires an additional amount of processing overhead before transmission.

To address these and other concerns, IBM developed the bit-oriented SDLC protocol. Under SDLC, data is not interpreted on a byte-by-byte basis; rather, it is interpreted as a series of bits, with control bits at the beginning indicating the size and length of the bit patterns to follow. This bit-level approach to data communications easily handles standard terminal input/output information as well as the special problems posed by binary data.

In fact, IBM was so pleased with its SDLC implementation that it submitted SDLC to the ANSI and ISO standards organizations for their approval. ANSI modified the basic SDLC definition and called it Advanced Data Communications Control Procedure (ADCCP), which is used today by many government organizations. ISO changed it into High-level Data Link Control (HDLC) and it is a model for many other computer manufacturers' communications protocols. Finally, the Consultative Committee for International Telegraphy and Telephony (CCITT) further modified HDLC into Link Access Procedure (LAP) and then into LAP-B (LAP-Balanced) as part of its X.25 network definition.

In SNA, SDLC is the main communications protocol used by workstations, controllers, and front-end processors alike. To accommodate the variety of devices (3270 versus 5250, for example), SDLC then carries the LU and PU assignments of the transmitting and receiving devices. Thus, an SDLC transmission can be identified as coming from a 3270 (LU 2) on a cluster controller (PU 2).

Another connectivity strategy is IBM's MQSeries, a messaging middleware that is used to connect applications across dissimilar environments. Different programs are capable of communicating with the MQSeries API, a high-level interface that shields developers from the various complexities of the different operating systems. MQSeries is often used by institutions, such as banks, that need to handle large numbers of transactions. Messages can be placed on queues and retrieved from queues instantly, and delivery is registered to ensure reliability.

APPN (Advanced Peer-to-Peer Networking)

APPN is a creation of IBM, which it originally positioned as the successor to SNA. APPN is used mostly in AS/400 environments, although it can support a mainframe network in a limited fashion. However, APPN is not able to provide native support for SNA 3270 datastreams, which makes up most mission-critical traffic.

Cisco Systems and Bay Networks, two major router vendors, both managed to overcome this limitation by enabling a routed APPN network to support SNA traffic from any SNA device. Without this solution, each device must contain its own dependent LU Requestor (dLUR) software. dLUR software is not widely available—it is offered only for 3174 controllers and OS/2 PCs. Cisco's and Bay's approach provides support for any SNA device, regardless of whether it possesses the dLUR software. With Cisco and Bay bridge/routers, it will be possible to run an APPN-based multiprotocol system that can support SNA traffic.

APPN has a number of strengths. It offers peer-to-peer networking, it can dynamically discover remote destinations, and it has a traffic prioritization mechanism. However, APPN does not support dynamic alternate routing. APPN might still be a good solution for complex networks because of its dynamic destination discovery service.

High-Speed Networking

IBM is working towards supporting Asynchronous Transfer Mode (ATM) in LAN/WAN environments. Price is one major barrier to wide area ATM, but another is the amount of work required to interface ATM with legacy networks.

IBM's solution for joining ATM with its SNA/APPN installed base uses the High Performance Routing (HPR) feature to provide native access to wide-area ATM networks for SNA/APPN. SNA is well suited for interfacing with ATM because of its service features. However, SNA routing is less suited to high-speed networking. HPR fills in for this area. IBM proposes that the native interface to ATM be through the HPR feature. Mainframe SNA and APPN would connect directly to ATM using either LAN emulation or Frame Relay emulation.

HPR is an open technology for routing data quickly and efficiently. The technology combines some features of APPN, frame relay, IP, and SNA. In case of a link failure, HPR's built-in rerouting capabilities relieves network managers from having to physically reroute sessions . In addition, HPR supports SNA priority and class-of-service features. HPR can run on existing hardware, and interoperates with existing SNA and APPN products.

HPR uses three separate techniques to improve data routing: Rapid Transport Protocol (RTP), Automatic Network Routing (ANR), and Adaptive Rate-Based (ARB) congestion control. RTP, a connection protocol, supports data transfer over a high-speed network. RTP automatically establishes end-to-end connections and generates the appropriate routing information. In the event of failure, RTP will detect the failure, and recalculate the path dynamically and automatically. Data that was sent at the time of failure will be automatically recovered.

ANR is a connectionless protocol used in the intermediate nodes of the HPR subnet. The ANR technology helps to control congestion between the various RTP endpoints by monitoring the amount of data flowing between the endpoints, and making adjustments to ensure against overload. ARB also guards against congestion by sending data only in measured amounts, as opposed to uncontrolled bursts.

Application/User Relationship

From the simplest of perspectives, the relationship between IBM users and applications is highly structured, highly controlled and menu-oriented. This is true of both the midrange (System/3X and AS/400) and the System/390 environments because both types of terminals (5250 and 3270) are block-oriented. Typically, users access the system and run the program they desire. Although accessing the program can be done in a conversational manner (as with TSO), the actual application program or utility normally uses some type of full-screen input/output.

Although IBM's environment is multiuser, each user's activities should not be construed as sessions, such as those with HP and DEC architectures. With sessions, users perceive that they have the computer to themselves and that their applications seem to function independently from other activities. In a multiuser environment like IBM's, each user accesses the system and then is given a controlled set of choices— the system guides the user through the selection process based on the user's profile.

Another key difference between the session-oriented computers and IBM computers is the level at which shared access to a program or system service occurs. With DEC and HP computers, each person runs, in effect, an individual copy of the program that shares system resources at a level typically below the visibility of the user. With IBM, this sharing occurs on a higher plane. In most cases, in fact, programs on IBM systems are written to accommodate concurrent access from multiple users.

The actual appearance of the user interface and the development of programs are disparate among the IBM platforms. Developing a program on an AS/400, for example, has a dramatically different approach and appearance than developing the same program on a 3090. These differences pose a real problem to IBM because it often prohibits an AS/400 customer, for example, from upgrading to a 9370, because the customer's AS/400 programs would not be compatible with the 9370 architecture (nor would the user's programming staff be competent with the new system).

To address this issue and to provide IBM-wide standards for programming and the program's appearance to the user, IBM introduced its Systems Application Architecture (SAA). SAA is a set of routines and transport mechanisms that (theoretically) makes it possible to develop and implement a program on one platform—a PS/2, for example—and then move that program to another platform—say, a 9370—with minimal effort. SAA programming routines perform the following functions:

- Provide a common means of accessing files and database information (regardless of where they reside).
- Supply a consistent way to access a terminal (regardless of the terminal's location).
- Define and implement both a universal character (workstation) and window-based (graphics) appearance to the user.

The full definition of SAA specifies and defines the underlying formats and transport mechanisms upon which these three higher-level functions rely. The term *SAA-compliant* indicates that a particular feature or function is included in the SAA definition. For example, the LU 6.2 interface is deemed SAA-compliant but LU 0 is not. Also note that the actual implementation of SAA is a long-term strategy that involves releasing pieces of SAA as time progresses.

Terminal Attachment Philosophy

IBM uses a hierarchical architecture between terminals and computers. This architecture is similar in the midrange systems and mainframes, although the midrange implementation cannot accommodate the large numbers of terminals supported by the mainframe architecture.

In the mainframes, the 3270 family of terminals and printers is the backbone of the user interface. In Figure 4.5, terminals attach to a cluster controller (also known as a remote control unit) via coaxial cable. Some example workstation controllers include the 3174, 3274, and the 3276 (which also features a built-in terminal). Each cluster controller can support multiple terminals and printers (typical numbers include 8, 16, and 32, although cluster controllers can be configured to support larger numbers).

Each cluster controller interfaces to the central mainframe (or a remote front-end processor). At the central site, the actual interface can be an Integrated Communications Adapter (ICA) for smaller networks or a front-end processor in larger networks. With the exception of small 4300 sites, the interface is normally to a front-end controller such as a 3705, 3720, 3725, or 3745.

The front-end communications controller is in itself an intelligent device. The front end runs software called the Network Control Program (NCP), which defines and controls the network. The NCP interfaces with VTAM (or some communications access method subsystem) in the host. The attachment between the front-end processor and the mainframe is a high-speed channel that facilitates a larger volume of high-speed data.

For the 5250 family of terminals and printers used with midrange systems, the architecture is similar but not identical. Like the 3270s, the 5250 terminals attach to a controller, but they use a twinaxial cable connection that daisy-chains the terminals on the cable to the controller (see Figure 4.6). In smaller networks, the controller is integrated directly into the midrange

FIG. 4.5
IBM 3270 Connectivity

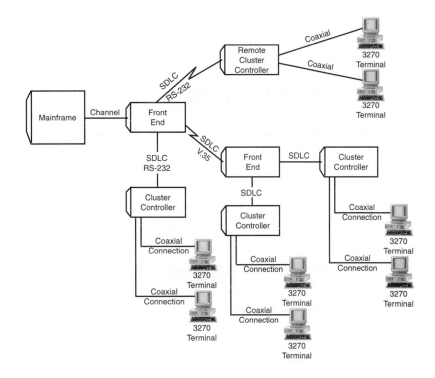

FIG. 4.6
IBM 5250 Connectivity

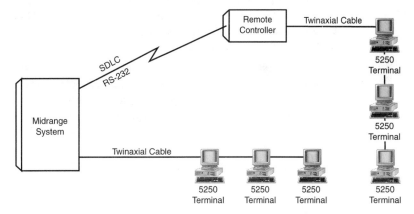

computer. In larger networks, remote controllers (5294 or 5394) serve to funnel the terminals back to the midrange host.

The critical difference between the midrange and mainframe terminal architectures, however, is the midrange's lack of a front-end communications processor. This device enables mainframes to handle large terminal networks.

Ch
4

N O T E   Both product families use SDLC as their communications methodology. Messages from the 3270 family are carried in the LU 2 and LU 3 formats, while messages from the 5250 family are carried in LU 7 format. ▩

Peer-to-Peer Relationships

Given the hierarchical nature of SNA and its structured PU layout, it is sometimes difficult to determine what is a peer to what else, let alone what relationship those two peers can have. Previously in this chapter, the fundamental concepts of PU 2.1, APPN, LU 6.2, and APPC were presented. However, it is often unclear how (or if) these topics are related.

Recall that a Physical Unit Type 2.1 device is an intelligent device capable of conversing with other PU 2.1 devices and is also capable of routing or rerouting messages through other PU 2.1 devices. Application Peer-to-Peer Networking (APPN) describes the interaction between PU 2.1 devices. A Logical Unit Type 6.2 is a data format that enables two programs to communicate across SNA. A program implementing the LU 6.2 interface must reside on a system that is operating at either the PU 2.1 or PU 5 level. Application Program-to-Program Communications (APPC) describes LU 2 conversations.

In addition to these concepts and implementations, SNA also supports the following interactions, which can be considered peer-to-peer:

- *SNA Distribution Services (SNADS)*. As the name implies, SNADS is a distribution service used to move information, such as documents, electronic mail, and files, throughout the SNA physical network. Please note, however, that the information sent through SNADS must be selected for distribution and that the distribution does not occur on demand (like the U.S. mail, things get there when they get there). SNADS uses both APPC and APPN as part of the delivery mechanism.

- *Network Job Entry (NJE)*. NJE exists above the Job Entry System (JES) and is used to distribute the processing aspects of batch jobs among systems. In other words, NJE links JES processing systems to form a loosely coupled batch system. With NJE, a job can be submitted on System A, processed on System B, and printed at System C. NJE uses bisynchronous links, SDLC links or direct channel-to-channel attachment to facilitate the communications between systems.

- *Distributed Data Management (DDM)*. DDM is used primarily in the midrange systems. DDM is a shared-file product that enables midrange systems to share access to data files on a file or record basis. DDM can be run over a Token-Ring network or over SDLC lines. Support for DDM is also available for versions of CICS, thus enabling mainframes and midrange system to share file-based information using DDM.

Again, given the size and complexity of SNA, other peer-to-peer facilities are available. The capabilities presented herein, however, are the most commonly used.

PC Integration Strategy

IBM has adopted the IEEE 802.5 Token-Ring specification as the basis for its PC and PS/2 LAN implementation. This ring topology features a central ring from which devices (such as PCs and PS/2s) are attached (see Figure 4.7). In this LAN architecture, a token is passed along the ring. When a unit stops transmitting or has nothing to transmit, it relinquishes the token to the next unit on the ring.

FIG. 4.7

Token-Ring Topology

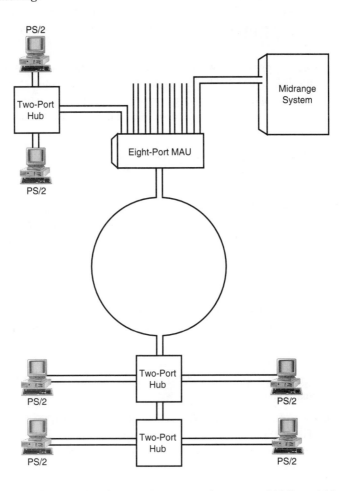

The original IBM Token-Ring implementation operated at a rate of 4 Mbps. A higher data rate, 16 Mbps, was made available in the late 1980s. To make the physical attachments to the ring easier, additional concentrators and attachment units were released. Two common units are the eight-port medium access unit (MAU) and the two-port hub; these units extend the ring without corrupting its fundamental topology. Gateways and bridges can be used to tie two or more Token-Ring networks together.

With the physical Token-Ring LAN, stand-alone PC networks can be implemented using IBM's network software or other network software such as Novell's NetWare. To incorporate a Token-Ring LAN into a global SNA network, however, IBM's networking software must be implemented with attachments to the SNA network. The nature of this attachment depends on the processor or terminal types closest to the LAN.

For example, in a small midrange environment, a Token-Ring LAN can be connected to the midrange via a midrange interface controller. In this case, the midrange system actually participates in the Token-Ring LAN; a PC product named PC Support is available to enable the PCs or PS/2s to access the midrange applications and files. (Moreover, when multiple midrange processors are present on a Token-Ring LAN, special peer-to-peer capabilities are available to share files and log on to the various systems.)

In larger SNA networks, however, the attachment of the LAN to the network depends on the location of the Token-Ring LAN. If the Token-Ring LAN is remote to the central mainframe, it can be attached to the remote cluster controller, which acts as a gateway to the SNA network. If, however, the LAN is near the central processor, it might also be connected to the front-end communications processor, which serves this gateway function.

For a more detailed comparison of the Token-Ring topology to other topologies (such as CSMA/CD), refer to Chapter 7, "LANs and WANs" (p. 139).

Office Automation

IBM offers several products to address the area of office automation. Its two basic products that offer office functions (a calendar, electronic mail, information management, and so on) are the following:

- *PROFS (PRofessional OFfice System)*. PROFS is a software package available for the VM operating system. Because PROFs depends on VM and because VM is not usually implemented on larger mainframes, the 9370 is often the host of choice. PROFS exchanges messages with other mail systems through SNA Distribution Services (SNADS) or DISOSS.

- *AS/400 Office*. AS/400 Office is a software package for the AS/400. AS/400 Office exchanges messages with PROFS or through SNADS or DISOSS (Distributed Office Support System).

To provide an office automation solution that integrates PC and PS/2 functions with the PROFS and AS/400 Office products, IBM developed OfficeVision. Like HP's NewWave Office, OfficeVision is a distributed solution that integrates the core services of PROFS or AS/400 Office with a network of PCs or PS/2s. OfficeVision was introduced as the first SAA-compliant IBM solution.

While both PROFS and AS/400 Office provide office automation features, the Distributed Office Support System (DISOSS) is also important to IBM's office automation strategy and its capability to interface with other non-IBM systems. DISOSS enables you to tie together a wide variety of word processing packages, office automation software, and non-IBM products. In a nutshell, it provides distribution and library services specifically for handling documents. DISOSS is not an electronic mail facility like PROFS and AS/400 Office; it is a network-wide document management facility.

DISOSS, AS/400 Office, and PROFS support a document format known as the Document Content Architecture (DCA). DCA defines the structure for revisable documents (documents that contain the entire editing history) and final-form documents (documents that are the final result of all edits). DCA establishes a common ground that most word processing systems can use. When DCA is coupled with DISOSS, documents can be imported and exported from virtually any source. For example, both HP and DEC support DCA document conversion in their word processors and also support DISOSS document exchange.

Also note that the term Document Interchange Architecture (DIA) is often used with DCA and DISOSS. DIA is the least known of IBM's three major distribution services (SNADS, DDM, and DIA). Whereas SNADS is a general-purpose distribution service and DDM is oriented toward record-level and file-level access in midrange systems networks, DIA is oriented toward the distribution and systematic storage of documents.

In most cases, SNADS is the facility through which electronic mail is distributed between systems. For example, if a PROFS message is sent to AS/400 Office, SNADS usually provides the delivery mechanism.

FIG. 4.8

Typical IBM SNA Network

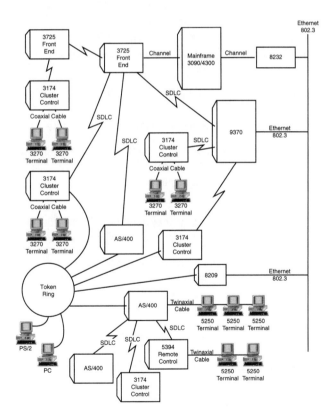

Ch
4

Network Architecture

A typical SNA physical network might contains a mainframe (3090 or 4300), a 9370, two AS/400s and some PS/2s or PCs. Each of these types of systems supports direct or indirect attachments to an SDLC-based SNA network, a Token-Ring LAN and an Ethernet (or IEEE 802.3) LAN. Standard SNA supports SDLC, X.25 and Token-Ring. The Ethernet/802.3 connections, in turn, can be used to implement IBM's variation of TCP/IP for multivendor connectivity (see Figure 4.8).

The mainframe supports connectivity to the terminal network via a front-end processor (the 3725 in Figure 4.8). From the 3725, connections can be made to the following:

- An X.25 network.
- Multiple, remote cluster controllers (the 3174 in Figure 4.8) that attach via coaxial cable to the 3270 family of terminals and printers.
- A second, remote front-end processor (the 3725) that interfaces with additional cluster controllers.

Connectivity between the mainframe and the Token-Ring LAN is shown at the cluster controller (3174) level, although that connection can also be made at the front-end communications processor. Because the mainframe does not support direct connection to Ethernet/802.3, a special device (the 8232 LAN/channel adapter) connects the mainframe to the LAN via a mainframe channel.

The ES/9370 uses the same general terminal network architecture as the mainframe, with the notable exception of no front-end processor. The 9370 interfaces with cluster controllers that in turn interface with the physical terminals via coaxial connections.

Figure 4.8 also shows a single SDLC line from the 9370 to the front-end communications processor of the mainframe. This connection enables the 9370 to participate in peer-to-peer interactions with the mainframe, and it also allows its own terminal network to access the mainframe.

The ES/9370 supports direct attachment to both the Ethernet/802.3 LAN and the Token-Ring network. Similarly, attachment to an X.25 network is made using an integrated controller.

The AS/400 supports attachment to both 3270 and 5250 terminals. Attachment to the 3270 terminal is made with a cluster controller (3174) that interfaces to an integrated controller in the AS/400. The native 5250 terminals can be directly connected to an integrated controller via twinaxial cable or through a remote cluster controller (the 5394 in Figure 4.8).

The AS/400 offers an integrated controller for connection to a Token Ring or Ethernet network. As shown, however, connectivity from Token Ring to an Ethernet/802.3 network can also be provided through an 8209 LAN bridge that converts Token Ring packets into either Ethernet or 802.3 packets.

Figure 4.8 also shows two additional SDLC links originating from the AS/400. One is routed to the front-end communications processor of the mainframe, and the other is routed to another AS/400. The link to the mainframe enables the AS/400 to participate in the SNA network with the mainframe; it also enables the local AS/400 terminals to access the mainframe via 3270 emulation.

The second SDLC link to the other AS/400 is typically for peer-to-peer relationships (PU 2.1/LU 6.2). This connection enables the two AS/400s to establish a direct link with one another (using APPN) and exchange program-to-program information (using APPC) without involving the mainframe. In effect, this link is independent from the main SNA physical network when used for this purpose.

Finally, the AS/400 supports an integrated adapter, enabling it to connect to an X.25 network.

The last elements in the network diagram are PS/2s or PCs. These devices can exist on a Token Ring network independent of the SNA network, or they can use the links available on the ring to access any of the processors via SNA.

Storage

The IBM Network Tape Access and Control System for AIX (NetTape) simplifies tape management and access in RS/6000 networks, and is capable of consolidating tape operations for all tape devices from a single GUI. With this system, you are able to transfer data between tape servers and clients over a high-speed TCP/IP network, such as FDDI, Fibre Channel, ATM, or High Performance Parallel interface (HiPPI).

ADSTAR Distributed Storage Manager (ASDM), a client/server storage management tool, provides disaster recovery support and more client capabilities. The Disaster Recovery Manager feature of ASDM can automatically generate a disaster recovery plan, manages off-site recovery media, and keeps an inventory of client and server systems for restoration of systems and data. ●

Ch
4

CHAPTER 5

Sun Microsystems

Company Background

Sun Microsystems incorporated in 1982 with Scott McNealy at the helm. Under McNealy's leadership, Sun (the company's name was derived from the Stanford University Network terminal) has become one of America's fastest growing and most efficient companies. McNealy is active in the open systems movement, and Sun was one of the early pioneers in this area. Today, Sun focuses on providing open solutions for enterprise-wide networks and developing Internet technology for the expanding needs of online users. During the first year of operation, Sun Microsystems sold approximately 400 workstations. It went on to experience phenomenal growth. Its revenue for the year 1989, only seven years after inception, approached $2 billion and by 1995 its revenues had reached nearly $6 billion.

Sun Microsystems has entrenched itself in the high-performance workstation and server market. In addition to providing high-speed computing units, however, Sun has staked its claim in the area of open systems computing. To this end, Sun uses UNIX as the basis for its Solaris operating systems, it uses TCP/IP over Ethernet for networking, and it uses the industry-standard VME bus. Solaris comprises nearly one-third of all UNIX systems sold worldwide. Similarly, Sun comprises 40 percent of the UNIX RISC workstation market.

Sun's strategic relationships with other manufacturers and vendors has certainly been instrumental in its success to date. Sun has granted commercial licenses on its Network File System (NFS) to a wide range of manufacturers, including the apparent competitors (such as DEC, HP, and IBM). By making NFS available to the industry as a whole, Sun has leveraged NFS as a de facto multivendor networking standard.

In the late 1980s, Sun took a dramatic step by allowing other manufacturers to produce clones of the Sun system hardware. On one hand, this is yet another example of Sun's efforts to transform its products into industrywide standards. On the other hand, many industry analysts regarded this move as an attempt to rekindle the explosive growth that occurred when the IBM clones were released.

Product Line Overview

Sun is a focused manufacturer. Sun doesn't do terminals; it doesn't do printers; it just does workstations. Sun is, however, the largest provider of UNIX workstations, servers, and software. Recently, Sun released a platform-independent programming language called Java, which provides a unique solution to programming for complex networks, including the Internet.

In the past, Sun produced workstations based on Intel and Motorola architectures. The most modern Sun systems use a Reduced Instruction Set Computer (RISC) architecture that Sun has termed SPARC (scalable processor architecture). Originally introduced as the Sun-4 line, SPARC systems have been scaled into a high-end group of uniprocessor and multiprocessor workstations (SPARCstations), a group of network file servers (SPARCservers), and the Netra Internet Server. The servers range from the single processor, 110-MHz SPARCserver 4 and 5, to the 20-processor SPARCcenter 2000E. The Netra Internet Server provides a complete Internet server solution; the Netra System Management Server is used for PCs on TCP/IP networks.

The latest evolution in the SPARC line, the UltraSPARC, puts Sun firmly in the lead of the workstation market by bringing supercomputer technology down to the workstation level. A switch-based interconnect typically found only in supercomputers, the UltraSPARC is based on Sun's Ultra Port Architecture (UPA), which permits multiple, simultaneous transfers between the processor, memory, graphics and I/O. The older, bus-based architecture common to most workstations is limited to a single data transfer at a time.

All Sun systems can support large amounts of memory (up to 512M per processor in some models) and a sizable amount of disk storage (up to 147G on the high end). The graphics resolutions on the workstations range from a low of 1024 x 768 pixels to a high of 1600 x 1280 pixels. The UltraSPARC's visual instruction set provides the technology for high-end graphics, including 3-D visualization, animation, and video processing.

Sun sponsors third-party programs to encourage independent companies to develop and market applications for the Solaris operating system. In 1990, Lotus Development Corporation committed to deliver its famous Lotus 1-2-3 spreadsheet to the SunOS platform, and became the first of many third-party companies to write software to run on the SunOS, and later, the

Solaris operating system. This was a coup for Sun because it was the first UNIX-oriented Solaris operating system (and because it was the first UNIX-oriented system Lotus agreed to port to). Although in retrospect this never resulted in the much hoped-for flood of PC applications being ported to UNIX, Lotus 1-2-3 operating on the Sun platform was a significant achievement in itself. Sun now offers versions of Solaris for several platforms other than SPARC, including Intel.

The latest version of the Sun's network operating system, Solaris 2.5, offers fully scalable NFS, NFS over TCP, and IPX/SPX connectivity. This support makes it possible for Solaris to integrate enterprise workgroups. Solaris for SPARC and UltraSPARC computers is highly scalable and secure, it is scalable up to the superserver level, and can handle databases at the terabyte level. Version 2.5 has been optimized to take advantage of the Ultra line of workstations and servers, and facilitates faster visual computing. Solaris uses the Common Desktop Environment (CDE), a product designed to give a common interface to all UNIX environments.

Sun offers a suite of infrastructure software along with Solaris, including:

- *Solstice*. Software for systems and network management.
- *WorkShop*. A set of visual tools for developing technical and business applications.
- *SunSoft NEO*. Software for building applications based on networked objects.
- *Java*. A network-enabled programming language.

Solaris is scalable and secure. It is ideal for use with an Internet server, application server, PC administration server, or high-performance workstation. Solaris is also available for Intel x86, Pentium, Pentium Pro, and PowerPC computers.

Strategy for Connectivity

Sun Microsystems refers to its approach to networking as the Open Network Computing (ONC) architecture. In implementing this architecture, Sun has recruited other computer manufacturers and related companies into the fold. Many of these companies have, in fact, bought into the Sun architecture—some completely, others restraining their commitment to a particular service or set of services.

Sun's unique contributions to ONC are mainly in the upper application and service layers (see Figure 5.1).

The lower layers of ONC are handled by TCP/IP running over Ethernet (or other TCP/IP-compatible networks). The portions of TCP/IP that are relevant to understanding ONC are as follows:

- *Transmission Control Protocol (TCP)*. TCP delivers information between systems participating in the TCP/IP network. As part of this delivery process, TCP confirms receipt of the information and handles the retransmission of corrupted information.
- *User Datagram Protocol (UDP)*. UDP is a facility available for applications to deliver information between systems. Although similar to TCP, UDP does not provide the automatic error correction facilities of TCP and cannot verify receipt of data.

FIG. 5.1

Sun's ONC Architecture

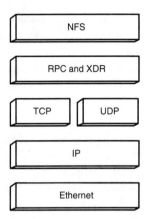

- *Internet Protocol (IP)*. While TCP handles the delivery of data, IP determines the best possible route between two systems. This might or might not include moving the information between LANs or across WAN bridges.

TCP/IP is discussed in more detail in Chapter 9, " PC LAN Network Operating Systems" (p. 198).

Sun's ONC services and functions lie on the standard TCP/IP layers as follows:

- *Remote Procedure Call (RPC)*. RPC provides a common set of routines that programs can use to communicate with each other throughout the network. Whereas the TCP/IP UDP service facilitates the movement of information between two programs in the ONC environment, RPC adds structure and context on top of the delivery mechanism. From a broad perspective, RPC provides a common interface that two programs can use to converse with one another.

- *External Data Representation (XDR)*. XDR furnishes a common format for information moved through the ONC environment. Because different systems in a network might represent data in many different formats (for example, signed, packed decimal fields are invariably unique to each system), a common format that does not sacrifice efficiency for compatibility is necessary. XDR is a data description language that applications can use with RPC to enable two programs sharing information on the network to use a common format (even though the information might actually be stored on the two systems in different formats).

- *Network File System (NFS)*. In many respects, Sun is best known in the networking world for its implementation of NFS. NFS provides a networkwide file system that enables other systems supporting NFS to mount and access files (or sets of files).

As previously noted, Sun's approach to ONC has been to recruit other vendors and manufacturers into the ONC fold, and NFS has been a key factor in the recruiting process. For example, DEC, HP, and IBM have NFS implementations for many of their proprietary operating systems. In the world of UNIX, NFS is frequently bundled with TCP/IP to provide a LAN-wide file system. In fact, nearly 100 different companies have implementations of NFS, XDR, and RPC for their particular systems or applications.

However, NFS, XDR and RPC are not the sole components of Sun's ONC environment. Other members of this environment include the following:

- *Secure RPC.* An implementation of RPC with additional security that verifies the identity of each RPC user.

- *RPC Generator (RPCGEN).* A high-level program development tool that simplifies RPC programming.

- *RPC Application Program Interface (RPC API).* The combined library of the RPC and XDR interfaces made available for applications development on a given system. This is normally a high-level interface used by programmers.

- *Automounter.* Works in conjunction with NFS to automatically mount and dismount files and file sets as they are needed.

- *Network Information Services (NIS).* Maintains a common list (database) of files that can be accessed by various systems in the ONC environment. NIS implements a form of network security. Note that NIS was formerly known as Yellow Pages (YP).

- *Network Lock Manager.* Provides record- and file-level locking of information accessed through NFS.

- *Status Monitor.* Enables one system to determine whether another system has been restarted.

- *Remote Execution (REX).* Enables a user on one system to execute commands and programs on other systems in the network.

- *NETdisk.* Provides a booting mechanism for diskless workstations in the network.

- *PC-NFS.* Provides services in support of PCs in the ONC environment. This topic will be discussed in more detail later in this chapter.

Application/User Relationship

Ch
5

Because Solaris combines two UNIX implementations (AT&T and Berkeley versions), it uses the same multiuser, multitasking capabilities as these mainstream versions.

For the most part, Sun systems are used as engineering workstations. In this highly graphical application, virtually every cycle of every available processor goes toward maintaining the display and display quality (especially when manipulating 2-D and 3-D objects).

Sun also produces systems targeted as servers in large, multiuser environments, and these models do not fall into the same general category of the engineering workstations. Instead, they typically fall into one of two extremes:

- *No-user systems.* These systems are used solely as network devices (normally file servers). Although other users access these systems, they are doing so through their own native systems.

- *Data center servers.* The high end of the server line includes large-capacity disk storage for local and networkwide use and support for a moderate number of terminals (up to 64). This size of device is, in fact, multiuser oriented and is similar in concept to the DEC VAX midrange systems.

The application's interaction with the user is somewhat at arm's length. The user interacts with the operating system in a session, as with DEC's VMS and HP's MPE. This session orientation gives the user a working area in which to function that is (theoretically) independent from other users on the same system.

The application program, however, relies on system-level (or network-level) routines to make the communications bridge between the user and itself. The information passing across this bridge might be simple character-oriented data or complex graphics-oriented information, depending on the application.

This approach to programming is common in the UNIX environment. In fact, in the UNIX environment, much effort is made to isolate the program from the physical aspects of the systems and the network. With Solaris and the ONC architecture, this same philosophy is extended to encompass a much broader range of possibilities.

Terminal Attachment Philosophy

Where Sun's older architecture was based primarily on freestanding workstations, Sun's new UltraComputing architecture is focused on the network. As Sun's products became more accepted in a broader range of functions, Sun began to push into the midrange computing market dominated by DEC, among others. In this market, the need to provide a reasonable per-user cost dictated that Sun offer basic terminal connectivity to the products they targeted toward this market. This terminal connectivity requirement was in addition to a requirement for LAN connectivity.

To address this requirement, Sun provides simple, point-to-point connections between terminals and its higher-end servers. The nature of this connection follows the approach used by other UNIX implementations: a standard RS-232C connection to a variety of character-oriented terminal devices (from a variety of manufacturers). Again, this is similar to the approach used by other midrange computer manufacturers (such as DEC and HP).

However, with the increased popularity in graphics-based user interfaces and X Window terminals, Sun—and the rest of the industry—was forced to take a stand on implementing a noncharacter terminal interface. Sun's response was to use a graphics-oriented user interface it had co-developed with AT&T for UNIX. This product was named Open Look, and it worked with existing X Window terminal standards. In the interest of establishing a common UNIX desktop, however, Sun agreed to forsake Open Look in favor of Motif, as specified by the Common Desktop Environment (CDE).

One of Sun's earlier GUI innovations was its SunTools product, which enabled a user to have more than a single terminal emulator on the screen at one time. SunTools included two terminal emulators, the Terminal Tool, which was a true VT100 emulator, and Command Tool, which recorded a history of the login session. SunTools later became OpenWindows, although it still required two separate terminal emulators. Later, the Open Software Foundation came up with the Motif interface—which Sun did not immediately embrace, despite a tremendous user demand for the Windows-like GUI. Sun now sells an implementation of CDE that runs on top of Solaris, which effectively put an end to OpenWindows.

In terms of actually manufacturing any character or graphics-oriented terminals, Sun has kept its distance. In fact, instead of embracing the X Terminal approach as a manufacturer, Sun has introduced diskless workstations that offer the functions of an X Terminal at a low price but with the advantages of an engineering workstation.

Sun unveiled this approach with the SPARCstation SLC, a SPARC-based workstation that comes close to the price of X Terminal offerings but still provides the basic functions of a workstation. Although the SLC is diskless, the ONC/NFS architecture enables the SLC to retrieve programs and data from the network to which it is attached. This is not altogether different from using diskless workstations in PC LANs.

Succeeding the SLC is the SPARC Xterminal 1, which boasts a clock speed of 50 MHz and runs the microSPARC processor. This X terminal offers strong performance, and a high-resolution color display. Besides running X terminal applications, the Xterminal 1 can run software that would otherwise require an additional system, such as Windows or Macintosh. The Xterminal 1 includes standard X11R5 software, giving it access to a variety of servers using TCP/IP, NFS, SNMP, BootP, Telnet, and several other networking protocols.

Peer-to-Peer Relationships

Peer-to-peer processing is a critical element within Sun's concept of workgroup computing, and it significantly influences Sun's approach to networking. In Sun's world, people with similar information requirements must be able to share this information with one another to reduce duplication and increase efficiency. Sun provides two critical functions to establish and maintain peer-to-peer relationships: Network File System (NFS) and RPCs.

NFS provides common access to shared information. Multiple programs and users can access the same set of information, such as files and records, as peers via NFS. Because NFS can oversee multiple systems accessing the same information, NFS can be a focal point for this sharing or exchange of data. A key factor in this technology is NFS's capability to perform record-level and file-level locking to prevent the simultaneous update of the same information (see Figure 5.2).

Ch
5

FIG. 5.2
Peer-to-Peer
Communications
via NFS

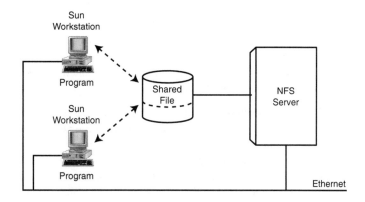

RPCs are used for customized program-to-program communications. From another perspective, programs on different systems can establish peer-to-peer communications with one another via Sun's RPC architecture. After the communications link is established, the two (or more) programs can freely exchange information with one another, regardless of their respective locations in the network (see Figure 5.3).

FIG. 5.3
Peer-to-Peer
Communications
via RPC

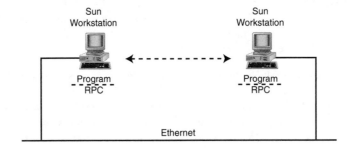

Furthermore, these functions are not mutually exclusive. Combined RPC and NFS solutions can, for example, be implemented to share data in localized work groups via NFS, while RPC functions are used to distribute a subset of the local information to a wider audience within the total network.

Thus, implementing NFS and RPC on a wide variety of systems produced by different manufacturers is an attractive possibility. NFS and RPC can be used in a multivendor environment to create peer-to-peer relationships between systems and programs that previously could not recognize one another or exchange information.

PC Integration Strategy

Sun's underlying approach to integrating PCs with its technology focuses on PCs operating on the same LAN as the Sun equipment or networking products. Within that LAN, Sun concentrates on enabling the PCs to access standard ONC/NFS services. In the case of file services, this means that the PCs can access a non-PC NFS server.

Sun's main product in the PC arena is PC-NFS, a PC-resident software package that permits DOS and Windows users to share data and resources with UNIX systems, minicomputers, and mainframes running TCP/IP and ONC/NFS. PC-NFS works with a PC Ethernet card and provides basic connectivity to the network (via TCP/IP) and to NFS servers. The three basic PC-NFS functions (see Figure 5.4) are:

- *NFS Client.* This function within PC-NFS handles the interface between MS-DOS and the NFS server. In this role, the NFS Client performs the necessary network activity (in concert with the network hardware) to communicate with the NFS server. Because the NFS file structure (native UNIX) is foreign to MS-DOS, the NFS Client function also handles the mapping of the NFS names into MS-DOS names. And finally, the NFS Client works with both MS-DOS and NFS to support and maintain networkwide record and file locks.

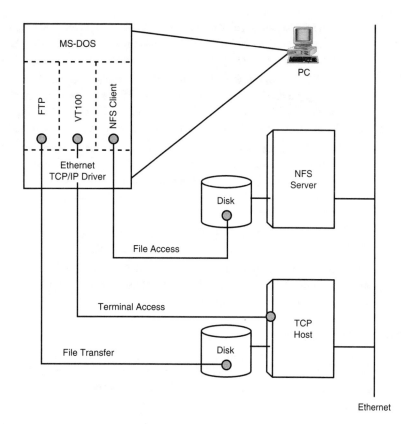

FIG. 5.4
Connectivity via Sun's
PC-NFS

- *VT100 emulation.* Because the lower layers of PC-NFS depend on TCP/IP to handle the networking services, the product also includes VT100 emulation for TELNET access. This enables the PC to act as a terminal to access other systems in the NFS and/or TCP/IP network.
- *File Transfer Protocol (FTP).* Most implementations of TCP/IP include FTP, which transfers files from one system to another. PC-NFS includes FTP to provide a high degree of functional compatibility with other TCP/IP systems in the network. Whereas the NFS Client can provide online access for a user or application to an NFS file, FTP makes a copy of a file on another system.

In addition to the main PC-NFS package, Sun offers the following add-ons:

- *SolarNet PC Management.* This software gives PC users access to the UNIX operating system, and permits administrators to manage networked PC systems. The system enables users to share enterprisewide data across multiple, heterogeneous servers through TCP/IP connectivity and NFS integration. PC clients can become equal members on the LAN and all resources will appear to the PC as if they were local.

Ch
5

■ *PC-NFS LifeLine Mail.* This package supports the TCP/IP standard Simple Mail Transfer Protocol (SMTP) and the Berkeley UNIX's Post Office Protocol (POP) to enable the PC to participate in electronic mail.

■ *PC-NFS LifeLine Backup.* Because NFS servers tend to have a large disk capacity, the Backup package enables a PC to use an NFS server as a backup device for local and network information. In addition to backing up to the NFS server, PC-NFS LifeLine Backup also supports networkwide backup to a tape drive attached to an NFS server.

■ *PC-NFS Programmer's Toolkit.* This product includes a set of Sun's XDR and RPC library routines that programmers can use to establish communications between PC-resident programs and other programs operating in the Sun RPC/XDR. These routines enable programs operating on PCs to establish peer relationships with programs operating anywhere on the network.

Another event that fortified Sun's PC integration strategy was a joint announcement in late 1989 by Sun, Novell, and Netwise, in which they revealed a plan to support Sun's RPC and XDR in Novell networks. Under this plan, Sun provided the ONC/NFS standard, Novell's NetWare was enhanced to support RPC, and Netwise revised its product, RPC TOOL, to include support for both Sun and OSI RPC formats.

Office Automation

To date, Sun has no strong offering of its own in the area of office automation. Instead, it relies on TCP/IP's SMTP, Berkeley's POP, and third-party products to provide stand-alone and integrated multivendor office automation solutions. This approach is really no different from their approach to any other general application.

Sun bundles the Ultra Pack with its Ultra workstations. Ultra Pack is a set of applications and tools, including several collaborative applications. Sun's ShowMe shared whiteboard application is included for collaboration. The Ultra Pack also includes the Netscape Navigator World Wide Web navigator, Sun's own Hot Java browser, several multimedia tools, an MPEG II player, and a music player.

The SunSoft WorkShop includes tools that permit developers to take advantage of the UltraSPARC instruction set. WorkShop includes the SunSoft Visual WorkShop for C++, SunSoft WorkShop for C, SunSoft Performance WorkShop for Fortran 90, SunSoft WorkShop for FORTRAN 77, and SunSoft WorkShop for Ada. These new compilers offer a significant performance improvement and require minimal code modification. The SunSoft Performance Library is an optimized implementation of common numerical algorithm libraries used for applications such as structural analysis, computational fluid dynamics, and simulation.

Network Architecture

At the simplest level, Sun's foundation for networking is based on running TCP/IP over an Ethernet network. In doing this, Sun uses the same network topology (bus), the same network discipline (Carrier Sense Multiple Access with Collision Detection), and the same basic medium attachments (transceivers) that Digital Equipment uses. In fact, Sun workstations are frequently found on the same physical LANs on which DEC equipment resides (although this does not necessarily mean that the two types of equipment communicate).

In a Sun network, then, the workstations and servers attach to a thick or thin LAN (see Figure 5.5). TCP/IP manages communications over the 10 Mbps Ethernet. Communications among the systems on the LAN can occur in two different fashions.

FIG. 5.5

Sample Sun Network
Architecture

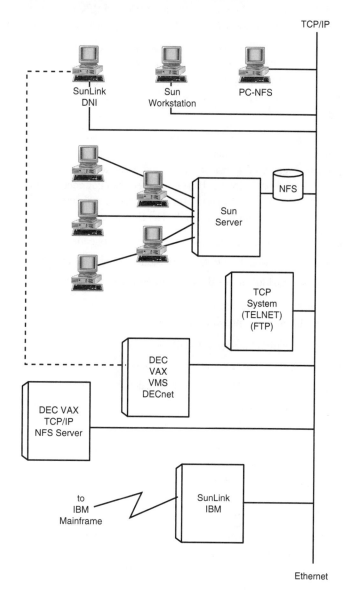

Because Sun's underlying network protocol is TCP/IP, the standard TCP/IP mechanisms for system-to-system communications can be used. In Sun's environment, the two most widely used communications are TELNET for terminal access and FTP for file transfer.

Sun has added its own network services above TCP/IP. These services are commonly referred to as Open Network Computing/Network File System (ONC/NFS). They include NFS for sharing files and records throughout the network, and RPC to enable a program running on one system to communicate with a program running on a different system.

Connectivity with PCs starts with the PCs being connected to the Ethernet LAN. Running with MS-DOS, Sun supplies PC-NFS to implement TCP/IP on the Ethernet connection and to provide three essential services that enable the PC to participate in the Sun network: NFS Client for access to files stored on NFS servers, VT100 to give the PC TELNET access, and FTP for file transfers.

In terms of interfacing with other systems, Sun has focused on connectivity with DEC and IBM, enabling its ONC/NFS partners to establish other connectivity options with other systems. Sun uses a gateway approach between the Sun and IBM network environments. Its SunLink connectivity solution for IBM equipment can connect to an IBM mainframe system via a channel attachment, a SNA SDLC data communications connection or a non-SNA bisynchronous data communication link. The SunLink IBM solution offers the following:

- IBM 3270 terminal emulation to access IBM applications.
- RJE and NJE emulation to facilitate bidirectional file transfer.
- LU 6.2 support for native IBM program-to-program communications (APPC).

For DEC connectivity, Sun supplies two approaches with SunLink DNI and implements support for DECnet. This solution provides the following:

- VT100 emulation for access to DEC systems.
- Support for standard DECnet file transfers.
- Support for standard DECnet task-to-task communications.

Alternatively, Sun provides a solution that implements NFS (and TCP/IP) in a VAX environment, thus enabling the DEC equipment to participate in the Sun network.

Other connectivity solutions are provided by the companies subscribing to the ONC/NFS strategy. Also, because Sun implements standard TCP/IP over Ethernet, virtually any standard Ethernet bridges can be used to tie Sun networks together over a wide area.

High-Speed Networking

Sun offers switched Fast Ethernet and Fast/Wide SCSI 2 functionality directly on the motherboard of the Ultra series of workstations and servers. No other workstation vendor is currently offering Fast Ethernet directly on the motherboard. Sun's SunATM Adapter 2.0 provides for 155 Mbps ATM networking. Sun also offers a 10/100 Mbps auto-sensing SunFastEthernet add-on adapter and the SuNFDDI adapter for connectivity to 100 Mbps FDDI networks.

The dual-speed Ethernet add-on is the most efficient way to migrate to high-speed networking; it can operate at either speed and automatically switch to the highest possible rate. The same gradual migration approach is taken with the SunATM Adapter. The ATM adapter includes an implementation of LAN Emulation 1.0, a specification that permits an ATM network to appear as an Ethernet LAN. (For more information on ATM and LAN Emulation, see Chapter 11, "Network Management," p. 242.) With LAN Emulation, a hybrid network can be created that leverages the higher bandwidth possibilities of ATM using existing wiring.

Java Internet Programming Language

The Internet presents a number of programming and networking challenges. Sun's Java is the first programming language to offer a platform-independent environment for programming for the Internet and other complex networks. Java is portable and secure, and offers a previously unavailable level of interactivity to programmers and users working on the World Wide Web.

Java is loosely based on C++ and has rapidly come to be an open standard for Internet programming. Hundreds of small Java *applets* have been created by Sun and third parties, which are downloaded across a network and run locally. Java applications are platform-independent, so long as the receiving platform holds the Java Virtual machine. This works as an interpreter between the end user's computer and the Java application. Potentially, Java could end the need to port applications to multiple platforms.

UltraSPARC Technology

Sun introduced its UltraSPARC technology in November, 1995. With the Ultra family of workstations (see Figure 5.6), Sun has raised the bar in workstation computing by bringing out technology for high-speed networking and collaborative computing and complex data designs.

The Ultra design replaces the bus-based interconnect with a faster, switch-based interconnect. The Ultra design is based on the Ultra Port Architecture (UPA), a switch-based interconnect that is typically found only in supercomputers, which can accommodate a data transfer of up to 1.3 Gbps. The UPA serves as a central switching mechanism for integrating all system components, creating a close integration and high-speed connection between the processor, I/O, graphics, memory, and networking. The UPA lends itself to efficient multitasking and significantly reduces memory latency. Consequently, users will experience fewer delays when running complex processes.

In any networking model, messages are broken up into packets, routed to a destination, and reassembled. Under the UPA model, packets from multiple subsystems can be interspersed, so multiple transactions can take place simultaneously. In the bus-based scheme, however, a single subsystem has complete and exclusive control over the bus while its message is being delivered; other subsystems are unable to use the lines during the transaction. Currently, Sun is the only vendor to offer this technology in workstation-class machines.

The UPA brings five innovative technologies to the UltraComputing architecture:

FIG. 5.6
Sun Ultra 1 Workstation

Photo courtesy of Sun Microsystems

- *UltraSPARC.* The latest of the SPARC family of microprocessors, the UltraSPARC has a 64-bit architecture and is one of the fastest microprocessors on the market. The superscalar design enables four instructions to be executed per clock cycle. The UltraSPARC has several advantages over traditional processors. Its non-blocking load/ store unit can continue functioning after a cache miss—that is, when instructions are not on the on-chip cache and must be located in external caches or main memory. In addition, its multilevel trap handling facilities provide for speedy context-switching and better multitasking performance.
- *Visual Instruction Set (VIS).* The VIS is built into the motherboard, and is able to significantly improve graphics and multimedia performance without the need for add-in cards. This set of instructions can execute 2-D and 3-D technology, image process- ing, real-time video decompression, pixel format/conversion, fast data transfer, and animation.
- *Creator Graphics.* A graphics engine that produces speedy graphics manipulation. It offers true 24-bit color, and accelerates windowing and graphics manipulations.

- *3D-RAM.* 3D-RAM is a subset of Creator Graphics that incorporates memory management technology to increase performance for 3-D graphics.
- *Fast Ethernet.* Fast Ethernet technology is built directly into the motherboard. The Ultra architecture remains compatible with 10BaseT Ethernet and supports other networking standards, including ATM and ISDN.

The Ultra is compatible with the existing base of applications developed for the Solaris operating system. Through Sun's Wabi (Windows application binary interface) emulation software, Ultra workstations can also run Windows applications. In addition, Wabi enables Solaris users to cut and paste between Solaris programs and several popular Windows applications. Typically, Windows emulation carries an excruciatingly high processing burden. Wabi eliminates much of this burden by mapping Windows function calls directly to native X services.

The Ultras run the latest version of Solaris, the Solaris 2.5 SPARC Edition. This version of Solaris has been optimized for the Ultra, and supports the Ultra's high-speed VIS instructions and 3-D graphics.

The Ultra family includes the following:

- *Ultra 1 Model 140.* An entry-level machine suited for computationally intensive desktop applications. It comes with a 143 MHz UltraSPARC processor.
- *Ultra 1 Creator Model 170E.* Uses a faster, 167 MHz processor and is better suited to computationally-intensive 2-D graphical applications.
- *Ultra 1 Creator3D Model 170E.* Has a 167 MHz UltraSPARC processor and is meant for higher-end 3-D and imaging applications, such as scientific visualization or CAD.
- *Ultra II Creator3D Model 2200.* A multiprocessor system with two 200 MHz UltraSPARC processors. It is best for extremely intensive applications, such as fluid dynamics or high-end animation.
- *UltraServer 1.* Model 140 (143 MHz), Model 170 (167 MHz), and Model 170E (167 MHz) combine the benefits of the UltraSPARC architecture and 100BaseT networking, with enhanced cache management and reduced memory latency (see Figure 5.7).

Through the UltraSPARC's UPA technology, these devices can offer superior server performance for common network applications, such as Lotus Notes or SAP R/3. The UltraServer can integrate with and manage PC, UNIX, and Macintosh networks. The servers support all major network protocols, including TCP/IP, SNA, OSI, and DecNet. This level of support permits end users to access data on mainframes, minicomputers, and desktop systems.

Sun's Ultra architecture optimizes computing to accommodate rapidly growing public and private networks. This model significantly reduces latency, and is able to accommodate a wide range of data types. The Ultra architecture addresses four challenges that have come to be pervasive in modern network computing: the need for superior computational performance, visual computing, fast networking, and network-based software.

Several software vendors support the Ultra platform. The systems are compatible, for the most part, with other Sun systems.

Ch
5

FIG. 5.7

Sun UltraServer 1
Workgroup Server

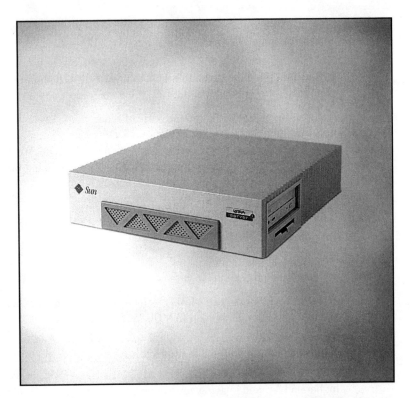

Photo courtesy of Sun Microsystems

The SPARCstation/SPARCserver family includes the following:

- *SPARCstation/SPARCserver 4 Series.* This is Sun's entry-level system. It is binary compatible with the entire family of SPARC systems and can be upgraded with a chassis swap. It is best for smaller workgroups of up to ten users and has up to 12G of disk storage.

- *SPARCstation 5/SPARCserver 5.* The SPARCserver 5 system is a mid-range workgroup server, intended for workgroups of up to 40 users, and has up to 25 GB of disk storage.

- *SPARCstation 20/SPARCserver 20 Series.* Several different models of the high end SPARCstation 20 series are available, from uniprocessing SuperSPARC machines, to multiprocessing hyperSPARCs. The hyperSPARC HS21, HS22MP, and HS14MP models are especially well-suited for compute-intensive applications. The hyperSPARC processor is an ideal platform for applications such as simulation and modeling, and the machines can easily connect with the enterprise through built-in 10BaseT and AUI Ethernet networking features.

The SPARCstation machines can integrate well into a multivendor environment. As with other Sun systems, the hyperSPARC machines support industry-standard Ethernet, Token Ring, Fast Ethernet, ATM, and FDDI. Mainframe and minicomputer connectivity can be achieved through Sun's support of SNA, TCP/IP, OSI, and DECnet protocols. The SPARCstation 20 might be well-suited for data warehousing and other high-capacity applications when used along with the SPARCstorage Model 200. The SPARCserver 20 is designed for up to 70 users and has up to 50 GB of disk storage.

■ *SPARC Storage Library.* This storage system uses a robotic handling mechanism to automatically transfer tapes. The library is a high-capacity system that can easily handle major backups on an unattended basis. This highly automated system is capable of performing a self-inventory and automatically cleaning its own drives. The Tower model works with mid-range servers and a rack-mounted model is available for larger systems. The device works with most data management software and it can support a hierarchical storage management environment. ●

Ch
5

CHAPTER 6

Standards

The Need for Standards

Most computer manufacturers would rather not participate in standards organizations or endorse any standards they did not develop. From the manufacturer's perspective, little is to be gained (and much lost) from producing products conforming to external standards; especially when these products might deviate from or conflict with the manufacturer's own internal standards. However, if a manufacturer can set a de facto standard, there is much to be gained. In other words, the issue is who is setting which standards for whom.

The psychology behind the use of nonstandard interfaces is certainly older than the computer industry—it is merely a different twist on the foot-in-the-door sales approach. When used in the computer industry, however, this tactic takes on epic proportions. First, you buy the basic system and a few user terminals. Then, you add some more terminals and a few printers. As you expand, you add network devices (modems, controllers, and so forth) to accommodate even more terminals and printers. Eventually, you realize you have invested so much money in a single vendor that it might no longer be economically feasible to consider any alternatives.

Fortunately, the economic impact of single-vendor sourcing has been diminished by third-party companies.

These companies provide compatible but often more economical terminals, PCs, printers, disk drives, tape drives, and so forth. At the same time, however, the compatibility of these third party products must remain so high that they are not, in a technological sense, much different from the manufacturer's versions of the same products. In other words, a third-party, 3270-type terminal cannot be dramatically different from an IBM 3270 terminal, or else it won't work.

In contrast, you can't buy a standard DEC VT220 terminal and plug it directly into a standard IBM 3174 terminal controller. They simply weren't designed to be interchangeable.

In the world of data communications, however, this story has a slightly different twist. While it is understandable that hardware and software products from different manufacturers cannot be interchanged like so many Lego blocks, most of the major manufacturers eventually understood that they would have to be able to exchange information. Because IBM took an early lead on the market, it became the focal point for the information interchange. Any serious contender to the IBM throne has to exchange information with IBM systems.

Beyond the realm of punched tape and punched cards, the first real means of data exchange was via magnetic tape. On the negative side, this solution is inelegant, is usually not well integrated with the mainstream applications, and requires operator intervention. On the positive side, however, tape transport can accommodate a sizable amount of data and does not require the permanent assignment of a systems analyst (although this systems analyst is invariably required during the first few attempts to define the required parameters on the tape load/unload commands).

Tape transport certainly has its limitations. For one thing, it is difficult to move a tape across the country in a couple of hours. For another, because tapes are a magnetic media, they are very susceptible to magnetic interference. Therefore, tapes and travel mix about as well as oil and water.

To address the need for reliable and more timely transfer of information, data communications-based alternatives were developed. The most popular and well-known solution is Remote Job Entry (RJE) workstation emulation. Here, rather than relying on tape transport, one machine emulates an IBM input or output device (each being a part of an RJE workstation). To send data to an IBM system, the non-IBM system emulates a remote card reader to transmit the data. To receive the data, the non-IBM system emulates either a remote printer or remote card punch.

Of course, the core of this approach is the function of the RJE workstation. Without the inception of that particular device (or set of devices), there would have been nothing to emulate.

When IBM developed the RJE workstation, it was, in fact, addressing a shortcoming in its own product line. Given the strategic and physical positioning of its mainframes in central sites, IBM needed to accommodate large batches of information coming from and going to remote satellite operations. To accommodate these remote sites, IBM manufactured RJE workstations. These workstations were really a combination of devices (a card reader, a card punch, a printer and a terminal, for example) but they were handled as a single logical unit over a single data communications link.

For non-IBM manufacturers, this presented an ideal way of interfacing their systems with IBM systems. Certainly their systems could emulate the different components of an RJE workstation—a card reader when transmitting a file, a card punch when receiving a file—and they could thus reliably exchange data in a real-time method. This type of RJE emulation became so widespread that it became an industry-wide de facto standard.

Furthermore, the popularity of emulating RJE became a standard that, in a sense, transcended IBM. The most popular implementation of RJE emulation involved emulating a 2780, a 3780, or both workstations. Because both workstations could, in fact, exchange information with another workstation, 2780/3780 RJE emulation became an ideal mechanism for exchanging information between any two systems—even if neither were an IBM system.

Standards Organizations

Although computer manufacturers would prefer that no standards be applied to them, they have indeed come to realize that some standards are necessary. For example, it is extremely convenient that most terminals use the same basic connector and that the wiring within that connector uses specified voltages and tolerances. For one thing, this agreement could prevent a possible explosion when a user plugs one type of terminal into another type of connector. (For a real-life example of this, talk to someone who has plugged an Apple laser printer set on the AppleTalk interface into an IBM PC serial port.)

After computer manufacturers realized that they could not avoid standards, they did the next best thing: Whenever possible, they started submitting their own standards to the various standard organizations in hopes of gaining a competitive edge. For example, IBM submitted its SDLC protocol to various organizations—it was subsequently transformed and endorsed as HDLC (ISO standard), LAP-B (CCITT standard), and ADCCP (ANSI standard). This is also an example of winning a battle but losing the war, because SDLC, HDLC, LAP-B, and ADCCP are similar—but incompatible.

Still, this level of participation remains extremely important to computer manufacturers, even when they do not always win a clear victory. By participating in the development of emerging standards, they can add their two cents, look at what all their competitors suggest, and most important, get feedback from the general scientific, and sometimes user, communities. For the manufacturers, these benefits justify the price of admission (even though they might secretly rather see the show close).

Ch
6

Standards organizations are often concerned about matters outside the somewhat limited sphere of computers. In the international world, standards regulate radio, telegraph, telephone and data communications within and between countries. In fact, many standards organizations predate the invention of the modern computers. The International Telecommunications Union (ITU), the parent organization of the Consultative Committee for International Telegraph and Telephony (CCITT), for example, was founded by treaty in 1865. Even within the more limited domain of the United States, some of the better-known standards organizations develop standards that are far beyond the realm of data processing—for example, ANSI also develops standards for ladders, car washes, and many other nondigital industries.

Standard-producing organizations can be government-sponsored or independent. Standards can be the by-product of computer-related associations in which the membership actively defines and develops standards, or they can be the direct result of extensive and intensive scientific research specifically aimed at developing a set of standards. Then again, some organizations do not participate in the development of standards at all but submit standards proposed by other organizations for broad approval.

There are thousands of organizations worldwide that participate, directly or indirectly, in establishing standards for the computer and data communications industries. Six of these organizations can be considered heavy hitters, capable of shaping the future of data communications.

American National Standards Institute (ANSI)

Although ANSI sponsors some research activities, it is primarily a clearinghouse for other organizations that develop and submit standards. These organizations include the Electronics Industries Association (EIA) and the Institute of Electrical and Electronics Engineers (IEEE). ANSI was established in 1918 by a consortium of engineering societies and government agencies, slowly evolving into its current structure. ANSI is a nonprofit, independent organization that also serves as the U.S. representative in the International Standards Organization (ISO). Like all of the larger standards organizations, ANSI is divided into smaller subcommittees to focus on and study various topics. One such committee of relative importance is the X.3 Standards Committee.

ANSI's X.3 Standards Committee is sponsored by the Computer and Business Equipment Manufacturers Association (CBEMA). The scope of this committee is computer technology. Technical Committees within the larger X.3 Standards Committee are appointed to focus on areas of public data networks, transmission formats, and other computer related topics.

International Telecommunications Union (ITU)

ITU was established by treaty in 1865 to define standards in the emerging telecommunications (that is, telegraph) industry. ITU was realigned into an agency underneath the United Nations in 1947. Most technical topics within ITU are handled by two committees: the Consultative Committee for International Radio (CCIR) and the Consultative Committee for International Telegraph and Telephony (CCITT).

The CCITT's focus includes the areas of data communications, telematic services (teletex, videotex, and facsimile), and Integrated Services Digital Networks (ISDN). The CCITT is further divided into study groups that research standards within each of those three key areas. Each study group works on its assigned topic for four years. The CCITT has adopted and developed many standards, including the popular V.35 standard for high-speed communications, but it is best known for the X.25 standard for public data networks. The U.S. involvement with the CCITT is coordinated through the State Department.

European Computer Manufacturers Association (ECMA)

Established in 1961, ECMA voting membership is composed of European-based computer manufacturers and has a nonvoting membership open to other parties that have marketing or technical concerns about the European market. ECMA actively contributes to both CCITT and ISO standards.

Electronic Industries Association (EIA)

EIA is a trade organization founded in 1924. With respect to data communications, EIA's prime concern is the interfacing of terminal, telecommunications and computer equipment. Undoubtedly EIA's best known contribution to standards is the famous RS-232C interface (although the group also engineered its replacement, the RS-449 interface). EIA works closely with ANSI toward the development of standards; therefore, ANSI quickly adopts many of the EIA recommendations as its own standards.

Institute of Electrical and Electronics Engineers (IEEE)

The IEEE is an extremely large professional society in which members participate in the development of standards that are forwarded to ANSI for approval. Like EIA, the IEEE's relationship with ANSI is a direct path for standards to become adopted. Specifically, the IEEE 802 series of standards (802.2, 802.3, 802.4 and 802.5) have been adopted by many manufacturers, including HP (802.3) and IBM (802.5).

International Standards Organization (ISO)

The ISO is a voluntary, independent organization founded in 1947 to find and define international standards that could be agreed upon by a large number of countries. The ISO's most significant contribution was the development of the Reference Model for Open Systems Interconnect (OSI). The work for the OSI Reference Model began in the late 1970s with the first drafts of the work appearing in the early 1980s. The purpose of the model is to define a layered architecture for the development of future standards.

The OSI Reference Model   The OSI Reference Model is often seen as a monolith much greater and far more awesome than intended by its creator, the ISO. The OSI model is not a mandate for computer manufacturers to produce systems that are of uniform design and use the same networking architecture. Instead, it is a layered architecture for the design and implementation of standards that relate to the interconnection of computer systems.

When the OSI model was introduced, compliance by the manufacturing community was purely voluntary. The promises of OSI, however, were very attractive to the international user community, so the private sector became a strong supporter of the OSI model. Following suit, both the U.S. and United Kingdom governments have also backed the OSI model through their respective Government OSI Profile (GOSIP) programs. With both private and government sectors lined up behind the OSI Reference Model, the computer manufacturers quickly stepped up to support OSI and its emerging standards.

Computer manufacturers generally have little direct experience or interest in networks composed of systems from multiple vendors. It is of no great concern to IBM engineers that IBM systems interface with those of Unisys. Nor do Digital executives stay awake all night worrying about linking their systems to HP.

Ch
6

The user community, however, neither enjoys nor appreciates these constraints. Their reality involves interfacing IBM systems with Digital systems, with HP systems, with Sun systems, and so forth. The fact that most vendors offer interfaces to IBM and UNIX-based systems as multivendor networking solutions is of little value or solace to them.

So the promise of OSI is to bring forth standards that provide points of connectivity among diverse systems. The OSI Reference Model should not, however, be thought of as the ingredients for multivendor soup. Instead, it is the cookbook from which many recipes can be selected, altered and tasted. Like most cookbooks, OSI represents a blend of the old with the new. Many existing products and standards have been included in the OSI architecture.

When the ISO began its work on the OSI model, it intended to define a layered architecture to facilitate the development or definition of standards that relate to the interfacing of open systems. An open system was defined as a system that elected to participate in the standards. This work was carved into layers to first define the working boundaries for the model and then enable separate small groups to work on the issues specific to each layer.

Logistics notwithstanding, the layered approach of the OSI Reference Model also relates to the historic view of data communications and networking and their relationships to applications, terminals and users. For example, IBM's Systems Network Architecture (SNA) is highly structured and layered in many aspects (consider the layered functions of SNA's physical units, for example). Digital's network involves layering networking services (DECnet) on top of transport services (Ethernet) to provide information flow between applications and users. So in the most general of terms, the world of networking lends itself to a layered dissection.

The OSI Reference Model is divided into seven layers. Each layer contains similar functions and is as localized as possible. This localization enables layers to change and evolve as new concepts and technology become available, without forcing changes in its neighboring layers. In brief, these seven layers are (from bottom to top):

- *Physical*. The physical transmission media.
- *Data Link*. Low level data packaging and transmission.
- *Network*. Management of the routes available for data.
- *Transport*. Delivery and delivery acknowledgment.
- *Session*. Link management between applications.
- *Presentation*. Data conversions and transformations.
- *Application*. End-user and programming services.

Information flows from one system down the OSI layers, across the physical media, and then back up the layers on the other system (see Figure 6.1). As it moves information from one system to another, each OSI layer communicates with the corresponding OSI layer on the other system. Please note, however, that although this peer-to-peer communication between layers is often shown as direct links, the actual path for the communications flows through the same layers. Each layer of the OSI model depends on the lower layers to prepare or transport information from one open system to another (see Figure 6.2).

FIG. 6.1

Information Flow
Through OSI Layers

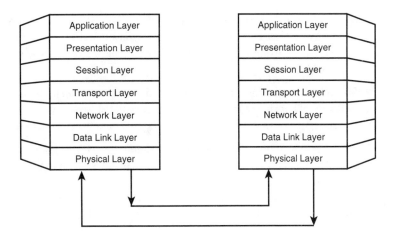

FIG. 6.2

Actual Communications
Path

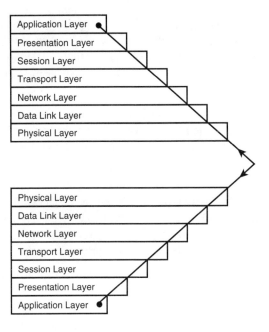

Ch
6

Another way to view the OSI Reference Model is to divide the seven layers into the following three logical functions:

- *Physical network.* Both the Data Link Layer and the Physical Layer are concerned with the movement of data between two points within the known network. Data integrity at these layers ensures that no errors are introduced during the transmission process—the concern is data content, not context.

- *System to system.* The Network, Transport, and Session Layers focus on moving information from one open system to another. These layers ensure that the correct data is delivered to the proper destination.

■ *End-user services.* Both the Presentation and Application Layers provide a range of services for the end user. These layers ensure that data is in the proper format for the context (for example, making sure that an application screen is correct for that user's actual terminal).

GOSIP   Not willing or able to be left out of the standards match, the U.S. government has thrown several hats in the ring. From an organizational perspective, the government has two significant agencies that define the standards used in networking and data processing.

The Federal Telecommunications Standard Committee (FTSC) develops or adopts standards for the government's telecommunications needs in advisement to the National Communications System (NCS). In defining these federal standards, the FTSC works with CCITT, ISO, ANSI and EIA. In some cases existing standards from these standards organizations are implemented directly, while in other cases the standards are altered to meet the specific needs of the government.

The U.S. Department of Commerce, in the form of the National Bureau of Standards (NBS), was given legal responsibility for the development of Federal Information Processing Standards (FIPS) relating to the government's data processing activities. Whereas the scope of the FTSC is confined to telecommunications, the scope of FIPS is much broader. As with the FTSC, the NBS tries to work with existing standards, especially the federal standards published by the FTSC.

The federal standards put forth by the FTSC are not mandates for all government agencies. Federal agencies must conform to FIPS by virtue of the same law that brought FIPS into creation. However, compliance need not be instantaneous; governmental entities have time to plan and adapt.

Another major offspring from the U.S. Department of Commerce is the Government Open Systems Interconnection Profile (GOSIP). In 1988, the National Institute of Science and Technology (NIST) developed GOSIP as a subset of the OSI Reference Model for the government. Once published, GOSIP then became a FIPS, thereby representing a major commitment from the U.S. government to embrace parts of the OSI Reference Model.

GOSIP was planned for implementation in two phases, the first phase taking effect in 1990, the second scheduled for 1992 (see Table 6.1).

Table 6.1   GOSIP Phases

Layer	Name	GOSIP Phase
1	Physical	Phase I: 802.3, 802.4, 802.5
2	Data Link	Phase I: CSMA/CD, Token Ring, Token Bus
3	Network (connectionless)	Phase I: X.25, ISO 8473 Phase II: ISDN
4	Transport	Phase I: ISO 8073 (connection oriented)

Layer	Name	GOSIP Phase
5	Session	Phase I: ISO session (8327 and 9548)
6	Presentation	Phase I: ISO presentation (8823 and 9576)
7	Application	Phase I: X.400, FTAM Phase II: X.500, ODA, CMIP/CMIS, VT, RDB Access

Provisions within GOSIP enable the government to continue to use and enhance TCP/IP-based products that might not be OSI compliant in the strictest sense. Furthermore, exceptions are granted to small expansions of existing networks as well as to situations in which total compliance represents an economic hardship (or impossibility).

The U.S. Government is not alone in its GOSIP approach. The United Kingdom has implemented a similar program and other governments are considering following suit. These tactics, coupled with the growing maturity of the OSI Reference Model, are laying the groundwork for practical and functional international OSI networks.

Since the implementation of GOSIP, however, U.S. government agencies have continued to use other networking protocols besides OSI, most notably TCP/IP. The government incorrectly expected GOSIP standards to displace proprietary protocols because of OSI's status as an international standard. Although OSI was expected to be universally implemented, GOSIP products have been slow to come to market, and have not been widely accepted or deployed.

The Internet Protocol (IP) suite, on the other hand, has been widely accepted, and products built on this standard have become widely used commodity products. In addition, the Internet, which supports IP, has developed substantially since the imposition of GOSIP; while there has been no such infrastructure developed for GOSIP itself. Those OSI products that have become available are more expensive, and less well integrated than comparable IP-based products.

In 1994, the Federal Internetworking Requirements Panel (FIRP) was established by NIST to reassess the government's requirement for open systems networks and compliance with the GOSIP standard. At that time, FIRP decided that no one protocol suite should be imposed to meet all government requirements for internetworking, and that it would be better to adopt the most effective solution in each of the different areas of information technology; rather than requiring absolute compliance to one set of standards. Although the reevaluation applies only to the federal government, it will ultimately have an impact on American industry as well.

NOTE The reevaluation of open systems networks applies only to the United States; other countries' OSI requirements still stand at this time. ▨

Ch
6

Exchange of Standards

As you can see, organizations often adopt each other's standards. For example, the EIA RS-232C standard was adopted by the CCITT as V.24 and V.28, and by ISO as 2110, and the IEEE 802.3 standard was adopted by ECMA as ECMA-80, 81 and 82, and by ISO as 8802/3.

Good news and bad news intertwine in this exchange of standards. The good news is that many different organizations with different origins and orientations can communicate with one another and share information in an open, honest format. The bad news is that, in many cases, a standard gets subtle changes by each organization that adopts it; or one organization might subsequently update an adopted standard while another organization might not. Thus, for example, an EIA standard might not be 100 percent compatible with what appears to be the equivalent CCITT standard.

Table 6.2 shows which standards are being exchanged among organizations; Table 6.3 lists the names of these and other popular standards.

Table 6.2 Examples of Standards Exchange

ISO	CCITT	ECMA	ANSI	EIA	FTSC	FIPS
646	V.3		X3.4			1-1, 7, 15
1155	V.4, X.4		X3.15, X3.16		1010, 1011	16-1, 17-1
1177	V.4, X.4		X3.15, X3.16		1010, 1011	16-1, 17-1
1745			X3.28			
2022			X3.41			35
2110				RS-232C		
2111			X3.28			
2628			X3.28			
2629			X3.28			
3309	X.25, X.75	40	X3.66		1003	71
4335	X.25, X.75	49	X3.66		1003	71
4902				RS-449		
	X.20bis			RS-232C		
	X.2lbis			RS-232C, RS-449		
6159	X.25	60, 71	X3.66		1003	71
6256	X.25, X.75	60, 71	X3.66		1003	71
8802/2			(IEEE 802.2)			
8802/3			(IEEE 802.4)			
8802/4			(IEEE 802.4)			
8802/5			(IEEE 802.5)			
10020-21	X.400					
9594	X.500					

ISO	CCITT	ECMA	ANSI	EIA	FTSC	FIPS
9594	V.22				1008	
	V.24			RS-232C, RS-449		
	V.26bis				1005	
	V.27bis				1006	
	V.27ter				1006	
	V.29				1007	

Table 6.3 Standards Descriptions

ISO	
646	Seven-bit character set
1155	Use of longitudinal parity for error detection
1177	Structure for start/stop and synchronous transmission
1745	Basic mode control procedures
2022	Code extension techniques based on ISO 646
2110	25-pin DTE/DCE connector and pin assignments
2111	Basic mode control procedures–code independent
2628	Basic mode control procedures–complements
2629	Basic mode control procedures–conversational
3309	HDLC frame structure
4335	HDLC elements of procedures
4902	37-pin and 9-pin DTE/DCE connectors and pin assignments
6159	HDLC unbalanced class of procedures
6256	HDLC balanced class of procedures
7498	OSI basic reference model
7776	HDLC–X.25 LAPB-compatible DTE data link procedures
7808	HDLC connectionless class of procedures
7809	HDLC consolidation of classes of procedures
8072	Transport Layer definitions
8073	Transport Layer connection-oriented services
8208	X.25 packet-level protocol

Ch
6

continues

Table 6.3   Continued

ISO

8326/27	Session Layer connection-oriented services
8348	Network Layer definitions
8473	Network Layer connectionless services
8571	File Transfer, Access and Management (FTAM)
8602	Transport Layer connectionless services
8613	Office Document Architecture (ODA)
8632	Computer Graphics Metafile (CGM)
8648	Network Layer internal organization
8802/2	Class 1 logical link control
8802/3	CSMA/CD
8802/4	Token Bus
8802/5	Token Ring
8822/23	Presentation Layer connection-oriented services
8832/33	Job transfer and manipulation
8878	Use of X.25 as a connection-oriented service
8879	Standard Generalized Markup Language (SGML)
8886	Data Link Layer definitions
9040	Virtual terminal services
9314	Fiber Distributed Data Interface (FDDI)
9548	Session Layer connectionless services
9576	Presentation Layer connectionless services
9594	Directory services
9595/96	Network management (CMIS and CMIP)
10020/21	Message-handling services
10026	Distributed transaction processing

CCITT

V.3	International alphabet #5
V.4	Structure for V.3 transmission over phone network

CCITT

V.5	Standard synchronous signaling rates for dial-up lines
V.6	Standard synchronous signaling rates for leased lines
V.14	Asynchronous to synchronous conversion
V.21	300-bps modem for switched phone lines
V.22	1200-bps modem for switched and leased phone lines
V.22bis	2400-bps modem for switched and leased phone lines
V.24	List of exchanges between DTE and DCE devices
V.25	Automatic calling/automatic answering equipment
V.26bis	1200/2400-bps modem for switched phone lines
V.27bis	2400/4800-bps modem for leased phone lines
V.27ter	2400/4800-bps modem for switched phone lines
V.28	Electrical characteristics for unbalanced circuits
V.29	9600-bps modem for 4-wire leased phone lines
V.32	9600-bps modem for 2-wire switched phone lines
V.33	12,200- and 14,400-bps modem for leased phone lines
V.35	Device interface supporting rates up to 48 Kbps (no longer recommended)
V.42	Error detection and correction scheme for modems
V.42bis	Data compression method for use with V.42
V.100	Interconnection between public data networks and public switched telephone networks
V.110	ISDN terminal adaption
V.120	ISDN terminal adaption with statistical multiplexing
V.230	General data communications interface (layer 1)
X.1	Class of service in public data networks
X.2	Services and facilities in public data networks
X.3	Packet assembly/disassembly (PAD) facilities
X.4	Structure of V.3 transmission over public network
X.20	Interfacing devices using asynchronous transmission
X.20bis	Use of DTE devices on public network via asynchronous modems
X.21	Interfacing devices using synchronous transmission

Ch
6

continues

Table 6.3   Continued

CCITT

X.2lbis	Use of DTE devices on public network via synchronous modems
X.25	Interfacing DTE and DCE devices over packet networks
X.28	Interface for start/stop device accessing a PAD
X.29	Exchange procedures for a PAD and a packet-mode DTE
X.75	Control and transfer between packet networks
X.400	Message handling services
X.500	Directory services
X.509	Authentication framework for X.500

ECMA

40	HDLC frame structure
49	HDLC elements of procedures
60	HDLC unbalanced class of procedures
61	HDLC balanced class of procedures
71	Transport protocol (for ISO/OSI layer 4)
80-82	Physical and logical link control for CSMA/CD
84	Data presentation protocol
85	Virtual File Protocol (File transfer)

ANSI

X3.4	Information interchange code
X3.15	Bit sequencing for X3.4 in serial data streams
X3.16	Character and parity structure for X.34 transmissions
X3.28	Standard for the use of communication control characters
X3.41	Code extensions for the 7-bit V3.4 interchange code
X3.66	Advanced Data Communication Control Procedures (ADCCP)
X3.92	Data Encryption Algorithm

IEEE

802.2	Data Link Layer
802.3	CSMA/CD
802.4	Token Bus
802.5	Token Ring
802.6	Metropolitan area networks
802.7	Broadband local area networks
802.9/802.10	Integrated LAN/MAN networks
802.11	Wireless LAN Medium Access Control and Physical Layer specification
802.12	100 Mbps (Fast Ethernet)
1003	Portable operating systems (POSIX)
1394	High Performance Serial Bus ("Firewire")

EIA

RS-232C	Interfacing DTE and DCE devices via serial exchange
RS-449	37- and 9-pin DTE interfaces for serial exchange

FTSC

1003	Synchronous data link control procedures (ADCCP)
1005	Coding and modulation requirements for 2400-bps modems
1006	Coding and modulation requirements for 4800-bps modems
1007	Coding and modulation requirements for 9600-bps modems
1008	Coding and modulation for 600/1200-bps modems
1010	Bit sequencing of ANSI X3.4 for serial transmissions
1011	Character/parity structure for ANSI X3.4 transmissions
1015	Analog to digital conversion of voice by 2400 bps linear predictive coding
1016	Analog to digital conversion of radio voice by 4800bps code excited linear prediction (CELP)
1026	Interoperability and security requirements for use of the Data Encyrption Standard in the physical layer of data communications

Ch 6

continues

Table 6.3   Continued

FTSC

1027	Security requirements for equipment using the data encryption standard
1028	Interoperability and security requirements for use of the Data Encryption Standard with CCITT Group 3 facsimile equipment
1045	High frequency radio automatic link establishment
1046	Radio Automatic Networking
1047	Radio automatic message delivery
1048	Radio automatic networking to multiple-media
1049	Radio automatic operation in stressed environment
1052	Radio modems
1101-1108	Land mobile radio

FIPS

1-1	Code for information interchange
7	Implementation of FIPS 1-1 and related standards
15	Subsets of the 1-1 code for information interchange
16-1	Bit sequencing of the 1-1 code for serial transmissions
17-1	Character and parity structure for FIPS 1-1 transmissions
35	Code extension techniques using 7 or 8 bits
71	Advanced Data Communication Control Procedures (ADCCP)
81	Data Encryption Standard (DES) Modes of Operation

Dramatic differences in standards were much more prevalent in the days before the OSI Reference Model. In today's world, each organization dances around the same OSI maypole, hoping to create a universal set of multifaceted standards. The fact that a given standard at a given layer was created by one organization or another becomes, for the most part, irrelevant—the ISO stamp of approval is the great equalizer.

Emerging Standards

New standards, and indeed, even new standards organizations are being created at an accelerated pace. In addition, there is a growing trend among companies to make informal alliances to create a de facto standard. Formalized or not, however, a new standard must prove its vitality in an ever-changing marketplace before being accepted by the user community.

Salutation Architecture

The Salutation Consortium, Inc.—whose members include IBM, Novell, and HP—is planning to release a specification that will let devices identify and communicate with each other. The consortium's middleware, Salutation Architecture, creates a handshake between several different types of devices, such as faxes, printers, and PCs. The consortium will release the specification to the developer community without royalty or fees. The middleware fits within the operating system and defines a set of APIs that applications are able to understand. It has discovery capability, so it can identify devices, determine their capabilities, and communicate. The middleware is similar in nature to Microsoft's Microsoft At Work, a project designed to connect office equipment to PCs. Salutation Architecture is more network-oriented, however, and At Work never took off.

SONET (synchronous optical network)

SONET is a high-speed transmission standard initially developed for fiber-optic systems. It has since been adapted for microwave radio systems, for use in areas where physical cabling is difficult.

Plug and Play Standard (Microsoft)

The Plug and Play standard is Microsoft's approach to multivendor compatibility. Although it enables users to easily integrate peripherals from many vendors, it is limited by its proprietary nature. However, the standard is supported by many vendors, and is likely to become a de facto standard. Plug and Play has been built into the Windows 95 operating system and enables PCs and peripherals from different vendors to work together under the Microsoft environment. Under this paradigm, if a PC user attaches a new peripheral, it can start working immediately. A Plug and Play hardware device automatically sends information to the host about its basic services, what it requires to operate, and which drivers it needs. The operating system software will then automatically configure the device. The catch is, the peripheral must be specifically designed for the standard.

Ch
6

Firewire (IEEE 1394)

This standard was designed to speed up LAN communications over high-speed serial ports. It can function as a local device interface for ATM or Fast Ethernet, enabling ATM to be routed to individual devices inexpensively. The standard might ultimately provide the framework necessary for multimedia LAN applications, and is designed to transport data at rates of up to 400 Mbps.

Common Desktop Environment (CDE)

There have been many attempts to unify a fractured UNIX market, but only the Common
Desktop Environment (CDE) has succeeded. Part of the Common Operating System Environment (COSE) agreement, CDE establishes several common features across all major UNIX
implementations. CDE does not actually implement any new technology; rather, it is a compos-
ite of bits and pieces of various UNIXs from HP, Sun Microsystems, and IBM. ●

LANs and WANs

The Many Faces of Networking

Before the great LAN explosion, networking, for the most part, addressed the connection of distributed devices to a central location. Although some pioneering companies, such as Digital Equipment, offered LAN technology in these early days, the bulk of the market was accustomed to a centralized computing environment.

In this centralized approach, the primary concern was to find the most practical and economical way to connect terminals, printers, and other data collection/reception devices to the primary location. When connectivity was required between systems, the link was approached typically as a special-case, point-to-point operation, rather than part of a peer-oriented, distributed processing network. However, as requests mounted to link computer systems over wide areas, multiple, point-to-point operations became very cost ineffective, and the door opened to such alternative wide-area connections as X.25 and ISDN. Wide-area technologies have continued to evolve, and now include Frame Relay, Asynchronous Transfer Mode (ATM), and Switched Multimegabit Data Service (SMDS).

All things considered, this system-to-system connectivity hardly concerned the end user—after all, this was the job of the communications analyst. But when the LAN wave finally reached the PC on the end user's desk, that user suddenly encountered and became concerned about connectivity issues. At first it was just local (LAN) connectivity and terminal emulation. Then, as networks grew and costs increased, products such as gateways, bridges and routers snaked their way into the LAN. Today, the end user has an unprecedented amount of power at his or her disposal. Consolidated, enterprise-wide data is no longer in the hands of a few technical elite; off-the-shelf desktop software now gives the end user the ability to access data anywhere in the enterprise—whether it is on the PC, server, minicomputer, or mainframe.

This progression of connectivity changed the role of the LAN. Whereas the LAN began as a local computing environment (usually an island unto itself) it grew into an area of computing, normally linked to other computing areas. The fact that one computing area might be a LAN, another a mainframe, and yet another a combined midrange computer and PC LAN has become almost irrelevant.

From this high-level perspective, the world of distributed networks can be broken down into two large categories: local-area links and wide-area links. A *local area network (LAN)* typically is limited to one geographic area and allows individual workstations to access data or applications on a server. In smaller LANs, a peer-to-peer arrangement can be deployed to allow each station to function as both server and client. A *wide area network (WAN)*, on the other hand, typically covers a large geographic area, and often links together multiple LANs. Within each category, however, are a wide variety of implementations and strategies.

LANs often play a pivotal role in modern networks. This chapter will address the following LAN issues:

- *Topology.* LANs can be implemented in a variety of topologies (or structures), such as star, bus, ring, hub, and so forth.
- *Protocols.* LANs can run token-passing or collision sensing protocols.
- *LAN implementations.* This section will examine IEEE standards and how they compare to each other (and to Ethernet).

WANs can be used in both centralized and distributed processing environments to tie all of the necessary devices together. This chapter will discuss the following WAN issues:

- *Point-to-point links.* In the most basic of cases, creating a WAN might simply involve tying together two LANs or two systems. These connections are most often implemented using standard telephone links.
- *Integrated Services Data Network (ISDN).* This service is offered by the telephone industry as a modern, high-speed, multi-point connectivity solution.
- *X.25.* This chapter will examine X.25 as a wide-area, packet-switching network. The use of such networks has become a low-cost solution for low-volume networking on a worldwide basis.
- *Asynchronous Transfer Mode (ATM).* ATM is a high-speed protocol that offers every client on the network the capability to send data at speeds of up to 155 Mbps, or nearly 15 times the speed of a standard Ethernet LAN. ATM is especially useful for those applications with high bandwidth requirements, such as videoconferencing.

■ *Frame Relay.* Frame Relay can carry multiple types of traffic, including voice and Systems Network Architecture (SNA). It is extremely fast, and less costly than a dedicated line solution.

■ *Switched Multimegabit Data Service (SMDS).* SMDS is a connectionless service and is simpler to implement than Frame Relay or ATM. SMDS is used to establish any-to-any connectivity and is a highly scalable solution. Technologies such as frame relay require permanent virtual circuits (PVCs) to be established between each and every location; SMDS, on the other hand, takes a much simpler approach. Each workstation on the network is given an address, and any site can communicate with any other site. The administrator does not have to set up individual connections ahead of time.

■ *Fiber Distributed Data Interface (FDDI).* This token-passing technology uses optical fiber cabling, and can transmit data at 100 Mbps. Because of its superior speed, FDDI is especially useful for sending large files such as graphics or digital video. It is a useful method of adding bandwidth without having to make a costly, long-term commitment.

FDDI switching can also have a big impact on a backbone network. Digital Equipment has led the way in FDDI switching with its GigaSwitch product; other vendors are also now starting to offer FDDI switching products. FDDI switching, like other types of LAN switching architectures, can significantly increase bandwidth and extend the lifetime of the network.

■ *Fibre Channel.* Fibre Channel is a high-speed architecture for connecting network devices and high-speed hardware. This ANSI standard supports speeds of up to 1.06 Gbps.

■ *Tools of the trade.* Implementing wide-area solutions requires some special-purpose devices or software that smooth out the differences between the local and wide-area connections. These tools include bridges, routers, and gateways. They enable the different LAN and WAN strategies to be mixed and matched in a single, unified network.

Local Area Networks

LANs became significant in the world of networking in the late 1980s, following on the heels of the PC to become the preferred method for connecting multiple PCs in a self-contained area.

Unfortunately, the networking software and operating systems used with the PC LANs were quite different from the networking software used on midrange and mainframe computers and office automation equipment (for example, dedicated word processing machines and intelligent copiers). This, of course, set up the inevitable conflict between PCs, office automation equipment, and the larger midrange and mainframe computers. Although many computer-savvy corporations saw the conflict coming and took steps to address it head on, other companies first became aware of the conflict when the requests to run cable hit the maintenance department.

Ch

7

After all, from a simple and fundamental perspective, the laying of the cable represents a major commitment. Installing the cable requires the unpleasant work of snaking cable through ceilings and down walls. It requires that the cable be arranged in such a way that it is manageable and easy to expand (from a networking perspective). And even worse, the placing of cable is often regulated by local ordinances that require special casings or materials (Teflon enclosures, for example) if the cable runs near pipes, electrical work or people. In short, putting the cable in is almost as much fun as simultaneously remodeling the kitchen and bathroom of your house.

LAN Topologies

Whether the purpose of the LAN is to interconnect PCs, minicomputers, or both is almost irrelevant—the first issue is often choosing the topology of the LAN. This choice dictates the cable, cabling methodology and the networking software that can operate on the LAN. The three basic topologies are the ring, star, and bus (see Figure 7.1).

FIG. 7.1
LAN Topologies

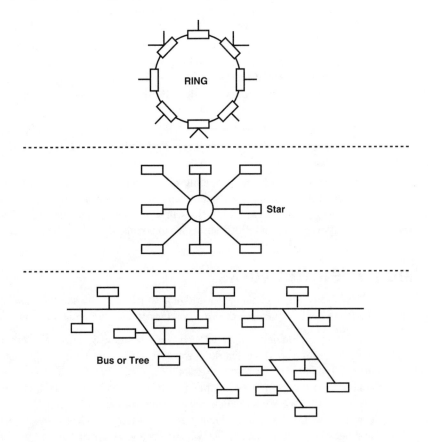

- *Ring.* As its name suggests, a ring LAN joins a set of attachment units together via a series of point-to-point connections between each unit. Each attachment unit, in turn, interfaces to one or more computers or computing devices. Information flows from attachment unit to attachment unit in a single direction, thus forming a ring network. Because each PC in a ring network acts as a repeater, performance degrades with each additional PC. Consequently, this is typically appropriate only in small networks.

- *Star.* In a star LAN, each computer or computer-related device is connected on a point-to-point link to a central device called a hub. The hub acts as the LAN traffic manager, setting up communication paths between two devices seeking to exchange information. This configuration makes it very easy to isolate problem nodes, and is one of the most common LAN models.

- *Bus.* The simplest form of bus LAN is a set of computers or devices connected to a common, linear connection. Under the bus topology, information is transmitted over the distance of the network, so each computer can pick up its intended information. Links from the main bus line might break off into additional linear links with multiple attachments; this type of bus structure is also referred to as a tree because multiple branches reach out from the main trunk. This model is used in high-speed PBXs.

Star and ring network topologies are sometimes combined into one network to provide a higher degree of fault tolerance. Because a star network is susceptible to a failure in the hub, and a ring network is sensitive to a break in the ring, combining both forms into one offers an alternate route in case one topology fails.

LAN Protocols

While the LAN topology defines the cabling methodology and the way that information flows through the network, the LAN discipline determines how the computers interact with each other on the LAN. The two most used protocols are *token passing* and *collision sensing.*

In a token passing network, a special token is passed from computer to computer. Possession of the token enables a computer to transmit on the network. When the original transmission returns to the computer that sent it, that transmission is regarded as complete (whether or not it was actually received) and a new token is generated to flow to the next station (based on the LAN topology). When a message is successfully received, the receiving station confirms receipt by changing a flag in the original transmission. Therefore, by examining the original message when it returns, the sending station can determine what happened at another end of the ring. Token passing dates back to 1969 and is one of the earliest multiple-unit, peer-to-peer control procedures. Token ring networks, although not as widely used as a CSMA/CD network, offer robust performance because they furnish only a single channel; thereby avoiding any possibility of collision.

The proper name for collision sensing is *Carrier Sense Multiple Access with Collision Detection (CSMA/CD).* With this discipline, each computer listens to the LAN to sense if another computer is transmitting. If someone else is active on the LAN, the computer wishing to transmit waits for a preset amount of time before trying again. When the computer perceives that the LAN is inactive, it transmits. In the event that two computers transmit at the same time (and

Ch 7

their data collides and is hopelessly corrupted), both sides wait for different lengths of time before attempting to retransmit. CSMA/CD dates back to the mid-1970s (when Ethernet was in its infancy) and has grown to be the most common discipline for PC LANs.

The biggest difference between the two disciplines is that token passing is termed a deterministic discipline while collision sensing is not. A token passing network is deterministic because each computer is given the opportunity to transmit, but only at preset time intervals, and only if it is in possession of the token. On a collision sensing network, however, each computer must, in effect, compete for the opportunity to transmit.

A third type of discipline, *time division,* is sometimes used in laboratory environments for specialized controllers, technical equipment or wireless communications networks. With this discipline, each unit is given specific amounts of time at specific intervals to exchange data. Using time division in a conventional data processing LAN, however, is extremely unusual, not to mention impractical.

LAN Implementations

Both the discipline and topology define a LAN implementation. Thus, a LAN might be a token passing ring, a token passing bus, or a collision sensing bus.

The standards for LAN implementations can be roughly broken into two groups: those that pre-date the work performed by the IEEE in this area, and those that were developed by the IEEE. Of the LAN implementations that pre-date IEEE's involvement, Ethernet and token ring implementations have stood the test of time and remain popular.

Ethernet was originally developed by Xerox Corporation in the 1970s as a 3 Mbps bus LAN using the CSMA/CD discipline. Following the initial release of Ethernet, both Digital Equipment and Intel joined the development effort and the three companies released the specification for Ethernet version 1.0 in 1980. The most notable improvement in Version 1.0 was the increase in the LAN speed from 3 Mbps to 10 Mbps. The Ethernet specification was then revised again several years later as Ethernet II to provide a higher degree of compatibility with the IEEE 802.3 standard. The 802.3 standard has since grown to include a newer specification, known as Fast Ethernet, which boosts the speed tenfold to 100 Mbps.

In addition, the IEEE 902.9a isochronous Ethernet standard provides a way for two networks to run over 10Base-T wiring. IsoEthernet permits the integration of LAN and WAN services, and can extend a company's existing investment in standard Ethernet. IsoEthernet can deliver voice and video as well. In the past, multimedia over Ethernet has been limited because of Ethernet's connectionless nature. Traditional Ethernet generates bursty traffic, which is excellent for sending data, not suitable for time-sensitive information such as video. This type of time-sensitive traffic is highly dependent on all packets arriving in the correct order. IsoEthernet is capable of multiplexing 56 Kbps/64 Kbps ISDN B channels and running both packet and wideband circuit-switched multimedia services over Category 3 UTP cable. Its encoding scheme also increases the available bandwidth from 10 Mbps to 16 Mbps. The extra 6 Mbps of bandwidth is used to create a multimedia pipe. IsoEthernet can be integrated into an existing 10Base-T Ethernet with the addition of an isoEthernet hub, which permits WAN and

LAN services to be synchronized. Workstations must be equipped with isoEthernet adapter cards, which are connected to the hub. An *attachment unit interface* (AUI) then connects the isoEthernet and Ethernet hubs.

Token ring networks have been implemented on a variety of media at a variety of speeds. Therefore, unlike Ethernet, token ring technology was not successfully introduced into a generalized data processing network. IBM implemented token ring in its early PC LANs, as did Apollo for its engineering workstations. But somehow, token ring did not catch on as Ethernet did. There were several reasons for this, including the fact that token ring is more expensive to deploy than Ethernet, requires more planning, and is more difficult to install. More recently, however, token ring networks have enjoyed a rebirth in popularity for several reasons.

The IEEE organization adopted token ring as a sanctioned network in its IEEE 802.5 specifications.

The market for token ring switches is enjoying tremendous growth as corporate networks continue to grow at an unprecedented pace. These switches provide users on overcrowded LANs with their own personal 4 Mbps to 16 Mbps piece of bandwidth. The switch can also be used to divide a large ring into smaller segments.

Until recently, equipment for switched token ring networks was largely unavailable. However, token ring networks can suffer from the same geographic limitations as Ethernet, and vendors are now stepping in to provide the switching equipment users require to expand their token ring networks. Traditionally, two-port bridges are used in token ring networks, which impose a significant limitation on its expandability. Token ring switches can connect the separate rings to each other and to servers, without the performance limitations of the past. Some products include both token ring and Ethernet switching facilities in the same box. Most switches also accommodate high-speed networking, such as ATM or FDDI; many also support RMON management.

Both token ring and Ethernet networks have bandwidth limitations. Many corporate networks are beginning to reach those limitations, as they bring in more and larger applications and experience a greater demand for data. Switching technology can help overcome these limitations by extending an overcrowded network. Whether the switch is used to divide the ring into smaller segments or to give each user a personal slice of bandwidth, switches can greatly enhance network performance, thereby extending the useful life of the existing network.

IBM has made a significant commitment to supporting token ring as the preferred SNA LAN and has, in fact, provided connections for its broad range of computers and communications controllers to token ring.

The architecture of the *Fiber Distributed Data Interface* (FDDI) is modeled after token ring. FDDI is a high-speed WAN technology that runs at 100 Mbps. Therefore, if you love FDDI, you must also at least have a passing respect for token ring.

Token ring technology was patented by a European engineer who forced those who adopted it to pay a royalty. However, this patent has been successfully challenged, so the economics of token ring networks has taken a turn for the better.

LAN Implementation Standards

Although both Ethernet and token ring networks function well, they were not recognized as official standards because they were developed in the private, commercial sector. To address this need for standardization, the IEEE studied these and other implementations and developed a series of standards to properly define a series of LAN specifications.

In developing its standards, the IEEE had to walk the line between the OSI Reference Model and the existing, well-known and widely accepted LAN implementations. In terms of the OSI Reference Model, for example, IEEE carved the Data Link Layer (layer 2) into two parts. The upper half of the layer that interfaces with the Network Layer (layer 3) was termed the *Logical Link Control* (LLC). The LLC provides a common, low level point of access, independent from the actual physical media.

The lower half of the layer that interfaces with the Physical Layer (layer 1) was termed the *Medium Access Control* (MAC). The MAC addresses the specifics of the physical network interface; therefore, separate MAC standards are defined for CSMA/CD, token passing bus and token passing ring. However, note that a single LLC specification addresses all three MACs.

A message passed from the Network Layer is processed by the LLC protocol, and an LLC header is added to the data (see Figure 7.2). This new data structure is then passed on to the MAC where another header and a trailer are added before the data enters the physical network. The resulting structure that includes the MAC header, the LLC header, the data and the MAC trailer is termed a *frame*.

IEEE 802.2

In IEEE terms, the 802.2 specification defines the LLC (see Figure 7.3). The 802.2 header consists of the following:

- *Destination Service Access Point (DSAP).* The DSAP is a seven-bit address with an eighth bit to indicate if it is a specific address (0) or a group (broadcast) address (1). The DSAP is not a station or device address; rather it designates the service control point where the message should be routed.

- *Source Service Access Point (SSAP).* The SSAP is also a seven-bit address, but in this case the eighth bit is used to indicate if the message is a command (0) or a response (1). Like the DSAP, the SSAP designates a control point and not a station address. In the case of the SSAP, this is the control point from which the message originated.

- *Control.* The control field is either 8 or 16 bits long, with the length indicated by the first two bits. The 16-bit fields are used to exchange sequence numbers, while the 8-bit variation is used for unsequenced information.

Below the 802.2 LLC are the MACs for the various physical LAN implementations. These standards are known as 802.3 for CSMA/CD, 802.4 for token passing bus, and 802.5 for token passing ring.

FIG. 7.2
IEEE LLC and MAC
Layers

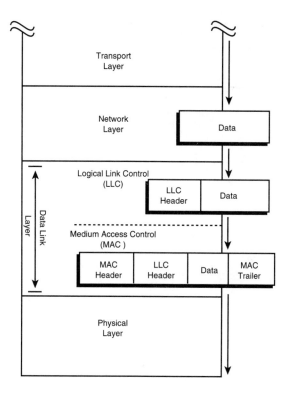

IEEE 802.3

The IEEE 802.3 standard specifies a CSMA /CD bus network that supports 10-Mbps transmission over baseband, broadband, and twisted pair cable. This networking standard closely resembles Ethernet. Both HP and IBM (and others) support the IEEE 802.3 networking standards (HP for their native NS networking product, and IBM for their TCP/IP products).

The 802.3 header (see Figure 7.4) includes the following:

- *Preamble.* An 8-byte pattern of binary 1s and 0s used to establish synchronization. The last bit of the preamble is always 0.
- *Start Frame Delimiter.* An 8-bit pattern indicating the formal start of the frame.
- *Destination Address.* An address specifying a specific destination station, a group of stations, or all stations in the LAN. This address can be 16 bits or 48 bits in length, but all stations in the LAN must adhere to one format or the other.
- *Source Address.* The address of the originating station. This address has the same length requirements as the Destination Address.
- *Length.* The length, measured in bytes, of the actual data, including the 802.2 header. This is a 16-bit field.

Ch
7

FIG. 7.3
IEEE 802.2 LLC Header

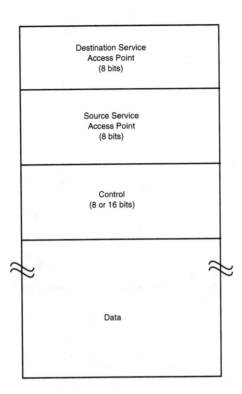

Following the header is the 802.2 header and the actual data. At the end of the data is the 802.3 trailer, which includes:

- *Padding*. Extra, nondata bytes can be inserted into the frame to make the overall frame length more palatable to the physical network.

- *Frame Check Sequence*. At the end of the frame is a 32-bit Cyclic Redundancy Check (CRC) on the data starting with the destination address and terminating at the end of the data (not including any padding).

IEEE 802.4

The IEEE 802.4 specification defines a token passing bus that can operate at speeds of 1, 5, or 10 Mbps. The 802.4 standard is, in many ways, a marriage of Ethernet and token ring technologies. The physical topology for 802.4 is a bus, much like in Ethernet, but the MAC-level discipline is a token-passing logical ring (as opposed to a token-passing physical ring). Although the 802.4 specification does not have as many active supporters as the 802.3 and 802.5 standards, its popularity is rapidly growing. The format for 802.4 transmissions (see Figure 7.5) is as follows:

- *Preamble*. One or more bytes used for synchronization patterns.
- *Start Frame Delimiter*. An 8-bit pattern signaling the start of the frame.

- *Frame Control.* A 1-byte field used to indicate if the frame contains actual data or if it is a control message.
- *Destination Address.* An address specifying a specific destination station, a group of stations, or all stations in the LAN. This address can be 16 bits or 48 bits in length, but all stations in the LAN must adhere to one format or the other.
- *Source Address.* The address of the originating station. This address has the same length requirements as the destination address.

Following this header is the 802.2 header and the actual data. At the end of the data is the 802.4 trailer, which includes the following:

FIG. 7.4

IEEE 802.3 CSMA/CD Frame

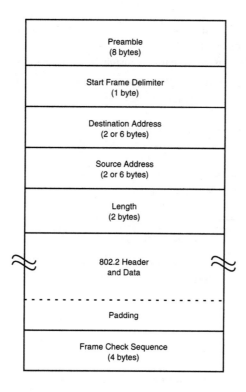

- *Frame Check Sequence.* At the end of the frame is a 32-bit Cyclic Redundancy Check (CRC) on the data starting with the Frame Control field and terminating at the end of the data.
- *End Delimiter.* The 8-bit pattern signaling the end of the frame. The last two bits of this field signal if the frame is the last frame to be transmitted and whether any station has detected an error in the frame.

Ch

7

IEEE 802.5

The IEEE 802.5 standard specifies a token passing ring operating over shielded twisted pair cables at speeds of 1, 4, or 16 Mbps. This standard is supported by IBM in its Token Ring implementation. The 802.5 construction (see Figure 7.6) is defined as follows:

■ *Start Frame Delimiter.* An 8 bit-pattern signaling the start of the frame.

■ *Access Control.* An 8-bit field used for priority and maintenance control. Most important, one bit of this field is the token bit. If set to 1, the frame contains data. If set to 0, the frame is actually a token that can be seized by a station waiting to transmit. Also note that when the token bit is set to 0, the entire frame consists only of the start frame delimiter, the access control byte and the end delimiter byte.

■ *Frame Control.* A 1-byte field used to indicate if the frame contains actual data or a control message.

■ *Destination Address.* An address specifying a specific destination station, a group of stations, or all stations in the LAN. This address can be 16 bits or 48 bits in length, but all stations in the LAN must adhere to one format or the other.

■ *Source Address.* The address of the originating station. This address has the same length requirements as the destination address.

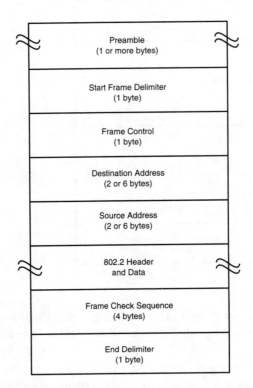

FIG. 7.5

IEEE 802.4 Token Bus Frame

FIG. 7.6

IEEE 802.5 Token-Ring Frame

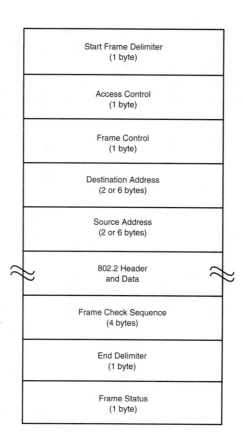

| Start Frame Delimiter (1 byte) |
| Access Control (1 byte) |
| Frame Control (1 byte) |
| Destination Address (2 or 6 bytes) |
| Source Address (2 or 6 bytes) |
| 802.2 Header and Data |
| Frame Check Sequence (4 bytes) |
| End Delimiter (1 byte) |
| Frame Status (1 byte) |

Following this header is the 802.2 header and the actual data. At the end of the data is the 802.5 trailer that includes the following:

- *Frame Check Sequence.* At the end of the frame is a 32-bit Cyclic Redundancy Check (CRC) on the data starting with the Frame Control field and terminating at the end of the data.

- *End delimiter.* The 8-bit pattern signaling the end of the frame. The last two bits of this field signal if the frame is the last frame to be transmitted and whether any station has detected an error in the frame.

- *Frame Status.* An 8-bit pattern indicating whether a station has recognized the frame and also if the frame has been copied (received).

802.3 Versus Ethernet

The implementations of Ethernet and IEEE 802.3 are so compatible that computer systems using each can coexist on the same network. The most significant difference between the two is the way information is formatted into frames. Although both specifications define the destination and origin of the information, the 802.3 frame includes significantly more detail.

Ch

7

The Ethernet frame begins in the same fashion as the 802.3 frame with a preamble, start delimiter, and then the destination and source addresses (see Figure 7.7). The similarity stops here, because in Ethernet these addresses are followed by a type field, which identifies which Ethernet service the frame applies to. However, because the headers are so similar, these frames can coexist on the same LAN without interfering with one another (providing that the 802.3 frame uses 48-bit addresses as does Ethernet).

FIG. 7.7

Comparison of Ethernet and 802.2/802.3 Frame Formats

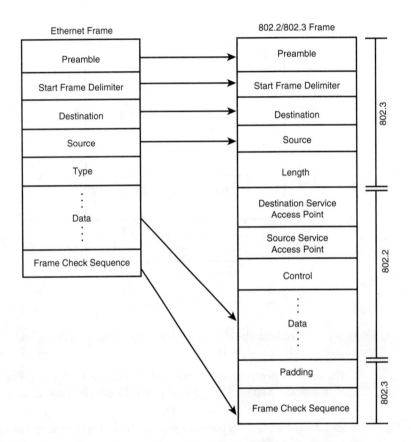

N O T E Ethernet Version 1.0 does not have the same level of compatibility with IEEE 802.3 as Ethernet II. Specifically, the primary difference is that Ethernet II and IEEE 802.3 both include a "heartbeat" function performed by the transceivers (units that attach computer and computer equipment to the physical LAN) to signal their ongoing operation (the absence of a heartbeat signals a failed or failing transceiver). ▪

Wide Area Networks

At a basic level, a WAN can be created by tying a series of simple, point-to-point links together. On the other end of the spectrum, a WAN might comprise many different systems and LANs, all interconnected using a variety of techniques, including standard telephone lines, packet-switching networks and ISDN links. Between the two extremes are networks that are superficially simple but technically complex, and those that are superficially complex but technically simple.

Unlike LANs, which all accomplish the same purpose, WANs offer a unique variety of technology and approaches. This discussion will focus on some of the better known approaches—standard phone links, ISDN networking, and X.25 packet-switching—as well as emerging methods such as ATM, Frame Relay, and SMDS.

Like LANs, WAN links are simply a way of transferring information from point A to point B. Running on top of both types of links are networking protocols and services that bring additional functions to the network. For example, IBM's SNA, Digital's DECnet, TCP/IP, and many other networking protocols all include services that operate over the physical links. Some protocols are specific to the LAN environment (such as Digital's LAT or Novell's IPX), while other protocols are better suited for wide area links (like IBM's SDLC or HP's implementation of HDLC).

The point is, in all cases, no network (wide or local) provides any value without upper layers of protocols, services and applications.

Point-to-Point Links

In most cases, long-distance point-to-point links are routed through a telephone carrier. From a practical point of view, the long-distance telephone carriers have already done the work of establishing a wide area of physical links, so it makes sense in some circumstances to use these existing connections.

Before the advent of high-speed digital lines, this world of long distance teleprocessing was composed of dial lines and leased lines. Dial-up *POTS (Plain Old Telephone Service)* lines are one of the few aspects of data communications that has not changed much over the years, although higher-speed modems have enabled data to be sent over them much faster. As the name implies, a dial line uses standard voice-grade lines to create a temporary connection between two computing devices. POTS lines can operate at speeds of up to 36,600 bps if a noise-free connection can be made.

A leased line is a permanent circuit installed between point A and point B. Because they are permanent, leased lines can be conditioned to provide less noise and therefore support high-speed operation (such as 28,800 bps) on a more reliable basis. Leased lines have been greatly affected by the advent of digital phone circuits.

Ch
7

Before the advent of digital lines, point-to-point links used the same basic approach to carry data as they did to carry voice. Although, as noted, leased lines could be purchased with various levels of conditioning, they still used the same analog approach for transmitting. Modems were developed to bridge the difference between the analog nature of the phone system and the digital nature of computers. Modems that translate between the digital and analog formats are described in greater detail at the end of this chapter.

N O T E   The analog/digital translation process, MOdulating and DEModulating, forms the etymology of the word "modem." ◼

As technology and phone systems matured, the nature of the phone network became much more sophisticated. Satellites were deployed to provide greater coverage without costly physical connections, and digital circuits were added into many phone systems to offer high transmission speeds with lower noise (and therefore fewer errors).

In particular, *Digital Data Service (DDS)* brought increased performance to leased lines. When compared to digital networking, the analog phone system is slow and error-prone. Furthermore, because the existing phone system was developed to address voice transmissions, the way it handles data communications is less than ideal. Digital service brought increased reliability and performance to leased line networks.

Higher rates are provided through the use of *T1 links.* T1 links are multiple, high-speed links packaged into a single unit. Specifically, a T1 line has an aggregate throughput of 1.544 Mbps but is, in reality, composed of 24 64-Kbps digital lines.

A T1 user can dedicate these 24 lines to separate functions—for example, some might carry voice, some video and some data. Or a T1 user can use multiplexing equipment to run data across all (or a subset) of the separate lines concurrently, to effectively achieve the full throughput. If a company does not need the full T1 bandwidth, it might also choose fractional T1 service. In this case, only some of the T1 lines are connected to the customer's premises. The availability of fractional T1 lines is dependent on the local phone company's ability to find enough fractional users to use up an entire T1 link.

Through bridges and routers, geographically distant LANs can be interconnected over a T1 link. However, since T1 is strictly a North American standard, it cannot be used to establish an intercontinental WAN.

N O T E   Because of the wide and diverse geography of the U.S., digital and T1 services are not available in all areas of the country. ◼

ISDN

ISDN is the planned replacement for the analog circuits used to provide voice and data communications services worldwide. Development on ISDN was begun in the 1970s by AT&T and formalized in the early 1980s under the mantle of the *Consultative Committee for International*

Telegraph and Telephony (CCITT). Under the direction of CCITT, ISDN became worldwide in scope, offering for the first time a fixed set of interfaces and interface devices that were applicable globally. Thus, the computer interface used in Germany for ISDN attachment would be the same interface used in the U.S.

The customer's interface to ISDN is through a *service node* (see Figure 7.8). The purpose of the service node is to provide an interface from ISDN to the customer phone system or PBX, a data communications device that interfaces to the local computer equipment (analogous to a modem or CSU/DSU), or a hybrid device that performs both functions. This service node interface enables the customer to access (given proper security and compatible equipment) any other system also connected to ISDN.

FIG. 7.8

ISDN Service Node
Concept Interface

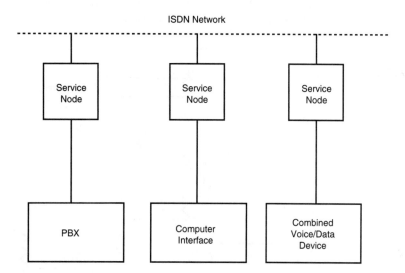

For data communications, this approach is more flexible than the traditional point-to-point leased line or dial-up connections previously discussed. Voice service, on the other hand, will not be dramatically improved because it also operates at the equivalent of 64 Kbps over the analog system. The digital nature of the network should, however, remove some of the static often heard over phones. (Also remember that while static is annoying to humans, it is devastating to data, and that's why data is not transmitted across analog lines at these extremely fast speeds.)

From a point of entry perspective, ISDN offers two types of user interfaces:

- *The Basic Rate Interface (BRI).* This interface offers two 64-Kbps data and/or voice circuits, known as the B channels, combined with a 16-Kbps management and service circuit, or D channel.

- *The Primary Rate Interface (PRI).* This interface features 23 64-Kbps data and/or voice circuits with an additional 64-Kbps circuit for management and ancillary services.

Ch

7

Because the costs for a PRI far exceed the cost for a BRI, most business needs are addressed by one or more BRIs. Still, given the higher speeds offered by the PRI (a total of 1.544 Mbps for the PRI versus a total of 144 Kbps for the BRI), the PRI is a viable contender to extending LANs using bridges and routers.

Also note that the PRI closely resembles a T1 link. The primary difference lies in their use and network architecture. T1 is most often used to facilitate high-speed point-to-point links, whereas ISDN is intended to interface a large number of systems on a global basis. ISDN also differs from the T1-style link in that it features a management circuit separate from the data circuits. This additional circuit is present in both the Basic Rate and Primary Rate Interfaces and delivers some benefits that are important to ISDN and its marketability. This circuit is separate from the data/voice channels (see Figure 7.9). In fact, it is termed a *D Channel,* as opposed to the *B channels* that carry the data and voice traffic.

FIG. 7.9
ISDN B and D Channels

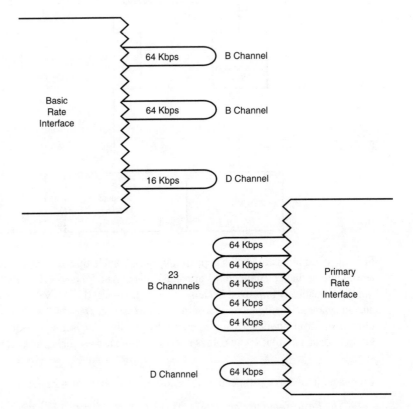

This type D circuit can be used for a number of functions:

- *Network management.* If network monitoring and management functions are separated from the network itself (which would be running over the D channels), then two benefits accrue. First, the monitoring and management function does not adversely affect network performance because it does not occur from within the network. Second, if a failure occurs within the network, the monitoring and management structure is still available to signal and alert operators to take corrective action.

- *Faster call servicing.* By using the D Channel to perform call set-up operations, ISDN dramatically reduces the amount of time necessary to initially establish a call. After the set-up occurs via the D Channel, the B Channel is instantly available for the actual voice transmission.

- *Automatic Number Identification (ANI).* Although the introduction of this feature has provoked political controversy in many states, ANI technology has many reasonable applications, especially in the customer service area. Specifically, it enables a phone call recipient to view (on a special display device) the phone number of the person who is calling. In addition, call center applications are available that will produce the caller's database record, order information, credit limits or other pertinent data instantly on a computer screen, before the call is even answered.

- *Advanced information forwarding.* As customers learn to use ISDN, they will invariably use the D Channel to send advanced information that relates to the call going over the B Channel. For example, customers might direct their PBX to send account information on the D Channel when they are making a voice call to a vendor. Because the account information arrives before the voice call, it can often be processed before the two parties converse. Thus, the vendor's representative might have the customer's file on his or her workstation when the phone rings.

Beyond establishing a digital international data network, ISDN is a key piece of the standards pie for several reasons:

- The U.S. government has developed federal standards based on ISDN and will soon require federal agencies to comply with these standards.

- The phone companies are committed to ISDN. Like it or not, you will be using ISDN at your home and office.

- ISDN has not overlooked fiber optic technology. Broadband ISDN (BISDN), which uses higher speed and more reliable fiber optic communications, is being analyzed as a transport within ISDN as well as a service in itself.

Laptop PC users now also have the ability to access a network with ISDN services through new ISDN Basic Rate Interface PCMCIA cards.

Ch
7

The various Regional Bell Operating Companies (RBOCs) are now providing ISDN service to most major cities, and the number of ISDN lines has increased dramatically over the past few years. Additionally, all of the major commercial on-line services offer ISDN access, and many Internet service providers are also offering ISDN Internet access. The advantages are obvious; file downloads are lightning fast, and there is less possibility of interruption due to line noise. PC vendors are accommodating the increasing demand for ISDN by releasing ISDN modems, also known as ISDN terminal adapters.

Although the cost of an ISDN connection is bound to decrease, costs vary tremendously from region to region.

Asymmetric Digital Subscriber Line (ADSL)

Although ISDN has been getting most of the press, a similar technology called *asymmetric digital subscriber line (ADSL)* promises even more throughput over an ordinary, narrow copper telephone line. ADSL accomplishes this remarkable feat through a series of complex compression and digital signal processing algorithms, and dynamic switching techniques. The ADSL transport technology boosts the capacity of the existing phone line significantly more than ISDN. Duplex ADSL offers a downstream data rate of up to 6 Mbps and an upstream channel running at 640 Kbps. ISDN, on the other hand, ranges from 64 Kbps to 128 Kbps—faster than a standard modem, but still too slow to handle that interactive TV and other services they keep telling us we'll all have one of these days.

Most of the regional Bell operating companies are testing ADSL and making plans to offer it to customers seeking high-bandwidth Internet access. Also, because it offers two-way communications, some entertainment companies are considering it a realistic possibility for interactive cable television.

ADSL gives the RBOCs an alternative to costly optical cables because it can transform their existing copper-wire network into a high-performance system. Here's how it works: The regular phone wire is configured for ADSL, and then connects to an ADSL modem on one end and an ADSL circuit switch on the other. The connection then creates:

- A high-speed, unidirectional data channel capable of running between 1.5 Mbps to 6.1 Mbps.
- A medium-speed duplex channel running between 16 Kbps and 640 Kbps.
- A standard analog connection.

Cable companies, set-top box makers, and TV couch potatoes drool over the possibilities. Look for this technology to be making big news in the near future.

X.25

The CCITT developed the X.25 standard to define a reliable, relatively low cost means of routing data through a shared network. An extremely important aspect of X.25 is that the information being transmitted has been converted into packets.

Packets can be thought of as small fragments of information. Specifically, a block of information is broken into smaller parts (packets) before being transmitted on the physical network. The packet methodology provides faster and more reliable error detection and correction; it also prevents a system with a huge volume of information to ship from tying up the network.

In addition to the raw information, each packet also contains information specifying its origin, its destination, and a number indicating the "piece" of the information to which it corresponds. This enables each packet to be treated as an independent entity, so that packets from many different systems can be intermixed on the network without concern about the order in which they are transmitted or even the order in which they arrive. Each packet might take the best possible route available at the time it is ready for transport.

The application end points of the information (that is, the terminal user and the application program) rarely see the information in its packetized form. As part of its interface with the network, the computer system converts the information into packets, and then subsequently reassembles the packets into the original information (see Figure 7.10).

FIG. 7.10

Conceptual Packetizing

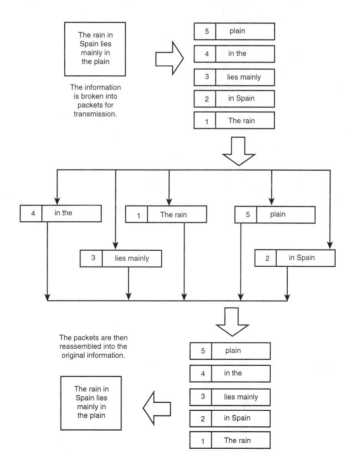

This packet approach to transmitting data is extremely pervasive in the networking world. In addition to being used by X.25, this approach is also used by most LANs and many other data communications protocols (although they are usually referred to as frames, as discussed in the LAN section of this chapter). Specific to X.25 networks, however, is the concept of a *packet switching network (PSN)*.

A PSN is a WAN through which packets are sent. The precise route that packets take from point A to point B is not fixed and is immaterial to the equipment at point A or point B, which checks only to see whether the packets arrive intact (again, order is not a major concern).

Because they don't have prescribed data routes, PSNs are often shown as clouds in many networking diagrams (see Figure 7.11). When depicted in this manner, information goes into the cloud at some point and comes out at another. What goes on within the cloud is not the concern of mere humans.

FIG. 7.11
Typical X.25
Representation

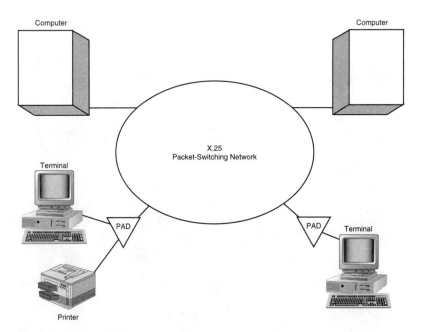

The inside of the cloud, however, is composed of *packet-switching nodes* (also called PSNs, just to make life confusing). The switching nodes can take routes to other switching nodes, and thus can route or reroute data as necessary. For example, if a switching node has a packet to forward and the best possible switching node to receive it is busy, the node holding the packet will reroute it to another node for subsequent rerouting (see Figure 7.12).

Packet-switching networks often are associated with public data networks (PDNs), but this relationship is certainly casual. A PDN is normally a telephone system (or telephone company in the U.S.) that offers data services to the public. It does not have to use packet-switching to move information from point to point. If a PDN does offer the services of a packet-switching

FIG. 7.12
Inside of the X.25
"Cloud"

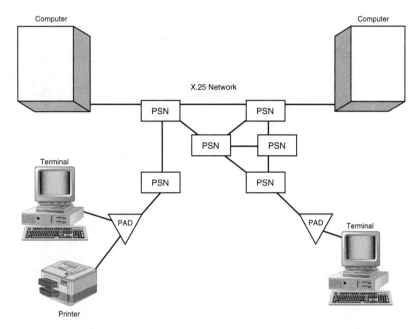

network, it might be referred to as a packet-switching data network (PSDN) or even a packet-switching public data network (PSPDN). Clearly, the abbreviations are almost endless.

Furthermore, implementation of packet-switching networks is not limited to telephone companies. In fact, PSNs can be constructed of telephone links, fiber optic links, microwave links, satellite links, and other forms of communications. Many large corporations have used these diverse communication techniques to construct their own private PSN. Because, in the final analysis, a packet switching network is a cost-effective WAN, organizations with widely dispersed equipment find this approach most effective in terms of both cost and function.

The traditional packet-switching cloud is shown in Figure 7.13.

FIG. 7.13
X.25 Interfaces

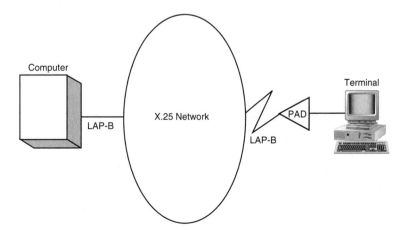

Ch
7

Moving outside of this cloud, the interfaces between the computer equipment and the cloud generally fall into one of two types of devices:

- *PAD.* The packet assembly/disassembly device is a piece of hardware that interfaces between the network and computer equipment incapable of sending or receiving packets. This function is defined in CCITT standard X.3. The purpose of the PAD, then, is to handle the conversion of the raw data into packets for transmission into the packet-switching cloud and, conversely, handle the reassembly of information from packets received from the cloud. PADs most often are used to interface terminals into the packet-switching network, but they are also used to interface computer systems that cannot handle packet transformations on their own.

- *A communications controller running (normally) the LAP-B protocol.* Rather than use an external device, such as a PAD, most computers use an internal interface to directly connect to the packet-switching network. These interfaces and their corresponding software drivers provide much of the same function provided by a PAD. The advantage to putting these interfaces into a computer is that computer software can directly access the link (whereas in the PAD the link was external and, for the most part, invisible to the software). For example, an office automation package can communicate with a counterpart package operating on the other "side" of the cloud.

For terminal traffic over packet-switching networks, two additional standards come into play. First, the *CCITT X.28* standard defines the interface between an asynchronous terminal and a PAD. Second, the *CCITT X.29* standard defines the control procedures for information exchanges between a PAD and another PAD (or an integrated controller). Just as X.25 has become synonymous with packet-switching networks, X.29 has become synonymous with interfacing terminals over packet-switching networks.

LAN Switches

Switches are used to extend overcrowded networks by providing each end user with his own piece of 4 Mbps or 16 Mbps bandwidth. In many cases, this might be more than each end user needs. In this event, the token ring switch can be used to break one big token ring into multiple, smaller rings. This approach will also significantly increase performance.

Switch Technology—Token Ring and FDDI

Many vendors are bringing token ring LAN switches to the market. A number of alliances illustrate the strength of this market, such as a recent noteworthy alliance between Bay Networks (Santa Clara, California) and IBM. Other network vendors, such as Cisco Systems and Cabletron Systems, have made similar deals with third parties. As more vendors go into this market and volume increases, token ring switch products are expected to come down in price and enjoy higher demand.

FDDI switching is another promising technology for extending network life and bandwidth. Digital's GigaSwitch is the leading FDDI switching product, although several other vendors are preparing to release FDDI switches as well.

Token ring networks, like Ethernet networks, have bandwidth limitations, and many are starting to reach those limitations because of the bigger applications and greater demands for data that companies are experiencing. The lower pricing structures of Ethernet and token ring LAN switching devices might encourage individual business units to make their own purchases. In terms of the overall enterprise, however, this can be disastrous. It is essential for individual departments to consider the overall corporate direction when making such purchases, and to make sure that the technology they are purchasing is compatible with the existing infrastructure and corporate data needs assessments. If not, they might wind up spending much more money because they now have to buy additional equipment to connect with the corporate switches and to address data type and volume transmission requirements decided on by corporate information communication needs.

Tools of the Trade

Needless to say, computers and networks do not connect to each other as easy as phones plug into wall jacks. In networks, the tools of connectivity handle conversion between analog and digital formats, between one type of physical interface and another, or between one transmission media and another. In short, these tools are the nuts and bolts of the erector set called networking.

For LANs, one set of tools is required to make the physical attachment between the interface in the computer (for example, an Ethernet adapter in a VAX or a token ring adapter in an AS/400) and the physical network. The tools include:

- ▪ *The Attachment Unit Interface (AUI)*. This is the cable that attaches the interface in the computer to the MAU described below.
- ▪ *The Medium Attachment Unit (MAU)*. Also known as a Multistation Access Unit when used with a token ring network. This device attaches one or more AUIs to the physical LAN. A MAU can provide one-to-one connection with a computer or it can be a hub to several systems.

When two LANs are joined together, a bridge or router is normally used. When a bridge links two or more LANs, those LANs form a single, logical LAN. In this case, all information routed through one LAN goes over the bridge and through the attached network. Because of this traffic, high speed links are normally required to keep the bridge from slowing the performance of the network. And finally, because bridges are implemented at such a low level, all protocols can operate over a bridge.

A router also connects two or more LANs, but routers are much more selective about the information that they allow to cross over. Specifically, routers are aware (through self-learning or manual configuration) of which computer addresses apply to which LANs. Therefore, rather than pass all information across, routers transmit only information pertinent to the other LAN. Because only selected traffic travels across the link, lower speed links can be used without affecting overall LAN performance. The router can also act as a *firewall* to prevent unwanted access to the network from outside.

Ch
7

Routers cannot be used in all types of networks, though. Because routers depend on the network to supply an internetwork address (an address that is globally unique), those network protocols that do not support this type of addressing cannot be used with routers. Digital's LAT protocol, for example, has no facilities for internetwork addressing, and therefore will not travel over a router (but it will travel over a bridge). And because routers and bridges have their advantages and disadvantages, the two are often combined into one piece of equipment (in this case some protocols are bridged and others are routed). These devices are often called *brouters*.

When a computer, bridge, or router must interface to the telephone system (analog, digital or T1), more special devices are needed. They are as follows:

- *Modem.* For traditional (analog) phone lines, modems (MOdulator/DEModulators) provide the conversion between the digital computer output and the analog phone transmissions. The interface between the computer (or router or bridge) and the modem is normally a well-defined standard such as EIA RS-232 or CCITT V.32.

- *CSU and DSU.* For digital links (DDS or fractional T1 lines), two devices are required. A channel service unit (CSU) interfaces with the telephone-side of the link and with a data service unit (DSU) that, in turn, interfaces with the computer system (or router or bridge). The attachment to the DSU is a well-defined standard like EIA RS-232 or CCITT V.35. In most cases, the CSU and DSU are combined into a single, physical unit.

- *Gateway.* A gateway attaches seemingly incompatible networks, such as IBM's SNA and Digital's DECnet. In a nutshell, a gateway is a complicated form of protocol converter—it converts multiple protocols and emulates multiple devices to provide a wide variety of services. Gateways can be used to link electronic mail systems, to enable one type or terminal to access another type of host, to provide file transfer between networks, or to perform all of these functions. ●

CHAPTER 8

Services

The Scope of Services

Services are a very elusive aspect of networking. Because
they cannot be seen or held in the palm of your hand, it is
difficult to envision connecting them together. Yet services are the make-or-break component of a network
implementation. If the underlying services cannot support the demands of the applications and the users, then
the network will collapse.

And while networks depend greatly on services, the
reverse is not true. In most cases, services are independent from the type of network on which they run. For
example, multivendor office automation services have
similar applicability and functions in both LANs and
WANs. The same is true of manufacturer-specific services, such as IBM's Systems Network Architecture
(SNA) and Digital's DECnet.

Sometimes, however, services are married to networks
for a reason. For example, PC (MS-DOS) virtual disk
services could technically be implemented on a midrange
host over a WAN or LAN, but the need for transmission
speed dictates a close marriage to the LAN environment.

In fact, the very nature of a LAN poses certain requirements for services. After all, if a LAN presented no
benefits, no one would consent to attach to it. For minicomputers and mainframes, the purpose of a LAN is to

share terminals, printers, and disk space. For PCs, however, the prime requirement is to share files and applications, and to promote communication.

Furthermore, not only do PC LANs and minicomputer/mainframe LANs have separate service needs, but when both types of systems need to be integrated as a whole, yet another set of services is necessary. In this arena, then, the choices become broader, the players grow in number, and the mind begins to boggle.

Rising to meet this need for better integration among all types of computers is the concept of *client/server computing*. This concept provides a distributed environment for all application programs, while still giving the user a consistent and understandable appearance.

The LAN environment contrasts sharply with that of a WAN. For one thing, transmission speed in a LAN is virtually free (in other words, there are no ongoing costs for daily operation of the network). In a WAN, however, you get what you pay for when it comes to speed. Sure, you can get breathtaking speed with T1 links, satellite links, and even microwave links, but these technologies don't come cheap.

At the other extreme of cost/performance is low-speed networking. Where high speed WANs engendered concern about optimum use, slower networks tend to be used for lower volume and less critical information. In this category fall the traditional phone-dial and packet switching networks. They are excellent, cost-effective solutions for occasional terminal access, intermittent and non-critical file transfers, or electronic mail.

In particular, electronic mail services have enjoyed explosive growth in WANs of all varieties. Electronic mail products have become much more sophisticated and have begun to offer real value to companies implementing them. And with this increase in use has come an increase in the need to expand the communications sphere of the product. Often, electronic mail starts in one department on one type of computer but grows into a corporatewide network encompassing many different departments and many different types of computers.

LAN Services

Despite the physical and logical connectivity provided by a LAN, a network has no functional capabilities until network services are added to the mix. These services facilitate shared files, shared printers, program-to-program communications, directory services, and other more specific functions. The implementation details for network services, however, differ from vendor to vendor and from system to system.

Perhaps the biggest difference is how PCs interact on LANs compared to how midrange and larger computers interact on them. This difference results partly from the fact that the needs of PCs on a network differ from the needs of traditional computers, and partly from the fact that much of the LAN networking software for PCs was developed from scratch (without respect to existing standards).

The requirements of a PC LAN are rapidly changing. In a larger environment, the network is used as a collaborative tool that enables individuals in different geographical locations to work together on individual documents. In a smaller environment, users may have more modest

Ch
8

needs from their networks, and may use them only for sharing files, peripherals or applications, and for e-mail. The network interface to handle files is at a very low (sector) level to maximize speed.

In minicomputer/mainframe computer LANs, however, the requirements generally focus more on the movement of files and the optimization of terminal resources. File access must be performed in a highly structured, secure manner, and files have specific places of residence and ownership. When an end user wants to alter a file in this environment, the file will probably be copied (transferred) to the user's computer and then modified there. Terminals are the user's way of accessing applications and information; therefore, this type of LAN maximizes the way a terminal accesses the various systems in the LAN. As in PC LANs, though, it is common to share printing and program-to-program communications between systems.

The heart of the contrast between the two operating environments lies in the operating systems. Operating systems written for midrange and mainframe systems (for example, VMS, MPE, OS/400, and Windows NT) are designed with networking in mind. File systems are designed to accommodate residence on different physical hosts, physical printers are isolated from the print generation process by print queues and spoolers, and program compilers are developed to accommodate all of these network-oriented operations. Thus, a program developed in this environment can immediately take advantage of the network architecture.

Originally, personal computers were largely stand-alone devices. One of the first PC operating systems was Microsoft's Disk Operating System (MS-DOS) with its IBM derivative (PC-DOS) and other OEM versions. DOS in its various incarnations was designed to control all resources directly. Files were on local disks, printers were locally attached, and every program was an island incapable of communicating with other programs—and that was that. Thus, when networking was introduced to the PC, it had to be crowbarred in between the operating system (DOS) and the hardware. In other words, a program operating on a networked PC had to think it was operating using its own local resources. Faster PCs eventually led to the development of more sophisticated PC operating systems, such as Microsoft's Windows 95 and Windows NT, which have networking features built in.

The presence or absence of tight integration between network services and the operating system makes a dramatic difference in how the network appears to the end user. In tightly integrated systems like DECnet, the network is a widely accepted and embraced part of the system. In loosely integrated systems, such as most implementations of TCP/IP, the network is a separate entity, accessed through a separate set of utilities and routines. And in between these two examples are networks that make a variety of compromises between tight and loose integration.

Minicomputer/Mainframe LAN Implementations

Given that networks and operating systems have a significant impact on one another, a brief recap of the networking architectures and philosophies of Digital, HP, IBM, and Sun is in order.

Digital Equipment   Digital Equipment's networking architecture is based on the IEEE 802 family of standards. In terms of networking software, Digital offers a range of utilities and services under the umbrella of DECnet. DECnet protocols and services allow remote file operations, print sharing, remote logon, program-to-program communications, and other functions. Because DECnet is tightly integrated with Digital's operating systems (VMS and ULTRIX), DECnet is part of the user and file-naming conventions and structures used by the operating systems.

Another Digital LAN protocol that has gained wide popularity is the *Local Area Transport (LAT)*. LAT is a protocol used by *terminal servers* (devices that attach terminals directly to the LAN) to route terminal traffic to and from one or more hosts on that LAN. LAT is not a formal part of the DECnet service suite and has gained some usage and acceptance in non-DEC networks and hosts.

All things considered, Digital Equipment has one of the most well-integrated network architectures—it was one of the first companies to integrate networking into their standard computing environment.

Hewlett-Packard   HP's primary LAN architecture relies on the IEEE 802.3 standard. It, however, does have some peripheral products that also use Ethernet.

HP's networking software is called NS and is similar to both TCP/IP and DECnet in its architecture and implementation. Because HP added networking to its core products much later in life than Digital, networking routines and utilities have been implemented as extensions to its existing products.

HP's most significant contribution to LAN computing has been its use and endorsement of the client/server computing architecture, which is discussed later in this chapter.

IBM   IBM's LAN strategy is primarily focused on its token-ring network, compatible with the IEEE 802.5 specification. For networking services, IBM has implemented those defined in its SNA.

Specifically, in a mainframe environment, token-ring networks can be used to tie workstations to controllers, and controllers to communications processors (front ends). Token-ring networks provide high-speed communication links for these traditionally distributed and hierarchical SNA connections.

Token-ring LANs can also connect AS/400 computers. With these implementations, IBM offers a set of services to enable file sharing between systems (the Distributed Data Manager) or the logging on to one system from another (Display Station Passthrough).

Again, because the token ring is part of the bigger SNA picture, standard SNA transports such as LU 6.2 can run across a token ring LAN just like they run across SDLC links.

In addition to its token ring implementations, IBM also offers a number of products to provide connectivity to both Ethernet and IEEE 802.3 networks. These connectivity products typically use IBM's implementation of TCP/IP for network services to non-IBM computers.

IBM has further reinforced its commitment to establishing connections between SNA and the LAN by purchasing Novell's NetWare for SAA (System Application Architecture) gateway business. NetWare for SAA is a leading LAN-to-SNA gateway, and connects NetWare LANs to IBM SNA applications. However, the deal now places IBM in the position of having two competing products. IBM's Communications Manager/2 accomplishes the same functions as the former Novell product. Both of these products in turn compete with Microsoft's PC LAN-to-SNA integration product, SNA Server.

Sun Microsystems   Sun Microsystems provides Ethernet connections with most of its equipment. Its networking services are layered on top of TCP/IP and are focused on Sun's Network File System (NFS) product, which provides transparent file access between systems participating on the same network.

In fact, Sun's approach to networking is an interesting hybrid between Digital's distributed processing techniques and the shared file server technology now commonly used in PC LANs. To a certain extent, Sun enjoys the best of both worlds.

Such functions as program-to-program communications, print services, and remote logon are handled through services integrated into the operating system. These services are based on the TCP/IP model.

For file services, however, Sun has introduced the concept of NFS servers to its LANs. In this approach, one or more systems contains the physical disk and the logical files used by other systems throughout the systems. As in PC networks, a user wanting to access a file on a server must issue special network requests (such as a mount command) to make the files available.

This use of NFS servers is quite different from Digital's approach of giving each system its own local disk to share. If nothing else, Sun's networking approach puts a new spin on traditional TCP/IP implementations.

And finally, note that standard implementations of TCP/IP are available for all of these vendors systems, although in some cases TCP/IP must be obtained through third-party sources. Unlike the manufacturer's proprietary networking services, TCP/IP has no particular ties to any one manufacturer or operating system. See Chapter 9, "PC LAN Network Operating Systems," for TCP/IP details.

PC LAN Implementations

Because most of the companies that developed LAN software for PCs have no vested interest in any particular LAN, their products can typically be configured for any type of network. This brings tremendous flexibility to the desk of the haggard network administrator who desperately wants only one network for the corporate equipment connections.

While achieving this distance from the manufacturers offers benefits (in the form of LAN independence), it also contributes complications because the network vendor and the operating system are not closely related. Again, this situation sharply contrasts with the implementation of networking services in the larger computers. In that environment, networking functions can often be incorporated into the operating system itself, offering a seamless, or nearly seamless, interface between the two.

In the land of the PCs, however, Microsoft dominates the market with its Windows family of operating systems. The bulk of network services have been designed around the Microsoft operating system structure. Windows 3.1 and previous releases are not true operating systems; rather, they are operating environments that run on top of MS-DOS. Windows 95 and Windows NT, however, are true operating systems that incorporate the functionality of MS-DOS within the overall operating system.

In order to understand how LAN services came to the PC environment, you need to look at the original MS-DOS architecture. As shown in Figure 8.1, the MS-DOS operating system uses two sets of low-level services for interface with the physical hardware. One set of services is provided through a ROM-based BIOS (Basic Input/Output System) program, and the other set is provided through a set of MS-DOS BIOS routines.

FIG. 8.1

Basic Input/Output System

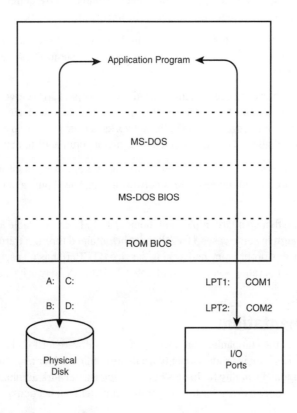

The two sets of BIOS services are not independent of one another. Specifically, the MS-DOS BIOS services provide generalized services that are requested by application programs (such as read a record in a file or send print to a printer), while the ROM BIOS provides extremely low-level services such as read a specific sector on a disk or write this information to a machine-level I/O port.

Ch 8

In practice, many MS-DOS BIOS services actually end up calling the lower-level ROM BIOS service. For example, when an application requests MS-DOS to read a record from a file, the MS-DOS BIOS service translates the request to a specific sector on the physical disk drive and then requests the ROM BIOS to read that sector. Similar relationships are in place for printer and communications services.

This channeling of basic input/output services through a common point gives networking software the opportunity to impose itself between the operating system and the hardware, without forcing any changes in the application program. This insertion can be done in several ways: by adding a device driver to the standard MS-DOS environments to redirect services on to the network; by replacing the MS-DOS BIOS routines with network-oriented routines compatible with the MS-DOS services; or by combinations of the two techniques.

When network services are put in place of or added to the MS-DOS BIOS services, requests for disk information and printed output can then be routed from one machine to another through the physical network (see Figure 8.2). Obviously, practical use of this technique also involves specifying which machines are servers for which services. But, when properly configured, a request to print a file on computer A can be routed to print on computer B. Furthermore, the disk resources of computer C can also be made available on computers A and B.

FIG. 8.2

Network Redirection

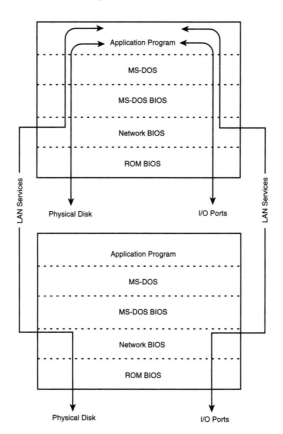

As mentioned earlier, disk sharing is a common function of most PC LANs. A network disk to be shared is normally mounted on the local workstation and accessed as if it were a normal, local drive. For example, a workstation might have two floppy drives, a local hard disk, and two network drives. The operating system and the application programs should not be able to distinguish the mounted network drives from local drives. This makes for relatively smooth integration.

Integration notwithstanding, the speed of performing network disk access is an issue. The issue is not the raw access speed of the physical disk drive (although it certainly is a factor), but how quickly and efficiently an access can be serviced over the network.

A PC can serve as both a workstation and as a network file server. However, PCs were originally designed as single-task machines, so only one operation could occur at a time. When the CPU is busy (doing a spreadsheet recalculation, for example), a network request would have to wait to be serviced. Newer PC operating systems are now based on multithreaded, multitasking architectures, and are able to accommodate several tasks at once (given powerful enough hardware). Still, larger LANs require a system to solely function as a file server. These file servers do not need to run the PC operating system. Thus, special operating systems were developed for network file servers to maximize performance and minimize the potential for disk errors.

PC LAN Players

Both Microsoft and IBM offer networking solutions to go along with their PC operating systems. Other networking products are available from Novell, Banyan Systems, and other companies, which provide high-performance networks that are compatible with an operating system over which they have no control.

Thus far, Novell has gained the greatest degree of acceptance and use in the corporate market. In a traditional Novell environment, one or more high performance computers are dedicated as the file servers. In terms of network-level communications, Novell has implemented its own protocols, named the *Internetwork Packet Exchange (IPX)* and the *Sequenced Packet Exchange (SPX)*, that run on top of IPX. Novell's software offering is referred to as *NetWare*. Several different implementations are available to accommodate different networking scenarios. Because the file server is central to the network, it must offer high performance.

The greatest changes in the PC networking arena are driven by the need to integrate PC information with minicomputer/mainframe information. As more and more devices reside on the same physical LAN, it becomes more difficult to overlook their inability to communicate with one another. Some of the most widely-used PC LAN operating systems include:

- *Banyan VINES*. Banyan Systems provides many of the same functions as NetWare, but Banyan's VINES (VIrtual NEtwork Software) products run with existing network standards. Thus, unlike Novell, which implements its own transport-layer protocol, VINES can run with TCP/IP, SNA, and other networking protocols. VINES is similar to Novell's NetWare in its use of servers, but Banyan claims that it is more unstructured and open, and therefore easier to use.

- *Novell NetWare.* For many years, Novell NetWare was the dominant file and print server in the PC LAN arena. NetWare runs in a designated server system and communicates with a variety of client systems (PC, Mac, UNIX) using either the IPX or TCP/IP protocol suite. Novell NetWare is the seasoned veteran of the industry, and has established a strong, loyal following in the corporate market. One of the key technological advantages of the current 4.x line of NetWare products is *NetWare Directory Services (NDS)*. NDS is a global directory service designed to manage LAN-based resources in large, enterprise-class environments. Although Novell went through a series of corporate twists and turns in the mid-1990s, the company has since refocused itself on its core NetWare technology.

- *Windows NT.* For years, Microsoft stayed out of the networking business. However, when Microsoft acquired 3Com's networking PC LAN technology, it began to integrate networking services into its operating system products. The first attempt at this integration was Windows for Workgroups, which was a difficult product because of the underlying DOS component. When Microsoft designed Windows 95 and Windows NT, however, it seized the opportunity to integrate core networking services right into the operating system. Microsoft took two tracks here, pushing peer-to-peer (workgroup) resource sharing via Windows 95 and Windows NT Workstation, and enterprise-scale file, print, and application serving via Windows NT Server.

Refer to Chapter 9, "PC LAN Network Operating Systems," for more information on these three key PC LAN operating systems.

Server Alternatives

Although Windows dominates the corporate desktop, UNIX is still widely used as a server platform due to its strong performance and robust features. Business-critical servers must be able to deliver high-end features and run the company's transaction-based applications. They also must be scalable enough to become part of a distributed network, which replaces mainframe and minicomputer-based networks. Additionally, as a mainframe replacement, a business-critical server needs to support security and systems management, and must be able to interoperate with other dissimilar resources throughout the enterprise. Specifically, it must be able to integrate with Windows PCs to make these critical resources available to PC users.

The *Common Desktop Environment (CDE)* is part of the Common Operating System Environment (COSE, pronounced "cozy") agreement, one of many attempts at unifying the UNIX market. Although COSE itself never took off, CDE has achieved some success—most notably, all the major UNIX vendors agreeing on the Motif interface as the basis for the Common Desktop Environment as well as establishing several other commonalities. Long overdue, this simple agreement will help make UNIX easier to run in a multivendor environment.

64-bit API

Another unification attempt involves an initiative to develop a common 64-bit UNIX API. Several UNIX vendors, including Intel, HP, SGI, DEC, Compaq, IBM, Novell, Oracle, and Sun, are hoping that the common specification will reduce more of the problems developers encounter in having to write for

continues

continued
   different implementations of UNIX. The alliance will build the 64-bit specification from existing 32-bit
   APIs, and will comply with existing standards, including CDE.

Despite its fractured nature, UNIX has a number of strengths. Many tools are available for free, and there are plenty of UNIX experts out there looking for something to do. UNIX is a strong platform for use as an application server. UNIX also offers the advantage of easy remote access—nearly any PC or Macintosh running any operating system can be made to work as an X Window terminal.

Finally, note that if you're on a tight budget (or have no budget at all), a UNIX-like 32-bit operating system called *Linux* (based on Berkeley Software Distribution, or BSD, UNIX code, which was developed at the University of California at Berkeley) is freely available. Linux is a non-commercial operating system, although implementations of Linux are available from commercial vendors complete with technical support. It might require some long hours and customization, because like most freeware products, it has a few rough edges. However, Linux has a number of fans, and a large informal support network offers technical help and advice, freeware products, and other services.

PC/Minicomputer/Mainframe LAN Integration

Although practicality might dictate that PC LANs and minicomputer/mainframe LANs share a common topology and discipline, no law dictates that they must communicate with one another on that same LAN. In fact, multiple sets of computers can implement different networking services, and each set might lead its life of quiet desperation independently of the other sets.

But when cross-communications are mandated by some foolish need or frantic demand, the broad scope of choices normally available in the data processing market narrows rapidly. In looking to integrate PC functions with the larger systems capabilities, you have to make some basic choices. Which architecture will be promoted over the others? Will the larger systems become servers for the PCs? Will the PCs become terminals to the larger systems? Or will a third LAN structure be implemented in which both the PCs and large systems conform to a common standard?

Most approaches provide similar results (shared disk space and shared printers), but each approach has its pros and cons:

- *System Servers.* If the larger systems become servers for the PC LANs, the PC file structure is imposed upon the larger system. In most cases, an area of the system disk is then unavailable to native system users. On the plus side, the PC LAN server information can be backed up along with all of the other system information (one procedure can address both needs). Manufacturers that support this approach include Digital Equipment and Novell. Digital markets a product that enables VMS systems to store MS-DOS files, and Novell has released NetWare for SAA, NetWare for DEC Access, and NetWare Connect. NetWare Connect provides a number of connectivity options: It permits remote Windows and Macintosh computers to access any resource available to the NetWare network, including files, databases, applications, and mainframe services; and it permits users on the network to connect to remote control computers, bulletin boards, X.25, and ISDN services.

■ *Terminal Emulation.* When PCs emulate native devices to the larger system, they lose some of their intelligence by emulating unintelligent terminals. File sharing in this environment is normally supported via file transfers between PCs and the larger system. This architecture is very centralized and favors the larger system by keeping PC access to a minimum. Digital, HP, IBM, and Sun all have sets of products that provide this type of centralized integration.

A number of third-party products are on the market to connect TCP/IP-based networks to mainframe and midrange hosts, potentially giving PC users access to CICS applications and facilitating file transfer between the LAN and the mainframe system.

■ *Peer Connections.* Introducing a new set of services to accommodate both small and large systems establishes an environment in which all computing nodes are peers. This approach, however, consumes additional resources (memory, CPU, disk) on each computer that participates in the shared environment. In such a system, TCP/IP might be implemented to allow file transfer between any two systems, to provide electronic mail services to all systems, and to enable the PCs to access the larger systems as if they were terminals.

All of these approaches share one fundamental concept: The application the user must be accessed at its native location. Therefore, to run a minicomputer program, you must log onto the minicomputer and have proper authority to run it. Similarly, to run a microcomputer program, you must mount and access the physical or logical disk where it resides. In both cases, the user must find a path to the remote application. This concept is changing, however, with the advent of distributed client/server computing architectures.

The Client/Server Model

To create more meaningful integration between PC LANs and LANs built on larger systems, a few manufacturers have developed some new approaches. They noted that the intelligence of the desktop device was rising increasingly, while the rule of dedicated *(dumb)* terminals was slowly crumbling. Emerging was a new breed of intelligent, low-cost, general-purpose computers that were quite capable of handling some of the applications-processing load. In short, the PCs had arrived.

To take these microcomputers and dedicate them to the task of terminal emulation was an obvious step in the evolution of the PC explosion, but was also, in many respects, a mismatch of power to purpose. To make a PC emulate a terminal sacrificed the ability of the PC to interact with data, and clearly a PC can perform data entry, do mathematical calculations and store information for subsequent retrieval. But when a PC is emulating a terminal, it performs none of those functions. Instead, it uses all of its own intelligence and resources to emulate a dumb device. Therefore, it would seem reasonable to let the PC take a more meaningful role in the processing of the data. But how?

Certainly the idea of distributed processing was nothing new. In fact, most operating systems and networks have basic task-to-task communication facilities. But in this case, the communications would not necessarily occur between similar computers. A PC might need to initiate a conversation with a midrange, or a mainframe might need to communicate with a PC. This was the interesting twist—how to implement a distributed processing environment that took advantage of computing power wherever it was in the network, without requiring all of the computers to use the same operating system or even the same primary networking services.

What formed as a possible solution to this puzzle was the concept of client/server computing. In the client/server scenario, the local computer (PC or a user's session on a larger computer) acts as the processing client. Associated with the client is software that provides a universal appearance to the user (be it a graphical, icon-oriented display, or a character, menu-oriented display). From that display, you can select the applications you want to use.

When a user selects an application, the client initiates a conversation with the server for that application (see Figure 8.3). This might involve communications across LANs and WANs or simply a call to a local program. Regardless of where the server resides, the client acts as the front end for the server and handles the user interface. Thus, the user is not aware of where the application actually resides.

FIG. 8.3

Client/Server Processing

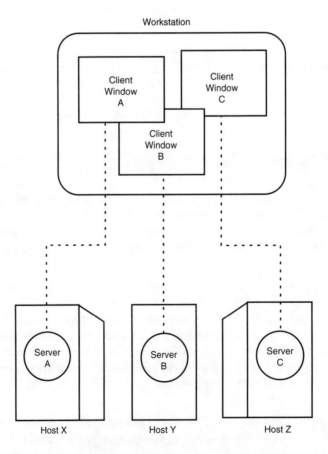

Furthermore, the client/server approach is dramatically enhanced when used with a windowing client platform. If, for example, the user is at a PC that is running a multitasking system, multiple windows can be used to initiate multiple client sessions, thereby enabling the user to hot-key between applications, with each application potentially running on a different computer system. This is a vastly superior method to having multiple terminals, each with a separate terminal emulation session logged into a specific host and running a specific application with specific keyboard demands. The client/server approach offers one consistent user interface for all screen and keyboard activities.

Ch 8

> **CAUTION**
>
> Hot-keying between applications can be a tremendous boon to end users, but if the network hardware is inadequate, this can cause performance problems. Some administrators might choose to limit the amount of active applications a user can have running at one time. Many network management systems give administrators the ability to enforce a "clean desk" approach by establishing a maximum number of simultaneous sessions.

When it was first described, client/server computing was intended as an enterprise solution, where users at all levels could work cooperatively across platforms. Client/server technology has gone a long way in enhancing departmental productivity, although further advances must be made before it can live up to its expectations on an enterprise level. One of the biggest challenges of implementing a client/server environment is establishing bridges between all of the various heterogeneous elements. Typically, client/server solutions offer only limited access to critical data. Also, because the environment is by its very nature decentralized, managing the environment is extremely difficult. In order for client/server to be useful as an enterprise solution, it must be able to access large amounts of data distributed over a heterogeneous environment and integrate it into a common report. This service is in fact being provided by executive information system (EIS) software and data warehouse technology.

There are many factors involved in designing a server system in a distributed computing environment. Application partitioning can follow one of three different paradigms:

- *Client-centric model.* Also called a "fat client" system, this model places all of the application logic on the client side. It requires higher-powered desktop machines, and requires substantially more administrative chores. Multiple copies of the applications, which have to reside on each and every client, must be synchronized. Additionally, this can cause the network to bog down, and the fat client system is vulnerable to security problems because of the unprotected client OS.

- *Server-centric model.* This model is easier to implement and less expensive than the client-centric model. It does not put critical data at risk. However, this model does not take full advantage of the Windows desktop. The client usually consists of only a terminal, or a PC running a terminal emulator with a minimal GUI front end.

- *Distributed transaction model.* This hybrid model places certain operations at the client, where the end user needs to take advantage of multimedia, or other features more common to the PC, and runs less intensive applications on the server. Multitiered distributed systems can be used in larger situations. This model divides the server logic across multiple servers, enabling functions to be divided between branches or divisions. UNIX is best-suited for distributed computing, and many companies put their critical operations on UNIX servers.

A newer model for client/server takes a three-tiered approach in order to avoid both fat-client and fat-server situations. A three-tier client/server model separates logic and compute-intensive calculations from the rest of the application. The first tier includes the GUI, the middle tier covers the logic and calculation components, and the third contains data management services. In some situations, the application logic can even be replicated over multiple servers, so the server with the most resources at a given time can handle a specific request for services.

Application development software vendors are starting to offer three-tiered development products in addition to their traditional environments.

Client/server products are relatively new, although each major manufacturer has its own applications architecture to implement client/server functions. Unfortunately, each manufacturer's implementation is very much geared toward its own product offering. If you're looking for an outside approach, X (Windows) marks the spot.

X Window Interface

By way of introduction, X Window strives to provide a common, GUI across systems. Under X Window, each terminal or workstation is, in fact, an intelligent graphics device that has multiple windows in it, each of which sponsors a different application. Consistent with the client/server model, the full scope of X Window enables each of these applications to reside on different systems.

Furthermore, because X Window is a third-party architecture, it is explicitly targeted to provide connectivity among different manufacturers. Because the user sees only one consistent interface, he or she is unaware of where the application program actually resides.

X Window is also a contender in the battle for presentation standards for graphical data. Specifically, X Window allows graphical data composed or stored on different systems to be displayed on a common terminal. This arrangement is significantly better than each manufacturer using its own format for graphics that will only display on its own graphics terminal. Under most implementations of X Window, a manufacturer's graphics format is converted to and from X Window's. As the popularity of X Window rises, however, more manufacturers will begin to include options for storing the data in the X Window's graphic format on disk, thereby eliminating any need for conversion.

The negative side of X Window is the relatively high cost for the workstations. Because X Window requires graphics processing capabilities, the X Window workstations are really specialized graphics computers that are far more expensive than the traditional, character-mode (nongraphic) terminals. However, an X workstation is still often more economical than a fully outfitted multimedia PC.

As PCs become less expensive and more widely deployed in the enterprise, X terminals will continue to fall out of favor. There are still a significant number of X terminals in use, but the market has reached its peak. Many companies are instead opting to purchase inexpensive PCs and run X terminal software on them. PC X servers, on the other hand, are gaining in popularity.

X terminals are associated with UNIX, but many X desktop users want to be able to access Windows applications. Fortunately, X terminals can become Windows displays by deploying Windows NT-based software products that permit an X device to function as a networked PC running Windows.

WAN Services

Although WANs are used for terminal access and file transfer, implementing these services in a wide-area environment is not all that different from implementing them in a local or metropolitan area. Therefore, viewing these services from the WAN perspective does not shed much new light on the subject.

The area of office automation and electronic mail, however, is a different matter. Here, a WAN is the best solution for tying together computer systems and LANs from different manufacturers for the purpose of enhancing human-to-human communications. Certainly, the fact that the communications links might not have speeds measured in millions of bits per second does not deter the effectiveness of electronic mail. Even the case where electronic mail goes through packet-switching networks and experiences delays at the packet level does not have an adverse effect.

But implementing office automation and electronic mail between systems is not a trivial task. For office automation, complex documents must be exchanged between systems that do not recognize each other's native file formats. Similarly, a mechanism is needed to enable one system to look across the network and see which files are where (this is also useful when performing general-purpose file transfers).

For electronic mail, the requirements are even more complex. Mail must be distributed to users who are often unknown to the system where the mail originates. The format for messages and documents might be different from system to system. And finally, the each type of system might use a totally different distribution technique.

This section will look at the following standards and services in this emerging area:

- *DCA/DIA.* Developed by IBM, the Document Content Architecture and Document Interchange Architecture have become de facto standards for exchanging documents between different manufacturers' systems.

- *X.400.* X.400 is a standard for interfacing diverse office automation systems. The number of products supporting this standard is increasing dramatically.

- *X.500.* X.500 is a standard for multivendor directory and file resources. Increasing acceptance of this standard has given birth to a number of X.500-compliant products. The directory services features of some network operating systems, including NetWare 4.x, Windows NT 5.0, and VINES, is based on this technology.

Ch
8

Document Content and Interchange Architectures

Even though from an application perspective the format of data is normally kept at a respectable distance from data communications and networking issues, the explosion of word processing and office automation tools has led to some key developments in the area of interoperability. The concern is not how the data gets from one system to another, but what format the data is in when it arrives.

For example, document interoperability is needed when two users are working on the same document, but each is based on a different computer system. Even in the simplest case where each user can work on his or her own separate section of the document, the final integration of each user's work still poses a problem. What if the two users needed to trade the document back and forth, each person adding his or her own edits and comments? Moreover, imagine how much more complicated the situation would be if more than two users were concurrently working on the same document.

IBM sought to address this dilemma with DCA/DIA. While the DIA addresses a much broader scope (specifically, the movement of documents among and between systems), the DCA has become a modern standard for document exchange. Specifically, the DCA defines two types of documents:

- *Revisable-form documents*. Contains the original document and its history of edits. This tracking of revisions not only allows changes to be removed, but more important, provides details on all changes made to the document. This type of historical tracking is often critical for maintaining contracts, specifications, and other documents of similar importance. Most modern word processors support the ability to convert to and from the DCA revisable-form document format.

- *Final-form documents*. The result of all edits; it is no longer truly revisable because the history of edits has been removed. The final-form document format is, however, supported by more hardware and software manufacturers, mostly because it is the easier of the two formats to implement.

Thus, DCA provides a common format that documents originating on different systems can convert to and from.

X.400

The X.400 standard specifies how to exchange electronic mail among diverse systems. In the context of X.400, electronic mail includes message exchanges, fully functional file transfers, and the transport of video images. Like X.25, X.400 is a standard, not a product, but X.400 products have taken to using the X.400 banner as an noun ("this product supports X.400") as opposed to a statement of compliance. And as with IBM's DCA/DIA approach, X.400 includes a set of formats for the mail it carries.

Within the structure of X.400, each user interacts with a *User Agent (UA)*. The UA is normally a software package that interfaces between the user and the X.400 electronic mail network. In the minicomputer/mainframe world, the UA could be, for example, Digital's ALL-IN-1, IBM's OfficeVision, or HP's Open DeskManager.

UAs never communicate directly with other UAs; instead, they forward their mail to a *Message Transfer Agent (MTA)*. The MTA then forwards the message to a UA or to another MTA if the final location for the electronic mail is not in the network domain of the first MTA (see Figure 8.4).

FIG. 8.4

X.400 User Agents and Message Transfer Agents

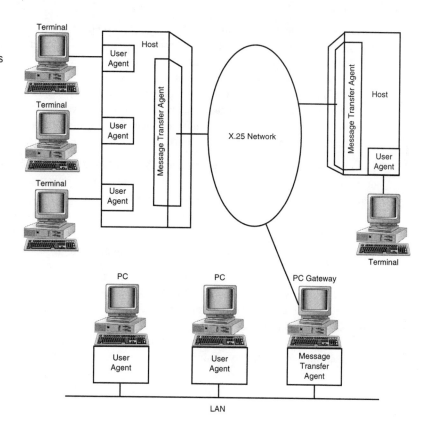

MTAs reroute mail until it reaches its final destination. These MTA routes are collectively referred to as the *Message Transfer Systems (MTS)*. Helping the MTAs move the data within the MTS is an additional utility called the *Reliable Transfer Server (RTS)*, which assists the MTA in determining the best route.

The X.400 standard has taken on a new life outside the dominion of the OSI Reference Model. Given the popularity of X.400 in the private sector, many computer manufacturers have adopted X.400 as a means of interfacing their office automation package with other vendors' office automation packages (providing they also support X.400). Thus, the X.400 standard is quickly giving birth to a large number of wide-area electronic mail networks.

The *X.400 Application Program Interface Association (XAPIA)* has released a new version of the *Common Messaging Call (CMC) API*. CMC 2.0 provides for greater interoperability between collaborative applications from different vendors. It supports features such as workflow, document management, and electronic data interchange; Version 1.0 of CMC only provided the capability to send and read messages, and to translate names into messaging addresses.

X.500

Whereas X.400 tackles electronic mail, X.500 focuses on user and resource directory services in large heterogeneous networks. While each computer manufacturer provides these services within its own proprietary network, the same services are, for the most part, unavailable when the network is composed of incompatible systems from different manufacturers. The X.500 standard is intended to provide this type of service within a global, multivendor network. Unlike the X.400 standard, X.500 has a relatively low profile because it is deeply integrated within other products and services that require multivendor access. For example, the X.400 electronic mail standard relies on the X.500 standard for its directory services.

The main point here is that a large company is likely to want a single, global directory for all users throughout the enterprise. This single directory might encompass multiple LAN systems. There are some difficulties involved in managing a global directory, including synchronization. Directory synchronization makes sure that each LAN directory is aware of any change in the enterprise.

There are a number of solutions for establishing a global directory:

- *StreetTalk.* One of the earliest directories, StreetTalk is part of the Banyan Systems VINES network operating system. The Universal StreetTalk directory service is being incorporated in equipment from a number of hardware and software vendors, including Cisco Systems, Oracle Corp., and SAP AG. However, until recently, Universal StreetTalk required a Vines server; but in order to compete in an increasingly tough market, Banyan has decided to unbundle its network services from Vines and offer them separately.

- *NDS.* Novell has now added the same facility for NetWare networks, in the NetWare Directory Service (NDS) product.

- *Windows NT 5.0.* Microsoft joined the fray late in the game, but plans to add global directory services in the newest release of Windows NT.

- *NIS+.* Sun's Network Information Services Plus (NIS+), bundled with several different UNIX operating systems, also competes in the global directory market. NIS+ is based on Sun's older NIS product, which was known as Yellow Pages. NIS+ uses a tree-based hierarchical directory, and keeps directories synchronized by transmitting only changes. The older version sent the entire directory map in the process of synchronization.

Although each of these vendor solutions has proprietary components, they are all moving toward supporting X.500 as a means of exchanging directory information between them.

X.500 Lite

X.500 Lite, also known as *Lightweight Directory Access Protocol (LDAP)*, presents users with a faster way to get data out of an X.500 directory. The full X.500 *Directory Access Protocol (DAP)* is much too processor-intensive to run on a standard desktop PC. Like DAP, LDAP takes information out of the X.500 directory service in response to queries. However, there are a few differences between DAP and LDAP that make LDAP much more bandwidth-conscious. With LDAP, there is a limit on the number of replies that can be returned in response to a query. LDAP also differs from DAP in that no referrals are allowed. Under DAP, if a server is unable to fulfill a query, a referral technique enables the search to continue on other servers. LDAP is easier to implement and use, and several vendors have announced plans to support the new standard, including Novell, Banyan Systems, Lotus Development and Netscape Communications.

LDAP supports these operations: search, add, delete, modify, modify RDN, bind, unbind, and abandon. It does not include the list and read functions found in the full X.500 implementation; rather, list and read are approximated with the LDAP search function.

An LDAP database record includes basic information, such as name and e-mail address, but can also include additional fields, such as address, phone, and public encryption key. LDAP was created at the University of Michigan under an NSF grant. A consortium of 40 companies have announced support for LDAP. If this type of support continues, the dream of an Internet-wide directory might eventually become a reality.

ON THE WEB

http://www.umich.edu/~rsug/ldap/   LDAP clients for several platforms are readily available from the University of Michigan Web site.

Emulation

Emulation is a software layer that enables one type of system to run applications meant for another type of system. Emulation software can display a PC window on a UNIX workstation screen, enabling the UNIX user to work as if she was working on a standard PC. Software that does the reverse (that is, it enables a PC to emulate UNIX) is also available. However, most emulation solutions suffer from sluggish performance and limited compatibility. There are several commercial emulation packages available. Some of the popular ones are the Macintosh Application Environment, which is a Motorola 68K emulator; Wabi (Windows application binary interface) from SunSoft (Chelmsford, Massachusetts); and Insignia Solutions Inc.'s (Inglewood, California) SoftWindows. Wabi and SoftWindows are x86 emulators that run on UNIX workstations.

Middleware

Application-to-application communications in a multivendor network can often be achieved through a new type of software, termed *middleware,* that sits between the application and the operating system. Developers can use it to accommodate multiple protocols, platforms, and languages, and exchange messages between applications. The goal of middleware is to give users seamless access to applications and data, regardless of platform or operating system. There are several types of middleware, including network gateways, Message-Oriented Middleware (MOM), remote procedure calls (RPCs), object request brokers (ORBs), and transaction processing (TP) monitors.

With *RPCs*, a client process calls a function on a remote server, waits for the result, then continues processing after the result is received. This synchronous model contrasts with the asynchronous techniques used with MOM and TP products, which queue messages. Synchronous middleware products are used in situations where bi-directional, real-time communications is essential; asynchronous communications are used where near-real-time is acceptable and high volume and speed are important.

MOM products handle message queuing in one of three ways:

- *Nonpersistent queuing* stores queue data in volatile memory, which increases performance, but is at risk of being lost in the event of network failure.
- *Persistent queuing* is slower than nonpersistent, but more secure. This type of queue data is stored on disk.
- *Transactional queuing* is also disk-based, but includes a mechanism for verifying that messages have been received.

TP monitors can maintain transactions over multiple servers, and are used in high-volume, critical environments.

Middleware is a vague term, and can have different meanings depending on the situation. Generally, middleware sits between the client and server, but it can also sit between the application and the database. Some middleware is based on messaging, while others are replication-oriented or transaction-oriented.

Object request brokers (ORBs) are not strictly middleware, but they might have a significant impact on the middleware market as the *Common Object Request Broker (CORBA)* architecture matures. One limitation of the ORB model is its limitations in connecting legacy systems to new architectures. Middleware is largely a custom business, with little available in terms of off-the-shelf, ready-to-run products. For more about CORBA and object technology, refer to Chapter 13, "Software Considerations."

Advances in middleware technology are permitting more end users to share information, regardless of the underlying network and operating system platform. For example, Teknekron Software Systems, Inc.'s Rendezvous Software Bus works as a communications software layer, which is able to translate data from different applications into a common format. Applications wanting to access data from a different application merely plug into the bus to access data from any source. With tools such as Rendezvous, it is no longer necessary to establish individual point-to-point links between many applications.

IBM's MQSeries middleware, a messaging and queuing technology, lets users establish links between client/server applications and legacy data. IBM has added object-oriented technology and asynchronous communications features to the middleware, which offers direct links to legacy TSO, IMS, and CICS packages. It is used to simplify the process of establishing application-to-application communications links, and permits applications to communicate asynchronously.

Novell's Tuxedo transaction processing monitor is being positioned as a key middleware tool for connecting Windows NT, UNIX, and mainframe systems into NetWare networks. With Tuxedo, developers can create distributed applications that are operating system-independent.

Fitting NetWare for a Tuxedo

Novell has established a partnership with BEA Systems (Sunnyvale, California) for future development of Tuxedo. The partnership will focus on integrating Tuxedo with NetWare. Tuxedo's namespace will be replaced with NetWare Directory Services (NDS), which will give NetWare users easy access to dozens of applications and processes running on multiple platforms. Under this scenario, a NetWare user could merely click an object in the NDS tree that represents a process or application running on any server. Consequently, users would no longer have to run live sessions in UNIX, NT, and NetWare simultaneously. Tuxedo would instead monitor calls to specific applications.

SNA-LAN Internetworking

As internetworks grow in size and complexity, many corporations are recognizing the need to integrate legacy data and applications with their LANs. Simply eliminating mainframes completely in favor of a distributed, client/server environment might initially sound attractive at first, but can be an enormously complex and costly procedure, especially if several mission-critical programs and datasets reside on a mainframe or midrange platform.

IBM has embraced the necessity for integration by enabling NetWare to be integrated with the AS/400. A new board-level file server for the AS/400 adds NetWare support to the platform. Previously, the AS/400 could only run IBM's own OS/2 LAN Server network operating system. Although LAN Server is faster than NetWare, NetWare integration is an important step because of NetWare's large presence. The addition of NetWare support will let the AS/400 run business applications perform file and print sharing, and eliminate costs by cutting out the need for additional PC servers.

There are a number of software options for connecting 32-bit Windows desktops to mainframe and midrange platforms. Vendors such as Wall Data, NetSoft, and Walker Richer & Quinn are offering connectivity software for this purpose. Wall Data is planning Windows 95 and Windows NT versions of the Rumba Office product; IBM is also getting into the game with the Personal Communications product family, available for Windows 95. Others include Attachmate's Extra Personal Client 6.0, NetSoft's NS/Elite and NS/Router, and WRQ's Reflection 3270 and Reflection AS/400. Many of these products offer much more than plain terminal emulation. Many support OLE 2.0 technology, and offer Windows users direct access to legacy databases.

IBM's 3172 Interconnect Controller Model 390 for the Network Control Program-Multinetwork Server (3172-390) attaches to a 3745 front-end processor, and is used to off-load SNA and

TCP/IP session establishment routines from the mainframe. This can significantly decrease WAN traffic, because administrative traffic no longer has to be sent across the WAN. The 3172-390 can be used as a tool to migrate to APPN. It supports TCP/IP routing as well as APPN, although this support can also be achieved with IBM's 3746-950.

IBM's front-end processor family, the 3746 Nways Multinetwork Controllers, can help you with the task of running SNA, APPN, and LAN traffic to the mainframe. Two models are available: the 900 and 950. The 3746-950 supports APPN, dependent LU Requestor (dLUR), and Enterprise Systems Connection mainframe links. dLUR is used to permit SNA devices to communicate over an APPN network. A later release of the 3746-950 will include support for TCP/IP routing protocols. IBM is also expected to add ATM and ISDN support.

The larger 3746-900 is used primarily in scenarios where you are migrating to APPN and deploying a multiprotocol backbone. The 3746-900, an expansion unit for the 3745 front-end processor, lets you retain your original investment in 3745s while participating in an APPN network.

One of the biggest factors in SNA/LAN integration is the availability of network management. Cisco Systems Inc. and Cabletron Systems Inc. have both released new products for managing routed networks carrying both SNA and LAN traffic. Cisco's CiscoWorks Blue and Cabletron's BlueVision 2.0 can consolidate management of an SNA/LAN internetwork.

One problem in integrating SNA with other systems is storage management. Storage Technology Corp. (Denver, Colorado) has a product called *Enterprise Volume Manager,* which unifies UNIX and mainframe storage management by allowing combined MVS/UNIX systems to share a single tape transport and library. The company has plans for multiplatform storage management products that accompany tape, disk, and solid state media. The *Expert Volume Manager* software is deployed by MVS users as a supplement to their tape management system and hierarchical storage management software, and brings many of the benefits of UNIX to the MVS environment.

Options for connecting Windows 95 to SNA environments emerged almost as soon as Windows 95 hit the streets. Microsoft's Windows 95 client for Microsoft SNA Server is an SNA gateway that lets Windows NT servers work as a bridge between Windows clients, IBM mainframes, and AS/400s. The Windows 95 client software serves as a platform for SNA applications running on Windows 95 and connecting to IBM hosts. Windows 95 Client for SNA Server provides Windows 95 users with access to the IBM mainframe for AS/400 applications and data. Those sites with large investments in IBM host systems can provide a Windows 95 desktop to their users, while still retaining their legacy systems. The client includes an ODBC driver that permits users to access all IBM DB2 databases. Windows 95 clients can also download large host files.

Third-party products are also widely available for connecting Windows 95 to host platforms. ●

CHAPTER 9

PC LAN Network
Operating Systems

As discussed in Chapter 8, "Services," PC LANs rely on a robust set of services delivered to PC clients by designated server systems. Originally, PC LAN servers only provided simple file and print services, but over time the role of a PC LAN server has expanded to include application serving, database support, transaction processing, and a variety of other client/server-related functions. In many ways, the growing and expanding role of the PC LAN server is challenging the traditional services offered by commercial midrange and mainframe computers.

Although a variety of vendors competed for the fledgling PC LAN market in the 1980s, one company managed to obtain the lion's share of the market—that company was Novell. Novell's product, NetWare, ran on a dedicated PC and provided simple file and print services to other PCs in the network. NetWare became widely popular largely because it was one of the few products on the market that enabled you to use whatever type of LAN you preferred— you could implement NetWare over ARCnet, Ethernet, or Token Ring. Most of the other contemporary PC LAN products were tied to specific LAN types or specific LAN adapters.

NetWare set the stage for the emerging PC LAN market by defining the capabilities consumers expected out of a file and print server. Of course, no leading product can stay unchallenged for long, and Novell's NetWare soon faced serious competition from products offered by Banyan Systems (VINES), IBM (LAN Server and then OS/2), and Microsoft (LAN Manager, Windows for Workgroups, Windows 95, and Windows NT).

The following is a quick overview of these four companies and their PC LAN products.

- *Novell*. As the market leader, Novell set the stage for a long line of PC LAN innovations that extend well beyond simple file and print services. Novell designed the *NetWare Load Module (NLM)* to enable third-party companies to write server-side NetWare applications and enterprise-oriented features, such as fault tolerance and data recovery. In terms of scalability, Novell extended the power and performance of NetWare by allowing other companies to port NetWare from its Intel-only origin to high-end RISC systems, such as the HP9000. At the network level, the routing capabilities and simple client configuration of Novell's IPX protocol suite enables NetWare customers to easily construct networks of any size. Novell has further reinforced the ease-of-installation and ease-of-maintenance of NetWare with the release of *NetWare Directory Services (NDS)*, a global directory structure for all NetWare resources.

- *Banyan Systems*. Banyan Systems' *VINES (VIrtual NEtwork Software)* provides file and print serving services similar to NetWare, but VINES runs with existing network protocols, such as TCP/IP, SNA, and others. More significantly, VINES was the first PC LAN product to support a network directory service, which Banyan named *StreetTalk*. StreetTalk presents a single directory that encompasses multiple servers and allows users to login only once to access multiple servers. Of course, Novell later added its own network directory service in version 4.1 of NetWare, and other network operating systems vendors are following suit. Banyan is, however, unbundling StreetTalk, and offering it for other platforms, such as Windows NT.

- *IBM*. IBM's original PC LAN product was the *LAN Server,* a dedicated server product that shares the same protocol suite (NetBIOS/NetBEUI) and same overall architecture as Microsoft's LAN Manager product. This should not be a big surprise because IBM was one of the core developers of the NetBIOS/NetBEUI protocol suite and the Server Message Block (SMB) architecture used by IBM, Microsoft, and others. IBM's DOS-based LAN Server technology was then integrated into it's *OS/2* server product. OS/2-based file and print servers have achieved a reputation for stability and reliability; however, OS/2 servers tend to be implemented in sites that have other IBM equipment—AS/400 and mainframes in particular.

- *Microsoft*. Microsoft acquired most of its networking technology from 3Com Corporation. Microsoft incorporated the 3Com technology in its main product lines, starting with *LAN Manager,* a dedicated file and print server similar to IBM's LAN Server offering. Microsoft then went on to extend its networking technology into workgroup environments with the release of *Windows for Workgroups* and *Windows 95*. None of these Microsoft products offered the stability or performance of a dedicated Novell NetWare server—but this changed with the advent of *Windows NT Server.* Windows NT Server is an enterprise-oriented product that can compete head-to-head with NetWare. Windows NT Server also offers additional features and value—most notably, the capability to run on a wide range of platforms, fully integrated support for TCP/IP, and support for a range of software products that enable an NT Server to function as a full-blown application server.

The PC LAN products offered by all four of these vendors (Novell, Banyan, IBM, and Microsoft) remain in use today, but two specific products are now competing to dominate the modern market: Novell's NetWare and Microsoft's Windows NT Server. With this in mind, the remainder of this chapter will focus on NetWare and Windows NT Server.

Novell NetWare

As discussed previously, Novell pioneered the PC LAN network operating system in the PC market. From a technology perspective, however, Novell offered few true innovations in the area of file and print sharing—most of the concepts Novell implemented were borrowed from other computer markets. For example, if you look closely you can see that the original NetWare implementation bears a striking resemblance to Sun's NFS implementation.

Although you can find fault with Novell's lack of technical innovation in its early days, you certainly cannot fault Novell's marketing expertise. In the early days of PC LANs, a number of companies—some big, some small—rushed products to market to claim space in the exploding market. In all fairness, many of these products offered technical features and functions superior to NetWare; however, none of the companies behind those products could match Novell's marketing effort. Novell took a solid, but hardly best-of-breed product, and leveraged it into a leadership position through salesmanship and marketing savvy.

Of course, after Novell gained control of the market, they made major develop investments in NetWare to shore up some of the technical inadequacies and insure it's longevity in the market. One of the key early developments was the release of a *System Fault Tolerance (SFT)* version of NetWare that addressed the data protection/data recovery demands of large businesses.

Another early criticism of NetWare was that it was a *closed* operating system—you had to run NetWare in a dedicated Intel-based system. Novell addressed this complaint two ways. First, Novell licensed other companies to port NetWare to non-Intel systems, such as high-performance UNIX systems. These systems were quite capable of running both NetWare and other business applications concurrently. Second, Novell developed an application environment inside the NetWare server that permitted third-party companies to write server-side programs. These programs are referred to as *NetWare Load Modules (NLM)* and can handle system-oriented functions, such as tape backup or application-oriented functions. When used in an application capacity, the server-side component is typically part of a larger, client/server application.

Like any large, prosperous, and fast-growing company, some of Novell's new products and new ideas were less than successful. For example, back in the early days of PCs, when PC hardware was still quite expensive, customers demanded a non-dedicated version of NetWare so they could also use the server system as a desktop system. Although Novell did, in fact, come out with a non-dedicated version of NetWare, the implementation was very awkward and desktop performance was so unpredictable that the product was impractical to use in most environments.

Novell also proved itself capable of making mistakes on an even grander scale. At one point Novell went through a phase of acquisition-mania, purchasing a broad set of companies and products that had nothing to do with NetWare. The intent of these acquisitions was for Novell to broaden its base beyond NetWare and to enter the highly competitive (and lucrative) application suite market. During this phase, Novell purchased high-profile products such as WordPerfect and Quattro Pro.

In addition to acquiring application-oriented products, Novell also acquired a full-blown implementation of UNIX that it renamed UnixWare. At the time, Novell's plan was to create a "SuperNOS" by merging NetWare and UnixWare. This SuperNOS would enable Novell to better compete with the emerging Windows NT product as well as with the ever-popular UNIX operating system.

Unfortunately for Novell, neither the application suite nor the SuperNOS strategy panned out—Novell succeeded only in wasting millions of dollars and years of research. Worse, Novell's lack of focus during this phase enabled Windows NT to penetrate deep into Novell's file and print server market.

Since that time, Novell has divested itself of both the application and UNIX products and has recommitted itself to enhancing NetWare on several fronts. On one front, Novell has launched a Smart Global Network initiative. Under this initiative NetWare services will be extended to the Internet and to other types of networks so NetWare can become the central focus of networking in a heterogeneous environment. Additionally, Novell's Net2000 initiative is targeted to establish an open set of APIs that will permit users to access network services from non-NetWare platforms and help ease the task of building distributed applications.

Novell has clearly realized that it is becoming rare for an enterprise to use a single server operating system. With this in mind, Novell plans to integrate Microsoft, HP, IBM, Sun, and SCO server platforms by making them all manageable via Novell's NetWare Directory Services (NDS). NDS, introduced in NetWare 4.1, is a global directory service that provides an organized, hierarchical structure for the administration and management of network resources (in other words, users, file servers, shared printers, and so on).

NDS offers a significant advantage over the older NetWare bindery. Under NDS, the entire network appears to the end user as a single entity, and permits a single log on to access all servers and shared network resources. Because the NDS structure is replicated across servers, there is no single point of failure. The NDS naming hierarchy can contain up to 15 levels of names (StreetTalk offers only a three-level naming hierarchy). This allows for a great deal of flexibility, but also raises the potential of creating overly complex or difficult-to-use names for network resources. In a very real sense, NDS has become Novell's key competitive advantage in the PC LAN market.

Integrating NDS

Rather than limiting NDS to a NetWare-only environment, Novell is extending NDS to other environments. For example, Novell is working with HP to join DCE software with NDS in a future 64-bit UNIX release. Novell is also collaborating with SCO so that it can merge NDS with the 32-bit SCO UNIX systems. Similar plans are underway for integrating NDS with other vendor operating systems, as well as for releasing NDS client software for a variety of desktop operating systems.

Finally, Novell is also improving NetWare's position in large enterprise environments. In large environments, NetWare worked well as file and print servers, but did not fare well as database or messaging servers. To address this limitation, Novell has introduced *NetWare Symmetrical Multi-Processing (SMP) 4.1,* which enables NetWare to take advantage of multiple processor hardware platforms. Under this release, an SMP NLM replaces the NetWare OS kernel that comes with 4.x. SMP's multiprocessor performance is comparable to that of NT, and scales well with additional CPUs. NetWare 4.1 SMP is currently available only from server hardware vendors, but Novell is also planning to introduce a shrink-wrapped version.

Ch

9

Basic Architecture

The server aspect of NetWare was designed to operate in a dedicated, Intel-based system. Although NetWare has been ported to non-Intel systems where it can run alongside other applications, the majority of NetWare installations are, in fact, dedicated, Intel-based servers. In this environment, the core NetWare system is launched from DOS—you boot up the server under DOS and then run NetWare. At that point, NetWare takes over the system and DOS is no longer the dominate operating system.

The configuration and management of a NetWare system can be performed at the system console, which is the keyboard and the monitor attached to the system. The system console provides a simple, character-mode interface for configuration and administration tasks. Alternatively, NetWare contains a remote console utility that enables you to perform most console functions from a client workstation. In contrast, the configuration and management of the NetWare user environment is typically performed from a client workstation using an administration tool.

Originally, NetWare used server-based security that required each user to log on to every server on which he or she needed resources. With the advent of NDS, however, user permissions can be set up on a network-wide basis, and each user simply has to log on to the network once. After a user logs on, NetWare can activate a user-specific batch program (a log on script) that allocates the resources the user accesses on a regular basis. For example, the log on script can mount NetWare directories as network disk drives so the user can access specific applications or business data.

The configuration of the client-side software that handles the communication between the client system and the NetWare server(s) has changed dramatically as NetWare has evolved. For NetWare releases prior to 3.12, the client-side software that handles traffic to/from the network adapter has to be "generated" using the NetWare utility WSGEN.

WSGEN is an interactive program that combines software that handles the physical network adapter in a client PC with software that implements the NetWare IPX protocol. WSGEN outputs a program file called IPX.COM that must be loaded in each PC prior to accessing the NetWare network. You need a version of IPX.COM for every unique type of network adapter in your PC network, and you must make sure each version of IPX.COM pairs with the network adapter it was generated to use.

In a pure NetWare environment, you load IPX.COM in the AUTOEXEC.BAT file. Because IPX.COM handles all the network adapter functions, NetWare requires no CONFIG.SYS device drivers. After IPX.COM loads, a second NetWare program, NETX.COM, is launched to integrate the NetWare functions into the DOS environment. After NETX.COM loads, you can log on to a NetWare server and start accessing NetWare services (for example, drivers, printers, NetWare Loadable Modules).

By most standards, interactively generating an executable file (in other words, IPX.COM) to handle each type of LAN adapter is less than ideal, especially if you have more than one type of adapter in your network. For example, if you're installing a workstation in a remote department and you bring the wrong IPX.COM file, you're basically out of luck. You also have an issue of version control—if you generate multiple IPX.COM files, you have to figure out how to identify which file applies to which adapter.

Given the awkward nature of WSGEN, network vendors looked at the problem of marrying proprietary protocols to a wide range of network adapters and tried to find a better approach. One of the key outcomes of this investigation came in 1988 when IBM, Microsoft, and 3Com introduced the *Network Driver Interface Specification (NDIS)* as part of the OS/2 LAN Server. NDIS addresses the problem of marrying adapter boards to protocols by dividing the functions into two logical layers:

- *Adapter interface layer.* Manages and communicates with the physical adapter. The adapter interface presents a "generic" interface to the network interface layer (described below), so every adapter essentially looks the same.

- *Network interface layer.* Implements the desired network protocols (for example, NetBIOS/NetBEUI or TCP/IP) and communicates with the physical adapter via the "generic" interface the adapter interface layer provides.

Novell was not blind to NDIS's development. But instead of embracing NDIS, Novell created its own solution—the *Open Data-link Interface (ODI)*. Like NDIS, ODI separates the physical network adapter's functions from those of the network protocol. Despite the apparent similarities, however, ODI is not compatible with NDIS (although NetWare does include an ODI "shim" module—*ODINSUP*—that enables NDIS and ODI traffic to coexist on the same physical adapter).

Novell's ODI standard requires certain files and programs to integrate network protocols with a wide variety of network adapters. Unlike Microsoft's Network Driver Interface Specification (NDIS), ODI does not require any device drivers in the CONFIG.SYS file. Instead, ODI operates from a batch file (normally the AUTOEXEC.BAT startup file) or directly from a command prompt. The ODI programs include:

- *LSL.COM.* The *Link Support Layer (LSL)* program is NetWare's ODI baseline program. It interfaces with vendor-supplied adapter programs and provides a consistent interface to the higher-level ODI modules.

- *XXXXXXXX.COM.* Each network adapter manufacturer provides a software driver that operates with the LSL program. For example, the SMC8000.COM program provides an interface to the Western Digital and SMC line of Ethernet Plus adapters.

Specific programs are then layered on top of the previous two files to implement network-specific features and functions. These files are:

- *IPXODI.COM.* This program implements NetWare's core IPX protocol suite over the underlying ODI drivers. It is analogous to the IPX.COM program used in pre-ODI environments.
- *VLM.EXE.* The *Virtual Load Module (VLM)* program starts specific NetWare work-station services based on the configuration file (described in the following paragraph). This program is the analogous to the NETX.COM program used in pre-ODI environments.

All the programs obtain configuration information from the NET.CFG file, a text file that defines the hardware's operational characteristics (for example, IRQ setting, port value, and DMA address), the operating parameters for the various ODI programs, and the interrelationships between the programs.

NetWare also includes client software for other, non-PC clients. Although the implementation details for these other environments are obviously different then for a PC environment, they all accomplish the same net result—a connection to a NetWare server.

Network Support

As previously noted, NetWare typically relies on the Internet Packet Exchange (IPX) protocol as the network transport between the client and server systems. Although Novell is aggressively moving toward supporting TCP/IP instead of IPX, the majority of NetWare installations still use IPX as the primary transport.

In reality, IPX is not really a single protocol, but actually a suite of protocols (much like TCP/IP). IPX can carry a number of service protocols, including the *Sequenced Packet eXchange (SPX)* protocol. By itself, IPX is a connectionless protocol that does not guarantee delivery of messages. SPX, on the other hand, is a connection-oriented protocol that runs as an extension to IPX and provides confirmation (or denial) of the end-to-end delivery of messages.

NetWare service protocols can run under just IPX, or the IPX/SPX combination. These services include:

- *NetWare Core Protocol (NCP).* This protocol handles the mainstream NetWare services, including accessing files and printers on NetWare servers.
- *Burst Mode Protocol.* This is a variation of the NetWare Core Protocol. Designed for high-volume applications, Burst Mode enables a client to request and receive more data in a single message than under NCP.
- *Service Advertising Protocol (SAP).* File, print, communication, and other types of servers announce themselves at regular intervals using this protocol. Client PC's "listen" for this protocol to determine what resources are available within the network. Clients can also use this protocol to inquire about the capabilities of specific servers.

Ch
9

■ *Routing Information Protocol (RIP)*. This protocol is used to help a message move from one NetWare network to a second NetWare network. Routing protocols like RIP is an important factor in how wide-area networks are constructed.

The IPX protocol suite is clearly one of the factors contributing to NetWare's success because IPX has a number of advantages over the two other protocol suites commonly used in PC LANs (in other words, NetBIOS/NetBEUI and TCP/IP). These advantages include:

■ Unlike TCP/IP, IPX does not require an extensive addressing scheme for clients and servers. IPX, like NetBIOS/NetBEUI, relies on the hardware addresses burned into network adapters.

■ Although IPX does not implement its own system-level addressing scheme, it is a fully routable protocol (that is, it supports network address assignments). Because IPX is fully routable, you can interconnect multiple NetWare LANs in a relatively simple fashion. In contrast, TCP/IP is also fully routable but NetBIOS/NetBEUI is not.

■ IPX is a relatively efficient protocol because it does not rely on client-initiated broadcast messages to establish client/server connections (as is the case in NetBIOS/NetBEUI) and it uses bit-based flags in its headers (unlike TCP/IP, which uses byte-based flags).

Microsoft Windows NT Server

Windows NT Server is the result of the successes and failures Microsoft has experienced with its earlier products and projects. Windows NT Server was clearly affected by the success of LAN Manager and Windows for Workgroups, as well as the failure of Microsoft's involvement with OS/2. If nothing else, Windows NT Server (and Windows NT Workstation) is a genuine commercial-class operating system—Microsoft's first entry into the marketplace of enterprise-oriented data processing.

Windows NT Server has not always been the darling of the industry. In fact, the early releases of the product weren't exactly welcomed with enthusiasm. The first change that steered Windows NT towards its current success came with the 3.51 release of Windows NT—a release that introduced support for native Microsoft file and print services over TCP/IP, IPX, and NetBEUI. This seemingly subtle change in networking support enabled Windows NT to be easily deployed in existing networks.

Although version 3.51 enabled Windows NT to enter into new corporations and gain new respect and appreciation in the industry, that change was nothing in comparison to the changes that occurred in version 4.0 of Windows NT. Version 4.0 featured the same user interface as Windows 95, which positioned Microsoft as a provider of a complete client/server solution with a consistent, easy-to-use and easy-to-manage user interface and user environment.

Of course, version 4.0 also contained significant improvements over 3.51. For example, all of the NetWare coexistence/migration tools (further discussed in the "NetWare/Windows NT Server Integration" section at the end of this chapter) were included on the distribution CD (they had previously been sold separately). Windows NT Server 4.0 also featured better TCP/IP integration, including the capability to operate as a DNS server and as a Web server (via the

Internet Information Server included on the distribution CD). Support for TCP/IP integration is proving to be a critical component for Windows NT.

Window NT 5.0 and the Internet

In the future (5.0) release of Windows NT, the desktop environment will be Internet aware—enabling you to open up a Web page just as easily as you can open a document on your hard disk. Furthermore, many of the enhancements to 5.0, including Microsoft's new directory services, are only targeted to run under TCP/IP. Microsoft is clearly betting that TCP/IP will be the protocol suite of choice in most public and private networks.

Another subtle change that occurred after the 4.0 release of Windows NT was Microsoft's approach to new products. Prior to 4.0, the details of new products and features were kept under wraps. After 4.0, however, Microsoft began a massive program of announcing and releasing beta versions of most of its new products via the Internet. Although Microsoft originally began this effort to better position its free Internet Explorer Web browser against Netscape's Navigator web browser, the program has since grown to epic proportions.

One final key point that separates Windows NT Server from NetWare is that Windows NT Server is clearly more than just a file and print server—Windows NT Server is an application server. Unlike NetWare, which requires vendors to write NLMs, Windows NT Server can host conventional, Windows-based applications. Client/server connections can be accommodated to these applications using direct program-to-program communication, ODBC (a distributed data base connection), and more recently ActiveX (a network-based Object Linking and Embedding solution).

Microsoft's commitment to delivering an application server can be seen in its investment in the *BackOffice suite* of programs. BackOffice contains a powerful database component (SQL Server), a mail/messaging component (Exchange), a legacy connectivity component (SNA Server), a system management component (SMS), and a fast-growing variety of Web-based applications built around Microsoft's Internet Information Server.

In fact, for several years Microsoft was willing not to challenge NetWare for traditional file and print business, concentrating instead on the application server focus. Microsoft's reasoning was that if it could get a Windows NT Server into a corporation as a mission-critical application server, the file and print business would eventually migrate to them anyway. This has proven to be a successful strategy, although recently Microsoft has become more willing to compete head-to-head with NetWare for conventional file and print server business.

Basic Architecture

Windows NT Server can be hosted by systems using Intel or DEC Alpha processors. Earlier in its history, Windows NT Server also supported MIPS processor systems; however, MIPS will no longer be supported as of the 5.0 release of Windows NT. Support for NT on the PowerPC has also been phased out by both Motorola and IBM, and it is unlikely that Microsoft will continue to support the PowerPC architecture in subsequent releases.

The basic functions of Windows NT Server are consistent across all these types of systems, but additional application programs might not be available for all processor types. For this reason, Intel-based machines are deployed in the majority of Windows NT Server installations.

In addition to supporting different types of systems, Windows NT supports Symmetrical Multi-Processing (SMP); therefore, Windows NT can immediately take advantage of systems with multiple CPUs. You can deploy a Windows NT Server in a one- or two-processor configuration and then upgrade it to a three- or four-processor configuration when you need additional performance improvements. Obviously, the base hardware system you're using to host Windows NT Server must support multiple processor configurations for you to perform this kind of upgrade.

Processor configuration aside, Windows NT Server runs as a non-dedicated operating system—you can use the same system for desktop applications if you so desire (however, most corporations prefer to run Windows NT Server as a dedicated system). In fact, Windows NT Server is very similar to its desktop counterpart, Windows NT Workstation. Detailed analysis has shown that the operating system kernel is the same for both products. Windows NT Server has, however, been fine tuned for server performance and includes additional software not available for Windows NT Workstation.

The fact that Windows NT Server has a full GUI appearance makes it relatively simple to configure and administer all aspects of the server environment. You can manage a Windows NT Server from the local keyboard and monitor and, as in the case of NetWare, you can manage it from other workstations in the network. However, many of the configuration and testing utilities are still command-line based.

In terms of security, Windows NT offers two types of security models: *workgroups* and *domains*. In a workgroup model, the user authentication process occurs on each system in the workgroup. Other workgroup systems "trust" that each system has performed the authentication. In a domain model, however, all users are authenticated by a central server (termed the domain controller). Using a centralized server provides greater control and security.

From a broader perspective, workgroups are informal groupings of systems that elect to share resources with one another. Domains, on the other hand, are formal collections of systems that can be centrally controlled and administered. The informal nature of workgroups makes it difficult to implement them as large, enterprise-wide solutions.

Unlike workgroups, domains can be interconnected. When you interconnect domains, you can establish trust relationships between them so a user logged on to one domain can access resources in another domain without being forced to log on to the second domain. Although this approach works well in simple organizations, trust relationships can grow very complex in large organizations. (For that reason, Microsoft is moving toward global, NDS-like directory services. These new directory services are planned for availability in the 5.0 release of Windows NT.)

One of the most unique aspects of Windows NT networking is how Windows NT separates client/server and peer-to-peer services from the underlying network protocol. Under Windows NT, you can choose the protocol you want to use in your network—NetBEUI, IPX, or TCP/IP—without worrying how it will affect Windows NT services for file sharing, printer sharing, and program-to-program communications. This flexibility enables you to construct and administer powerful networks that can address the needs of your company without being compromised by the demands of your existing client or server computers.

Microsoft's model for integrating network protocols with network adapters is, of course, the NDIS model previously discussed in this chapter. Microsoft's implementation of NDIS has, however, gone through dramatic changes to keep pace with Microsoft's relentless march of new operating systems.

For example, when NDIS originally started out in the DOS environment, it was a completely static model where all protocols had to be bound to the network adapters at boot time via the CONFIG.SYS file and then activated via a "NETBIND" command in the AUTOEXEC.BAT file. The detailed information about adapter settings (IRQ, DMA, port address, and so on) and about the protocols was placed in a separate PROTOCOL.INI file.

Ch
9

After all of the protocols were locked and loaded, you could not add new protocols nor could you unload any running protocols without reconfiguring your system and rebooting it. This structure worked fairly well for DOS but it proved to be difficult to operate under Windows. Therefore, Microsoft made some subtle changes to its NDIS support when it introduced Windows for Workgroups.

Under Windows for Workgroups, Microsoft moved the PROTOCOL.INI file into the Windows directory and moved some of the information that had been contained in the file into some of the standard Windows configurations files (for example, SYSTEM.INI and WIN.INI). Microsoft also introduced the NDIS *Demand Protocol Architecture (DPA)*. Under DPA, network interface drivers can be loaded as terminate-and-stay-resident (TSR) routines from the DOS command line (or AUTOEXEC.BAT file) instead of as device drivers from the CONFIG.SYS file.

Despite the integration into Windows for Workgroups, NDIS support remained mainly under the control of DOS. The network protocols were set up and activated before Windows was even launched. This same strategy could not work under Windows 95 and Windows NT because neither of those operating systems feature an underlying DOS layer to handle NDIS functions. As a result, NDIS had to be completely integrated into Windows 95 and Windows NT. Of course, you still need to reboot your system to activate any changes you make to your protocol environment.

Windows NT Server contains client software for all PC environments (DOS, Windows, Windows for Workgroups, and Windows 95). Windows NT Server has the capacity to emulate a Macintosh file and print server; therefore, some level of integration is available with Macs without requiring any changes or new software in Mac clients. Support for UNIX clients and other clients must be obtained from third-party companies.

Network Support

In order to appreciate the advantages of the Windows NT multi-protocol network support, you need to look back at the original networking model used by IBM, Microsoft, and others. This model was created in 1984 when IBM and Sytek released a LAN-based message interface system named the *Network Basic Input/Output System,* better known today as *NetBIOS.* NetBIOS is a generalized program-to-program communication facility that enables peer-to-peer and client/server communications between PCs operating in a LAN environment.

NetBIOS facilitates communication through three key services:

- *Name service.* Each PC using NetBIOS is assigned a logical name (for example, MKT1, SALES, KELLY, and so on), and other PCs use that name to communicate with that PC. PCs learn about one each others names by listening to announcements PCs make when they join the LAN (for example, "MKT1 now available for service") or by broadcasting a discovery request for a name (for example, "KELLY, are you there?"). Each PC keeps track of the names of other PCs in a local, dynamic table. No centralized name servers are required (or supported).

- *Session service.* A PC can establish a session with another PC by "calling" it by name. After the target PC agrees to communicate with the requesting PC, the two PCs can exchange messages with one another until one of them "hangs up." Session service is a connection-oriented service, so while the two PCs are communicating with one another, NetBIOS provides message sequencing and message acknowledgments to insure that all messages sent are properly received.

- *Datagram service.* Datagram service is a connectionless service that does not require a PC to establish a session with another PC in order to send messages and does not guarantee the receipt of any messages sent. Datagram services can be used to deliver broadcast or informational messages. Application-level session controls and acknowledgments can also be placed on top of datagram services to make them more reliable.

In addition to these three core services, NetBIOS provides a limited number of status and control functions. For example, these functions can be used to cancel a NetBIOS request, discover the current status of the NetBIOS interface, or start a NetBIOS-level trace.

When NetBIOS was first released, the term NetBIOS encompassed both protocol-level and service-level functions. As the industry moved toward using well-defined computing models that separate protocols from services (among other things), the NetBIOS protocol and service aspects were formally separated and the term *NetBIOS Extended User Interface (NetBEUI)* was adopted to define the protocol-level functions.

Microsoft pioneered the usage of the term NetBEUI and included support for the NetBIOS/ NetBEUI combination in its DOS-based LAN Manager product, in its Windows for Workgroups (WFW) offering, and, of course, in its Windows NT Workstation and Server products. Unfortunately, while Microsoft clearly distinguishes between the NetBIOS and NetBEUI functions, many other vendors continue to use the term NetBIOS to refer to both protocol and service functions.

As noted, NetBIOS provides a generalized interface for program-to-program communications. NetBIOS does not, however, provide specific services to facilitate file, print, and other user-related services in a peer-to-peer or client/server LAN. That task falls on the shoulders of *Server Message Blocks (SMB).*

Like NetBIOS, SMB is an interface system. But where NetBIOS is a generalized interface system, SMB is a specific interface system that enables file sharing, print sharing, and user-based messaging. Some of the specific services supported by SMB include:

- *Connection Related Services*

    Start/end connection

- *File Related Services*

    Get disk attributes

    Create/delete directory

    Search for file name(s)

    Create/delete/rename file

    Read/write file

    Lock/unlock file area

    Open/commit/close file

    Get/set file attributes

- *Print Related Services*

    Open/close spool file

    Write to spool file

    Query print queue

- *User Related Services*

    Discover home system for user name

    Send message to user

    Broadcast message to all users

    Receive user message(s)

In the Windows NT environment, SMB functions are integrated into the operating system. For example, when you use File Manager to connect to a network drive (or you issue a "NET USE" command), you are invoking SMB functions. Also note that NetBIOS and SMB often work together. For example, when you go to connect to a network drive, you rely on NetBIOS services to find the name of the system sponsoring the directory you need, but you actually connect to and access that network drive using SMB services.

As successful as the SMB/NetBIOS/NetBEUI architecture has been, it is not without its limitations:

- As discussed earlier, NetBIOS uses system names to enable and manage end-to-end connections. Under NetBIOS, names are resolved using broadcast-oriented techniques. For example, when a system joins the LAN it broadcasts its name and when a system wants to establish a connection to a system it has not previously heard from, it broadcasts a name discovery message. Unfortunately, broadcasts create overhead in a LAN and can negatively affect overall performance.

Ch
9

- NetBEUI does not use any addresses other than the physical LAN adapter address (also known as the *Medium Access Control,* or *MAC,* address). In contrast, protocols like IPX and TCP/IP add a second level of addressing that defines a network address. This second level address enables IPX and TCP/IP to quickly determine if a transmitted message needs to be routed to another physical network (because it has a different network address) or if it can be serviced on the local network. Because NetBEUI does not use a second level address, NetBEUI cannot distinguish between local and non-local messages, and is therefore considered a non-routable protocol.

When you combine the NetBIOS limitation with the NetBEUI limitation, you end up with network traffic that is difficult to manage over multiple, interconnected LANs or in a complex LAN/WAN environment. Specifically, you have NetBIOS generating lots of broadcast messages to resolve names, and because NetBEUI does not support network addressing, these broadcasts must be sent to all of the attached LANs. In effect, NetBIOS and NetBEUI aggravate each other's limitations.

Fortunately, Microsoft recognized the limitations of NetBIOS and NetBEUI and included alternate approaches in the network architecture for Windows NT. Under Windows NT, you are not forced to run NetBIOS and SMB over NetBEUI—you can, in fact, choose the network protocol that makes the most sense for your organization's overall network composition. Because you are no longer forced to use NetBEUI for native Microsoft networking traffic, you are no longer constrained by the NetBEUI limitation.

What LAN-level protocols can you choose from? Microsoft provides three protocols that can be used to carry NetBIOS and SMB traffic:

- *NetBEUI Frames (NBF).* This is an enhanced version of NetBEUI that supports a larger number of systems than the original NetBEUI protocol. Unfortunately, the enhanced version does not include any network addresses and therefore still suffers from the same internetworking limitation as the original protocol.

- *Internetwork Packet eXchange/Sequenced Packet eXchange (IPX/SPX).* As noted, IPX and SPX are the main protocols used in Novell NetWare networks. IPX is a connectionless protocol with no guaranteed delivery and SPX is a connection-oriented protocol with guaranteed delivery.

- *Transmission Control Protocol/Internet Protocol (TCP/IP).* TCP/IP is actually a suite of protocols that include TCP, IP, the User Datagram Protocol (UDP), and several other service protocols. TCP is a connection-oriented protocol with guaranteed delivery and UDP is a connectionless protocol with no guarantees. Both TCP and UDP rely on IP to resolve network addresses and facilitate the end-to-end delivery of messages.

As previously noted, TCP/IP and IPX implement network addresses; therefore, they are both considered routable protocols that can easily be integrated into multi-LAN environments and large wide area networks. This makes either protocol a superior choice to NetBEUI for most applications.

Unfortunately, the standard implementations of TCP/IP and IPX do not address the broadcast-intensive nature of NetBIOS. Because NetBIOS operates above the LAN-layer protocol, it is isolated from the technical details of the underlying protocol, and by the some token, the underlying protocol is isolated from the technical details of NetBIOS. That means that NetBIOS name resolution will, by default, be handled using broadcast techniques, regardless of which LAN-layer protocol is in use.

Microsoft did, however, address this problem by creating optional enhancements for the TCP/IP implementation in Windows NT—and only for the TCP/IP implementation. Specifically, Microsoft borrowed an idea (or two) from the way TCP/IP is implemented in a UNIX environment and implemented three ways of resolving NetBIOS name requests without generating broadcasts:

- *LMHOSTS*. You can configure a LMHOSTS file in each Windows NT system. LMHOSTS is a simple text file that contains a list of NetBIOS names and the corresponding TCP/IP address for each name. This is similar to the way that UNIX hosts use a HOSTS file to resolve native TCP/IP name-to-address translations. (You should note that Windows NT also supports a HOSTS file for TCP/IP traffic that does not involve NetBIOS.)

- *WINS*. You can implement a *Windows Internet Name Service* server. A WINS server provides a centralized database that maps NetBIOS names to TCP/IP addresses. When a WINS client wants to know the address for a NetBIOS name, it simply asks a WINS server. This is similar to the way that UNIX hosts use Domain Name System (DNS) or Network Information Service (NIS) name servers.

- *DNS*. You can also use a DNS server (UNIX or Windows NT Server) to resolve NetBIOS names into TCP/IP addresses. Microsoft is currently moving away from WINS and toward DNS as its preferred method of NetBIOS name resolution.

A given Windows NT system can use any one or a combination of any of these approaches. In the event none of the above approaches are used, the NT system will resort to using broadcasts for name resolution. Assuming, however, that one of these approaches is in place, the TCP/IP software in a Windows NT system will look for NetBIOS name discovery requests. When it sees such a request, it will send an inquiry request to a WINS server or look for the name in its local LMHOSTS file.

Finally, please note that the Windows NT implementation of TCP/IP also supports a dynamic IP address assignment protocol—the *Dynamic Host Configuration Protocol (DHCP)*. DHCP greatly simplifies the configuration of client systems in a TCP/IP network. Instead of assigning and configuring unique IP addresses in each client PC, you simply configure them to use DHCP and they will automatically receive an IP address assignment from a DHCP server system (typically a Windows NT Server system).

The real beauty (from a networking perspective) of the Windows NT environment is that it enables you to deploy multiple protocols on a concurrent basis. With Windows NT you can run native Windows NT networking services over IPX and run native TCP/IP services (in other words, Telnet, and ftp) over TCP/IP. Alternatively, you can run native NetWare services over IPX and run native Windows NT networking services over TCP/IP. You can even deploy all three protocol suites—NetBEUI, IPX, and TCP/IP—and enable native and non-native services over all of them.

Microsoft and TCP/IP

As Microsoft continues to enhance Windows NT, the multi-protocol scenario will begin to change because Microsoft is making a greater investment in TCP/IP-based services. For example, in the 5.0 release of Windows NT, all of the new directory services will only be available if you are using TCP/IP as your primary transport. Microsoft clearly believes that TCP/IP will be the de facto network protocol for the majority of the industry. You will, of course, still be able to run the other protocols, but if you do not run TCP/IP as well, you will find yourself feature-limited.

NetWare/Windows NT Server Integration

The reality is that many organizations choose to deploy both NetWare and Windows NT Server. For example, a company might use NetWare for file and print serving, but use Windows NT Server as a data base server for client applications. This kind of coexistence results in a requirement for a client systems to be able to access both types of servers.

Because Microsoft operating systems control the majority of desktop environments, it should be no big surprise to discover that Microsoft is the primary provider of NetWare/Windows NT Server coexistence solutions. NetWare/Windows NT Server coexistence solutions take on three forms:

- *Concurrent access.* Running two sets of client software in each desktop system so each client system can access both servers concurrently.
- *Emulation.* Using a Windows NT Server to emulate a Novell server so clients can use existing NetWare client software to access NT resources.
- *Gateway.* Using a Windows NT Server as a gateway so that clients see the NetWare server as part of the Windows NT Server system.

The first solution—running two sets of client software in each desktop system—is really only practical if the desktops are running Windows for Workgroups, Windows 95, or Windows NT Workstation. These three operating systems can easily support concurrent access to two different types of servers. You can use Novell-provided client software in all of these three cases, or you can use the Microsoft-provided NetWare client software in the Windows 95 and Windows NT Workstation environment.

Although concurrent access to both types of servers is technically possible in DOS and Windows environments, it is very difficult to implement and manage. If you are operating in either of these environments, you are better off looking at the other two approaches.

The second solution—having a Windows NT Server emulate a NetWare server—is accomplished via the NetWare file and print services included in the 4.0 release of Windows NT Server. After this software is installed, the Windows NT Server emulates a NetWare server and clients can connect to it to access file and print resources using standard, client-side NetWare software. In most cases, this solution is implemented as a migration strategy—clients are given access to both servers as information is moved from the NetWare server to the Windows NT

Server systems. After everything is moved, the clients are then switched to native Microsoft client software.

The final solution—using Windows NT Server as a gateway to a NetWare server—is implemented by using the NetWare gateway software included in the 4.0 release of Windows NT Server. This software establishes a connection to a NetWare server and remaps all of the files and printers into native Windows NT Server format—client systems see the NetWare resources through standard Microsoft client software. This approach is somewhat limited in that access to the NetWare server is performed via a single-user id—all of the client systems share the access rights of the gateway user-id.

Ch

9

Finally, you should note that a wide variety of third-party software is available to integrate both NetWare and Windows NT Server into UNIX and other operating system environments. The bottom line is that neither of these products suffer from a lack of connectivity options—either to one another or to the rest of the world. ●

CHAPTER 10

TCP/IP

An Overview of TCP/IP

The TCP/IP network architecture distinctly influences how multiple vendor networks are constructed and operated. The importance of TCP/IP in today's market is particularly amazing when you consider that TCP/IP is a *public domain* architecture. Unlike most private, commercially developed network architectures (for example, IBM's Systems Network Architecture (SNA) or Digital's DECnet), TCP/IP was developed under the auspices of the U.S. government. This development environment made TCP/IP an *open* network because the TCP/IP architecture was not aligned with any particular vendor or machine architecture.

A Brief History of TCP/IP

Just how did TCP/IP rise to such a level of importance? To fully understand this you must go back to 1957—the year the Soviet Union launched Sputnik, the world's first artificial satellite. When Sputnik went into orbit, President Eisenhower decided that the United States needed to focus its efforts on meeting and exceeding Soviet technology, so he created the *Advanced Research Projects Agency (ARPA)*. The purpose of ARPA was to conduct long-term research and development projects on behalf of the U.S. government.

As the number of research projects handled by ARPA grew, so did the number of researchers and sub-contractors, and the need to share resources. When computers and computing devices became important research tools in the late 1960s, ARPA decided to create a network that would enable ARPA researchers and sub-contractors to share the growing number of computer systems. This network came to be known as *ARPANET.*

Originally, ARPANET used packet-switching technology that was the precursor to the X.25 standard for packet-switching networks. Simple tools were created and deployed to allow terminal access, file transfer, and simple mail—these tools exist today under TCP/IP as Telnet, File Transfer Protocol (FTP), and the Simple Mail Transfer Protocol (SMTP).

ARPANET use continued to grow steadily through the 1960s and into the 1970s. In the 70s, however, the fledgling networking industry was going through significant technology and design changes. On the technology front, the Ethernet LAN hit the market, offering new levels of performance for local connections. In the same timeframe, the X.25 standard was approved by the CCITT, creating a universal standard for packet-switching networks.

On the design front, Xerox released its Xerox Networking Services (XNS) architecture. Although XNS was not a commercial success, it was a major influence on the design and implementation of Novell NetWare and IBM/Microsoft's LAN Manager. However, Xerox was not alone in developing and offering formal *network architectures*—IBM released its System Network Architecture, and Digital Equipment Corporation introduced its Digital Network Architecture (DNA), better known as DECnet.

Given this backdrop of new network links and architectures, ARPA decided to adopt TCP/IP as the *standard* network architecture for the ARPANET. ARPA saw TCP/IP as a tool that would enable them to quickly embrace new technology (like Ethernet and X.25) as it became available. As a result of ARPA's interest and investment, most of the major TCP/IP protocols were developed and deployed by the end of the 1970s.

The use of TCP/IP in ARPANET proved so successful that ARPA issued a directive for all ARPANET hosts to use TCP/IP by the mid-1980s. This directive is a milestone in the history of TCP/IP, because it insured that any computer manufacturer who wanted to sell equipment to ARPA had to support TCP/IP, regardless of what their "native" network architecture happened to be. So, thanks to the U.S. government, some level of TCP/IP has been implemented in virtually every mainstream computer system.

As the use of ARPANET continued to grow and prosper, the network underwent dramatic changes in the 1980s. President Reagan renamed ARPA to Defense Advanced Research Projects Agency (DARPA) and thus ARPANET became DARPANET. Military agencies became uncomfortable with the amount of non-military activity occurring over DARPANET and so they split off and formed their own network, named MILNET.

The beginning of the end of DARPANET occurred when the National Science Foundation (NSF) formed a separate network for science and academic research in 1985. The network, NSFnet, was modeled after DARPANET, and in the spirit of sharing, the two networks were interconnected. Over the course of the late 1980s, NSFnet absorbed DARPANET and became what we now know as the Internet (but that's another story).

More importantly, although ARPANET never made it into the 1990s, the network architecture it gave birth to—TCP/IP—lived on and prospered. For years, TCP/IP was the protocol suite of choice for UNIX networks. Then, in the 1990s, almost all of the major computer and network manufacturers followed suit and incorporated support for TCP/IP into their products.

For example, Microsoft now looks at TCP/IP as its protocol of choice for NT networks, and IBM has migrated a number of connectivity services from SNA to TCP/IP. In short, TCP/IP has established itself as the premier protocol suite for many corporate networks.

Core TCP/IP Protocols and Services

The TCP/IP network architecture is named after its two core protocols—the Transmission Control Protocol (TCP) and the Internet Protocol (IP). In truth, these two protocols are only the tip of the iceberg—when you start digging into a TCP/IP network, you typically encounter dozens of lower-level service and utility protocols. In this chapter, you will review a number of these protocols, starting with the following core TCP/IP protocols:

- *The Internet Protocol (IP).* This protocol is responsible for the delivery of messages between systems operating within the same network or operating in different (but interconnected) networks. As part of this function, the Internet Protocol handles all network-level addresses—for example, the Internet Protocol is ultimately responsible for moving a message from a system at address "192.0.0.101" to a system at address "192.0.0.102". (And that's also why these addresses are referred to as *Internet addresses* or *IP addresses*.) The Internet Protocol is a network-level protocol that acts as a carrier for transport-level protocols. The two main protocols that operate at the transport level are TCP/IP and UDP.

- *The Transmission Control Protocol (TCP/IP).* This is a connection-oriented protocol that guarantees end-to-end delivery. TCP is used as the primary transport for the majority of the TCP/IP utilities.

- *The User Datagram Protocol (UDP).* This is a connectionless protocol that does not guarantee end-to-end delivery. Because it is connectionless, UDP is faster than TCP. UDP is typically used for real-time (client/server) program-to-program applications or networking services that require the fastest possible response time.

TCP and UDP, in turn, carry application-oriented services (sometimes referred to as *application protocols*). Although there are literally hundreds of services that can run under the umbrella of TCP or UDP, the four major services are:

- *Telnet.* This service provides a means for a TCP/IP workstation or a terminal attached to a TCP/IP host to access a second host system. Telnet will be discussed in more detail later in this chapter.

- *The File Transfer Protocol (FTP).* This service enables the movement of text and binary files between systems. FTP is a *bulk* file transfer service that is unaware of field-level contents, although most FTP implementations have provisions for ASCII/EBCDIC conversion. FTP can be used on an interactive or programmatic basis.

- *The Simple Mail Transfer Protocol (SMTP).* This service handles the routing of mail in a TCP/IP network. Note that SMTP is a delivery service that does not communicate directly with end users. The end-user side of mail is handled by a front-end program that deals with the user-oriented mail issues (that is, composing, reading, forward, filing, and so on).

■ *The Simple Network Management Protocol (SNMP).* SNMP provides the framework for systems to report problems, configuration information, and performance data to a central network management location. Like SMTP, SNMP is not an end-user service—SNMP reports its information to a central programs that analyzes the data and interacts with an operator.

Figure 10.1 illustrates how these core protocols and services relate to one another. And remember, these protocols and services are really just a sample of the entire set of TCP/IP protocols and services. Later in this chapter we will look at additional protocols and services commonly used in many TCP/IP networks.

FIG. 10.1

Relationship of Core Protocols and Services in a TCP/IP Architecture

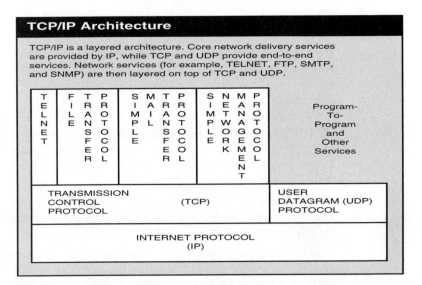

The TCP/IP Client/Server Model

Services such as Telnet, FTP, and SMTP follow the client/server model. This means that a user initiating a service request uses client software and the request is received by server software operating in the background of the target system. The client/server model is certainly not new to the TCP/IP environment—in fact, the entire architecture for TCP/IP is client/server oriented.

Under the TCP/IP client/server model, services are assigned *sockets*. Sockets are logical ports associated with the TCP and UDP transport protocols. Programs can attach to sockets in order to communicate with other partner programs. All of the major TCP/IP protocols and applications services have defined socket numbers. For example, Telnet uses TCP socket 23, FTP relies on TCP sockets 20 and 21, and SMTP is assigned TCP socket 25.

When a client wants to establish a connection to its server counterpart, it initiates either a TCP or UDP connection to the corresponding socket number on the target system. For example, when you run the Telnet client and initiate a connection to a host, the Telnet client requests a TCP connection to socket 23 on the target system. Figure 10.2 shows this basic connection architecture.

FIG. 10.2
Basic Connection Architecture in a TCP/IP Client/Server Model

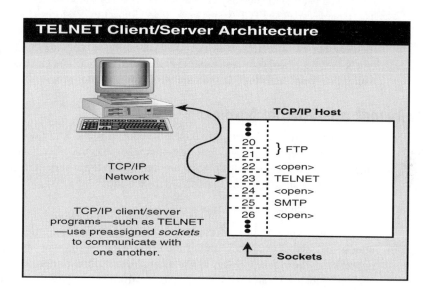

On the other side of the equation, when the server system receives a socket connection, it normally starts a new copy of the server program to handle the new client connection. The client and server then establish a new socket assignment they can use for the duration of the connection. This approach enables multiple client/server conversations to use the same socket number to initiate connections.

After the client and server programs have established a link to one another, they can start interacting. In many cases, the initial interaction often involves *negotiation* a process where the client and server module agree on what special functions or capabilities will be available during the session. After negotiation is complete, the end-user can begin using the service.

How exactly does a client system initiate a link to a server system? Under the TCP/IP architecture, connections can be initiated using the IP name of the server system or IP address of the server system. As explained in the following sections of this chapter, the IP name and IP address define the network path that leads from the client system to the server system.

TCP/IP Host Name Resolution

Every system in a TCP/IP network normally has both an IP name and an IP address. These two variables work together to enable end-to-end connections between TCP/IP hosts.

Unfortunately, all TCP/IP hosts do not support the same methods and protocols for assigning IP numbers and translating IP names into IP addresses. In this section you will see the common methods used to resolve IP names into addresses—in the next section you will take a closer look at IP addresses.

Before you get into the details of IP names, be aware of a little secret—you don't really need to use IP names at all in a TCP/IP network. If you know the IP address for every system you want to contact, you're all set. IP host names are merely tools that assist your personal analog-based memory. For example, IP names free you from having to remember that your production system is "192.0.0.1" and your test system is "192.0.0.2"; instead you can assign them descriptive names like "prod" and "test" (or cute names like "kirk" and "spock").

Informal and Formal Names

If you are operating in the confines of a self-contained network (termed a *domain*), you can reference another system using just its system name. On the other hand, if you function in a large network where multiple domains are interconnected, a system name must be expanded into an fully qualified IP name that follows the format:

<host name>.<domain name>.<type>

In this format, <host name> refers to the name of a specific system (for example, **kirk** or **spock**) and <domain name> identifies the name of the organization, institution, or enterprise network that the system belongs to (for example, **ieee**, **ibm**, or **netcom**). Domain names can contain multiple components. For example, **as400.ibm** and **java.sun** are both legitimate domain names.

The final component, <type> classifies the type of business or organization serviced by the domain. Some of the more common <type> values include:

- **.gov**   government body (for example, **whitehouse.gov**)
- **.edu**   educational institution (for example, **msu.edu**)
- **.com**   any commercial institution (for example, **ibm.com**)
- **.org**   organizations/standards bodies (for example, **ieee.org**)

For international access, <type> can be further broken down into multiple components. For example, **co.uk** and **co.nz** refer to institutions in the United Kingdom and New Zealand respectively.

Again, you often need to use the full IP name when you leave your domain; otherwise, you can just use the system name. For example, if you want to send something from **kirk.trek.com** to **spock.trek.com**, you can simply use the address **spock**. If, however, you want to send from **kirk.trek.com** to **xena.warrior.com**, you typically have to use the fully qualified name (in other words, **xena.warrior.com**). In a network environment where you frequently work with multiple local domains you can, in fact, set up a domain search list to look for a host name in a series of domains.

Making the Address Translation

You can invoke all TCP/IP services using either the IP address or IP name of the target system. For example, you can initiate a *File Transfer Protocol (FTP)* session using either of the following two commands:

- FTP SPOCK
- FTP 192.0.0.2

Assuming that the system named **spock** has an IP address of **192.0.0.2**, both of these commands accomplish exactly the same thing, but the first variation is certainly easier to remember.

Because the underlying TCP/IP protocols can't do much with the system name, TCP/IP services such as Telnet, FTP, SMTP, and others invoke a translation process that converts the host name into its corresponding IP address. This translation occurs "under the covers," so you never see it happening—you only see the results.

The first step in the translation process is to look up the host name in a *host table* file stored on the originating (local) system. This file—normally named *hosts*—is manually maintained, and it contains a list of system names and the corresponding IP addresses for those systems. If the specified host name is present in the local host table, the process is complete, and the IP address is returned to the requesting service. That service then initiates activity over the network using the IP address. If, however, the specified host is not present in the local host table, the translation process will turn to one or more systems in the network that have been designated as a *name server*.

A name server is a system on the network that maintains a database of host names and their corresponding IP addresses. In a nutshell, a name server provides a way of centralizing the information contained in various systems' host tables—name servers were developed to eliminate the need for each system to download a single master hosts file whenever a network change was made. Any given host name can appear in both a name server database and in a local host table. However, using both host tables and name servers creates a reasonable balance between speed and manageability.

On one hand, it is difficult and often unreasonable to try to maintain a current list of all host names and IP addresses on every system in the network. On the other hand, retrieving an IP address from a name server takes more time than retrieving it from a local host table file. By using both approaches, individual system administrators or users can maintain a short list of frequently accessed host names in the local host table file so access to those hosts can proceed at best possible speed. The IP address for less frequently accessed hosts can be retrieved over the network from a name server.

Finally, note that whenever a system resolves a name into an IP address, it stores the results in a memory cache. The memory cache is always consulted first for name-to-address resolution. If an entry isn't in the cache, then the system uses the hosts file and/or the name server to resolve the name. Memory cache speeds up the process of accessing the same host over and over again, but the cache is lost whenever a system reboots.

Ch
10

Name Servers

TCP/IP often provides several different ways of performing the same task. Names servers are no different. In today's TCP/IP market, you will run into three common name server implementations:

- *Domain Name Server (DNS)*. DNS is the most wide-spread implementation of a name server—for example, DNS is the preferred name server implementation on the Internet. DNS is a sophisticated implementation that even allows name servers to contact one another in the event they cannot resolve a name in their own databases. When most people say *name server,* they are referring to the DNS implementation.

- *Network Information Service (NIS)* (formerly called yellow pages or yp). NIS was developed by Sun Microsystems as part of its TCP/IP network architecture. Although there are plenty of technical differences between DNS and NIS, they can be viewed as functionally identical (but not interoperable) solutions for the purpose of this discussion.

- *Windows Internet Naming Service (WINS)*. This is a relatively new service that, despite the name, is not really used for native TCP/IP traffic. WINS is a facility that allows NetBIOS-based host names to be resolved over TCP/IP. It is an important component in Microsoft's implementation of native Windows networking services over TCP/IP.

Interestingly enough, these name server implementations are not exclusive of one another—a system can engage them as needed. For example, if an HP system can't resolve a name via NIS, it may invoke DNS. Similarly, a Windows 95 or Windows NT system can use both WINS and DNS to resolve names.

As you can see, IP names play an important role in TCP/IP networking because they add structure to the network and they allow users to reference systems by easy-to-remember names. Just remember, all IP names eventually get translated into IP addresses before action can be taken.

IP Address Construction

Under the TCP/IP architecture, each system in a network is assigned a four byte (32 bit) address, termed the *IP address.* Instead of representing these bytes as hexadecimal values, however, they are normally represented using the format **w.x.y.z**, where w, x, y, and z are replaced with a decimal number between 0 (hex 00) and 255 (hex FF). For example, **192.0.0.12** is a valid IP address.

This four-byte address is then further broken down into a network address and a system address. For example, the IP address **192.0.0.12** identifies system "12" within network "192.0.0". Similarly, IP address **128.10.20.12** identifies system "20.12" within network "128.10". The breakdown of how many bytes are used for the network portion of the address and how many bytes apply to the system is predetermined based on the *class* of the IP address. There are three real address classes, and they are as follows:

- *Class A.* This class follows the format "network.host.host.host," with the network byte falling in the range between 0 and 127 (exclusive of 0 and 127), and the host bytes being greater than 0. For example, in the address "64.0.1.12", "64" identifies the network and "0.1.12" identifies the host system. In case you're wondering, "0" is not a legal network address and "127" is used to define a "loopback" address within an IP host system.

- *Class B.* This class follows the format "network.network.host.host," with the first (leftmost) network byte falling in the range from 128 to 191 (including 128 and 191), and the host bytes being greater than 0. For example, in the address "130.101.0.68", "130.101" identifies the network, and "0.68" identifies the host system.

- *Class C.* This class follows the format "network.network.network.host," with the first network byte falling in the range from 192 to 223 (including 192 and 223), and the host bytes being greater than 0. For example, in the address "200.1.1.37", "200.1.1" identifies the network, and "37" identifies the host system. Class C is the most common implementation because it provides the greatest flexibility for creating multiple networks.

NOTE There is a fourth type of address—*Class D.* This virtual address class is used for multi-cast addresses, which are intended for multiple systems that possibly reside in different networks. Class D addresses have no network or host components and addresses begin with a byte that falls in the range of 224 to 239 (including 224 and 239). ▓

Ch
10

Note that in all classes, you cannot assign "0" or "255" as host numbers. These numbers are reserved for TCP/IP broadcast messages. As a general rule, you can select whatever address class makes sense for the composition of your enterprise-wide network. If you're going to hook up into the Internet, however, you need to obtain approval for your class assignment and address range through your local Internet access provider.

Assigning IP Addresses

Once you've determined and possibly registered the class and range of addresses you are going to use, you can go about the business of configuring your systems. All systems can be manually configured to use a specific IP address. Alternatively, some systems (for example, PCs, Macintoshes, and UNIX systems) can dynamically set their IP addresses using the services of an *address server*.

NOTE You *must* take Internet access into consideration when you develop your IP address plan. If you are never going to connect your network to the Internet or if you are only going to connect through a proxy server (which hides your internal IP addresses), then you can use whatever addresses you desire. If, however, you are going to connect to the Internet using a conventional gateway or router, then you must *only* use the IP addresses you registered. ▓

Before you set up an IP address server, you must decide on which dynamic address protocol you can (and want to) use. The three popular choices are the Reverse Address Resolution Protocol (RARP), the boot protocol (bootp), or the Dynamic Host Configuration Protocol (DHCP).

- *RARP and boot.* These two protocols were developed to handle diskless UNIX workstations. When a system boots up using RARP or bootp, the system broadcasts its LAN adapter address, and the address server returns an assigned IP address. In order to use

RARP or bootp, a network administrator must manually create and maintain a file on an address server that maps specific LAN adapter addresses to specific IP addresses. Bootp has the added capability of downloading additional configuration information, such as the addresses of the name servers and gateways.

■ *DHCP*. This protocol was developed as an alternative to bootp. Unlike RARP and bootp, a DHCP address server does not need to be configured with the hardware address of each and every system it will service. Instead, the DHCP server assigns IP address from a *pool* of addresses. Therefore, when a system makes a DHCP request, it will receive an IP address from the pool that may or may not be the same IP address it used the last time. Like bootp, DHCP can also download additional configuration information to the requesting system.

Although DHCP was developed as a general purpose TCP/IP protocol, its popularity and use have soared because Microsoft has adopted DHCP as its preferred methodology for IP address assignment in Windows 95 and Windows NT TCP/IP networks. Microsoft's decision has, in turn, convinced a number of PC and Mac network software vendors to introduce support for DHCP in their client software packages. And with Service Pack 2 of NT Server 4.0, Microsoft broadened the scope of DHCP by enabling an NT-based DHCP server to handle address assignment requests from bootp clients.

You can mix and match your IP assignment methodologies. Some systems, such as AS/400s and dedicated servers, can have manually configured IP address. Other systems can use bootp, and still other systems can use DHCP. The flexibility (and related administrative complexities) are yours to choose.

IP and MAC Addresses

As important as IP addresses are (and they are very important), they are not the only requirement for delivering a message to a system in a TCP/IP LAN environment. IP addresses are logical addresses that operate above the level of the physical LAN adapter address (the MAC address). In order for a system to have the opportunity to examine the IP address in a message, that message must get past the LAN adapter.

Specifically, when a LAN adapter card sees a message on the LAN, it will only look at the contents of the message under two circumstances:

■ The message is a *broadcast* message for all systems in the LAN.

■ The message contains the LAN adapter's address.

In both of these cases, the LAN adapter passes the message on to the operating system so the operating system can determine what protocol the message applies to (for example, TCP/IP, APPC, IPX, and so on). In the case of a TCP/IP message, the receiving system will then verify the IP address contained in the message. If the IP address doesn't match, it will, in most cases, be ignored.

TCP/IP networks could function by broadcasting every single message and forcing all the systems to look at each message. As you can probably imagine, this would create extra overhead on the systems because they all must examine every single TCP/IP message. Thankfully, however, TCP/IP provides a protocol to discover the LAN adapter address that corresponds to an IP address. That protocol is the *Address Resolution Protocol (ARP)*.

Here's how ARP works. The first time System A wants to send a message to System B, it sends out a broadcast message using ARP. Because it is a broadcast message, each system in the local LAN sees it. When System B sees the message, it finds its own IP address in it, recognizes that it is a ARP request, and returns a message to System A containing its LAN adapter address. From that point on, System A can directly address System B using both its LAN adapter address and IP address.

Combining Name and Address Resolution

The IP name, IP address, and LAN adapter address come into play whenever you begin communicating with a TCP/IP system. For example, when you initiate a Telnet connection to a host, the following steps occur:

1. The IP name is translated into an IP address using a hosts file or a DNS/NIS/WINS lookup.
2. The IP address indicates if the target system in the same LAN (in other words, it has the same network address as the source system) or if the message needs to be forwarded through one or more gateways (as explained in the next section of this chapter).
3. Once the message reaches the LAN where the target system resides, the target system's LAN adapter address is discovered via ARP. This discovery will be performed by the source system if it is on the same LAN as the target system, or by the gateway servicing the target system.

The beauty of TCP/IP is that these steps happen behind the scene. You simply enter **telnet <host name>** or **ftp <host name>** and all of the underlying services and protocols kick in to take you to your destination, wherever it happens to be.

IP Routing

The network portion of an IP address determines which computers a system can connect to without requiring the services of a router or gateway (TCP/IP networks generally use the term *gateway* even though a TCP/IP gateway is really a router). Under the TCP/IP architecture, two systems with different network assignments can only communicate with one another through a gateway—even if they are located immediately next to each other and connected to the same physical network.

A TCP/IP gateway can be a dedicated router or it can be a computer system that also acts as a router. For example, you can configure an NT Server system to be a gateway by adding the *Multi-Protocol Routing (MPR)* network service. MPR can run concurrently with other network services (for example, file sharing, printer sharing, or Web serving). Most UNIX systems can also provide gateway service (either *routed* or *gated*) in addition to their normal application loads.

Regardless of what type of device it is, a *gateway* system maintains a table of network addresses and a record of the physical connections associated with those addresses. Therefore, when a gateway receives a request to forward a message, it simply looks at the network address of the target system, finds the physical interface associated with that network address, and forwards the message over that interface.

How does a system know when it needs to forward a message to a gateway? Whenever a system goes to send a message to another system, it compares the network address of the target system with its own network address. If the two are different, the originating system must forward the message to a gateway.

Needless to say, each system must know what gateways are available for use. In the easiest scenario, each system is configured with the address of a single *default* gateway, and all cross-network messages are delivered to that gateway. That gateway can, in turn, forward the message on to other gateways, but this additional routing is not visible to the original system.

In more complex networks, multiple gateways might be available to service different networks. For example, one gateway might be available for traffic to and from a business partner's private TCP/IP network, and a second gateway might service general Internet traffic. Although, you can configure all of the traffic to go to the default gateway and let the default gateway handle re-routing the messages through another gateway, this approach creates additional overhead, and it introduces a single point of failure.

Alternatively, you can configure routing information in each system that tells it which gateway to use to reach what network. In this example, you tell the systems to use the first traffic for messages explicitly addressed to the partner's network and use the second gateway for all other traffic (the second gateway is the default gateway).

As discussed previously in the "IP Address Construction" section of this chapter, IP addresses fall into different classes that determine which portion of the address is used for network identification and which portion is used for system identification. The way that these classes are interpreted on each system is actually handled through something called a *sub-net mask*.

A sub-net mask is a series of 1 and 0 bits that are logically "ANDed" to the IP address of the target system in order to determine which address bits are used for network identification. For example, the three common IP classes use the following default sub-net masks:

- Class A: network.host.host.host
  Mask: 255.0.0.0
- Class B: network.network.host.host
  Mask: 255.255.0.0
- Class C: network.network.network.host
  Mask: 255.255.255.0

You can, however, extend a subnet mask to create network divisions that deviate from the standard class assignments. For example, you could break a Class C network into two additional subnets by extending the mask one more bit. Addresses with a 1 in that bit location would belong to a different subnet than addresses with a 0 in that bit location. The mask in this case would be: 255.255.255.128 (128 decimal = 10000000 binary).

Extending subnets is frequently done in private networks that have outgrown their original IP address assignments. Some Internet access providers also use this technique to assign IP address ranges to their local customers.

Once a system has determined the network address of the target system using a subnet mask, it can make the decision if that message needs to be routed through a gateway and, if so, what gateway needs to handle the message.

Additional TCP/IP Protocols and Services

As discussed earlier in this chapter, there are hundreds of protocols and services associated with TCP/IP. So far in this chapter you have explored many of the most essential—and most common—of these protocols and services. Chances are better than average that you will run into additional protocols and services in any reasonable size TCP/IP network.

Ch
10

From a networking perspective, some of the additional TCP/IP and TCP/IP-related protocols and services you might encounter include the following.

■ *AnyNet* and *Data Link Switching (DLSw)*. These are tunneling protocols used to transport SNA traffic through a TCP/IP network. In effect, both protocols establish end-to-end SNA connections through a TCP/IP network.

■ *The Internet Control Message Protocol (ICMP)*. ICMP is responsible for reporting link-level errors and routing information to TCP/IP systems.

■ *NetBIOS over TCP/IP (NBT)*. This is a protocol used by Microsoft to enable NetBIOS/SMB services (for example, NT-based file and print serving) to operate over a TCP/IP network.

■ *Routing Information Protocol (RIP)* and *Open Shortest Path First (OSPF)*. Both of these are protocols used by TCP/IP gateways and routers to share route information with one another. This is how gateways inform other gateways of the routes they are responsible for.

■ *Serial Line Internet Protocol (SLIP)* and *Point-to-Point Protocol (PPP)*. These two protocols enable full-function access to TCP/IP networks over leased line or dial-up connections. PPP was developed as a replacement for SLIP and offers both performance and security advantages.

■ *Point-to-Point Tunneling Protocol (PPTP)*. PPTP is the general tunneling service for virtually any LAN-based protocol. Microsoft's NT Server and NT Workstation use PPTP to transport IPX, NetBEUI, and NBT traffic over TCP/IP links, enabling you, in effect, to tunnel your local LAN traffic through any TCP/IP network (including the Internet).

In addition to the network-related services, you might also run into the following application and service-oriented protocols.

- *Gopher.* This is a service that lets you list, search, and browse text files stored on a server.
- *HyperText Transfer Protocol (HTTP).* HTTP is the underlying protocol used by World Wide Web (WWW) servers. HTTP provides a means of transferring files and HyperText Markup Language (HTML) documents from a Web server to a Web browser.
- *Internet Message Access Protocol 4 (IMAP4).* IMAP4 for is a client/server protocol for mail retrieval and management. Using IMAP4, a client-side mail program can view or retrieve mail stored on an SMTP server. IMAP4 is more sophisticated than POP3, which is described later.
- *Internet Relay Chat (IRC).* This service enables multiple clients to establish a common link on a server so they can "chat" with one another in real-time by typing information and reading the responses.
- *Line Print Daemon/Line Print Requestor (LPD/LPR).* LPD/LPR provides a means to print a file from one system on a printer attached to another system. LPR is the client-side of this service, and LPD is the server-side.
- *Network File System (NFS).* The NFS service provides a means of sharing directories and files in a TCP/IP network. Two NFS follow-up services are also used for this same purpose: the Andrew File System (AFS) and the Distributed File System (DFS).
- *Post Office Protocol 3 (POP3).* POP3 is a mail-retrieval protocol that lets a client-side mail program retrieve mail messages from a mail server and store them locally. POP3 is often used by PC/Mac-based mail programs (for example, Eudora) to download mail from an SMTP server.

TCP/IP Drawbacks

Most TCP/IP serviceprotocols operate using English-like commands. HTTP employs commands such as GET, SEARCH, and LINK. Similarly, FTP uses basic directives such as DIR, GET, and PUT. Even those protocols that don't use English commands still rely on simple, byte-oriented command sequences and responses (for example, under the Telnet protocol, option negotiation begins with the **255 250** command sequence and ends with the **255 240** sequence).

Consider the following Simple Mail Transfer Protocol (SMTP) conversation that sends a message from **john@enck.com** to **morrison@lizard.king.com** via the mail gateway **gateway2.heaven.com**:

Client	*Server*
	220 gateway2.heaven.com Sendmail ready
HELO mail.enck.com	
	250 gateway2.heaven.com Hello mail.enck.com
MAIL From:enck@mail.enck.com	
	250 enck@mail.enck.com... Sender ok

RCPT To:morrison@lizard.king.com

  250 morrison@lizard.king.com... Recipient ok

DATA

  354 Enter mail, end with "." alone

Dear Jim:

How are things in lizard land?

— John.

  250 Mail accepted

QUIT

  221 gateway2.heaven.com delivering mail

It's important to note that the preceding conversation is not pseudocode; this is how the SMTP protocol really operates. The SMTP client transmits the keyword **HELO**, and the server does, indeed, reply **250**. In fact, the entire SMTP protocol consists of English-like commands and numerical responses. (Note that the exact phrasing that follows each keyword might vary slightly from one machine to the next, but they all follow the same general format.)

Basing TCP/IP service protocols on high-level commands and responses makes them extremely easy to learn, easy to program, and easy to debug. Unfortunately, while this approach makes life easier for programmers and protocol developers, it presents significant headaches for network managers. In particular, there are three major drawbacks:

- *TCP/IP is not kind to network bandwidth.* Since its inception, TCP/IP has assumed it will have sufficient bandwidth at its disposal. Other network protocols (for example, IBM SNA, Digital DECnet, Novell IPX) are more sensitive to the fact that bandwidth is a valuable commodity that is hard to come by. These other protocols use bit-oriented flags for commands and responses instead of TCP/IP's multiple-character sequences.

- *TCP/IP is open to view.* Anyone with a network monitor can see everyone's dirty laundry (so to speak). You could certainly argue that anyone with a network monitor can see everything in the network anyway. But, with TCP/IP, you don't have to work very hard; all the information is laid out bare. You don't even have to decode bit-level flags as you do with SNA, DECnet, or IPX.

- *TCP/IP makes it easy for humans to masquerade as protocols.* Most of its application-level protocols use sockets as a means of communication. Using Telnet, for instance, you can attach to a specific socket and start manually typing in the protocol. So a hacker can Telnet into an SMTP socket and type HELO, and so on. You'd be surprised (and horrified) to learn what you can accomplish when you disguise yourself as a protocol.

None of these drawbacks have slowed down the growth and acceptance of TCP/IP. Nonetheless, they all raise issues that you should address during the design and operation of any TCP/IP network. You need to watch your available bandwidth, control who has access to network monitor software, and most importantly, keep close tabs on who is accessing your TCP/IP servers and why.

Telnet and IBM Systems

In most TCP/IP environments, Telnet functions as an interactive, character-level service. That means that when you type a character on the keyboard, the Telnet client sends that character over the network to the Telnet server, which then passes the character on to the application. Furthermore, Telnet was designed with the ASCII character code in mind—Telnet clients assume they will be communicating with the Telnet server using ASCII encoding.

Unfortunately, character-level operation and the use of the ASCII character set are contrary to the way that IBM terminals function in mainframe, System/3X, and AS/400 environments. In particular, IBM 3270 (mainframe) and 5250 (System/3X and AS/400) terminal types use these alternate approaches:

- IBM terminals are oriented toward block-mode operation instead of character-mode operation. In the IBM environment, information typed on the keyboard is stored locally until an Enter key or function key is pressed. At that point the input data is transmitted as a block of information. As shown in Figure 10.3, this is a stark contrast to character-mode operation, where each key is transmitted over the network as it is being pressed.
- IBM terminals use the EBCIDC character code instead of the ASCII character code.

These two differences affect how IBM devices operate in the Telnet environment from both the client and server perspective. For example, if an IBM terminal initiates a Telnet client connection using VT100 emulation, the Telnet client must provide EBCDIC to ASCII translation and provide terminal emulation for the following reasons:

- To translate display highlights.
- To translate function key operations.
- To compensate for the difference between block-mode and character-mode operations.

From a purely technical perspective, the EBCDIC/ASCII translation is a minor issue while the terminal emulation issue is significantly more difficult (but certainly not impossible).

Using an IBM mainframe, System/3X, or AS/400 as a Telnet server for VT100-style traffic causes similar difficulties. As in the case of the client, the IBM Telnet server must provide EBCDIC/ASCII translation and terminal emulation, but for the server, terminal emulation means:

- Translating display highlights sequences into IBM highlight attributes.
- Translating keystrokes into standard IBM function keys (for example, PF1–PF24).
- Translating character-mode operations into block-mode operations.

The server side of IBM Telnet also has one other interesting consideration. Because the IBM terminal environment is block-oriented and Telnet is traditionally character-oriented, a lot of unnecessary traffic is generated on the network. As noted, the Telnet client typically sends out characters as they are being typed. If these characters are going to an IBM Telnet server, the server simply collects them until it receives a termination key (for example, the Enter key) at which point it sends the block to the application. From a networking perspective, the overhead

FIG. 10.3

Character-Mode and
Block-Mode Operations

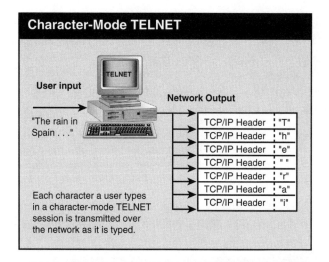

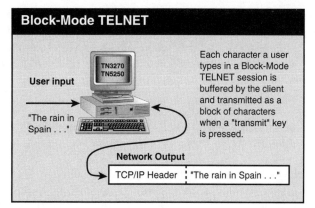

of sending characters out one at a time is much higher than the overhead of sending them out as a block (which is the traditional IBM approach).

TN3270

In order to alleviate many of these concerns, IBM developed an IBM 3270 terminal type for the Telnet environment. Released in 1988, the Telnet IBM 3270 terminal type is a negotiated option between the Telnet server and client that addresses many of the difficulties associated with Telnet and the IBM environment. These difficulties are addressed by instilling greater awareness for the IBM environment into the Telnet 3270 client program. Some of the benefits of the IBM Telnet 3270 solution include:

■ *Support for block-mode operations.* The Telnet 3270 client collects keystrokes and forwards them on to the Telnet server as a block when a trigger key (for example, Enter or a function key) is pressed.

Ch
10

- *Flexible mapping for IBM 3270 keys.* Keyboard mapping files enable terminal keys to be mapped into IBM 3270 keys (including function keys) as desired.
- *Translation of display attributes.* The Telnet 3270 client translates IBM field attributes into the appropriate highlight sequences for the client terminal.
- *EBCDIC/ASCII translation.* The Telnet 3270 client can translate and switch between EBCDIC and ASCII character codes as needed.

These features work together to create a Telnet client environment that has the look and feel of an IBM 3270 terminal. Thus, information can be entered into structured display forms; the Tab key can be used to move from field to field; and incorrect information entered into fields can be changed prior to transmission.

The Telnet 3270 solution can be used by ASCII terminals accessing IBM systems, by IBM terminals accessing a UNIX systems, and by IBM terminals accessing IBM systems over a TCP/IP network. Use of Telnet 3270 to accommodate ASCII terminal access is by far the most popular scenario.

IBM 3270 support is typically included in a separate Telnet program—usually called *TN3270*. This means it is not uncommon to find Telnet client environments that feature multiple Telnet programs. For example, the IBM RS/6000 includes both Telnet and TN3270 programs. The Telnet program negotiates for the current terminal type while the TN3270 negotiates for the IBM 3270 terminal type.

N O T E   An enhanced version of TN3270 is also available. This version—termed TN3270E— enables some addition 3270 features in the Telnet environment, the most important feature being printer support. ▦

TN5250

When TCP/IP connectivity was first introduced to the IBM AS/400 environment, the AS/400 supported Digital VT100 and IBM 3270 Telnet terminal types. Telnet access using the VT100 terminal type posed exactly the same difficulties found in the mainframe environment (for example, ASCII instead of EBCDIC and character-mode instead of block-mode), so Telnet 3270 access seemed a more logical choice. Unfortunately, 3270 access into the AS/400 had its own set of problems.

Telnet 3270 traffic going into the AS/400 goes through the exact same handling routines applied to "real" IBM 3270 terminals attached to the AS/400. These routines translate the 3270 data streams and function keys into 5250 data streams and function keys, so application programs only "see" 5250 terminals. Because 3270 and 5250 terminals are not functionally identical, the translation process introduces new considerations regarding keyboard support, data entry field handling, and screen display attributes.

To address these considerations, IBM developed a definition for a new Telnet terminal type: the *Telnet 5250* terminal. Introduced in 1991, Telnet 5250 operation provides all of the benefits of Telnet 3270 operation (for example, block-mode support, EBCDIC/ASCII translation, and so on), and also addresses the limitations of the 3270-to-5250 translation process by making the Telnet client program aware of the unique characteristics of the 5250 terminal. Thus, a Telnet 5250 client provides the following features not found in a Telnet 3270 client:

- *Support for 5250-specific keys.* The Telnet 5250 client permits flexible keyboard mapping like Telnet 3270 and also provide client-based emulation of the "Roll Up", "Roll Down", "Field Exit", "Field +", and "Field -", and other unique 5250 keys.

- *Enforcement of numeric-only fields.* The Telnet 5250 client recognizes numeric data entry fields and restricts data access on a local basis.

- *Support for the full range of highlight attributes.* The Telnet 5250 client provides direct translation between 5250 highlight attributes and the actual terminal running the Telnet client program.

The enhancements available in the Telnet 5250 solution make it superior to Telnet 3270 for accessing an AS/400 via Telnet. As in the case of Telnet 3270 clients, IBM 5250 support is normally available as a separate client program, often called *TN5250*. ●

Ch
10

CHAPTER 11

Network Management

In the past, network management was primarily a centralized endeavor carried out by a virtual priesthood of technicians who stared at arcane command-line screens all day. The growth of the distributed, client/server enterprise model has significantly changed the face of network management—simplifying it in some areas, while clouding it even further in others. Management tasks can now be distributed to the most appropriate machine, and various tasks executing on different platforms can now, under some circumstances, be integrated.

The Problems of Problem Determination

Networks were once either centralized or covered a relatively small local area. When data communications or networking problems involved leased or dialable lines, the long distance carrier stepped in and ran loopback tests until the problem was isolated (or until the data communication analyst resolved it out of boredom or desperation).

Today's networking picture is much larger and more complicated. Simple coaxial-based LANs now interface with fiber-optic *metropolitan area networks (MANs)* that, in turn, interface with one another to form WANs. The centralized point-to-point connections used in the past have been replaced with large, gray clouds of packet/cell switching networks or dual-purpose voice/data ISDN connections.

Not all of these changes create problems. In fact, the opening of voice circuits to the general (albeit often unsuspecting) public has enabled many companies to implement combined voice/ data networks. These have resulted in highly effective, multiple vendor networks that also produce large cost savings—not a bad package.

These types of combined networks are extremely frequent in large manufacturing operations, such as U.S. car manufacturers. In this scale of operation, it is often typical to find a broadband network running through the local plants to handle the combined voice/data traffic. The broadband networks within the plants can then be tied together via direct satellite (effective, but a little pricey), more conventional T1, X.25, or ISDN links, or high-speed ATM or frame-relay connections.

Because such large operations typically involve many different computer systems that must exchange data having a variety of networking protocols, using a common set of transports can be more effective than implementing multiple networks and attempting to bridge them together.

Problem Determination: Centralized Networks

From a human perspective, fault isolation is normally a rudimentary, logical process of elimination. The application of this logic is most readily apparent in the case of centralized (or hierarchical) networks, which feature a rigid and well-defined structure. If, for example, a user's terminal fails, the problem can be pursued in one of the following manners, depending on the network architecture (see Figure 11.1).

If the terminal is on a point-to-point line to the computer, only three items need analysis: the terminal, the line, and the line interface in the computer. Running diagnostics on the terminal and line interface is normally a straightforward procedure. If devices on both ends pass, the problem is probably in the middle. Line-level diagnostics can then be performed at the modem level through the use of loopback tests.

The seemingly more complicated case, in which a terminal is on a controller that interfaces to the main computer via a line, is actually easier to diagnose. In this scenario, the failure could be at the terminal, the terminal controller, the line, or the line interface in the main computer. However, because the terminal controller provides a critical function between the terminals and the computer, the failure can be more easily isolated. For example, if the terminal controller handles 16 terminals and only one of the terminals has failed, the problem can be isolated to the terminal (or its connection to the terminal controller). Diagnostics can then be run on the terminal to determine if it indeed is the point of failure. If all terminals fail, the problem should be pursued first at the terminal controller. Because most terminal controllers are intelligent devices, diagnostic routines can be used to further determine whether it has a failure.

Most terminal controllers will report the loss of a line (indicating problems at the line or line interface level). Therefore, further isolation can be performed by running the line interface diagnostics in the mainframe, or by running loopback tests on the line. The key point in all of this is that the introduction of additional hardware (in other words, the terminal controller) in a hierarchical network does not complicate problem analysis; instead, the structure of the

FIG. 11.1

Points of Failure in
Point-to-Point and
Hierarchical Networks

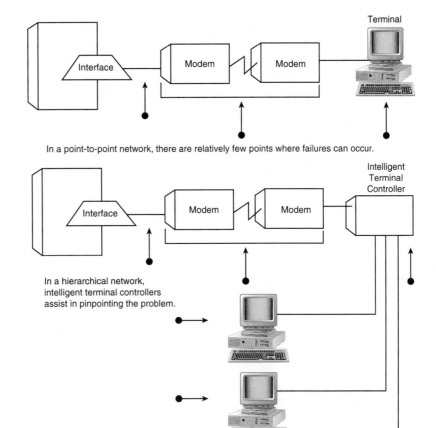

In a point-to-point network, there are relatively few points where failures can occur.

In a hierarchical network,
intelligent terminal controllers
assist in pinpointing the problem.

network and the well-defined relationship between network components actually assists in the troubleshooting process.

Although both of the previous environments might seem relatively easy to troubleshoot, in actual environments the problem is usually compounded by the sheer number of devices involved. In a large SNA network, it is not unusual to find thousands (or even tens of thousands) of terminals distributed across hundreds or thousands of line controllers, lines, and terminal controllers. So although a failure in a terminal might not be very difficult to diagnose, determining which terminal controller, line, and line interface is associated with that terminal can be an awesome task.

Problem Determination: LANs

The degree of difficulty of problem determination in a LAN depends on both the topology and the discipline of the LAN. The three basic topologies (ring, star, and bus) all require different types and amounts of cables and connection devices. As with virtually every manufactured product, when the component count increases, so do the possible points of failures. The three general LAN types (see Figure 11.2) have specific peculiarities, as described in the following paragraphs.

In a token-passing *ring network* (for example, IEEE 802.5), the frame being passed from one computer to the next is on the ring. Therefore, any break in the ring is critical to the operation of a token-ring network. To prevent this tragedy, the cabling and connection systems of most ring networks are self-healing—specifically, circuits automatically close when cables are detached from computers on the ring. In fact, most token-ring networks are cabled using central hubs, resulting in a physical layout that looks very much like star networks (described next).

In a *star network,* individual computers are attached to one another via hub units. Star networks can be operated on either a contention basis, where each computer competes with the other computers for access to the network, or can be token-passing. In either case, the hubs are common points through which all data flows.

FIG. 11.2

Examples of Ring, Star, and Bus Networks

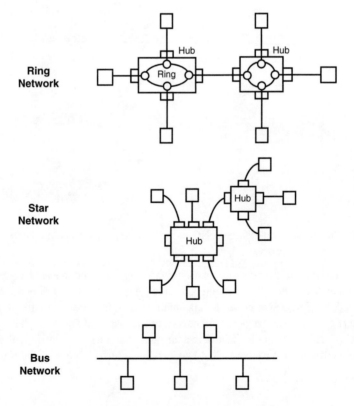

Ring
Network

Star
Network

Bus
Network

Bus networks are widely used in contention networks (as in Ethernet and IEEE 802.3 networks), although they are occasionally used with token passing networks (as in IEEE 802.4). In the most basic case, a bus LAN is a single main cable to which computers attach. As in the case of the ring, the integrity of the main path must be kept intact and all connections must be properly terminated—if an "open" connection is present in the network (in other words, a cable run with no termination at the end), the network will be unusable.

Despite these differences, any malfunction in any of these networks translates into one common problem: finding the point of failure. And regardless of the LAN of choice, discovery is no cake walk. One reason for this difficulty is that LANs do not have the direct user-to-node relationships that centralized networks have. For example, a terminal failure in a centralized network is normally reported by the user who wants to use that terminal. Therefore, if a terminal is broken and no one wants to access it, it might go unreported for a long time. On the other end of the spectrum, if the central computer fails, all users will notice it and the source of the problem will become quickly evident.

In a LAN, however, each node is a potential resource for other nodes. Even though no one might be directly attending a PC, it might be in use by the network at large because it contains files or controls a printer used by other PCs in the network. Because of these interdependencies, the absence of a resource is normally evident more quickly and is usually more critical to the overall operation.

Although the discussion to this point has focused on hard failures in a node, more serious problems are a node that intermittently fails or a malfunction that corrupts the information (and therefore degrades performance). These types of problems are much more difficult to diagnose than hard failures, because there is rarely a point from which to start. The use of monitoring equipment or software is instrumental in isolating these types of problems, because the condition is rarely reproducible or trackable by mere mortals.

Ch
11

And finally, some problems cannot be diagnosed—no matter how much diagnostic equipment and software is used. If, for example, a network goes into an extremely degraded condition every Thursday between 2 and 3 p.m., it might take months or years to learn that an overhead Air Force plane is performing advanced radar testing on that same schedule. Sometimes the big picture of network troubleshooting gets pretty large.

Problem Determination: WANs

Whereas LANs are more complex to troubleshoot than centralized networks, MANs and WANs are more difficult to manage than LANs. For one thing, both MANs and WANs typically interconnect other networks, so a MAN or WAN is a collection of networks, each of which is difficult to manage in itself.

Consider the network pictured in Figure 11.3. A LAN of PCs performs manufacturing functions, while a LAN of PCs with an attached midrange computer handles shipping functions. Two central systems servicing traditional terminal networks are then responsible for the accounting and administrative/sales functions, respectively. And all four of these networks are tied together through high-speed, digital (T1) links.

FIG. 11.3
Sample WAN

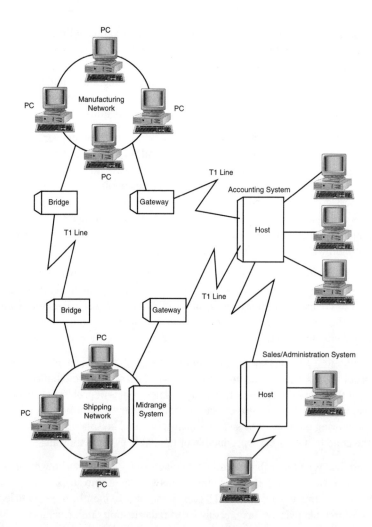

In this example environment, the flow of information between Manufacturing, Shipping, and Accounting is critical. It enables the company to track and coordinate parts received, final goods in inventory, shipments, and billings. The Sales/Administration system relies on information maintained by the other systems for tracking the status of customer orders or finding the availability of inventoried goods.

Each of the self-contained networks within the larger WAN has critical dependencies on one or more of the other small networks. If, in the example, the manufacturing LAN fails to communicate with the accounting system, important information is no longer being reported—parts received can no longer be tied to accounts payable, and new inventory cannot be added into assets. Therefore, any problem within any of the networks is critical to the entire network.

But the network analyst (who is probably not located where the failure is) must determine if the problem is in the manufacturing LAN or in the link between the LAN and the accounting system. Fortunately, the approach taken here is similar to the approach used for centralized networks. A quick call to the manufacturing operation should determine if the problem is the LAN itself or the link between the LAN and the accounting system. If the problem is in the link, the troubleshooter needs to pursue the bridge between the LAN and the link, the line interface on the manufacturing system, and, of course, the line itself.

Again, the problem is not insurmountable when analyzed in its own right. But when the network grows to worldwide size and interconnects many different centralized systems, LANs, and MANs, the problem becomes much more intense because of the scale and number of variables. A link between Kansas and Ohio might use T1 transmission, but a link between New York and Denmark might use a third-party, worldwide packet-switching network (PSN).

A WAN-wide failure can be simultaneously evasive and disastrous. Let's go back to the example of the large manufacturer using a broadband network. Broadband is a high-bandwidth data communications scheme capable of transmitting voice, video, and data simultaneously. Therefore if a forklift runs over the broadband cable and severs it, all kinds of systems will be affected (for example, computers, telephones, and teleconferencing equipment) If, on the other hand, a minor electrical component fails in a computer or interface device causing distortion or degradation on the broadband network, only selected operations will be affected, and sorting through the confusion will be a chore.

Given these large networks and the complex problems they pose, the need for network diagnostic equipment and software should be obvious.

Approaches to Network Management

Network management is best facilitated when the lowest layers of the networking and data communications software are sensitive to failures and capable of reporting them. Furthermore, the best possible network management solution uses intelligent equipment at all levels— equipment that is capable of detecting errors in itself and in the equipment with which it interfaces, automatically notifying personnel of the situation, and executing the repair of some common problems. Ideally, terminal controllers report workstation failures, modems report line problems, and LAN interfaces in computers report any irregularities they experience.

Many vendors and data communication providers have started to provide this level of intelligence in their products. However, because networking solutions often involve mature (or old) data communication solutions, the data communications protocols often cannot carry (let alone detect) this special information to a common networking management point.

This lack of integrated network diagnostic products has long fostered the use of independent, nonintrusive diagnostic products. These products grant visibility to low-level data communications activities without interfering with the activities. These types of products include breakout boxes, line monitors, and LAN monitors.

Breakout boxes serve to isolate and display the electrical signals within an interface. For example, an RS-232 breakout box shows when data is transmitted, when data is received, and the various electrical interface handshakes that accompany the transfer of data (that is,

Ch
11

Request-to-Send, Clear-to-Send, and so on). Although these devices do not actually display the data being carried over the interface, they show all of the other characteristics of the interface. Breakout boxes are available for a wide variety of interfaces, including LAN interfaces.

In contrast, data communications *line monitors* can be used to view the electrical signals and digital information being passed on a standard data communications line. These monitors perform no detection or isolation on their own; they just provide a viewport from which the data communications analyst can diagnose the problem. The evolution of the line monitor was an important step in the development of data communications management. Before this type of equipment, traditional electronic instruments like oscilloscopes had to be applied to the individual signal lines, and data was viewed as analog electrical patterns (square waves, sine waves, and so forth). With line monitors, the same information appears as digital data that can be viewed in binary or character format. Line monitors are specialized electronic devices produced, for the most part, by third-party companies such as Digilog Inc. and Tektronix Inc.

LAN monitors are similar to line monitors, except that they monitor the traffic and electrical signals operating on a LAN. This equipment tends to be more sophisticated (and expensive) than line monitors because it must actually interpret and present the frames (for example, 802.3, 802.5, and Ethernet) for analysis. By viewing the data at this low level, one monitor can track multiple LAN disciplines (for example, DECnet, TCP/IP, and Novell IPX) operating on the same physical LAN. Some LAN monitors can be further keyed into monitoring one or more specific disciplines. HP is a leading manufacturer of this type of LAN monitor.

Because any computer in any LAN looks at every frame that passes by, software has been developed for PCs and workstations to perform the function of a LAN monitor. While operating in this mode, the PC does not typically participate in the network (although it technically can). Rather, it displays and breaks out frame level and protocol-level traffic. The popularity of this approach has risen to the point that many manufacturers (lead by HP and Digital) promote the dedication of PCs or workstations to this task. In effect, that computer becomes the full-time network monitor. All major manufacturers and many third-party companies produce software that performs this function.

N O T E   Microsoft now includes a basic Network Monitor application in its Windows NT 4.0
operating system. Although it is has only limited functionality, it has the advantage of being free with Windows NT, and can be very useful in basic troubleshooting and for viewing network traffic.

Most of the intelligent devices used in networking have special internal diagnostic routines that perform some confidence testing of the raw hardware and interfaces. For example, terminals, terminal controllers, modems, and computer interface cards normally have these diagnostics available. Unfortunately, operating the diagnostics often involves removing the unit from the network. In many highly distributed WANs, this might not be a practical approach because the technical personnel might not be near the equipment in question.

Emulation and exercise equipment is often used to diagnose these remote problems. This type of equipment emulates the controlling equipment, but instead of running the live environment, it sends and receives test messages to exercise the remote equipment and then records and reports any failures. Exercise routines can also be run by computers instead of specialized instruments. When used in this fashion, the diagnostics might run concurrently with other network operations (although the devices being tested will not participate in the normal network activities).

In TCP/IP networks, you do have one other important diagnostic tool: the ping command. The ping command is a simple TCP/IP utility that sends a test message out to a system in the network and waits for a response back. If you receive a response, you then at least know that the system you are testing is properly connected to the network, and you can then move your tests up to the next level and look at configuration issues instead of network attachment issues.

It must be noted that the primary purpose of monitoring these diagnostic products is to aid the network or data communications analyst in determining the problem. These products do nothing on their own and have little value to non-technical personnel. In fact, there is a risk associated by allowing non-technical personnel to use monitoring products, because they will gain visibility to all kinds of information traveling through the network—for example, passwords, personnel information, and financial details normally flow through networks unencrypted. This is clearly a good reason to control who has access to network monitoring products.

Monitoring and diagnostic products are, in reality, just simple tools that pale in comparison to full-blown network management products. There are a variety of network management products on the market that range in price from hundreds to millions of dollars. Originally these products were implemented using proprietary interfaces, but the industry is know moving toward standards-based network management.

Ch
11

The *Desktop Management Interface (DMI),* a standard promoted by the *Desktop Management Task Force (DMTF),* provides a common management framework for products and management protocols from different vendors. DMI establishes a standard interface for communications between management applications and system components. More products are starting to comply with the specification, which revolves around a *Management Information Format (MIF) database,* a language used to specify the manageable attributes of DMI-compliant devices. MIFs have been released for several basic components, such as the CPU, operating system, and disk drives. Further MIFs are under development for network interface cards (NICs), printers, and other devices. Openview for Windows (HP), LANDesk Manager (Intel), and Systems Management Server (Microsoft) all use the DMI.

The DMI's Service Layer runs locally, and collects information from devices by accessing the MIF database. Compliant devices communicate with the Service Layer through a Component Interface, and pass information to the management applications. There are some similarities between DMI and SNMP. SNMP, instead of a MIF, stores data in a *management information base (MIB).*

In the past, DMI has been limited in scope. The DMI itself, although it specifies a definition for collecting management information, has no guidelines for passing data across the network. Without the ability to get information from a remote machine, DMI is very limited in its usefulness and requires proprietary means to move the information. The DMTF's *Remote Desktop*

Management Interface (RDMI) standard remedies that deficiency, enabling management products to share information across multiple platforms and operating systems.

Apple Computer Inc., IBM Corporation, Ki NETWORKS Inc., and Sun Microsystems have formed an alliance to implement a common agent technology, which facilitates collection of network management information from hardware and software components from multiple vendors. The common agent technology consolidates and synthesizes this information, using existing management protocols including both SNMP and DMI. Common agent technology permits DMI-enabled network components to be managed in an integrated fashion, and provides existing management consoles with immediate access to DMI information. The common agent technology is actually an SNMP implementation that supports integrated management of DMI-compliant components and SNMP subagents. It is also capable of converting DMI data into SNMP format. Consequently, network managers can support both SNMP and DMI resources.

Network Management Products

Network management products operate on at least two levels. At the lower level, a network management protocol must be in place to ferret out problems in the network. These problems are then presented to the upper level, which collects and correlates the information so it is understandable by humans (or application programs written by humans). Generally speaking, the functions provided by network management products include:

- *Network status.* Network management products enable the current state of the network to be monitored. This includes showing which devices are online and which are not, as well as the following information:

    - *Error reporting.* If information is being corrupted in the network or devices are not performing properly, these events will (or should) be reported with the status information. Often, you can use this information to solve problems before they become more serious.

    - *Performance.* In the context of network management, performance normally refers to line use. By showing the amount (percent) of usage on a line-by-line (or controller-by-controller) basis, performance information enables you to review the effectiveness of the network layout.

- *Hard fault alarms.* One of the primary purposes of network management products is to provide an immediate alert in the event of a serious failure in the network. To accomplish this, the product must detect and isolate the failure.

- *Network modifications.* Network management products provided by a vendor for use on a specific type of computer often integrate the procedures for implementing changes in the network under the large umbrella of network management. The theory is that modifications to the network are important and directly affect the state of the network, so the change procedures should be part of the network management product. However, if the product is from a third party or is intended for use on many different computer systems, this level of functionality will probably be absent.

In terms of the OSI Reference Model, network management functions are defined by the Common Management Information Service (CMIS) and Common Management Information Protocol (CMIP) standards. CMIS and CMIP were developed by the ISO as part of the application-layer Network Management standards. In the context of network management products, CMIP performs the lower-layer data collections functions and reports its finding to CMIS.

Network management is one area where the demand has exceeded ISO's ability to define standards. Witness the increasing popularity of *Simple Network Management Protocol (SNMP)*. The SNMP definition facilitates the reporting and collection of network errors. Originally targeted to bring network management tools to the TCP/IP environment, SNMP provides functions similar to those in CMIP.

As a result of the decline in popularity of the OSI Reference Model (following its de-emphasis by the U.S. government), the popularity of SNMP has increased in the eyes of most vendors. From the manufacturer's perspective, SNMP represents a relatively simple network management tool. Implementing SNMP involves having computers and intelligent network devices report errors to SNMP and designating one or more computers to receive the report of the errors collected from SNMP. Therefore, in a multivendor network where some (or all) of the computers report to SNMP, a single SNMP monitor station can track the network operations of several computer types. End users appreciate that SNMP can be used in a multivendor environment.

There are many vendors in the world of network management, with each offering its own sophisticated network management architecture. Note, however, that the architectures are not mutually exclusive, and there are some advantages to running all three architectures together. While the low end of the market is quite open and includes numerous products such as ManageWise, a joint venture of Novell and Intel, the high end of the market is largely dominated by HP, IBM, Cabletron Systems, and Sun Microsystems. The various company approaches are explored in the following sections.

IBM SystemView/NetView

NetView is the network management element of IBM's systems management software, SystemView. IBM has improved performance over older offerings by enabling CPU-intensive GUI processes to be offloaded to client workstations.

In 1990, IBM's SystemView Series was never widely accepted, largely because it depended on the OSI CMIP protocol at a time when SNMP was beginning to be more widely used. Current versions of SystemView are unrecognizable when compared to the 1990 CMIP versions. IBM has now embraced SNMP as the de facto management standard of the day, and has even embraced object technology in an attempt to make systems and network management a little easier. While the earlier versions focused mainly on the mainframe and SNA architecture, SystemView today is offered on four platforms: MVS, OS/400, AIX, and OS/2. SystemView consolidates many systems and network management applications into a single product; previously, IBM customers had to purchase management applications separately.

Ch
11

In releasing the SystemView Series, IBM has acknowledged the growing trend toward multi-vendor, client/server systems, and has given the product the ability to manage resources from many different vendors. SystemView provides utilities for change and configuration management, scheduling, workload balancing, storage and print management, software distribution, systems administration, and many additional functions. Additionally, its point-and-click interface and use of a process-oriented model marks a move towards simplified and more integrated management.

Features of SystemView   All four implementations of SystemView support all of the systems management functions defined by the SystemView architecture, which include business management, change management, configuration management, operations management (including network management), performance management, and problem management. Features include:

- *Client Support.* SystemView is able to manage clients including IBM OS/2, HP-UX, Macintosh, NetWare, SCO UNIX, Sun Solaris, SunOS, Windows NT, and Windows 3.x.

- *Storage Management.* SystemView's Hierarchical Storage Management (HSM) facility, part of the ADSTAR Distributed Storage Manager (ADSM) feature, automates the process of moving infrequently used files to lower-cost storage media. HSM retains files that are more frequently accessed on local file systems, which results in a faster response time. With the HSM system, users access all files, regardless of location, as if they were local.

- *Data Management.* The DataHub for UNIX Operating Systems data management facility permits the administrator to manage multiple databases from a single control point, and without having to know the different SQL syntaxes of the different databases.

- *Change Management.* Increasingly, mobile workers can cause the network manager more than a few headaches. Change management is not a simple task, although SystemView's Software Distribution for AIX facility offers significantly more automation than previously available for this task.

- *Performance Monitoring.* The Performance Reporter facility tracks system resources, such as disk utilization, and checks them against pre-set parameters.

- *Remote Monitoring.* The Nways Campus Manager Remote Monitor provides real-time performance monitoring across a multivendor network.

SystemView for MVS   SystemView for MVS, running on a System/390 MVS platform, permits the management of a distributed enterprise from a single control point. SystemView for MVS is able to manage MVS, VM and VSE hosts, SNA and IP resources, AIX and OS/400 systems, NetWare and other LANs, and several other network resources. It combines more than 36 systems and network management applications, providing access from a single, graphical window.

SystemView for OS/400   SystemView for OS/400 is a modular solution, also controllable from a single point. Its Automation Center/400 application automates the runbook, enabling the administrator to define important system conditions and define actions to take automatically should those conditions occur. For managing and analyzing performance data, the

Performance Tools/400 application is included. The System Manager/400 application is used to centrally manage distribution, operations, software, and problems from a single AS/400 system.

SystemView for OS/2   The newest addition to the SystemView family, SystemView for OS/2 is best used in small to medium-sized networks. It is based on IBM's NetFinity product, and integrates NetFinity's features for hardware management, inventory, file transfer, and more. Some of the features included in SystemView for OS/2 include real-time monitoring, software process monitoring, performance monitoring metrics, and a software inventory dictionary for automatically finding already-installed applications. Also featured is support for DB2/2 and Lotus Notes, which can be used to store and reuse configuration and performance data.

SystemView for AIX   SystemView for AIX can manage an enterprisewide, heterogeneous environment of multi-vendor devices and operating systems. Like the other SystemView products, it manages the network from a single console. However, the administrator can choose to share management functions and distribute some processes from the server to client workstations. Operational tools include: the LAN Management Utilities, for managing and monitoring IP, IPX, and NetBIOS devices; LAN Network Manager for AIX, for viewing status information about the LAN; LoadLeveler, for job management and balancing; and NetView for AIX, for managing multivendor TCP/IP networks.

NetView for AIX, the network management element of SystemView for AIX, supports up to 30 operators who can share access to management functions. System access is controlled through the distributed security features, and a sequential logon function is included for seamless transfer of control from one operator to the next.

Ch
11

IBM's SystemView Advance Team program might ultimately result in even more integration and features. This program invites third-party vendors to integrate their products into the SystemView framework. The plan makes alliances with vendors offering network and systems management products that support SystemView platforms. Members of this team include Bay Networks, Boole and Babbage Inc. (San Jose, California), and Cisco Systems Inc. (San Jose, California).

IBM and Tivoli

IBM has entered into an arrangement to acquire Tivoli Systems, a provider of systems management software. The deal will bring Tivoli's innovative management technology into IBM's family of systems management products, and will ultimately provide for an even more comprehensive solution.

Cabletron Systems' SPECTRUM

Cabletron is positioning its SPECTRUM product as an alternative to products like HP OpenView or IBM SystemView. SPECTRUM 3.1 runs on several operating systems, including HP-UX (it is the only other network management system other than OpenView to run on that platform). OpenView does not have a distributed architecture, which might make SPECTRUM a better alternative for some sites. Cabletron is attempting to extend SPECTRUM into the enterprise client/server arena with new systems management applications that facilitate policy-based management. Besides Cabletron, several third-party companies offer products that enhance the functionality of SPECTRUM with extra features such as performance and capacity measurement and configuration management.

SPECTRUM is protocol-independent and uses an artificial intelligence technology Cabletron calls *Inductive Modeling Technology (IMT)*. Through IMT, SPECTRUM can find solutions and solve problems on its own, with no human intervention. SPECTRUM creates a model that pictures every single entity in the network, including cabling, devices, topologies, and applications. The objects not only have intelligence about themselves, but also about their relationships to other objects. Version 4.0 of SPECTRUM gives the administrator the ability to manage not only the local domain, but any network that has been configured by SPECTRUM—giving SPECTRUM enterprisewide capabilities.

HP OpenView

HP OpenView, like SystemView, is an integrated network and systems management environment consisting of several related products. It is capable of managing NetWare and Windows NT servers and PCs, and a large variety of server platforms. There are a wide variety of third-party management solutions written for OpenView available on several platforms, including HP 9000 systems, Sun Solaris workstations, and Windows NT-based systems.

The HP OpenView Network Node Manager is at the center of OpenView. Network Node Manager, a network management platform, provides a full view of the network through TCP/IP and SNMP management. The utility runs the OpenView OSF/Motif interface, and permits many tasks to be carried out with little or no programming. The Network Node Manager includes the following subsystems:

- *Event Browser.* This subsystem permits event filtering and prioritization, and enables the administrator to set and customize alarms and configure events on a per-node basis.
- *Discovery.* This subsystem will automatically generate a map of a TCP/IP network, monitor the status of network nodes, and discover devices across WANs.
- *MIB Application Builder.* This enables the administrator to create MIB applications for MIB objects with no programming.

For larger networks, tasks can be distributed among several operators to reduce the processing load on the management station. This is accomplished with the OperationsCenter application, which offers manager-to-manager communications and hot-backup facilities, two important steps towards increasing OpenView's overall scalability. By distributing these tasks to up to 15 other operators, it becomes possible to manage a much larger network through cooperative management of multiple domains. This application will also offload much of the GUI processing from the server to operator consoles, thereby freeing up the server for more management tasks.

The AdminCenter portion of OpenView provides configuration change management functions for the enterprise. AdminCenter graphically displays the entire administration domain. All network objects are discovered automatically, and their status is represented with a color-coded schema.

HP entered into an alliance with Novell in 1996 to integrate its HP OpenView systems management platform with Novell ManageWise. The alliance further opens up OpenView, giving users of OpenView the ability to manage NetWare environments from the OpenView framework.

HP is also making available its long-awaited Windows NT-based agents, extending its reach further to the Windows world. The combination of NT and NetWare support significantly expands the reach of OpenView and provides for a much more comprehensive view of a multi-vendor enterprise. The Windows NT agent will also facilitate integration between OpenView and Microsoft Systems Management Server.

HP is planning a number of enhancements to the OpenView for Windows platform to enhance its PC management capabilities and bring the Windows version closer to the UNIX implementation in terms of functionality. HP plans to add support for the DMTF's *Desktop Management Interface (DMI)*, thus enabling users to monitor the configuration and inventory of desktop workstations. The DMI Browser facility will also permit users to perform remote locking and booting. However, users will need two browsers: one for monitoring SNMP MIBs and another for DMI MIFs.

Sun Microsystems Solstice SunNet Manager

Sun Microsystems is following the same path as HP and IBM, and merging systems and network management. In the past, a major complaint about Sun's management platform was that it could not scale to very large networks. Sun has significantly expanded its SunNet Manager over the past year with new implementations, including the Solstice Site Manager for smaller networks and the Solstice Domain Manager for large or multiple sites.

Ch
11

Solstice Enterprise Manager

The high-end version, Solstice Enterprise Manager, is still in the works—but will be capable of managing in excess of 10,000 nodes. Sun Microsystems' recent alliance with Computer Associates will ultimately produce a single product, meant to control an entire enterprise network. The new product will combine CA's Unicenter systems management and OpenIngres database, with Sun's Solstice SunNet manager network management platform.

Site Manager can support a LAN of up to 100 nodes, and can report to Domain Manager, which can handle up to 3,000 nodes. Site Manager and Domain Manager offer a consistent interface and feature set, which makes it much easier to run both systems. Domain Manager can be configured to receive information from multiple Site Managers, and can also send and receive information to other Domain Managers. Site Manager can access Novell's NetWare Management Agent (NMA) agent, which permits Site Manager to access the NetWare server's file system and print queues, and other key attributes. Domain Manager is available in one of three configurations: a standalone platform, as a central manager where multiple Site Managers are connected to one or more Domain Managers, and where multiple Domain Managers are interconnected as a cooperative management platform. The ability to enable multiple Domain Managers to share information gives the system a great deal of power and scalability;

the Domain consoles can be connected in a peer-to-peer fashion, thus permitting multiple administrators to share the administration of the network.

By distributing the management processing load throughout the network, Solstice Domain Manager is capable of handling a very large network. This is done through one of two different types of agent technologies. The first agent directly accesses managed objects, and the second is a *proxy agent,* which works as a middle manager. The proxy agents communicate with the management platform through ONC/RPC, translating the RPC protocol into a protocol that the managed element can understand. This mechanism permits Domain Manager to control a large range of resources.

Three application program interfaces (APIs) are provided for building tools to complement Domain Manager's functionality. These include the following:

- *Manager Services API.* This API provides ONC/RPC-based communication services as an alternative to SNMP or OSI. These services permit both Domain Manager and Site Manager to extend to other protocols, and scale well to large networks. This API also provides access to Solaris' access control and authentication mechanisms.

- *Agent Services API.* This API is used to manage multiprotocol environments through an intermediary protocol. A proxy agent can be written to this API, effectively extending Domain Manager's reach even more.

- *Database/Topology Map Services API.* This API gives managers the means to modify the management database and customize the topology display.

LAN Alternatives

While IBM's NetView is very effective in centralized networks and WANs, its applicability to a LAN environment is less than ideal. In a LAN environment, all network activity flows through the common LAN, and this LAN can be tapped and monitored, whereas in central and WAN environments, there is no single common thread for communications.

In this LAN environment, multivendor equipment can operate multiple protocols in the same physical network. At the lowest possible level, they all share the same (or very similar) data link and physical interfaces. Thus, in a single network, the Digital LAT protocol might run alongside HP's NS protocol, Digital's DECnet protocol, TCP/IP, and Novell IPX, but they all use either the 802.2/802.3 frame definition or the Ethernet frame definition. By focusing in on this lowest common denominator, a LAN monitor can track all of these protocols and more.

This is the approach taken by Digital, HP, and Sun. All three provide products to monitor the LAN operation at this low level. Thus, nonresponding addresses can be detected, along with excessive retries or rejections. In addition to these low-level functions, they also provide products to monitor their own specific protocols—so Digital products monitor DECnet and LAT, HP products monitor NS, and Sun products monitor TCP/IP.

Unfortunately, when a LAN extends into a WAN, these monitoring tools do not also reach out into the wide area. Thus, in a WAN composed of multivendor equipment, multiple products from multiple companies must be employed to track the network beyond the LAN. Fortunately, as the use of WANs has begun to spread, so has the development of comprehensive network management tools like SystemView. This remains a fast-paced area of growth.

Centralized consoles, such as HP's OpenView and IBM's SystemView, are used in the management of complex networks. However, these central consoles have not been as useful as they could be for enterprise networks. The root of their problem is scalability; the console gets bogged down when it reaches a certain number of devices. Typically, after this threshold has been reached, an additional management console must be added. Unfortunately, information is not shared between consoles. *Intelligent management agents (IMAs)* and *mid-level managers (MLMs)* address this problem. The IMA is able to act as an intelligent manager, diagnosing and repairing problems as they occur. The MLM is similar, but is able to manage other agents. The IMA typically resides in a managed device, while the MLM resides in the workstation and oversees a certain domain within the network. The enterprise console then manages a group of MLMs. The MLM sends summary reports to the enterprise console, so the console is less likely to become overloaded. Cabletron Systems' SPECTRUM network manager offers a good example of MLM features.

There are many obstacles to efficiently managing a network, particularly in a multivendor environment. Hubs, routers, NICs, workstations, and servers might all come from different companies.

Traditionally, network management products have come to run on UNIX platforms. However, Microsoft's Windows NT is gaining recognition as an acceptable platform for these critical applications. Several products, including SPECTRUM and Digital's PolyCenter NetView, now support Windows NT.

Ch
11

Cabletron Focuses on Integration

Cabletron is also planning integration with Microsoft's System Management Server (SMS). This integration will enable a SPECTRUM console to issue SMS commands; in a future release of SPECTRUM, data sharing between the two will be permitted. Cabletron has focused on ease of access in SPECTRUM 4.0, which will be able to send network management reports to a Web server. This feature will enable anyone with a Web browser and proper access to view management reports from any location.

The trend towards integration is being seen throughout the network management industry. Novell Inc. (Provo, Utah) and Intel Corp. (Santa Clara, California) have a new version of the ManageWise network management suite that better integrates the two companies' management applications. ManageWise 2.0 combines separate consoles for Intel's LANDesk and Novell's NetWare Management System. It integrates the NetWare Directory Services (NDS) and unifies network management and administration for the two management platforms. NDS maintains a central directory of authorized users, and provides for a single point of administration for enterprises with multiple servers. ManageWise 2.0 will also offer better SNMP support. Through ManageWise, an SNMP console will be able to manage a NetWare server.

Products like SystemView and OpenView often work with third-party products to expand their reach into other areas—such as a NetWare network. Novell's network management products are supported by both IBM and HP; users of SystemView and OpenView can gain immediate access to NetWare statistics through Novell's products.

Novell offers two network management products: LANalyzer for Windows and ManageWise. *LANalyzer* is an inexpensive, software-only network analyzer meant for smaller networks or for portable use. Running on an IBM 80386 processor, LANalyzer will continuously monitor traffic on an Ethernet or token-ring segment, capture and decode NetWare packets, and derive a variety of statistics such as bandwidth usage, traffic patterns, and packet counts. However, because it can only monitor a single segment at a time, it is usable only on smaller networks.

For managing multiple segments simultaneously, Novell offers their ManageWise network management software. *ManageWise* is a more full-featured, integrated set of management services that is used for controlling the network on an end-to-end basis. Like LANalyzer, it manages Ethernet and token-ring networks running NetWare 3 or 4. It offers extensive standards support, including SNMP, IP, IPX, and RMON; and several enhancements are available from third parties. IBM, SunSoft, and Hewlett-Packard have all agreed to support ManageWise 2.0 in their own systems management offerings.

Novell takes the approach of offering network management as a network service, integrated into the network itself, as opposed to presenting it as a centralized system. ManageWise is installed on each NetWare server, and enables an administrator to manage all NetWare servers from a single site. Because it is a distributed service, it can take advantage of the processing power that exists on the network, and minimize network traffic. Because ManageWise enables for shared access to the management information it collects, multiple consoles can cooperatively manage a heterogeneous environment. Users of IBM's SystemView can take advantage of the ManageWise network agent to get a dynamic view of the NetWare topology directly from SystemView. Similarly, users of HP's OpenView gain immediate access to NetWare statistics from the OpenView enterprise console.

Version 2.0 of ManageWise permits managers to move easily between SNMP management and NDS network administration. It uses NDS as a security measure for SNMP management by enabling staff to authenticate managers on the network and restrict access to management functions. ManageWise's SNMP agent technology permits NetWare servers to be managed from any SNMP management console, and also makes its network mapping services available to other consoles. Because it distributes its intelligent management agents throughout the network, the need for continuous polling is kept to a minimum.

Remote Monitoring (RMON)

RMON technology makes management tasks that were previously available only in the SNA environment possible for a distributed, internetworking environment. These features include network security, network design, and simulation. An embedded RMON agent can be beneficial to the corporate network, as the number of interconnected LANs and desktops continue to increase. RMON lends stability to the network, and enables network managers to support more users and segments without incurring bandwidth usage penalties. Most major internet-working vendors support embedded RMON, including 3Com (Santa Clara, Cailfornia), Bay Networks (Santa Clara, California), and Cisco Systems (San Jose, California).

The RMON and RMON 2 standards were created to permit troubleshooting and diagnosis of problems in an enterprise network, and to provide the means to proactively monitor and diagnose a distributed LAN. In the RMON model, a monitoring device, known as an *agent* or *probe,* monitors a network segment, gathers statistics, and monitors for user-defined thresholds that, when exceeded, trigger an alarm. These probes communicate via SNMP with a central management station. As networks get more complex and far-reaching, standards such as RMON are becoming essential. The original RMON 1 standard supported the monitoring of traffic only through the MAC (Data Link) Layer of the OSI model, and was limited in its usefulness. RMON 1-based probes only viewed traffic on the local LAN segment, and did not identify hosts beyond the router level.

The RMON 2 standard supports the Network Layer and Application Layer as well, making it usable for managing an enterprise network. The RMON 2 standard, however, does not support high-speed LAN/WAN topologies, switched LANs, or monitoring of network devices (the as-yet-undefined RMON 3 standard might accommodate these technologies). RMON 2 still goes far beyond the previous specification in providing a more complete view of network traffic, because the RMON groups map to the major Network Layer protocols, such as IP, IPX, DECnet, Appletalk, Vines, and OSI.

The importance of Network Layer support is evident when looking at a distributed environment, where resources might be on different physical LAN segments. These multiple LAN segments might be connected by routers or switches. Any user, given the right authorization by the administrator, can access any remote resource in the distributed network. RMON 2-based products are available for deployment in switched internetworking environments.

RMON can be used by managers to go beyond those functions afforded by SNMP for network management, and can accommodate a much larger enterprise. SNMP is used to configure and monitor network devices, but there are some limitations. SNMP management software usually polls the software agents on a continual basis. As a result, there is a finite amount of devices that can be monitored before the amount of traffic reaches an unacceptable level. The IETF (Internet Engineering Task Force) Remote Network Monitoring Management Information Base (RMON MIB) specification adds an extra MIB that defines managed objects, using standard SNMP mechanisms. The RMON MIB is mainly used to support monitors or probes that are not constantly connected to the management software. The RMON MIB also diagnoses and logs events on network segments, detects and reports error conditions, and expands SNMP's two-level hierarchy to provide the network manager with more flexibility. A RMON monitor can send data to more than one management application, and the alerts can be sent to the most appropriate station.

There are 10 basic RMON MIB groups, nine of which support Ethernet topologies and the tenth reserved for parameters that are specific to token ring. The 10 groups are:

- *Statistics.* This group shows data concerning network uses, traffic levels, and other information for troubleshooting. It counts Ethernet or token-ring frames, octets, broadcasts, multicasts, and collisions.

■ *History.* Provides trend analysis of the data in the above Statistics group.

■ *Alarms.* Permits thresholds to be configured, such that events can be triggered when those thresholds have been exceeded.

■ *Hosts.* Permits SNMP managers to receive information on network nodes that lack SNMP agents.

■ *Host TopN.* Permits reports to be defined, such that the top "n" ranking hosts are listed for different variables. For example, a report can be generated that shows the top "n" number of nodes that generated a specific number of errors over a time period.

■ *Traffic Matrix.* Permits a matrix that cross-references destination addresses against source addresses, and plots values for frames, octets, and errors for each traffic pattern. This permits the manager to discover which conversations generate the most traffic or errors.

■ *Filters.* Enables the manager to define packet match conditions to capture relevant data for analysis.

■ *Packet Capture.* This group provides capture buffers to hold information derived from actions taken by the Filters group. Captured packets are used by several network analysis software tools, such as Novell's LANalyzer.

■ *Events.* Generates an events log.

■ *Token Ring.* Actually several groups rolled into one, the Token Ring group includes token-ring-specific functions, such as ring station order and source routing.

Large token-ring internetworks often must be managed with minimal management and monitoring tools, simply because of limited availability. Token-ring RMON represents a standards-based approach to managing a token-ring LAN. However, many of the existing token-ring probes lack support for token-ring-specific features, such as autosensing ring speed or the ability to stop beaconing after a number of unsuccessful insertion attempts. There are also, of course, bandwidth issues to consider. The RMON management application accesses the RMON probes through in-band SNMP functions, which means that the bandwidth consumption of information requests can be a major consideration.

Major vendors of RMON products include Armon Networking (Santa Barbara, California), Frontier Software (Tewksbury, Massachusetts), and Hewlett-Packard (Palo Alto, California). In terms of the OSI model, RMON 2 supports Layer 1 (Physical), Layer 2 (Data Link), Layer 3 (Network), and Layer 7 (Application). Most RMON products, however, do accommodate all seven layers, although support for the Transport, Session, and Presentation layers are not yet standardized and are implemented through proprietary extensions.

RMON Agents

Both 3Com Corp. and Cisco Systems Inc. have plans for offering RMON agents that pass data to RMON management applications. The agents will be built into the companies' switches as a standard feature. RMON agents send data from each port on a switch to a management application. The agents perform the same task as RMON probes, which are attached to the links between switches, although the stand-alone probes are a more costly solution.

Frontier Software has created a superset of RMON 2, known as *EnterpriseRMON,* that overcomes the limitations of RMON 2 and supports all seven layers of the OSI model. Frontier's *NETscout* further extends RMON by supporting switched LANs and high-speed LAN/WAN topologies. (In the future, Frontier is also planning on adding support for Fast Ethernet and ATM.) The ability to monitor LAN switch and interswitch traffic permits NETscout to manage a virtual LAN (VLAN) environment. A NETscout probe device can be managed from any RMON-compliant management software product; similarly, the NETscout Manager application can manage any RMON probe.

VLAN (Virtual LAN) Technology

VLANs represent software-defined groups of endstations that communicate as though they were physically connected. The end stations can, however, be located on different segments throughout the greater network. VLANs also carry the advantage of allowing for policy-based management, which permits the network manager to assign priorities to different types of traffic. This model permits the network manager to manage the network from a business perspective, instead of a purely technical one. The network manager would, under this paradigm, be able to establish policies that would limit the amount of time a user could be on the net-work, the amount of bandwidth each user would have access to, and which applications are accessible.

The logical grouping of VLANs make it easier to do moves and changes, and provides for better use of bandwidth. One of the biggest problems of VLAN technology has been lack of interoperability. Cisco Systems is addressing this problem by spearheading a standard that could be used to create multivendor VLANs. The lack of interoperability has, until now, meant that in order to deploy VLAN technology, a company must stay with a single vendor. Several other networking vendors are supporting the standard (the IEEE 802.10 Interoperable LAN/ MAN Security standard) as a way to build multivendor VLANs.

Ch
11

IEEE 802.10, Cisco, and VLANs

IEEE 802.10 was originally created to address security within a shared LAN environment. Under Cisco's plan, the spec does not have to be modified to apply to VLANs. Cisco proposes that 802.10 be used in routers and switches for identifying network traffic that belongs to specific VLANs. Cisco supports 802.10 in its own routers.

The IEEE 802.10 Interoperable LAN/MAN Security standard would be used as a way to identify VLANs by tagging frames for delivery to different VLAN segments. However, a method for sharing address data still must be defined. Cisco proposes that a 4-byte field in the 802.10 frame be used to hold VLAN ID data; that field was originally intended to carry security information. Network hardware from multiple vendors would then be interoperable because they would all be able to send frames to different VLAN segments.

VLAN technology could potentially add a great deal of flexibility and security to a network, and save a tremendous amount of time and money (not to mention headaches). In a large, increasingly mobile enterprise, managers must spend an increasingly high percentage of their time accommodating moves, additions, and changes. The VLAN model would significantly reduce the time spent on these tasks, and enable users to move more freely between logical LANs.

Switches must also be able to share address table data, and there are no proposals for how switches could exchange frame information. Management is another issue of VLAN interoperability that needs to be addressed. There have been no definitions laid out for VLAN management objects, and all switches have different proprietary MIBs.

Most VLAN systems require users to define the VLAN based on LAN segments or Media Access Control (MAC) addresses. Although VLANs simplify management, one major limitation that existed until recently is that the manager had to issue new IP addresses manually whenever a new VLAN is established. More recent developments permit a single station running multiple protocols to belong to multiple VLANs. This technology creates virtual workgroups based on protocol type or subnetwork address, and requires less configuration on the part of the network manager.

The enterprise-wide VLAN is destined to become a reality, due in part to IBM's Switched Virtual Network architecture. This architecture provides a definition for grouping users over an ATM backbone using software, on its Nways switches and hubs. For more information about virtual LANs, see the "LAN Emulation" section in Chapter 12, "High-Speed Networking."

Managing Mobile Computers

Businesspeople carrying laptops to their homes and with them on business trips have become a common sight. These traveling road warriors often have the ability to dial into the corporate network to access applications, data, and critical corporate information. However, for the network manager, this increased mobility brings new challenges.

The MMTF

How do you manage something that is only occasionally connected and has no fixed geographic location? The *Mobile Management Task Force (MMTF)* might have the answer. The MMTF was organized to create extensions to SNMP 2, which would permit network managers to troubleshoot and control mobile clients using low-bandwidth remote or wireless links.

A proposed SNMP agent will provide for better network administration over mobile users. The MMTF has proposed a specification for a mobile Management Information Base (MIB) extension for TCP/IP networks. This MIB will permit SNMP consoles gather configuration and location data from dial-in devices.

Wireless Communications

Wireless is not likely to ever replace traditional wired networks, but there are areas where it can be useful. Wireless is not suitable for a data-intensive corporate environment, but might make sense for temporary connections, shop-floor applications, or in other situations where wiring might not be practical. Most wireless LANs send data much slower than standard 10 Mbps Ethernet—usually at about 1 or 2 Mbps, although frequency-hopping can speed up the throughput somewhat. The three types of wireless systems are: *Wireless LANs,* which establish a link within a limited area, such as a building; *wireless remote bridges,* which connect buildings within a 25-mile range; and *nationwide WANs,* which can maintain a connection between a large mobile workforce.

Commercial IP software products are starting to appear that enable mobile PC users to keep a wireless network connection over multiple segments in a large TCP/IP network. With such a system, proprietary protocols are no longer required for large wireless networks. Typically, if a user moves between segments, the wireless connection gets dropped. Users on multi-campus networks often are required to restart their hardware because of this limitation.

Mobile IP

IP6, currently under development by the IETF, includes specifications for mobile IP that will enable mobile users to maintain these types of connections more efficiently. Under this draft, a mobile node will always be identified by a fixed home address, regardless of where it is physically plugged into the Internet. The remote node will have a "care of" address that specifies the current location. Packets addressed to the fixed home address will be transparently routed to the "care of" address.

Of the many types of wireless technologies, *Cellular Digital Packet Data (CDPD) technology* holds perhaps the greatest potential, although it has not been widely deployed. CDPD technology sends data over a cellular network that is already being used for voice transmission; as such, it does not require establishing an entirely new infrastructure. It sends data packets between voice transmissions on an existing cellular channel without having any negative impact on the voice communication. The packets merely fill up unused voice spaces in a cellular transmission. The CDPD standard is non-proprietary, and allows existing applications to be adapted to the wireless environment. It supports multiple protocols, including IP, and uses cellular telephony standards already in use by cellular telephone users.

Ch
11

CDMA

Code Division Multiple Access (CDMA) is another emerging digital wireless technology that promises improved call quality and new wireless features. (The key word here, as in all wireless technologies, is "emerging.") Like CDPD, CDMA holds great potential in promoting open wireless standards, and ultimately more widespread commercial acceptance of wireless services. A new industry group, the CDMA Development Group (CDG), plans to address international development of CDMA standards, which will eventually permit wireless systems in all countries to interoperate.

Security and Firewalls

The move to open computing and client/server architectures has brought a great many advantages, but administering security has become a greater problem than ever before—especially in situations where the corporate network is connected to the public Internet. For example, by itself, TCP/IP has no inherent security. Many a worried administrator has spent more than a few sleepless nights wondering when the next hacker will wander into his domain.

Firewall products enforce strict control over access to the network, usually taking the approach of denying any type of access that is not expressly permitted. However, although these tools might keep hackers at bay, they might also keep legitimate users from taking full advantage of technologies that might otherwise be at their disposal—such as streaming video.

Proxy servers, on the other hand, will permit access to all Internet resources while still maintaining security. Under this type of system, a command is executed to an HTTP proxy server running on a separate firewall machine. The proxy takes requests and executes them, requesting whatever information is required from outside remote servers, and then delivers the response to the protected machine. A proxy server can also retain a cache of data, which returns requested documents more quickly. Because the data is then stored locally, it is available immediately, and the proxy does not have to go out and look for it each time it is requested. Caching is done usually on the proxy server, rather than the local client. Although proxy software is widely available, each protocol requires its own proxy server, which means a lot of administrative overhead.

IPSec

As previously mentioned, TCP/IP has no inherent security of its own. A proposed IETF security standard, IPSec (Internet Protocol/Security), will be appearing in firewall and TCP/IP stacks soon. IPSec is not specifically mandated for the next version of TCP/IP, version 6, although it will work with both version 6 and the current iteration.

The other type of firewall is a simple packet-filtering router, which decides whether to forward a packet based on the IP address and TCP port number in the packet header. These are much less secure than proxy server solutions, but are more transparent to the end user.

The *Security Administrator Tool for Analyzing Networks (SATAN),* a security tool designed by Dan Farmer, stirred up some controversy when Farmer decided to make it freely available on the Internet. SATAN detects vulnerabilities in networks, and can be a valuable tool that helps administrators find their networks' weak spots. However, it can also be used by a hacker to find the network's weak spots.

The application can be valuable to the administrator who runs it, reads the report of vulnerabilities, and fixes all the holes. If the administrator does so first, any hacker that subsequently applies SATAN to the network will come up empty-handed. SATAN is easy to use, although its intuitiveness is a double-edged sword. First-time hackers with little experience can easily break into a system, and the report clearly describes any vulnerabilities and tells how to fix them.

If you're worried about an outside SATAN attack, get a copy of *Gabriel,* a free SATAN detector that warns administrators of network intrusion. ●

CHAPTER 12

High-Speed Networking

Asynchronous Transfer Mode (ATM) Networking

Asynchronous transfer mode (ATM) technology lends itself to applications with high bandwidth requirements, such as video and multimedia. ATM not only enables the network to ship huge amounts of data, it can also reduce use of the server. With an ATM configuration, a NetWare server, for example, no longer has to wait for an Ethernet transmission that would otherwise cause data to get backed up in the cache.

ATM networks are built on a star topology, with a centrally located ATM switch and each desktop wired directly to the switch. ATM is a high-bandwidth packet-switching and multiplexing mechanism. Network capacity is divided into cells of a fixed size, which include header and information fields. These cells are allocated on demand. This high-speed protocol will ultimately bring many advantages to wide-area networking. However, the technology can be costly and might require other parts of the network to be upgraded to handle the load. A server optimized for a 10Base-T network will probably require upgrading to handle the increased amount of data flowing in from the clients. Besides the servers, the clients might also need a hardware upgrade.

More than ever, computer networks are being pushed to their limits. Huge applications, increased end-user demand for data, and high-demand applications such as videoconferencing and multimedia are creating a need for more bandwidth than is often available on a traditional 10 Mbps LAN. ATM, unlike Ethernet and token ring, is a connection-oriented technology. In an Ethernet LAN, the amount of bandwidth available to each user decreases as more people use the network. However, in an ATM network, the amount of bandwidth available to each connection remains constant.

Earlier implementations of ATM used fiber optic cable and optical transceivers, although commercial acceptance of ATM depends on its effective deployment on a variety of media. ATM technology is rapidly moving towards the desktop level, and is now available over Category 5 unshielded twisted pair (UTP) and Type 1 shielded twisted pair (STP) cabling. UTP and STP are the most commonly used types of media in the typical LAN environment. Category 5 UTP and Type 1 STP both support ATM transmissions up to the full 155 Mbps. Cable lengths can reach 100 meters, and a maximum of two connections per 100 meters is allowed.

Support for Category 5 UTP copper wiring means that ATM can now be brought to the desktop in a manner that is transparent to end users. FORE System's (Warrendale, Pennsylvania) PC ATM product line recognizes the need to bring ATM to the desktop, and includes driver support for NetWare, Windows NT, and the Macintosh OS. In addition, LAN Emulation techniques will permit existing applications running over NetWare, Windows, DECnet, TCP/IP, MacTCP, and AppleTalk to run unchanged over an ATM network. LAN Emulation also provides the means to establish internetworking between the ATM and Ethernet or token ring LAN.

A recent LAN emulation specification, suggested by the ATM Forum, enables ATM to be deployed in a LAN environment without having to change the system software. In addition, the price is gradually decreasing on all fronts as competition increases and new vendors enter the market. However, before ATM is widely accepted, more telephone service providers must establish their ATM services, and ATM interfaces must be built into network operating systems.

If ATM is brought to every desktop, every client gains the ability to send data at speeds of 25 Mbps–155 Mbps, or more than 15 times the existing data rate of a standard Ethernet LAN. The ATM architecture itself, however, has no upper speed limit.

ATM technology is still young, expensive, and lacking in standards, and an end-to-end ATM network is still not a realistic possibility. It is used primarily to support more specific, highly demanding applications that a traditional network would not be able to support. A network with only ordinary, run-of-the-mill needs and productivity applications running, for example, some database programs, productivity apps such as word processing, spreadsheets, and e-mail, can run on a standard 10Base-T network for quite some time without slowing down. Implementing an ATM network for these ordinary tasks is like driving to the corner supermarket in an Indy 500 racecar.

ATM takes all types of traffic, including data, voice, and video, and transforms it into 53-byte packets, which can then travel directly over a network via switching. This small packet size lends itself to real-time applications, such as video. In order to increase speed, the switches can route traffic through multiple paths. The link, however, will appear as a point-to-point connection, or virtual circuit. Bandwidth is available on demand, and users do not need to bear the expense of a dedicated line.

Because of the lack of standards, various ATM switches are often incompatible. The ATM Forum has done a considerable amount of groundwork for defining ATM standards, however, and more vendors are starting to comply and offer complete ATM product lines. An ATM solution can be costly by the time the switching equipment is paid for, workstations are upgraded, and training has been planned. (In the near future, however, it is likely that ATM will come to be accepted as a robust and complete backbone technology.)

The ATM Forum is a consortium of over 500 organizations. One of the first companies to release ATM products was Fore Systems, one of the ATM Forum's principal members. Fore released the first ATM adapter cards in 1991, the first ATM LAN switches in 1992, and remains the leader in this market. Fore approaches ATM with a four-tiered architecture, as follows:

- *Layer 1: ATM Transport Services.* These services convert non-ATM traffic to ATM cells, allowing all types of traffic to make use of ATM features.
- *Layer 2: VLAN (Virtual LAN) Services.* A VLAN is a logical association of users with a common broadcast domain. VLAN technology permits a network to be designed based on logical relationships, instead of physical connections.
- *Layer 3: Distributed Routing Services.* Although VLANs eliminate a substantial amount of routing, some routing might still be required, such as establishing communications between different VLANs, or conversion between different MAC types (Ethernet to token ring).
- *Layer 4: Application Services.* This layer makes the services in the above three layers available to existing applications.

An ATM network can carry three types of traffic: *constant bit rate (CBR), variable bit rate (VBR),* and *available bit rate (ABR)*. CBR accommodates voice and video, and requires the ATM network to act like a dedicated circuit and provide sustained bandwidth. VBR traffic is similar, except that the bandwidth requirement is not constant. ABR traffic does not require a specified amount of bandwidth or delay parameters, and is useful for most common applications such as e-mail or file transfer.

Ch
12

The ATM network uses three techniques to manage traffic. They are as follows:

- *Traffic shaping.* This is performed at the user-network interface level and ensures that the traffic matches the negotiated connection between the user and the network.
- *Traffic policing.* This is performed by the ATM network and ensures that traffic on each connection is within the parameters negotiated at the establishment of the connection. An ATM switch uses a buffering technique called a "leaky bucket" in order to police traffic. In the leaky bucket system, traffic flows (leaks) out of a buffer (bucket) at a constant rate, regardless of how fast the traffic flows into the buffer.
- *Congestion control.* This is still being defined by the ATM Forum.

More on Congestion Control

The ATM Forum is still defining the congestion control technique of traffic management, although two schemes have been proposed to control traffic flow, based on either an end-to-end, or link-by-link basis. End-to-end schemes control the transmission rate where the LAN meets the ATM device. The drawbacks of this method are that some cells can be lost and it requires a considerable amount of buffer space. A link-by-link flow control mechanism can support more users and uses less buffer space. This too, has its drawbacks: it is more expensive and equipment to implement link-by-link control is not commercially available. An integrated proposal, being considered by the ATM Forum, would establish a default end-to-end mechanism, with an optional link-by-link scheme.

For ATM to be widely accepted, however, switching systems must be capable of interoperating. The ATM Forum's Private Network-to-Network Interface (PNNI) is a dynamic routing protocol that can be used to build a multivendor ATM switching network. PNNI permits different vendors' switching hardware to interoperate and establish a switched virtual circuit (SVC) routing system. Under this model, several switches can work together and act like a single switch. PNNI distributes information about network topology between switches, so that paths can be calculated. It also provides for alternate routing in the event of a linkage failure.

ATM Management

ATM networks, like traditional networks, need tools for analyzing and managing switches and connections. However, these types of tools are in short supply for ATM networks. As more software vendors respond to the demand, the availability of ATM analysis tools will be another contributing factor to the widespread acceptance of ATM. (A consortium led by Fore Systems has created a solution to the lack of management tools for ATM networks. Fore proposes to extend *Remote Monitoring,* or *Rmon,* to ATM networks, providing fault and performance monitoring services on ATM networks.)

Slow ATM

You might not need ATM if you don't have demanding applications like videoconferencing, but you might still want more speed. AT&T Corp. is offering a new option, referred to as "slow ATM." The service runs at 1.5 Mbps, instead of standard ATM's minimum of 45 Mbps. The ATM Forum is, however, working on a standard for 25 Mbps ATM. Either service would add extra speed over a standard network configuration, while being less costly than standard ATM service. Many more low-end users could be expected to move from 56 Kbps frame relay to the 1.5 Mbps service, rather than moving immediately to high-speed ATM. The low-speed ATM network technology lets you move gradually to high-speed ATM, as the need arises; this is an ideal solution for easing into ATM technology without having to make a big commitment.

ATM and Frame Relay Internetworking

The ATM Forum and the Frame Relay Forum have jointly established a new standard—the *Frame relay to ATM PVC (Permanent Virtual Circuit) Service Internetworking Implementation Agreement*—to let users mix frame relay and ATM traffic on the same high-speed network.

This will permit frame-relay sites to move to higher-bandwidth ATM without having to make an absolute choice between the two technologies. As a result, protocol conversion software is unnecessary. The ability to use a mixed model permits a company to use ATM at high-volume sites, while retaining frame relay at lower-volume sites such as branch offices, and enabling the two to communicate.

If you use frame relay, but want to upgrade to ATM as a central hub, a hybrid frame-relay/ATM internetworking service might do the trick. Protocols adopted by the Frame Relay Forum and ATM Forum facilitate the establishment of such a hybrid network. Under the service, the carrier provides protocol translations that enable the ATM switch to talk to the frame-relay switch. The system lets you bring ATM into an existing frame-relay network, instead of having to decide on deploying one or the other.

FUNI

Frame relay to ATM internetworking provides for transparent linking of frame relay sites to ATM sites. One way to achieve this is through a new standard known as the Frame User Network Interface (FUNI), a service that performs a protocol conversion between frame relay and ATM. This service permits a network manager to use existing frame relay equipment, while gradually scaling up to ATM without having to make changes to the existing frame relay network. FUNI is actually a low-speed, frame-based ATM solution. The FUNI standard is still under development, while frame relay is widely available and fairly stable. The difference between FUNI and frame relay is that FUNI allows signaling and flow control to be extended to equipment on the customer premises, and it might be an attractive solution for sites with many different applications needing low-speed connections into an ATM network.

SNA Access to ATM

IBM is also working to support ATM in LAN/WAN environments. Price is one major barrier to wide area ATM, but another is the amount of work required to interface ATM with legacy networks. IBM's solution for joining ATM with its SNA/APPN installed base uses the *High Performance Routing (HPR)* feature to provide native access to wide-area ATM networks for SNA/APPN. SNA is well suited for interfacing with ATM because of its service features. However, SNA routing is less suited to high-speed networking. HPR overcomes these limitations. IBM's proposal is that the native interface to ATM take place through the HPR feature. Under this model, mainframe SNA and APPN would connect directly to ATM using either LAN emulation or Frame Relay emulation.

The *APPN/ATM Internetworking specification,* submitted by IBM to the APPN Implementers Workshop, defines a method for SNA users to migrate existing applications to ATM. The AIW is a consortium of vendors that includes IBM, Cisco Systems, and 3Com. The specification maps IBM HPR class-of-service routing to ATM's Quality-of-Service specification. The specification will permit APPN/HPR users to make use of APPN's class of service across an ATM net, without having to change existing APPC applications. The APPN class of service defines route security, transmission priority and bandwidth between session partners. HPR is an APPN extension that provides the ability to bypass failures and eliminate network congestion. The specification would permit users to deploy SNA class-of-service routines over an ATM net, without having to change existing applications. IBM's HPR/ATM proposal is part of its strategy of helping users migrate to switched network environments.

ATM Inverse Multiplexing

The ATM Forum is working on another way to ease the migration to IBM environments. Their *Asynchronous Transfer Mode inverse multiplexing (AIM)* technique provides for a more cost-effective deployment of broadband ATM over a WAN, by allowing a manager to stay with their less expensive T-1 links as opposed to moving to a more costly T-3 connection. T-3 runs at 45 Mbps, whereas a T-1 link runs at 1.544 Mbps. AIM establishes a high-speed connection using multiple, point-to-point T1 links that are managed collectively. The AIM specification permits ATM devices to be linked with a single T-1 link; as the network requirements grow, additional links can be added, until volume justifies the use of a T-3 link. AIM sends parallel streams across multiple T-1 lines and dynamically balances the cells over all available links.

Quantum Flow Control

A consortium of vendors known as the Flow Control Consortium are proposing an alternative to ATM, making it even more confusing for potential ATM users. The group, which includes Digital Equipment and ten other companies, says that their *Quantum Flow Control (QFC)* specification complements the ATM Forum's Traffic Management Working Group's work on the Available Bit Rate (ABR) specification. QFC is designed to interoperate with the ATM and Forum's Explicit Rate specification for ABR services.

LAN Emulation

LAN Emulation (LANE) defines how existing applications can run unaltered on the ATM internetwork, and how the ATM internetwork itself can communicate with Ethernet, token ring, and FDDI LANs. LANE, a specification of the ATM Forum, is an internetworking strategy that permits an ATM node to establish connections to the *Media Access Control (MAC)* protocol section on the Data Link Layer. This capability permits most major LAN protocols to run over an ATM network, without having to modify the LAN applications. LANE does this through three distinct techniques: data encapsulation, address resolution, and multicast group management.

Each end station in the ATM network possesses a LANE driver, which establishes the IEEE 802 MAC Layer interface. The driver will translate the MAC-layer addresses to ATM addresses through the LANE Server's Address Resolution Service. Furthermore, the MAC layer interface is transparent to high-level protocols, such as IP and IPX. It is through this mechanism that a point-to-point ATM switched virtual circuit (SVC) connection is established and data can then be transmitted to other LANE end nodes.

Multiple LANs can be emulated on a single ATM network, allowing for the creation of *virtual LANs (VLANs)*. A LANE driver located on an access device, such as a router or hub, functions as a proxy for multiple end stations connected to the device.

LANE offers advantages over a traditional LAN bridge environment, which is not scalable enough to support a large internetwork. In addition, the LANE model supports dynamic configuration, making it unnecessary to define physical connections and allowing a host to be physically relocated, while remaining with the same VLAN.

Because existing 802 frame types are used in the LANE environment, an ATM adapter can appear to an end station as an Ethernet or Token Ring card. Consequently, any protocol that runs on Ethernet or token ring can also run on the ATM network.

The ATM Forum's *LAN Emulation Over ATM 1.0* specification describes how an end station communicates with the ATM network. The specification consists of two parts: the *LAN Emulation Client (LEC)* and *LAN Emulation Services.* The latter includes the *LAN Emulation Server (LES), Broadcast and Unknown Server (BUS)*, and *LAN Emulation Configuration Server (LECS)*. The ATM Forum has gone out of its way to demonstrate the computer industry's affinity for bizarre acronyms, by collectively referring to this mechanism as the *LAN Emulation User-to-Network Interface* (LUNI).

Despite the strange name, LUNI (pronounced "looney") goes a long way toward providing multivendor compatibility. Through the LUNI specification, vendors can easily establish interoperability between their various end stations.

Each ATM LAN end station has a unique MAC-layer address, as do standard 802 LAN end stations. When one ATM end station is transmitting data to another ATM end station, the first station will look for the second station's MAC address. After the first station has discovered the second station's ATM address, any existing LANE connection between the two can be used. If there is no existing connection, the first station will initiate a connection using ATM signaling.

If an end station on an ATM LAN wishes to connect with an end station on an Ethernet LAN, a few more steps are involved. Suppose John sits in front of a workstation on an ATM LAN and wants to send the results of the World Series to Dan, whose machine is connected to an Ethernet LAN. This is where the LAN Emulation Services (LES) come into play. John's machine will send an address request message to the LES which sends the request to a router on the Ethernet LAN. The router acts as a proxy LEC for the end stations on the Ethernet LAN, and stores all the addresses of all the Ethernet stations, including that of Dan's machine. When the address request is sent to the Ethernet router, it is then broadcast to all of the end stations on the Ethernet LAN. Dan's machine will eventually receive the request and respond to the router, which then uses its own ATM address to make the connection.

Ch

12

Typically, connectionless LANs use bridges or routers to add additional end stations to the internetwork. ATM, on the other hand, is connection-oriented, and data sent between devices on an ATM network is seen only by the destination station. An ATM network can use two types of connections: a *permanent virtual circuit (PVC)* or a *switched virtual circuit (SVC)*. The PVC is manually configured, where the SVC is dynamically created by the ATM switch.

Also, the ATM network uses a different address structure from the connectionless LAN. LANE takes care of the PVC and SVC connections transparently, using an address resolution procedure to bridge the different addressing schemes and enable the two to be connected. Products such as Fore Systems' ForeThought 4.0 include ATM Forum LANE 1.0 software, which establishes a seamless connection between the ATM and Ethernet LAN.

ATM LAN emulation mitigates much of the complexity of the ATM network, but is only an interim approach on the road to full-scale ATM. Through emulation technology, a shared-media LAN, such as Ethernet and Token Ring, can co-exist with ATM. This permits a company to retain their original investments, while implementing a gradual migration to ATM.

Multiple Protocols Over ATM (MPOA)

MPOA, an extension of the LAN emulation concept, is used to map network layer addresses—such as IP or IPX—to ATM. Under an MPOA scenario, routing protocols such as IP can use the *ATM Quality of Service (QoS)* features, with the ultimate goal of allowing a LAN to work over ATM without having to migrate the LAN to native ATM. As with LAN emulation, MPOA creates an ATM SVC (switched virtual circuit) whenever a data relationship is established, creating a virtual router of sorts. This permits network managers to create virtual subnetworks that go beyond routed boundaries regardless of physical locations. The MPOA architecture is compatible with all routing protocols capable of carrying addresses used by ATM, and is compatible with ATM's P-NNI specification.

There are three components to the MPOA architecture:

- *Edge devices.* These intelligent switches forward packets between legacy LAN segments and the ATM infrastructure.

- *ATM-attached hosts.* Adapter cards that implement MPOA and enable the ATM-attached hosts to communicate with each other and with legacy LANs connected by an edge device.

- *Route server.* This is actually a virtual server, not a physical device. It permits the network-layer subnetworks to be mapped to ATM.

Frame Relay

Frame relay switching is a type of packet switching that uses small packets. It also requires less error checking than other packet switching mechanisms; instead, it relies more on end user devices, such as routers or front-end processors, to provide error correction. Frame relay is similar to X.25 in that it is a bandwidth-on-demand technology. It establishes a pool of bandwidth which is made available to multiple data sessions sharing a common virtual circuit.

The *Frame Relay Implementors Forum,* a consortium that includes Cisco Systems, Digital Equipment, Northern Telecom, and StrataCom, has established a common specification for frame relay connections. The specification is based on the ANSI frame relay standard and includes an extension that establishes a local management interface.

In the past, frame relay networking technology was used only in large WAN environments, although it is coming to be used as a tool to carry multiple types of traffic, including data, fax and even SNA traffic. It is less costly than a dedicated private line solution, and extremely fast.

Frame relay offers a number of benefits. SNA over frame relay adds savings by enabling users to eliminate private lines typically used to support critical applications. A high-speed frame relay network will let users transmit data at a rate of 1.544 Mbps.

Voice Support and NNI

Although it does not currently support voice transmission, the potential of voice support is tantalizing. Frame relay voice support would let you make voice calls on the frame relay net, potentially saving big money on international calls.

However, Network-to-Network Interfaces (NNI) have not yet been sufficiently developed. NNIs are used to let carriers interconnect their separate networks, and are an essential part of international frame relay.

Frame relay technology is becoming much more attractive economically, and carriers are getting intensely competitive. In many circumstances, frame relay is superior to a private line for data networking scenarios. The carriers' pricing models should be taken into account when considering a frame relay solution. Pricing schemes are complex, and include port charges for physically connecting to the network, charges per PVC (permanent virtual circuit), and charges for local access. Other charges include *COC (central-office connection)* tariffs, which cover the cost of the connection between local access service and the interexchange carrier.

The lack of switched virtual circuit (SVC) services has delayed the widespread implementation of frame relay in the past. However, manufacturers and service providers are starting to implement these services in earnest. The lack of SVC services caused customers to instead rely on frame-relay PVCs. SVCs would permit a network manager to establish a frame relay connection on demand, and replace the need for PVCs between sites.

Software is starting to become available to integrate voice, fax, and data networks over frame-relay. Products are available to enable a frame relay network to handle all three types of traffic. This type of software would naturally give priority to voice traffic, sending it at a Committed Information Rate—which reduces delays typically associated with sending voice over frame relay.

Switched Multimegabit Data Service (SMDS)

Switched Multimegabit Data Service (SMDS), a connectionless service, can be advantageous in some multivendor networks over ATM or frame relay technologies. Network design under an SMDS architecture is actually quite simple. With frame relay, on the other hand, you have to assign and configure PVCs (permanent virtual circuits) between locations. ATM has similar complex design requirements. SMDS, on the other hand, establishes any-to-any connectivity. Each location has its own E.164 address, so all you have to do is assign it a port connection speed. After a site is hooked up, it can communicate with any other site on the SMDS net.

SMDS is a scalable solution, and is capable of keeping pace with an increased number of sites at a low incremental cost. SMDS port speeds are also scalable. In addition, the ATM Forum and SMDS Interest Group have established a specification for internetworking SMDS and

ATM services. SMDS networks have a group addressing feature, which can be used to create multiple virtual private networks that can be easily modified as needed. However, it is limited to data only, and is not suited for real-time multimedia as is ATM.

Fibre Channel

The ANSI *Fibre Channel* standard offers higher available bandwidth than ATM, and more products supporting Fibre Channel are available in the marketplace. Sun and HP both have workstations that support Fibre Channel networks. ATM was designed as a cell-based, high-speed network architecture for data and voice traffic. Fibre Channel, on the other hand, is a high-speed architecture for connecting network devices, such as PCs and workstations, and high-speed hardware (such as hard drives) that are usually connected directly to a system bus. The bus (channel) offers the combination of high transmission speed with low overhead. The standard supports four speeds: 133 Mbps, 266 Mbps, 530 Mbps, and 1.06 Gbps. Fibre Channel NICs supporting these speeds are currently available. ANSI has approved 2.134 Gbps and 4.25 Gbps Fibre Channel specifications (although the technology for these rates have not yet been made commercially available). Commercially available ATM products, on the other hand, usually support only the middle of the ATM transmission rate range.

Switching in Fibre Channel networks is done by ports logging directly onto each other, or to connecting devices (the "fabric"). Fibre Channel architecture consists of five layers:

- *FC-0.* This is the physical layer, and includes the Open Fibre Control system. If a connection is broken, Open Fibre Control permits the receiving device to change over to a lower-level laser pulse.
- *FC-1.* This is the transmission protocol layer,
- *FC-2.* This is the Signaling Protocol layer. FC-2 defines three service classes: Class 1 is a dedicated connection, class 2 provides for shared bandwidth, and class 3 is the same as 2 except that it does not confirm frame delivery.
- *FC-3.* This layer defines common services.
- FC-4. This layer includes the Upper Layer Protocols (network and channel protocols).

High-Performance Parallel Interface (HIPPI)

Fibre channel is meant to be the successor to *HIPPI (high performance parallel interface)*, which was developed to connect heterogeneous supercomputers with IBM mainframes. Like HIPPI, the primary application for fibre channel has been clustering, or joining processors together in a point-to-point link for parallel processing. It can also be used to link the processor to a storage array. The advantage of frame relay over HIPPI is that processors can be located several kilometers apart, whereas HIPPI had a much shorter maximum distance (at least during its earlier incarnation). Fibre channel is not currently used as a LAN backbone technology (although it is being proposed for that purpose).

Is Fast Ethernet still not fast enough? Although 100Base-T, ATM, and other fast networking technologies are probably more than most people need. Some areas, such as scientific visualization, fluid dynamics, structural analysis, and even cinematic special effects, require a gigabit-per-second throughput. HIPPI, a connection-oriented, circuit-switched transport mechanism, offers an incredible data rate of up to 1.6 Gbps. Originally designed in the late 1980s as a supercomputer technology, the latest incarnation of this ANSI standard is now applied to workstation clusters and internetworks. Although it is limited to a distance of 50 meters in a point-to-point connection over copper wire, it can reach 300 meters over multimode fiber, and up to 10 kilometers over single-mode fiber. In addition, the original specification has been extended to allow the 50 meter copper wire connection to be extended to 200 meters by cascading multiple switches.

Much has been done to extend the capabilities of HIPPI below the supercomputer level; it can now be applied to an Ethernet internetwork or workstation cluster. HIPPI works well with most LAN and WAN technologies, including all varieties of Ethernet, FDDI, ATM, Fibre Channel, and standard TCP/IP protocols. It is capable of linking workstations and other hosts, and connecting workstations to storage systems at very high speeds. While HIPPI offers greater potential than other high-speed technologies such as ATM, HIPPI can coexist well with an ATM network, combining ATM's wide-area possibilities with the super high speed throughput of HIPPI over the local area. (HIPPI-ATM interfaces are still under development by the ANSI committee and HIPPI Networking Forum. Such a connection would encapsulate HIPPI data, send it over the ATM network, and then rebuild it at the other end.)

Fast Ethernet

The *Fast Ethernet* specification provides ten times as much bandwidth as a traditional 10Base-T network. Some consider the technology to be overkill, especially for smaller networks running standard productivity applications. Very few corporate users even use more than a few Mbps of bandwidth, and do well with their existing Ethernets. However, there are cases in which 100Base-T and other fast networking scenarios are practical and economical. Fast Ethernet networks might prove invaluable to professionals in the fields of engineering, CAD, and multimedia. Using Fast Ethernet as a backbone in a client/server network might make sense, especially if a high number of clients want to access the backbone network.

Ch
12

100BaseT is an extension of the IEEE's official 802.3 Ethernet standard. The 100Base-T network interface cards are fairly easy to install and widely available, and use standard two-pair UTP wiring (category 3, 4 or 5). Chances are, you already have category 3 or 4 wiring in the walls, which makes upgrading to 100BaseT fairly economical. There are actually three physical layers to the 100Base-T specification:

- *100Base-TX.* The most common layer, 100Base-TX is full-duplex capable but supports only category 5. Most Fast Ethernet products target category 5 installations only.
- *100Base-T4.* This is a four-pair system for category 3, 4, or 5 UTP cabling. 100Base-T4 can be more difficult to install and maintain because it requires four pairs of wiring, and there are fewer products available.

■ *100Base-FX.* This is a multi-mode, two-strand fiber system. Use of fiber optic cable yields a maximum distance of 2 kilometers.

All three types of systems can be interconnected through a hub.

Hybrid 10/100 Mbps network interface cards (NICs) can run $100 more than straight 10 Mbps cards, (although prices are likely to come down when the market for Fast Ethernet matures). These hybrid cards are usually software-configurable and capable of running at either speed. They can also include an auto-negotiation feature, which is a technique used by the card to communicate with the hub to automatically determine the environment. It will automatically sense whether it is 10 Mbps, 100 Mbps, half-duplex, or full-duplex. Some Fast Ethernet products might permit cables for both 10BaseT and 100BaseT networks to be directed to a single hub.

Despite advancements in 100Base-T, 10Base-T is still the most widely used network infrastructure, typically implemented in a star configuration with a central hub. However, as demand for data increases and applications grow in size, high-speed LANs are gradually becoming more important. Technology such as Fast Ethernet can provide the faster response times that impatient end users need, as well as the additional bandwidth that is required by high-end applications.

The Fast Ethernet standard has become the predominant standard for high-performance networking. Like 10Base-T, 100Base-T is based on the Media Access Control (MAC) protocol section of the Data Link (Layer 2) section of the OSI model. As a result, 100Base-T can be easily integrated into an existing 10Base-T network and run over existing cabling. Because many vendors now support 100Base-T with new products, including hubs, routers, bridges and interface cards, Fast Ethernet networks enjoy a high level of multivendor support. Adding 100Base-T to an existing 10Base-T network can be a gradual process and is often largely determined by existing cabling. As new stations are added to the network, dual-speed 10/100 adapters can be installed in anticipation of full migration.

Data can move between 10Base-T and 100Base-T stations without protocol translation because Fast Ethernet retains the same protocol as plain Ethernet—*Carrier Sense Multiple Access Collision Detection (CSMA/CD)*. A simple bridge will carry out this movement between 10Base-T and 100base-T. Migration from 10Base-T to 100Base-T is quite simple, because of the high level of compatibility and because it is based on the same technology and protocols. Most 100Base-T NICs are actually 10/100 cards and can run at either 10 or 100 Mbps. Many cards are auto-sensing and will automatically detect whether it is connected to a 10Base-T or 100Base-T hub.

An alternative to 100Base-T is *100VG-AnyLAN*. This 100VG technology eliminates packet collisions and provides for more efficient use of network bandwidth. The 100VG also provides some facilities for prioritizing time-sensitive traffic. Despite these technical advantages, many network professionals still prefer 100Base-T simply because it is more familiar—it uses many of the same access mechanisms found on standard 10Base-T nets. However, being based on the same mechanisms means that 100Base-T is not suitable for time-sensitive or real-time applications, such as videoconferencing.

Gigabit Ethernet

Gigabit Ethernet is the next step in the evolution of Ethernet. This wondrously fast gigabit-per-second Ethernet technology is still a long way off, and is currently little more than vaporous talk coming out of standards committees. However, this promising technology is likely to be less expensive than ATM and more scalable, not to mention less expensive to deploy because the costs normally associated with frame conversion are absent. The IEEE 802.3 working group studying Gigabit Ethernet might, if all goes well, have a specification by 1998. Under the group's initial design, Gigabit Ethernet would retain 100Base-T's frame size and CSMA/CD scheme, but would use the physical layer of the Fibre Channel architecture as underlying transport mechanism.

CHAPTER 13

Software Considerations

The advent of multivendor networks and client/server architectures has resulted in more software being cross-platform in nature. Cross-platform software development is simple for programs without a GUI; a simple recompile of a C program will do the job. It is more complicated for programs with a graphical front-end, but end users now expect this front-end from developers. Fortunately, there are several development tools available for this purpose. These include:

- *Uniface 6 (Uniface Corp.).* Uniface can be used to create a generic interface, which is defined in an object repository instead of in code.

- *Zapp Developer's Suite (Inmark Development Corp.).* This suite is actually an application framework, which includes a set of C++ class libraries with prebuilt services. Screens can be designed by dragging and dropping interface objects, and the resulting C++ code that is automatically generated can be compiled for either UNIX or Windows.

- *UIM/X (Bluestone Communications, Inc.).* UIM/X is an object-oriented development tool. It uses native libraries to create a more compliant look and feel, and has an interactive GUI builder. The UIM/X Cross Platform Toolset provides developers with a set of cross-platform interface components.

WinSock

WinSock (Windows Sockets) is an open API designed by Microsoft that provides the means of using TCP/IP with Windows. The newest version, WinSock 2, will add support for IPX/SPX, DECnet, and OSI. WinSock 2 is transport independent, and includes a complete set of APIs for programming to multiple network transports concurrently. (In addition, WinSock 2 will permit applications to take advantage of high-speed ATM switching technology. The API will permit existing applications to be adapted to ATM with only a minimal amount of reprogramming.)

The OAG and Multivendor Application Integration

The Open Applications Group (OAG) has demonstrated a specification for multivendor application integration. Two members of the consortium plan to deliver systems with snap-together functionality by next year. The OAG specification will enable client/server applications to be integrated "out of the box," without having to add on extra software interfaces. The applications will pass data directly between one another in a common format. Compliant applications will contain an API written to the OAG message format specification, known as the Business Document Exchange. If widely accepted, applications written to this specification will be capable of recognizing each other's data.

Macintosh File Sharing

The Macintosh is not widely used in corporate networks, although it does have its niche areas, such as graphics and multimedia. Several utilities are available to enable PCs to recognize Macintosh files. TCP/IP ships with the Macintosh hardware and is actually simple to configure on the Apple Macintosh platform. Any TCP/IP application can work with the Macintosh TCP/IP drivers.

AppleTalk is the Macintosh's native network protocol, although TCP/IP might actually be simpler. Some network managers prefer to avoid AppleTalk on the corporate net, despite the fact that there is actually little justification for this. Although AppleTalk uses a small packet size, this does not necessarily mean it will generate more traffic. AppleTalk does generate, however, some additional traffic because of the automation inherent in the protocol. Devices communicate with each other over the AppleTalk network in order to make AppleTalk a plug-and-play network; it is not necessary to have to type in addresses and setup data for each device. TCP/IP is moving more toward this model with *Dynamic Host Configuration Protocol (DHCP),* which is very similar to the *AppleTalk Address Resolution Protocol (AARP).*

Tools such as Wall Data Inc.'s *RUMBA* enable the Mac to participate in IBM-based networks. With this tool, Mac users can communicate with IBM mainframes and minicomputers, and with other platforms. Mac RUMBA client software integrates Wall Data's (Kirkland, Washington) SNA*ps mainframe gateway technology with the company's RUMBA PC-to-mainframe client software.

Component Technology

The concept of distributed objects holds great potential. A distributed object is a software component that performs functions for other objects. They can be distributed throughout the network and accessed by any network user with authorization, and the objects can be assembled into complete distributed applications.

There are four separate, and sometimes conflicting, standards for distributed objects: OLE, CORBA, DCE, and OpenDoc. These standards offer a way for different objects to communicate, regardless of vendor origin, and bring developers a higher level of abstraction. Instead of focusing on clients and servers, the developer works with users, objects, and methods. It is no longer necessary to track which server process is executing each function because this information is encapsulated within each object. When a message is sent to an object requesting action, the object will then execute the appropriate methods. The object encapsulates data, functions, and logic, which is then shielded from the receiving application.

Object technology can also simplify maintenance and network management tasks. For example, changes and adds can be abstracted to the point of plugging or unplugging visual objects in a graphical interface.

OLE

Component technology's goal is to permit development, management, and other tasks through interoperable, cross-platform, off-the-shelf components. Windows developers have at their disposal a large collection of Visual Basic ActiveX custom controls. Based on Microsoft's *OLE (object linking and embedding)* technology, ActiveX has evolved from the earlier VBX and OCX models. OLE, however, carries a high learning curve and lacks object-oriented features such as inheritance, a technique whereby both data and functions are moved from one object into a new object.

Network OLE

Microsoft is working on a version of Network OLE to provide this same functionality. Network OLE will use RPCs to distribute components throughout the enterprise. Network OLE will be released with the next version of Windows NT. It adds a third tier to a client/server network, with business rules and code encapsulated into components and distributed across the network. This third layer is transparent to the end user, who will not have to know where the OLE objects are located.

Ch
13

OLE (Microsoft) is based on the *Common Object Model (COM)*, an open spec for object technology. OLE objects are interoperable, and can be created in any one of several languages. OLE is only available on Windows platforms. Microsoft's Visual Basic 4.0 takes some steps towards a *Distributed OLE* model, which permits VB functions to be declared remote.

Under pressure to at least marginally embrace open systems and the World Wide Web, Microsoft has come up with an OLE enhancement technology it calls *ActiveX*. Besides Windows, ActiveX supports Macintosh and UNIX, and supports a large set of tools and programming languages. Microsoft's goal in releasing ActiveX is to make it easier to create interactive applications and World Wide Web pages. Already, there are more than 1,000 reusable ActiveX controls—which means that when you are building a Web page, you don't have to build every piece from scratch. Although it doesn't compete directly against Sun Microsystem's enormously popular Java language, Microsoft certainly had Java's market in mind when they created this little gem. Java programmers can access ActiveX controls from Java applets, and ActiveX also establishes a bridge to Java to let other programming languages use Java applets as reusable components. Microsoft's *Visual J++* Java development tool integrates the Java language with ActiveX.

NeXT Computer is planning to beat Microsoft at its own game, by offering distributed OLE technology before Microsoft releases its own distributed OLE products. NeXT plans to ship an extension of its current OLE object environment, called *Distributed OLE for Windows*. With this tool, developers can create Windows applications that send OpenStep objects across a distributed network.

CORBA

Common Object Request Broken Architecture (CORBA), however, does support object-oriented development. *OpenDoc* is a CORBA-based platform developed by an industry alliance led by Apple Computer, Inc. OpenDoc is better suited to cross-platform development and works well on UNIX, Mac, and OS/2 environments. OpenDoc does support OLE and an OLE 2.0 object can be embedded in an OpenDoc component. Because OpenDoc is a derivative of CORBA, it is networkable. CORBA 2.0 has a method for distributing objects throughout the enterprise.

CORBA's *ORB (Object Request Broker)* architecture affords developers more freedom than OLE in terms of programming languages and operating systems. OMG's (Object Management Group) CORBA 2.0 is based on the ORB structure. ORBs facilitate interoperability and establish a single platform on which objects request data and services on the client side or provide them from the server side. TCP/IP is used by CORBA as a standard communications protocol. Compared with the other standards for distributed objects, CORBA is still immature and lacks some features for large-scale production.

Version 2.0 of the CORBA specification includes the *Internet Interoperability Object Protocol (IIOP),* which provides for multivendor connectivity. The previous implementation of CORBA, although it provided for portability, did not include a specification for interoperability. The availability of IIOP will significantly increase CORBA's potential to become widely accepted.

The ORB model is rapidly maturing, and several vendors are bringing ORBs to market. Some of these products extend the CORBA specification to support mission-critical applications, by providing fault tolerance, support for shared memory, and multithreading. Microsoft OLE-based applications will communicate with CORBA applications through a CORBA 2.0 ORB.

CORBA (Object Management Group) provides the specifications for the development of ORBs. An ORB instantiates objects, establishes communications between objects, and invokes methods on behalf of objects. The *CORBA Interface Definition Language (IDL)* is used to define the object's interface, but the existing specification, 1.2, does not provide for a standard communications protocol. As a result, few ORBs are interoperable between vendors. (The next version, 2.0, will specify such a standard.) CORBA does not specify a mechanism for locating or securing objects.

ExperSoft's *PowerBroker 4.0* is an extension to the XShell 3.5. It is the only product available that supports both the Common Object Request Broker Architecture (CORBA) 2.0 and Microsoft's OLE. This is accomplished through the product's *Meta object request broker,* which works as a translation layer that understands the two object models, as well as the predominant object-oriented programming languages. CORBA 2.0 defines mappings between object-oriented languages. ORBs are a type of software that defines how a software object is identified and used across the network. CORBA and OLE are integrated through the PowerBroker OLE feature, which automates interactions between OLE automation clients and PowerBroker objects.

OpenDoc

OpenDoc developers are currently able to more easily migrate a component between platforms, and OpenDoc is much more interoperable than OLE. OpenDoc is promoted by Component Integration Laboratories (Sunnyvale, California), an Apple-led consortium.

The OpenDoc (Component Integration Laboratories) consortium comprises several vendors, including Apple, IBM, and Novell. Similar to OLE, OpenDoc is based on IBM's System Object Model (SOM) and presents a visualization system for compound documents. (Members of the consortium are planning to provide OpenDoc support in their applications, and development kits have become available.) However, OpenDoc is a latecomer into the distributed object market.

OpenDoc introduces a component-based architecture suitable for cross-platform development. It is implemented as a set of shared libraries, which include the protocols for creating software components across a mixed environment. The standard is vendor-independent, and has a layered architecture that offers five services: Compound Document Services, Component Services, Object Management Services, Automation Services, and Interoperation Services. Many of the features of OpenDoc can be accessed through API calls. OpenDoc is based on the CORBA-compliant *System Object Model (SOM)*. Developed by IBM, SOM is a tool for creating cooperative objects, it's used in the OS/2 Workplace Shell, and has proven itself to be a reliable and mature technology.

The goal of OpenDoc is to enable users to call up compound documents that might include graphics, text, or other elements, without having to invoke all the various applications involved in creating them. Under the OpenDoc view, vendors replace their traditional large applications with part editors and part viewers, and therefore represents a significant change in the way software is created and used. This differs from the traditional, application-centered model, where users call up specific applications to create platform-specific documents. Despite large vendors' attempts at throwing everything imaginable into one large application, it is impossible to provide every feature that every user could possibly want. OpenDoc instead makes features separately available as parts, so end users can customize their application environments to suit them. Companies are starting to deliver OpenDoc parts to the market.

Ch
13

DCE

Distributed Computing Environment (DCE) is one of the most mature standards. Microsoft's OLE, because it is proprietary, is not a true standard, but has become a de facto standard for Microsoft environments. OLE is widely used, but specifications have not been provided to other vendors. OpenDoc is not widely accepted.

A product of the Open Software Foundation (OSF), DCE is fully vendor-independent and is widely available from several vendors and most operating systems. It includes services for locating distributed objects, and secure access facilities. It also includes a protocol for communicating in a heterogeneous environment.

The widespread availability of DCE objects makes it a good framework for building applications. The DCE *Remote Procedure Call (RPC)* is not dependent on one protocol or network type. The DCE RPC lets a server communicate with multiple clients on different types of networks, and DCE's *Global Directory Service (GDS)* and *Cell Directory Service (CDS)* is a useful technique for managing an internetwork. In this model, a local node set is represented as a CDS on the bigger GDS hierarchy.

DCE has been commercially available only for a short time, and supporting commercial software products are still not widely available or are in their early stages of development. When better tools become available, managing the distributed environment will be easier.

OSF's *Distributed Management Environment (DME)* is DCE-enabled management services. DCE's administration is consolidated under DME, providing a programmable process for managing the distributed environment. Implementing a successful DCE migration might take years and it requires detailed planning and strategies. Migration is hindered by DCE incompatibilities, a slow emergence of standardization, and resistance by users and management. While major vendors have announced DCE support, there are not yet any application development or management tools; although some products do offer DCE support. DCE decreases the complexity of a migration to a distributed computing environment by reducing the amount of variables, simplifying transition, and lessening dependence on multiple vendors.

The Motif GUI was one of the earliest successes of OSF. Motif has been accepted as a standard open systems interface by most major UNIX vendors. DCE includes RPC technology, which provides application and file sharing, enterprise security, and directory services. These are all transparent to operating systems, hardware, and protocols.

More widespread availability has led to an increase in DCE's popularity: DCE is now available on Windows NT, MVS, and AIX. DCE is a set of integrated directory, security, and transport services for building distributed applications that can run over multiple operating systems. It can support large-scale distributed environments in a multivendor environment. Other object technologies lack the same level of standardization and security to be effective in an enterprise-wide multivendor environment. More tool vendors are bringing products to the market that make DCE programming easier. Several UNIX vendors have shipped DCE code with their operating systems, including IBM (AIX) and HP (HP-UX).

Although DCE was originally targeted strictly at interoperability between UNIX systems, there has been a migration to accommodate many different operating systems. Microsoft is planning to use the specification as a way to move into the enterprise.

Data Warehouses and Repositories

The combination of larger networks, multiple database products, and a greater demand for business information on all levels demands new tools and technology. In striving for an inter-connected enterprise, made up of heterogeneous hardware and software, the data warehouse can provide an excellent solution. Imagine an enterprise with a legacy mainframe system, a transaction processing environment, and several departmental LANs. Imagine again, an executive coming to you and saying, "Give me a report on the Big Picture." You sweat a little as you imagine trying to gather all this information from these various systems and then integrate it all into a single report. You know you will spend weeks on the report and then the executive will look at it for ten seconds and file it, having no idea the amount of trouble it took you to prepare it.

The data warehouse can be used to bring together a variety of information from legacy systems, transaction processing environments, and other areas. Furthermore, an *Executive Information System (EIS)* can be deployed on top of the data warehouse, which will provide the executive or manager with direct access to this data. The executive no longer has to wait for reports, and you no longer have to spend precious time preparing endless management reports.

Systems within the enterprise are too often incompatible or just unconnected. Take, for example, the poor fellow who has to generate a series of monthly reports based on mainframe data. Every month, he has delivered to his desk a familiar wide printout, that after unfolding eventually drops down to the floor and across the hall. It is a major accomplishment when the mainframe guys even convert the dataset into a delimited ASCII file! Of course, they have to deliver it by hand, on a floppy disk, and then this unfortunate soul has to massage and rekey the data into a Lotus spreadsheet.

However, if he had one of the many data mining applications that are currently available, not only could he have directly accessed that data, but he could have "drilled down" to any level of detail down to an individual transaction.

Is this a familiar scenario? It is likely that most large companies have situations like this, where data has been entered once but must be entered again because of a computer incompatibility. What makes it even more frustrating is that it is no longer even necessary. Yet, the problem continues to increase as data gets more spread out and departmental LANs are created as autonomous entities. A centralized management of this wealth of information is absolutely essential.

This centralization can be achieved through the *repository*—a "meta" data system that collects information about the various data that exists through the enterprise. The repository provides information about data relationships, regardless of format. It does not actually hold the databases, but rather provides a sort of central, overall view.

Ch 13

Running on top of this repository is the *data warehouse,* which is able to bring together and manipulate corporate data, and make it more accessible for the end user. The warehouse puts data into a consistent format for simplified access. The repository/warehouse model provides an effective platform for connectivity throughout a heterogeneous enterprise. By having access to all corporate data, end users are empowered and the company maintains a competitive edge.

The data warehouse does not necessarily take the form of a central physical data store. Although this is one option, the distributed *data mart* approach to data warehousing lets the end user select a subset of a larger scheme, which is organized for a particular usage.

The data from the data warehouse appears to the end user as a single, logical database. In reality, the information might come from multiple databases and heterogeneous platforms. The differences between these DBMSs and platforms become transparent to the end user.

End users are able to access this information without having to access the production applications that were used to create the data in the first place. One of the most effective approaches to data warehousing is a three-tiered architecture that uses a middleware layer for data access and connectivity. The first tier is the *host,* where the production applications operate; the second tier is the *departmental server;* and the third tier is the *desktop.* Under this model, the host CPU, or first layer, can be reserved for the operation of the production applications; the departmental server handles queries and reporting; and the desktop manages personal computations and graphical presentations of the data. The data access middleware is the key element of this model. *Middleware* is what translates the user requests for information into a format to which the server can respond. This three-tiered architecture can then establish connections with many different types of data sources on different platforms, including legacy data.

Tasks involved in building a data warehouse include extracting the production data on a scheduled basis, removing redundancies, and cataloging the metadata. After extracting and restructuring operational data, the data warehouse environment then places it in a database that can be accessed by the end user. A traditional RDBMS can be used, although multidimensional databases offer special advantages for the warehouse environment.

With the increasing use of data warehouses, companies might need to extend the capabilities of the network to provide access to the warehouse across the enterprise. The number of end users needing access to the data warehouse is increasing, partly due to the trend towards downsizing and elimination of middle management. One solution is the establishment of the data mart, a smaller, departmental database that contains a relevant subset of the larger data warehouse, and is synchronized with the central data warehouse. The data mart might contain information that is most frequently requested, or relevant to only specific departments. This can keep the load on the data warehouse down, and make it easier to retrieve information.

World Wide Web

The *World Wide Web* is emerging as a tool for internal corporate networking and communications. Some large companies are deploying Web servers strictly for internal communications and applications (often referred to as intranets), and a way for employees, regardless of location, to access databases and other information. Because data written for posting on a Web site is created in a common format, using the HTML mark-up language, the originating platform is irrelevant.

Through these types of internal *intranets,* users can access applications through their Web browser, instead of having to log in through a remote access program.

The Internet and World Wide Web are also being widely used to offer publicly accessible data such as customer contact systems, where customers can check bank balances, order status, or other information.

Networking vendors are using the Web to deliver network management information. Viewing this data over the Web presents many obvious advantages. Network managers can access this critical information from any location, from any computer equipped with a modem and a Web browser. With this capability, it is no longer necessary to logon to the internal network or be physically in front of a specific management console to view network management data.

Web Plans—Cabletron, NeXT, and IBM

Cabletron Systems Inc. (Rochester, New Hampshire) is planning a Web reporting utility in the next version of its enterprise network management software. Cabletron's Spectrum 4.0 enterprise management software will include a reporting option that will send updated information to a Web server.

NeXT Computer has a software object library that will permit developers to write Web applications that can link with a back-end, object-oriented, client/server system. The tool set will include a number of objects for building electronic commerce-enabled Web sites, including credit card authorization objects, catalog objects, and inventory objects.

IBM is offering a solution for linking IBM PC Servers to the Internet that will enable customers to manage LANs through the Internet, from any PC, or from a workstation equipped with a Web browser. The solution will permit the management of remote locations around the world, while also permitting the administrator to perform management tasks from any desktop. This function is included in IBM's PC SystemView 4.0 systems management software.

The Web is emerging rapidly as a tool to make networks more powerful. This attractive section of the Internet is an effective way to make information readily available, both internally and externally. IBM has made a commitment to Web technology with its *MVS Web Server,* which can enable a mainframe to be used as a Web site. (IBM is also planning a similar access tool for the AS/400.) Lotus Development Corp., now an IBM subsidiary, also has a product to incorporate the Web in internetworks. The *InterNotes Web Publisher* permits a Lotus Notes database to be published and accessed over the Web.

Standardizing on the Web for internal publishing addresses many network limitations and compatibility problems. The Web is the easiest way available for enabling Macintoshes, UNIX workstations, and Intel-based PCs to share information. Anyone can create a page in HTML from any platform, which can then be made available to anyone with a Web browser, regardless of operating system or hardware.

Ch
13

Glossary of Terms

Numerics

10BASE2   A specification for thin coaxial cable often used with the IEEE 802.3 LAN standard.

10BASE5   A specification for thick backbone cable often used with the IEEE 802.3 LAN standard.

10BASET   A specification for twisted-pair cable often used with the IEEE 802.3 and 802.5 LAN standards.

100BASET   Also known as Fast Ethernet. An extension of the IEEE 802.3 LAN standard that boosts the speed of an Ethernet network from 10 Mbps to 100 Mbps. The three layers of 100BASET include 100BASE-TX, supporting Category 5 UTP and STP cabling; 100BASE-T4, supporting Category 3, 4 and 5 UTP cabling; and 100BASE-FX, supporting two-strand fiber optic cable.

20/20   A VAX-based spreadsheet package developed by Access Technology and often used in conjunction with Digital Equipment's ALL-IN-1. *See also* ALL-IN-1.

360   *See* System/360.

370   *See* System/370.

390   *See* System/390.

802.2   *See* IEEE 802.2.

802.3   *See* IEEE 802.3.

802.4 *See* IEEE 802.4.

802.5 *See* IEEE 802.5.

2780/3780 IBM Remote Job Entry (RJE) stations. This symmetrical protocol is often used in the context of the IBM bisynchronous contention protocol that directs the flow of activity between these RJE stations and the mainframe. It is also frequently used to implement RJE from one type of computer to another. 2780/3780 stations are non-SNA devices. *See also* RJE.

3080 An IBM System/370 mainframe.

3090 An IBM System/370 mainframe.

3151 An IBM ASCII workstation (for multivendor compatibility).

3164 An IBM ASCII workstation (for multivendor compatibility).

3174 IBM control unit for the 3270 workstation family. An SNA Physical Unit (PU) Type 2. *See also* 3270, 3274 and 3276.

3178 A 3270 workstation (LU 2). *See* 3270.

3179 A 3270 color workstation (LU 2). *See* 3270.

3180 A 5250 workstation (LU 7). *See* 5250.

3196 A 5250 workstation (LU 7). *See* 5250.

3197 A 5250 color workstation (LU 7). *See* 5250.

3262 A 3270 printer (LU 3). *See* 3270.

3268 A 3270 printer (LU 3). *See* 3270.

3270 A family of IBM workstations and printers generally used with IBM mainframes (9370, 4300, and 3090). Members of the 3270 family include the 3178 display station, 3179 color display station, 3278 display station, 3279 color display station, 3287 printer, and others. These units interface with the 3174, 3274, or 3276 control unit. In SNA terms, they are defined as Logical Unit (LU) Types 2 (3270 workstations) and Type 3 (3270 printers).

3274 An IBM control unit for the 3270 workstation family. The 3274 connects one or more 3270 devices with a host computer via a communications control node (3705, 3720, 3725 or 3745) or Integrated Communications Adapter. In SNA terms, the IBM control unit is defined as a Physical Unit (PU) Type 2. *See also* 3270, 3174, and 3276.

3276 IBM control unit for the 3270 workstation family. The 3276 is a 3274 with a built-in terminal. Like the 3274, it is a Physical Unit (PU) Type 2 but also includes a Logical Unit (LU) Type 2. *See also* 3270, 3174 and 3274.

3277 A 3270 workstation (LU 2). *See* 3270.

3278 A 3270 workstation (LU 2). *See* 3270.

3279 A 3270 color workstation (LU 2). *See* 3270.

3287   A 3270 printer (LU 3). *See* 3270.

3289   A 3270 printer (LU 3). *See* 3270.

3705   An IBM communication control node. Interfaces the mainframe to 3274 control units. In SNA, this is a Physical Unit (PU) Type 4. *See also* 3270, 3720, 3725, and 3745.

3720   IBM communication control node. In SNA, a Physical Unit (PU) Type 4 device. *See also* 3270, 3705, 3725, and 3745.

3725   A later model of the IBM 3720 communications control node and an SNA Physical Unit (PU) Type 4 device. *See also* 3270, 3705, 3720, and 3745.

3745   An IBM communications control node. In SNA, a Physical Unit (PU) Type 4 device. *See also* 3270, 3705, 3720, and 3725.

3770   An IBM RJE workstation that supports a console, printers, card readers, and card punches. The 3770 is similar to the 2780 and 3780 RJE workstations in function but interacts with the host (mainframe) in a slightly different manner. The 3770 is a Logical Unit (LU) Type 1 SNA device. *See also* RJE.

3780   *See* 2780/3780.

3812   A 5250 printer (LU 4). *See* 5250.

4210   A 5250 printer (LU 4). *See* 5250.

4214   A 5250 printer (LU 4). *See* 5250.

4224   A 5250 printer (LU 4). *See* 5250.

4225   A 5250 printer (LU 4). *See* 5250.

4234   A 5250 printer (LU 4). *See* 5250.

4245   A 5250 printer (LU 4). *See* 5250.

4250   A 3270 printer (LU 3). *See* 3270.

4300   An IBM System/370 mainframe.

5210   A 3270 printer (LU 3). *See* 3270.

5219   A 5250 printer (LU 4). *See* 5250.

5224   A 5250 printer (LU 4). *See* 5250.

5225   A 5250 printer (LU 4). *See* 5250.

5250   A family of IBM workstations and printers used with IBM's mid-range computer line (AS/400, System/36, and System/38). Members of this family include the 5251 display station, 5291 display station, 3197 color display station, 5256 printer, and others. These units interface with the 5294 or 5394 control unit. The 5250 family is classified as an SNA Logical Unit (LU) Type 7 device for workstations and a Type 4 device for printers.

5251   A 5250 workstation (LU 7). *See* 5250.

5256   A 5250 printer (LU 4). *See* 5250.

5262   A 5250 printer (LU 4). *See* 5250.

5291   A 5250 workstation (LU 7). *See* 5250.

5292   A 5250 color workstation (LU 7). *See* 5250.

5294   An IBM control unit for the 5250 workstation family. The 5294 interfaces with a mid-range host. In SNA terms, the 5294 is an SNA Physical Unit (PU) Type 2. *See also* 5250 and 5394.

5360   An IBM System/36 mid-range system.

5380   An IBM System/38 mid-range system.

5394   Like the 5294, a control unit for the 5250 workstation family (and a PU 2 device). *See also* 5250 and 5294.

9402   The system unit designation for the low end of the AS/400 mid-range system line. The 9402 system unit includes the D04 and D06 models.

9404   The system unit designation for the middle of the AS/400 mid-range system line. The 9404 system unit includes the D10 through D25 models.

9406   The system unit designation for the high end of the AS/400 mid-range system line. The 9406 system unit includes the D35 through D80 models.

9370   An IBM System/370 mainframe.

A

Accumaster Integrator   An AT&T network management product that collects and reports network information generated by AT&T's Network Management Protocol (NMP).

ACF   Advanced Communications Functions. An IBM prefix attached to products that support SNA functions. For example, ACF/VTAM indicates that this version of VTAM supports SNA devices.

ACK   Acknowledgment. A control character transmitted by a receiver as an affirmative response to the sender.

ACU   Automatic call unit. A device used with a standard modem to dial the telephone number for the originating equipment. Dedicated ACU devices were popular (and necessary) before the advent of Hayes and Hayes-compatible modems. ACUs work with asynchronous or synchronous modems.

ADCC   Asynchronous Data Communication Controller. An HP asynchronous controller card for the CISC models of the HP 3000 computer line. The ADCC is used to interface terminals with the computer via either the RS-232C or RS-422 standards. *See also* ATP and DTC.

ADCCP Advanced Data Communications Control Protocol. The ANSI implementation of a bit-oriented, symmetrical protocol based on IBM SDLC. Because of the ANSI endorsement, support for ADCCP is often specified in connectivity situations involving the U.S. government.

address A set of bits (or bytes) that uniquely identifies a device on a multidropped (or multipoint) data communications line or in a network.

ADSL Asymmetric Digital Subscriber Line. A transport technology capable of significantly increasing the capacity of existing phone lines.

Aegis A proprietary operating system for Apollo's Domain engineering workstations.

AIX Advanced Interactive Executive. IBM's primary (but not only) implementation of UNIX. Versions of AIX are available for IBM engineering workstations, PS/2s and for the System/370 mainframe systems. *See also* IX.

ALLBASE/SQL A HP product for the HP 3000 to implement networkwide databases.

ALL-IN-1 DEC's electronic mail and office automation product for the VAX system.

analog transmission Transmissions in which the native data processing digital signals are converted into waveforms for transmission. This transmission is used when sending information over voice-grade phone lines. *See also* digital transmission.

ANI Automatic number identification. A service implemented by ISDN that enables the receiver of a phone call to see the phone number of the caller on a special display. *See also* ISDN.

ANSI American National Standards Institute. ANSI is a nonprofit, nongovernmental body supported by more than 1,000 trade organizations, professional societies and companies. ANSI is the American representation at ISO.

API Application program interface. Originally an IBM term, API has now taken on a much broader usage. API refers to an interface available to an application for communicating with other applications. *See also* APPC, IPC, and RPC.

Apollo An engineering workstation manufacturing company that was acquired by HP in 1989. Apollo's products, its Domain line, used both conventional (Motorola MC68000-series processors) and parallel RISC technology (which Apollo termed PRISM).

APPC Advanced Program-to-Program Communications. An IBM term used to refer to an interface that enables two programs running on separate systems to communicate with one another. In most cases, APPC refers to the LU 6.2 interface. *See also* API, IPC, and RPC.

AppleTalk Apple's CSMA/CD-based LAN technology.

Application Layer The seventh (top) layer of the OSI Reference Model. The Application Layer defines services available to the application and to the user. This layer includes utility functions such as file transfer and virtual terminal services. *See also* OSI Reference Model.

APPN Advanced Peer-to-Peer Networking. An IBM term that refers to the capability of two intelligent microcomputer systems in a network to communicate directly without involving any higher-level SNA devices. In most cases, APPN refers to the capability of two PU 2.1 devices to communicate with one another.

Arcnet   A LAN implementation developed by Datapoint that uses a token-passing discipline operating over a 2.5 Mbps physical network. Arcnet became popular in implementing early PC networks because it offered a reasonable level of performance at a reasonable price. Arcnet can be implemented in many topologies, but it is usually implemented as a star.

ARPA   Advanced Research Projects Agency. Now called DARPA. *See* DARPA.

AS/400   Introduced in 1988 as the flagship of IBM's mid-range product line. The AS/400 (Application System/400) was modeled after both the System/36 and System/38—the two systems the AS/400 was targeted to replace.

AS/400 Office   IBM's electronic mail and office automation product for the AS/400.

ASCII   American Standard Code for Information Interchange. An ANSI-defined code that defines the bit composition of characters and symbols. ASCII defines 128 different symbols using 7 binary bits (the eighth bit is reserved for parity). DEC, HP, and Sun all use the ASCII encoding system, although larger IBM platforms use EBCDIC—a similar but incompatible code. *See also* EBCDIC.

ASP   Attached Support Processor. An IBM Job Entry Subsystem for the OS/SVS operating system. *See also* JES.

Asynchronous   A data transmission method in which each character (eight bits) transmitted is bounded by a start bit and one or more stop bits. Under asynchronous communications, no timing or clocking information is exchanged between parties. *See also* Synchronous.

Asynchronous Transfer Mode (ATM)   A high-speed protocol that offers every client on the network the capability to send data at speeds up to 155 Mbps.

ATP   Advanced Terminal Processor. A HP asynchronous controller card for HP 3000 CISC computers. The ATP interfaces terminals with the computer using either RS-232C or RS-422 standards. The ATP is similar to the ADCC, but can perform more functions locally. *See also* ADCC and DTC.

AUI   Attachment unit interface. The interface on a LAN between a network device (for example, a workstation or computer) and a medium attachment unit. Often used to describe a cable (in other words, the AUI cable attaches the workstation to the MAU). *See also* MAU and transceiver.

Automounter   Part of Sun's Open Network Computing (ONC) architecture. Automounter works with Sun's Network File System (NFS) to automatically mount and dismount files on demand. *See also* NFS and ONC.

B

Backbone   The main cable of a bus or tree LAN to which nodes or other LAN segments can attach.

Baseband   A data communications medium (such as coaxial cable) used to carry data in many LANs. *See also* Broadband.

Batch A self-contained task that requires little or no operator input to run. Batch jobs are normally run as background tasks in most computers (in other words, no specific terminal or input devices are associated with it).

Baud A measurement of speed as sampled in seconds. Although baud is often interchanged with bits-per-second (bps), the two units of measurement are not necessarily the same. While bps always refers to bits, baud encompasses greater dimensions. If the sampling resolution is bits, then baud equals bps. If, however, the sampling is based on two bits, then baud and bps are not equal.

BCC Block check character. The result of a transmission verification algorithm performed on the block of data being transmitted. The one- or two-character result is normally appended to the end of the transmission. *See also* CRC and LRC.

Bell 103 AT&T modem that either originates or answers phone transmissions using asynchronous communications at speeds up to 300 bps.

Bell 113 Same as Bell 103, except the 113 modem can only originate or only answer (and not automatically switch between answering and originating).

Bell 201 AT&T modem providing synchronous data transmission at speeds up to 2400 bps.

Bell 202 AT&T modem providing asynchronous data transmission at speeds up to 1800 bps. Requires a four-wire line for full duplex operation.

Bell 208 AT&T modem providing synchronous data transmission at speeds up to 4800 bps.

Bell 209 AT&T modem providing synchronous data transmission at up to 9600 bps.

Bell 212 AT&T modem providing full duplex, asynchronous or synchronous data transmission at speeds up to 1200 on a dial network.

BSD Berkeley Software Distribution. Part of the University of Berkeley responsible for the on-going maintenance and distribution of Berkeley's version of UNIX.

BIOS Basic Input/Output System. In PCs, the BIOS is a central service loaded from ROM chips that provides the core services for accessing devices (for example, the monitor, keyboard, diskette, hard disk and so forth).

BISDN Broadband Integrated Services Data Network. An ISDN implementation that uses high-speed fiber-optic links. *See also* ISDN.

Bisync Binary Synchronous Communication. A byte-oriented protocol using synchronous transmission. Bisync was widely used by IBM before its transition to the bit-oriented SDLC protocol.

BIU Basic information unit. The SNA data format that consists of the RH and RU information. *See also* BLU.

BLU Basic link unit. The information contained in an SDLC frame that is composed of SDLC control data plus PIU plus SDLC control data. The PIU, in turn, is composed of the TH and BIU, with the BIU being the combination of RH and RU information.

BPR Business Process Re-Engineering. A method of restructuring business processes to achieve a greater level of automation, a more efficient flow of information throughout the business, and a better understanding of the critical business processes by its participants.

BRI Basic Rate Interface. The low-end interface of the Integrated Services Data Network (ISDN) that offers two 64-Kbps data/voice lines and a third 16-Kbps management circuit. *See also* ISDN and PRI.

bridge Normally a set of devices used to connect two remote networks, with each network unaware that the other network is, in fact, remote. Bridges operate on Layer 2 (data link layer) of the OSI model. They can be used to form WANs and differ from gateways and routers in that they do not perform any emulation or translation services. *See also* gateway and router.

Broadband A data communications medium (such as CATV cable) capable of transmitting voice, video and data simultaneously. *See also* baseband.

BSC Binary Synchronous Communication. *See* Bisync.

BTAM Basic Telecommunications Access Method. An IBM mainframe subsystem that handles application access and routing within the network. *See also* TCAM, RTAM and VTAM.

BTOS An UNIX-like operating system for the Unisys microcomputer line that originated from its Convergent Technology subsidiary. BTOS is a modified version of Convergent's own CTOS operating system. *See also* CTOS.

Bus topology A LAN topology that features a linear backbone on to which nodes are connected. *See also* tree topology, ring topology, and star topology.

C

CAD Computer aided design. Design and engineering processes aided by the use of computers. In most cases, CAD contributes to the initial design and test phases through the use of sophisticated design and modeling packages normally run engineering workstations.

CAM Computer aided manufacturing. Manufacturing processes aided by computers. With respect to manufacturing, CAM contributes in the area of process control and quality assurance.

CASE Computer aided software engineering. An approach to the development of application programming that uses other programs to help generate parts of (or all of) the final product. At a minimum, CASE might be thought of as a programming tool.

CBEMA Computer and Business Equipment Manufacturers Association. An association of U.S. manufacturers that, among other things, sponsors the X.3 standards committee of ANSI. *See also* ANSI and X.3.

CBX Computerized branch exchange. A telephone routing exchange driven by an intelligent device (in other words, a computer).

CCIR Consultative Committee for International Radio. An international standards body that sets the rules and requirements for radio communications. CCIR is a committee within the International Telecommunications Union (ITU). *See also* ITU and CCITT.

CCITT Consultative Committee for International Telegraphy and Telephony. An international standards body which sets the rules and requirements for international communications. CCITT is a committee within the larger International Telecommunications Union (ITU) and is best known for the development of the X.25 standard for public data networks. *See also* CCIR and ITU.

CCN Cluster controller node. *See* cluster controller.

CD Carrier Detect. A lead in the RS-232C interface that signals that information is being received over the data link. CD is also sometimes called Data Carrier Detect (DCD). In the full 25-pin RS-232C standard, CD is pin 8. In the abbreviated 9-pin PC interface, CD is pin 1. *See also* CTS, RS-232C and RTS.

CDE Common Desktop Environment. Part of the COSE agreement between major UNIX vendors to present a common interface to all UNIX implementations.

CGM Computer Graphics Metafile. A device-independent format for the presentation of graphics. Defined as ISO standard 8632.

CI Computer Interconnect. A high-speed, fault-tolerant connection between DEC VAX systems and a Star Coupler in VAXclusters. *See also* Star Coupler and VAXclusters.

CICS Customer Information Control System. An IBM transaction-oriented, database/data communications system for mainframes.

CIM Computer integrated manufacturing. A total solution to the computerization of manufacturing operations that integrates as many related functions as possible (for example, administration, engineering, purchasing, and manufacturing).

CISC Complex (or complete) instruction set computer. The traditional architecture for computers in which useful software functions are supported by hardware. *See also* RISC.

CIXCD DEC's improved version of its basic CI link between VAX systems and Star Couplers in VAXclusters. The CIXCD is used with the VAX 9000 systems.

Classic HP applied the term Classic to its HP 3000 CISC models after it released its HP 3000 RISC models.

Cluster controller A device used to control the interface to multiple workstations. Cluster controllers are commonly used in remote locations to interface multiple workstations with a single data communications line. IBM cluster controllers (often referred to as CCNs) include the 3274 and 5294. Under SNA, a cluster controller is a PU 2 device.

CMIP Central Management Information Protocol. An OSI standard for the low-level functions required to perform network management. *See also* CMIS.

CMIS   Central Management Information Service. An OSI standard for the high-level functions required to perform network management. *See also* CMIP.

CMS   Conversational Monitor System. In an IBM mainframe environment, CMS is the interface between the user and the central Control Program (CP) of the VM operating system. Multiple copies of CMS are used to support multiple users (but still only one CP). *See also* CP.

coaxial   In general, a cabling system that uses a central conducting core that is surrounded by an insulating medium that is, in turn, surrounded by a protective sheathing. Coaxial cable is used by IBM to connect its 3270 family of workstations. *See also* twinaxial.

COMMAND.COM   A program supplied with MS-DOS and PC-DOS that performs the built-in DOS commands. For example, DIR and TYPE are internal commands, while FORMAT and COPY are external commands. All internal commands are contained within COMMAND.COM.

common communications support   One of three SAA interfaces. The common communications support interface defines the data formats and protocols that can be used in an SAA environment. This includes, for example, the SNA 3270 data format, DIA/DCA and SNADS. *See also* common programming interface, common user interface, DCA, DIA, SAA, and SNADS.

common programming interface   One of three SAA interfaces. The common programming interface defines a set of routines for accessing files, programs and communications devices under SAA. *See also* common communications support, common user interface, and SAA.

common user interface   One of three SAA interfaces. The common user interface defines the characteristics of text and graphics screens generated by SAA-compliant programs and how the user interacts with those displays. *See also* common communications support, common programming interface, and SAA.

communications controller   In an IBM mainframe environment, a communications controller is channel-attached to the host and serves to control the data communication network. IBM communication controllers (often referred to as either CUCNs or FEPs) include the 3705, 3725, and 3745. Under SNA, a communications controller is a PU 4 device. *See also* FEP and ICA.

compound document   A document that can include text, graphics, video and voice data.

conditioning   A process applied to standard analog phone lines to provide filtering in support of less error-prone data transmission. Various levels of conditioning are available at various costs and are implemented through specialized equipment.

connectionless   A type of networking service in which the sending side requires no direct or indirect access to the receiving side(s).

connection-oriented   A type of networking service in which the sending and receiving sides are in direct or indirect contact with one another.

CORBA Common Object Request Broker Architecture. A specification for the development of ORBs. CORBA establishes an environment for software objects to communicate with each other.

CP Control Program. In an IBM mainframe environment, CP is the central management facility under the VM operating system.

CPF Control Program Facility. An IBM operating system used on the System/38 computers.

CP/M An operating system for microcomputers created by Digital Research. CP/M was king of the hill among microcomputer operating systems prior to IBM's adoption of MS-DOS (PC-DOS).

cps Characters per second. A measurement of data communications speed and throughput.

CPU Central processing unit. The core processing unit of a computer system, in most cases contained in a single chip.

CRC Cyclic Redundancy Check. An error detection scheme in which the block check character (BCC) is derived from dividing all the serialized bits in a block by a predetermined binary number. *See also* BCC and LRC.

CSMA/CD Carrier Sense Multiple Access with Collision Detection. The LAN discipline (protocol) used by both Ethernet and the IEEE 802.3 standard. Under CSMA/CD, a device that wishes to transmit on the network first listens for other activity. If the network is quiet, the device then attempts to transmit. Data collisions are detected and result in both transmitters retrying their transmissions after a random amount of time.

CSU Channel service unit. The interface to a Digital Data Service line. The CSU takes data off the DDS line and feeds it to a Data Service Unit (DSU) that, in turn, interfaces with the terminal or computer equipment. In many cases, a CSU is combined with a DSU, into a single unit called an integrated service unit (ISU). *See also* DDS, DSU, and ISU.

CTERM A DECnet protocol used by one DEC host to forward information from a terminal to another host. This is the protocol used by the standard DECnet SET HOST command.

CTOS An operating system produced by Convergent Technology (Unisys) for its line of microcomputers. CTOS is a multitasking, multiuser operating system that is similar in structure to UNIX.

CTS Clear to Send. A lead in the RS-232C interface. CTS is raised in response to receipt of the Request to Send (RTS) signal. In brief, when one side of the link wishes to transmit, it raises the RTS line. If the other side is ready to receive, it responds by raising the CTS line. Once transmission has begun, the Carrier Detect (CD) line is also raised. In the full 25-pin RS-232C standard, CTS is pin 5. In the abbreviated 9-pin PC interface, CTS is pin 8. *See also* CD, RS-232C, and RTS.

CTS-300 DEC's commercial operating system for the PDP-11 family of computers. *See also* DSM-11, RSTS, and RSX.

CUCN Communications controller node. *See* communications controller.

CUT Control unit terminal. Another term used by IBM for its general-purpose workstations.

D

DAP Data Access Protocol. A low-level DECnet protocol responsible for the movement of information from system to system.

DARPA Defense Advanced Research Project Agency, formerly known as ARPA. An agency within the U.S. Department of Defense that was instrumental in the development of TCP/IP. The agency's ARPANET network was the precursor of the modern Internet. *See also* TCP/IP.

DASD Direct access storage device. An IBM term that refers to IBM mass storage devices (disk drives).

Data Link Layer The second (from the bottom) layer of the OSI Reference Model. The Data Link layer defines the protocols used to move data across the Physical Layer (for example, HDLC, LAP-B or IEEE 802.2). The Data Link Layer is sometimes also called the Logical Link Layer. *See also* OSI Reference Model.

DB2 IBM's relational database for mainframes running the MVS or VM operating systems.

DCA Document Content Architecture. An IBM document specification that defines the structure and contents of documents in both revisable and final forms. Under DCA, revisable documents include their editing history, while final form documents are the net result of all edits.

DCD Data Carrier Detect. *See* CD.

DCE Data communications equipment. A device such as a modem that facilitates a data communications link. The DCE interfaces with the data terminal equipment (DTE), which is the origin or destination of the information. A complete link includes a DTE interfacing with a DCE that interfaces with another DCE that, in turn, interfaces with another DTE. In direct connection environments, one side of the connection (normally the computer) emulates a DCE interface. *See also* DTE.

DDCMP Digital Data Communications Message Protocol. A DECnet byte-oriented protocol that ensures the integrity and correct sequencing of messages between adjacent nodes. DDCMP can be used for synchronous or asynchronous transmissions and is most frequently used to implement DECnet wide-area connections over conventional leased lines.

DDM Distributed Data Management. An IBM product geared for its mid-range machines. DDM enables a system to access remote files over a network at both the record and the file level. *See also* DIA and SNADS.

DDN Defense Data Network. The multivendor WAN used by the U.S. Department of Defense.

DDS Digital Data Service. A leased line using digital transmission that can provide data communications rates up to 56 Kbps. When DDS is employed, the modems used with analog lines are replaced by a Channel Service Unit (CSU) and a Data Service Unit (DSU). *See also* CSU and DSU.

DEBNA Digital Ethernet VAXBI Network Adapter. Replaced by the DEBNI. *See* DEBNI.

DEBNI Digital Ethernet VAXBI Network Interface. A DEC controller card for VAX computers that interfaces the VAXBI bus with the Ethernet LAN. The DEBNI replaced the DEBNA. *See* DEBNA.

DEC Digital Equipment Corporation.

DECmate An office automation (word processing) microcomputer.

DECnet Digital's line of products that allow communications between DEC systems.

DECnet-DOS A DEC software product for PCs and PS/2s running MS-DOS (or PC-DOS). DECnet-DOS enables the PC to participate in a DECnet network (normally through a Ethernet adapter in the PC). The functions provided by DECnet-DOS include task-to-task communications, remote file access and VT 220 terminal emulation.

DECnet/SNA Gateway A LAN-attached gateway between SNA and DECnet. The IBM side of the gateway might attach via an SNA SDLC connection or via a direct channel attachment to a mainframe. Specific SNA services are run in other DEC hosts to provide functional services across the gateway (such as terminal access, file transfer and document exchange). *See* gateway.

DECrouter LAN-attached bridges to facilitate wide-area connections within DECnet networks. A router can be used to connect two Ethernet LANs using DDCMP or X.25. A router on one LAN can communicate with another router or with an integrated communications card within a DEC host system.

DECserver Digital's LAN terminal server. *See* terminal server.

DECstation Digital's line of PCs based on Intel processors and their line of engineering workstations based on RISC technology. The DECstation 3100 and 5000 use a RISC design while the DECstation 200, 300, and 400 models use standard PC architectures. *See also* VAXstation.

DECwindows DEC's architecture for a graphical user interface that provides a common, multiwindowed graphical environment from which the end user can access applications residing on other systems. DECwindows is part of DEC's Network Application Support (NAS). *See also* NAS.

DELNI Digital Ethernet Local Network Interconnect. Provides connection to eight Ethernet segments with a ninth connection that can be used to optionally attach the DELNI to the LAN backbone. The DELNI can be used as a stand-alone device to create a small DECnet network, or can be networked into a main LAN as described.

DELQA Digital Ethernet LAN-Q-bus Adapter. A DEC controller card for Q-bus computers that interfaces the computer with the Ethernet LAN. The DELQA replaces the DEQNA.

DELUA Digital Ethernet LAN-Unibus Adapter. A DEC controller card for Unibus computers that interfaces the computer with the Ethernet LAN. The DELUA replaces the DEUNA.

DEMCA Digital Ethernet MicroChannel Adapter. An Ethernet ThinWire adapter card for PS/2 computers. DEMCA uses a standard MCA slot.

DEMPR Digital Ethernet Multi-Point Repeater. A DEC LAN product that provides eight ThinWire ports, with a ninth port to optionally connect to the standard Ethernet cable. Like a DELNI, a DEMPR can be used to implement a standalone ThinWire LAN or to integrate ThinWire devices into a main Ethernet LAN.

DEPCA Digital Ethernet PC Adapter. An Ethernet ThinWire adapter card for PCs. DEPCA uses a standard 8-bit PC slot.

DEQNA Digital Ethernet Q-bus Network Adapter. The DEQNA was replaced by the DELQA. *See* DELQA.

DeskManager HP's electronic mail and office automation product for the HP 3000 computer.

DESPR Digital Ethernet Single-Port Repeater. A DESPR provides conversion between an Ethernet transceiver connection and a ThinWire connection. A DESPR is used to attach a ThinWire device to a standard Ethernet transceiver. *See also* DESTA.

DESTA Digital Ethernet Station Adapter. A DESTA provides conversion between a ThinWire connection and an Ethernet transceiver. A DESTA is used to attach a standard Ethernet device into a ThinWire network. *See also* DESPR.

DESVA Digital Ethernet MicroVAX 2000 Adapter. A DEC controller card for the MicroVAX 2000 that interfaces the computer with the Ethernet LAN.

DEUNA Digital Ethernet Unibus Network Adapter. The DEUNA was replaced by the DELUA. *See* DELUA.

DHCF Distributed Host Command Facility. An IBM product running as a remote processor, DHCF interfaces with the mainframe-resident HCF subsystem to provide distributed access. In a pure IBM environment, it is often used to gain 3270 terminal access from a mainframe to a remote, nonmainframe system. In the multivendor arena, DHCF is often emulated to allow 3270 terminals to access the non-IBM system via the mainframe HCF facility.

DIA Document Interchange Architecture. One of three distribution techniques used by IBM to move information from system to system in an SNA network. DIA is specifically focused on the movement of documents in both revisable and final form. *See also* DCA, DDM and SNADS.

digital transmission. Transmission in which information is sent in its discrete bit form. That is, each bit is represented as a 0 or a 1. *See also* analog transmission.

DISOSS Distributed Office Support System. An IBM product that enables documents created by different products to be distributed and shared among IBM systems. DISOSS is commonly used as an interface point for transmitting documents to and from non-IBM computers.

DMA Direct Memory Access. A hardware method of reading and writing directly to memory without involving the main CPU.

DNA   Digital Network Architecture. DEC's architecture for the interconnection of its computer and computer-related devices. This is equivalent to IBM's SNA, HP's AdvanceNet, and Sun's ONC.

DoD   U.S. Department of Defense. *See also* DARPA.

Domain   **1.** A set of hosts on a LAN that share a single database, typically for moving mail between hosts. **2.** The name for Apollo's (now HP's) line of engineering workstations. *See also* Apollo.

DOS   Disk Operating System. Introduced in 1981 by Microsoft Corp. as the operating system for IBM's 8080-based IBM PC.

DOS/VS   Disk Operating System/Virtual Storage. An IBM System/370 architecture operating system.

DOS/VSE   Disk Operating System/Virtual Storage Extended. An IBM System/370 architecture operating system.

dpi   Dots per inch. A term used to describe the resolution of printers. Most dot-matrix printers offer less than 200 dots per inch resolution, while most laser or inkjet printers offer at least 300 and as high as 1,200 dots per inch. The higher the density of dots, the better the resolution of printed characters, graphics and images. In contrast, typesetting equipment can offer dpi resolution of 1,270, 2,540, and even higher amounts.

DS/1000 and DS/3000   HP 1000 and HP 3000 networking services that have been replaced by NS/1000 and NS/3000. The DS services relied mostly on HP HDLC links for networking, while the NS products use standard IEEE 802.3 links.

DS0   Digital Service rate 0. The transmission rate (64 Kbps) of each of the 24 circuits in a T1 connection. *See also* T1.

DS1   Digital Service rate 1. The combined transmission rate (1.544 Mbps) of all 24 circuits in a T1 connections. *See also* T1.

DSM-11   DEC's business-oriented operating system for the PDP/11 series computers. *See also* CTS-300, RSTS, and RSX.

DSR   Data Set Ready. A lead in the RS-232C interface, DSR is used to signal that the modem (or DCE device) is ready for communications. The counterpart to DSR is Data Terminal Ready (DTR), which is the computer/terminal's signal that it is ready to communicate. In most cases, no communication can take place unless both the DSR and DTR signals are raised. In the full 25-pin RS-232C standard, DSR is pin 6. In the abbreviated, 9-pin PC interface, DSR is pin 4. *See also* DTR and RS-232C.

DSU   Data service unit. A device that interfaces between a channel service unit (CSU) and a terminal or computer. The DSU and CSU work together to interface the computing device to a digital data service (DDS). *See also* CSU, DDS, and ISU.

DTC   Distributed terminal controller. For the RISC-based HP 3000 systems, DTCs are used to interface the asynchronous terminals into the LAN-based system. *See also* ADCC and ATP.

DTE   Data terminal equipment. A device such as a terminal or computer that is the origin or destination of information flowing over a data communications link. The DTE interfaces with data communication equipment such as a modem, that handles the actual data communications processing and interfaces with another DCE device (that interfaces with another DTE device). When direct connect links are used, one side emulates a DCE while the other performs normal DTE functions. *See also* DCE.

DTP   Distributed Transaction Processing. An OSI upper-layer service for implementing transaction-based processing. Defined as ISO standard 10026.

DTR   Data Terminal Ready. A lead in the RS-232C interface. Data Terminal Ready is used to signal to the modem (or DCE device) that it is ready for communications. The counterpart to DTR is Data Set Ready (DSR), which is the modem's signal that it is ready to communicate. In most cases, no communication can take place unless both the DTR and DSR signals are raised. In in-dial situations, DTR is normally raised when the Ring Indicator (RI) is raised to tell the modem to answer the phone. In the full 25-pin RS-232C standard, DTR is pin 20. In the abbreviated, 9-pin PC interface, DTR is pin 4. *See also* DSR, RI, and RS-232C.

Duplex   *See* half duplex and full duplex.

E

EBCDIC   Extended Binary Coded Decimal Interchange Code. A definition for the bit compositions of characters and symbols. EBCDIC uses 256 eight-bit patterns to define 256 different characters, numbers and symbols. IBM mid-range and mainframe systems use the EBCDIC standard. *See also* ASCII.

ECMA   European Computer Manufacturers Association. A standards organization composed of European computer manufacturers. ECMA participates in both CCITT and ISO activities.

ECMA 40   ECMA specifications for HDLC frame structure. *See also* HDLC.

ECMA 49   ECMA definition of HDLC elements of procedures. *See also* HDLC.

ECMA 60   ECMA definition of HDLC unbalanced class of procedures. *See also* HDLC.

ECMA 61   ECMA definition of HDLC balanced class of procedures. *See also* HDLC.

ECMA 71   ECMA standard for transport protocol (for ISO/OSI layer 4).

ECMA 80-82   ECMA definitions of the physical and logical link control for CSMA/CD. *See also* CSMA/CD.

EDI   Electronic data interchange. A set of services for information and document exchange. The intent of EDI is to reduce or eliminate paper flow for common business transactions.

EIA   Electronic Industries Association. A U.S. trade organization specializing in the electrical and functional characteristics of interface equipment. EIA has a close working relationship with ANSI.

EISA Extended Industry Standard Architecture. An alternative to IBM's MCA bus structure for the PS/2. EISA was developed by a group of nine manufacturers led by Compaq Computer. *See also* MCA.

EMA Enterprise Management Architecture. DEC's products and services that implement network management.

EMI Electromagnetic Interference. Electromagnetic waves that can potentially interfere with the operation of electronic devices. The U.S. Federal Communication Commission (FCC) is responsible for deciding whether an electronic device (such as a computer) generates too much EMI or radio frequency interference (RFI). *See also* FCC and RFI.

end node A node in a network that cannot forward or reroute packets intended for other nodes. *See also* node.

ESDI Enhanced Small Device Interface. A disk interface standard that offers storage of 34 sectors per cylinder. Because of its speed and density, ESDI is used in both PCs and mid-range systems. *See also* MFM, RLL, SCSI, and ST506.

Ethernet A LAN standard that uses the Carrier Sense, Multiple Access with Collision Detection (CSMA/CD) discipline. Ethernet was originally developed by Xerox Corporation. *See also* IEEE 802.3.

EU End User. An IBM SNA term.

F

FAL File Access Listener. FAL is a DECnet module that listens for network requests to access its local files. In effect, FAL is a network file server for DECnet.

Fast Ethernet *See* 100BASET.

FCC Federal Communications Commission. An agency of the U.S. government that regulates the use of electromagnetic waveforms, such as television waves, radio waves and other electronic and magnetic emissions. *See also* EMI and RFI.

FDDI Fiber Distributed Data Interface. FDDI is an ANSI standard for fiber-optic networking. FDDI uses a token-passing discipline over a ring topology at speeds up to 100 Mbps. Interfaces to traditional LANs enable the FDDI network to act as a WAN or MAN for the LANs attached to it. *See also* MAN and WAN.

FEP Front-end processor. A phrase often used to refer to intelligent communications controllers. *See also* communications controller.

Fibre Channel. A high-speed architecture for connecting network devices and high-speed hardware. Sometimes seen as a replacement for HiPPI.

FIPS Federal Information Processing Specification. Specifications adopted and published by the U.S. government that are mandated for use by the government and its agencies.

FIPS 1-1   FIPS code for information interchange.

FIPS 7   Implementation of FIPS 1-1 and related standards.

FIPS 15   Subsets of the FIPS 1-1 code for information interchange.

FIPS 16-1   Bit sequencing of the FIPS 1-1 code for serial transmissions.

FIPS 17-1   Character and parity structure for FIPS 1-1 transmissions.

FIPS 35   Code extension techniques using 7 or 8 bits.

FIPS 71   Advanced Data Communication Control Procedures (ADCCP). *See also* ADCCP.

Firewire   *See* IEEE 1394.

fractional T1   One or more of the 24 64-Kbps channels of a T1 line, broken out by the local telephone office and offered to local customers. Fractional T1 enables a range of customers to share the benefits (and cost) of a full T1 line. *See also* T1.

frame   A block of information organized in a specific format. Depending on the network, a frame might have origin and destination information in it, or might be included as part of another structure (such as a packet) that defines the routing information. *See also* packet.

FTAM   File Transfer, Access and Management. An OSI upper-level service for file transfer between open systems. FTAM is defined as OSI standard 8571.

FTP   File Transfer Protocol. FTP is a TCP/IP application that enables the transfer of files between host computers.

FTSC   Federal Telecommunications Standards Committee. A U.S. government advisory body to the National Communications System agency.

FTSC 1003   FTSC definition of synchronous data link control procedures (ADCCP). *See also* ADCCP.

FTSC 1005   FTSC definition of coding and modulation requirements for 2,400-bps modems.

FTSC 1006   FTSC definition of coding and modulation requirements for 4,800-bps modems.

FTSC-1007   FTSC definition of coding and modulation requirements for 9,600-bps modems.

FTSC-1008   FTSC definition of coding and modulation for 600/1200-bps modems.

FTSC 1010   FTSC definition of bit sequencing the ANSI X3.4 information code for serial transmissions.

FTSC 1011   FTSC definition of character and parity structure for ANSI X3.4 transmissions.

Full duplex   Simultaneous, independent bidirectional transmission.

FUNI   Frame User Network Interface. A service that performs protocol conversion between Frame Relay and ATM networks.

G

Gabriel A software product that detects the presence of SATAN. *See also* SATAN.

Gateway A device that permits the network activity on one type of network to flow into another type of network. A gateway is different from a bridge or router in that it must perform conversion and/or emulation tasks to tie two (or more) heterogeneous networks together, while bridges and routers link two homogenous networks. A gateway maps to all seven layers of the OSI model. *See also* bridge and router.

GCS Group Control System. In an IBM mainframe environment, GCS is used with the VM operating system to host SNA-oriented subsystems such as ACF/VTAM.

GOSIP Government OSI Profile. A set of requirements issued by the U.S. and United Kingdom governments to dictate the use of OSI-compliant products within the government and its agencies.

GPI Graphics Programming Interface. A generalized interface within OS/2 controlling fonts and graphics as displayed and printed on a variety of devices.

Groupware A type of software that facilitates sharing of electronic data and processes throughout a group of end users.

GUI Graphical user interface. A term used to describe a graphical interface as seen by the end user of a computer system. Specifically, a GUI enables a user to select applications by selecting icons and graphics representations presented on the screen. GUI products include the Apple operating system, Microsoft Windows, the OS/2 Presentation Manager, HP's NewWave and DEC's DECwindows.

H

H4000 and H4005 *See* transceiver.

half duplex Transmission in one of two directions at any given time, but not both directions simultaneously.

HASP Houston Automatic Spooling Program. An IBM Job Entry Subsystem (JES) for the OS/SVS operating system.

HCF Host Command Facility. An IBM package originally designed to interface mainframes with 8100 Information Processing machines running the companion DHCF package. HCF is commonly used as an interface from IBM to non-IBM computers. *See also* DHCF.

HDLC High-Level Data Link Control. A bit-level protocol for data transmission. HDLC is ISO's implementation of the IBM SDLC standard. HDLC is often used as a high-speed, general-purpose computer-to-computer link.

heartbeat A function performed by transceivers on Ethernet and 802.3 IEEE networks that signals their continuing operation.

High Performance Routing (HPR)   A mechanism used in IBM networks to provide an SNA/APPN network with native access to a wide-area ATM network.

HiPPI (High Performance Parallel Interface)   A method for connecting heterogeneous supercomputers with IBM mainframes.

HP   Hewlett-Packard Company.

HP 125   HP's implementation of a combined terminal and PC system. The HP 125's memory capacity was, however, rather limited.

HP 150   HP's revised implementation of a dual terminal and personal computer. The HP 150 also featured touch-screen operation.

HP 700   A monochrome HP terminal.

HP 1000   HP's line of real-time technical minicomputers. The HP1000s use a proprietary CISC architecture.

HP 2620   A monochrome HP terminal.

HP 2640   A monochrome HP terminal.

HP2697   A color HP terminal.

HP 3000   HP's line of general-purpose business computers. The HP 3000 product line includes both CISC and RISC models. The CISC models include the MICRO 3000 and Series 70. The RISC models include the HP 3000 Series 900 Series.

HP 9000   HP's line of engineering workstations. The HP 9000 line includes both RISC and CISC models.

HP-GL   Hewlett-Packard Graphics Language. The command set used by HP plotters. HP-GL is a vector-oriented interface that describes the objects to be printed/plotted as a series of mathematical shapes. HP-GL also supports color. Because of its widespread use, HP-GL is often used as an intermediary format for converting graphics from one system (or package) to another.

HP-IB   HP's implementation of the IEEE 488 general-purpose, bus interface used to interface tape and disk drives to system processors.

HP Portable   The HP Portable and HP Portable Plus were HP's initial MS-DOS, portable PC offerings. Unfortunately, they lacked such things as built-in disk or diskette drives.

HP-UX   HP's UNIX implementation for the HP 9000 Series computers.

HSC   Hierarchical Storage Controller. A DEC device that allows shared access to a set of disk drives. The HSC is used in VAXclusters to act as the intermediary between a Star Coupler and the drives. *See also* CI, Star Coupler, and VAXcluster.

I

ICA Integrated Communications Adapter. An IBM device used in a 9370 and 4300 Series mainframes as a communications controller. For the 4300, an ICA is an alternative to a stand-alone 3705 or 3725 communications controller.

ICMP Internet Control Message Protocol. ICMP is responsible for the detection and reporting of link-level errors.

IEEE Institute of Electrical and Electronics Engineers. A professional society that often participates in the development of standards. IEEE recommendations are usually forwarded to ANSI for its endorsements. Among the best known IEEE standards are the 802.2, 802.3, and 802.5 LAN specifications.

IEEE 488 A general-purpose bus interface most commonly used to interface tape and/or disk drives to system processors.

IEEE 802.2 A standard that defines the Logical Link Control (LLC) level of LAN communications. IEEE 802.2 is used with the 802.3, 802.4 and 802.5 medium access control (MAC) standards. In terms of layers, 802.2 resides above the MAC standards.

IEEE 802.3 A standard that defines the medium access control (MAC) layer for a Carrier Sense Multiple Access with Collision Detection (CSMA/CD) bus network. The IEEE 802.3 standard is not identical to Ethernet; however, both Ethernet and 802.3 devices can coexist on the same cable. The IEEE 802.3 standard has been adopted by ECMA as ECMA-80, 81 and 82 and by ISO as ISO 8802/3. *See also* Ethernet, ECMA and ISO.

IEEE 802.4 A standard that defines the medium access control (MAC) layer for a token-passing bus network.

IEEE 802.5 A standard that defines the medium access control (MAC) layer for a token-passing ring network. IBM's Token Ring conforms to this standard.

IEEE 802.6 A standard defining a MAN based on a fiber-optic ring 30 miles in length. The standard supports data rates of 1.5 Mbps to 155 Mbps.

IEEE 902.9a A standard for running two networks over 10BaseT wiring. *See also* isochronous Ethernet.

IEEE 1003 IEEE definition of portable operating systems (POSIX). *See also* POSIX.

IEEE 1394 A local device interface for ATM or Fast Ethernet, which permits either to be routed to individual devices. *See also* Firewire.

IMF/3000 and IMF II/3000 HP 3000-based software that provides interactive (virtual terminal and batch) capability with an IBM mainframe. IMF/3000 uses bisynchronous communications, and IMF II/3000 uses SNA SDLC communications. IMF II is also known as SNA IMF.

INP   Intelligent Network Processor. An intelligent HP controller card for the HP 3000 CISC computers that provides bisynchronous, SDLC, and X.25 communications.

Internet Interoperability Object Protocol (IIOP). A part of the CORBA 2.0 specification that adds multivendor connectivity to the ORB model.

IP   Internet Protocol. *See* TCP/IP.

IPC   Interprocess communications. A mechanism that enables two programs to communicate with one another. The term Net-IPC is often used to describe a network-level interface between two programs. *See also* API, APPC, and RPC.

IPX   A datagram protocol established by Novell for use in sending data over Netware networks. In the OSI model, IPX is a network-layer protocol. *See also* NetWare.

ISA   Industry standard architecture. A term used to describe the original bus structure used in the PC/AT and subsequently adopted by the industry as a de facto standard. *See also* EISA and MCA.

ISDN. Integrated Services Digital Network. A digital-based network for voice and data lines. From a broader perspective, ISDN is targeted to be an international service for the integration and networking of voice and digital information.

ISO   International Standards Organization. A voluntary, independent organization chartered to define international standards for communications of all types. ISO is best known for the development of the seven-layer Basic Reference Model for Open Systems Interconnection, termed the OSI Model. *See also* OSI Reference Model.

ISO 646   ISO definition of a seven-bit character set.

ISO 1155   ISO standard for the use of longitudinal parity for error detection.

ISO 1177   ISO structure for asynchronous (start/stop) and synchronous transmission.

ISO 1745   ISO basic mode control procedures.

ISO 2022   Code extension techniques based on the ISO 646 seven-bit character set.

ISO 2110   ISO definition of a 25-pin DTE/DCE connector and pin assignments. *See also* RS-232C.

ISO 2111   ISO basic-mode control procedures for code-independent information transfer.

ISO 2628   Complements to the ISO 2111 basic mode control procedures.

ISO 2629   ISO basic mode control procedures for conversational information message transfer.

ISO 3309   ISO definition of HDLC frame structure. *See also* HDLC.

ISO 4335   ISO definition of HDLC elements of procedures. *See also* HDLC.

ISO 4902   ISO definition of 37-pin and 9-pin DTE/DCE connectors and pin assignments. *See also* RS-232C and RS-449.

ISO 6159   ISO definition of HDLC unbalanced class of procedures. *See also* HDLC.

ISO 6256   ISO definition of HDLC balanced class of procedures. *See also* HDLC.

ISO 7498   The ISO Open Systems Interconnect basic Reference Model.

ISO 8072   Transport layer definitions for the OSI Reference Model.

ISO 8073   Transport layer connection-oriented services for the OSI Reference Model.

ISO 8208   ISO standard for X.25 packet level protocol.

ISO 8326-27   Session Layer connection-oriented services for the OSI Reference Model.

ISO 8348   Network Layer definitions for the OSI Reference Model.

ISO 8473   Network Layer connectionless services for the OSI Reference Model.

ISO 8571   ISO definition of the File Transfer, Access and Management (FTAM) application. *See also* FTAM.

ISO 8602   Transport Layer connectionless services for the OSI Reference Model.

ISO 8613   ISO definition of Office Document Architecture (ODA). *See also* ODA.

ISO 8632   ISO definition of Computer Graphics Metafile (CGM). *See also* CGM.

ISO 8648   Network Layer internal organization in the OSI Reference Model.

ISO 8802/2   ISO standard for class 1 logical link control.

ISO 8802/3   ISO's equivalent of the IEEE 802.2 and 802.3 standards for a CSMA/CD LAN. *See also* IEEE 802.2 and IEEE 802.3.

ISO 8802/4   ISO's equivalent of the IEEE 802.2 and 802.4 standards for a token-passing bus LAN. *See also* IEEE 802.2 and IEEE 802.4.

ISO 8802/5   ISO's equivalent of the IEEE 802.2 and 802.5 standards for a token-passing ring LAN. *See also* IEEE 802.2 and IEEE 802.5.

ISO 8822-23   Presentation Layer connection-oriented services for the OSI Reference Model.

ISO 8832-33   ISO definition for Job Transfer and Manipulation application (JTM). *See also* JTM.

ISO 8878   ISO standard for the use of X.25 as a connection-oriented service.

ISO 8886   Data-Link Layer definitions for the OSI Reference Model.

ISO 9040   ISO definition of the Virtual Terminal Services (VTS) application. *See also* VTS.

ISO 9314   ISO standard for Fiber Distributed Data Interface (FDDI). *See also* FDDI.

ISO 9548   Session Layer connectionless services for the OSI Reference Model.

ISO 9576   Presentation Layer connectionless services for the OSI Reference Model.

ISO 9594 ISO standard for directory services based on the CCITT X.500 standard. *See also* X.500.

ISO 9595-96 ISO definition of network management applications (CMIS and CMIP). *See also* CMIS and CMIP.

ISO 10020/21 ISO standard for message handling services based on the CCITT X.400 standard. *See also* X.400.

ISO 10026 ISO standard for Distributed Transaction Processing (DTP). *See also* DTP.

Isochronous Ethernet *See* IEEE 902.9a.

ISU Integrated Service Unit. The combination of a channel service unit (CSU) and data service unit (DSU) into one device. The ISU is used to interface computers and terminals to a digital data service (DDS) line. *See also* CSU, DDS, and DSU.

ITU International Telecommunications Union. The ITU is an agency under the United Nations charged to define standards for international telecommunications. The CCITT is a committee of the ITU. *See also* CCITT.

IX Interactive Executive. An IBM implementation of UNIX that runs as a guest operating system under the VM operating system on mainframes.

J

JCL Job Control Language. An IBM term for the instructions used to control execution within a Job Entry Subsystem (JES). JCL is also often used as a general term for the instructions required to define a sequence of events to be run on a computer.

JES. Job Entry Subsystem. A specific IBM Job Entry Subsystem for the OS/VS1 operating system that is also known as JES1 and RES. In more general terms, a job entry subsystem controls the batch job environment and, as part of that environment, collects information from Remote Job Entry (RJE) workstations and distributes information to RJE workstations.

JES1 Job Entry Subsystem version 1. An IBM Job Entry Subsystem (JES) for the OS/VS1 operating system. *See* JES.

JES2 Job Entry Subsystem version 2. An IBM Job Entry Subsystem (JES) for the MVS operating system. *See* JES.

JES3 Job Entry Subsystem version 3. An IBM Job Entry Subsystem (JES) for the MVS operating system. *See* JES.

job In general, a specific task or set of tasks associated with a given user or application. *See also* Batch.

JTM Job Transfer and Manipulation. An OSI upper-layer service for the transfer and sharing of jobs between open systems. Defined as ISO standard 8832/33.

K

Kbps   Kilobits per second. 1,024 bits per second (approximately 128 bytes per second).

KBps   Kilobytes per second. 1,024 bytes per second (approximately 8,192 bits per second).

Kermit   A file transfer protocol developed by Columbia University in the city of New York and often used to transfer files between PCs and mid-range computers. In most implementations, Kermit also includes terminal emulation. Kermit was indeed named after the Muppet.

L

LAN   Local Area Network. A communications architecture that passes information between multiple systems over relatively short distances at very high speeds.

LANIC   Local Area Network Interface Controller. An HP controller card that interfaces the HP 1000 and HP 3000 to an 802.3 LAN.

LanWorks   A set of products jointly developed by DEC and Apple Computer that enable VAX and Macintosh systems to share files, printers, documents and mail in a common network. Later combined into PathWorks.

LAP-B   Link Access Balanced, revision B. CCITT's implementation of a balanced, bit-oriented protocol based on the IBM SDLC standard. LAP-B is most widely known as the protocol of choice to connect a computer to a packet-switching X.25 network.

LAT   Local Area Transport. An Ethernet-based DEC protocol implemented for terminal servers to enable terminals connected to a server to establish logical sessions on DEC host nodes without connecting through intervening host nodes (as in the case of a SET HOST command). LAT also attempts to minimize network usage by grouping individual characters into a single transmission. *See also* CTERM and terminal server.

LAVC   Local Area Vaxcluster. A DEC VAXcluster solution that uses standard LAN connections to share access to a set of disk drives between multiple VAX systems.

LDAP   Lightweight Directory Access Protocol. A subset of the X.500 standard designed for interoperability and ease of use. LDAP and X.500 provide the means to create a universal network directory system.

Leased line   A permanent circuit provided by the telephone company (or similar organization). A leased line can be a direct point-to-point connection or a multipoint connection. Leased lines are available for either analog (voice grade) or digital transmission. Analog lines can also be conditioned to reduce errors. *See also* conditioning.

LEN   Low-Entry Networking. An IBM standard that enables adjacent nodes to initiate and terminate communications with one another using LU 6.2 APPC.

LLC   Logical Link Control. The highest sublayer in Layer 2 (data link layer) of the OSI model. In the IEEE standards, 802.2 is the LLC. In Ethernet, the LLC and the medium access control (MAC) are enmeshed. *See also* MAC and OSI Reference Model.

LocalTalk   Apple Computer's cabling for the AppleTalk LAN.

Location Broker   Part of HP/Apollo's Network Computing System (NCS) architecture. Global and Local Location Brokers determine what local services will be available on a network-wide basis. *See also* NCS.

logical unit   *See* LU.

LRC   Longitudinal redundancy check. An error detection scheme in which a check character is generated on the basis of the exclusive OR of all the characters in the block. *See also* BCC and CRC.

LSI   Large Scale Integration. An approach to printed circuit board design that uses a small number of individual components (chips), with each component being responsible for a range of functions. *See also* VLSI.

LU   Logical unit. Logical units are part of the IBM SNA structure and correspond to entities (for example, users, programs) that request or transmit information through the network.

LU Type 0 (LU 0)   Direct-link communications.

LU Type 1 (LU 1)   Data processing workstation communications.

LU Type 2 (LU 2)   3270-type workstation communications.

LU Type 3 (LU 3)   3270-type printer communications.

LU Type 4 (LU 4)   5250-type printer communications.

LU Type 6.1 (LU 6.1)   Program-to-program communications using one of the following SNA data stream formats: character string, 3270, logical messages services, or user-defined.

LU Type 6.2 (LU 6.2)   Program-to-program communications using either the SNA general data stream format or a user-defined data stream.

LU Type 7 (LU 7)   5251-type workstation communications.

LUNI   LAN Emulation User-to-Network Interface. Part of the ATM Forum's LAN Emulation Over ATM specification, which enables multivendor end stations to communicate with an ATM network.

M

MAC   medium access control. The lower level of LAN communications that handles discipline and topology of the LAN. MAC corresponds to the Physical Layer (layer 1) of the OSI Reference Model. *See also* LLC and OSI Reference Model.

MACH   A multiuser, multitasking operating system directly descended from UNIX that offers lower overhead and higher performance than UNIX.

MAN   Metropolitan area network. A somewhat smaller, special implementation of a WAN. MANs use fiber-optic transmissions to provide high-speed communications over relatively small distances (but distances that are beyond the range of a traditional LAN). *See also* FDDI and WAN.

MAP Manufacturing Automation Protocol. A transport system defined by the manufacturing industry to accommodate its specific needs and requirements.

MAPI Messaging Application Programming Interface. A proprietary protocol created by Microsoft that permits developers to create mail-enabled applications.

MAU Medium attachment unit. A device that physically attaches to a LAN to permit the connection of one or more devices (or LAN segments) to that LAN via an AUI. *See also* transceiver and AUI.

Mbps Megabits per second. 1,048,576 bits per second (approximately 131,072 bytes per second).

MBps Megabytes per second. 1,048,576 bytes per second (approximately 8,388,608 bits per second).

MCA Micro Channel Architecture. IBM's improved, proprietary architecture for the PS/2 that replaced the bus architectures used in the original PC/XT and PC/AT.

MCP Master Control Program. The operating system for the Burroughs line of Unisys computers.

MFM Modified frequency modulation. A disk encoding technique that results in 17 sectors per cylinder. MFM is the original (and still widely used) encoding technique for PC disk drives and uses the ST-506 interface. *See also* ESDI, RLL, SCSI, and ST-506.

MFT Multiprogramming with a Fixed number of Tasks. An IBM System/360 architecture operating system.

MHz One million cycles per second. The usage of MHz has dramatically increased since its associated with PCs. In that arena, the higher the MHz, the faster the processor can operate (because there are more available cycles per second).

MicroVAX The low end of DEC's VAX line. The MicroVAX line includes the MicroVAX 2000, MicroVAX II, and MicroVAX 3000 series.

MicroVMS DEC's implementation of the VMS operating system for the MicroVAX computers.

Millisecond One thousandth of a second.

MIPS Million instructions per second. A unit of measurement applied to the performance of computer systems. For example, a computer rated at 3 MIPS can perform 3 million instructions in one second. The higher the MIPS rating, the higher the performance.

modem Modulator-Demodulator. A device that converts between the digital data format used by computers and the analog signals transmitted over a telephone circuit.

MPE MultiProgramming Environment. HP's operating system for the HP 3000 Series computers. Note that a special version of MPE (MPE-XL) runs on the HP 3000 RISC systems.

MPOA   Multiple Protocols Over ATM. An extension of the LAN emulation concept, used to map network layer addresses—such as IP or IPX—to ATM.

MRJE/1000 and MRJE/3000   HP 1000- and HP 3000-based software products that provide bisynchronous multileaving RJE support to IBM mainframes.

MS-DOS   Microsoft Disk Operating System. An operating system acquired and modified by Microsoft Corporation for use in microcomputers.

MS Windows   Microsoft Windows. Microsoft's graphical user interface (GUI) that enables the user to select from multiple on-screen applications, each application occupying a screen window. *See also* GUI.

MTA   Message Transfer Agent. In an X.400 network, the MTA forwards messages between User Agents (UA) or among other Message Transfer Agents. *See also* MTS, UA, and X.400.

MTBF   Mean time between failure. The length of time (on average) a unit should operate without failures.

MTS   Message Transfer System. The network of routes available between Message Transfer Agents in an X.400 electronic mail network. *See also* MTA and X.400.

MTTR   Mean time to repair. The amount of time (on average) it should take to repair a specific failure.

multidrop   A connection enabling multiple devices to share one physical line. This is often used in the context of a data communications line that has multiple terminals attached to it. *See also* multipoint.

multipoint   A connection between multiple devices that enables all attached devices to share a common link. This is often used in the context of sharing a leased telephone line among three or more points. *See also* multidrop.

MVS   Multiple Virtual System (also known as OS/VS Release 2). An IBM System 370 architecture operating system. MVS is available in several packages.

MVS/ESA. MVS/Extended System Architecture. The top of the MVS operating system line. The resource requirements of MVS/ESA dictate that it can only be used on top-of-the-line mainframes.

MVS/SP   MVS/System Product. The low-end MVS operating system line, requiring the least amount of memory and storage.

MVS/XA   MVS/extended architecture. The middle of the MVS operating system line, requiring more resources than MVS/SP, but less than MVS/ESA.

MVT   Multiprogramming with a Variable Number of Tasks. An IBM System 360 architecture operating system.

N

NAK Negative acknowledgment. A transmission-control character transmitted by a receiver as a negative response to the sender. The normal response to a NAK is to retransmit the previous sequence.

Nanosecond One billionth of a second.

NAPLPS North American Presentation Level Protocol Syntax. An ANSI standard for the presentation of text and graphics.

NAS Network Application Support. A set of software products developed by DEC to integrate products on different systems. NAS is similar in concept to IBM's SAA.

NAU Network address unit. Any of the three addressable units in an IBM SNA network (in other words, SSCP, PU, and LU).

NCCF Network Communications Control Facility. An IBM NetView module that collects maintenance and status information from the SNA network. *See also* NetView.

NCP **1.** Network Control Program. In IBM environments, the NCP is the software running in the communications controller to control the data communications environment. In DEC environments, the NCP is a utility that interfaces with lower-level network management modules. **2.** In Novell environments, the Netware Control Protocol.

NCS Network Computing System. An architecture developed and promoted by Apollo (now HP) for implementing Remote Procedure Calls in a heterogeneous computer environment.

NETBIOS Network Basic Input Output System. A low level interface developed by IBM to allow PCs to share files and communicate with one another over a network. In brief, NETBIOS enables a PC program to open, close, read, write and lock network-based files. NETBIOS is often emulated by other network systems and forms the basis of Microsoft networking architectures.

NETdisk Part of Sun's Open Network Computing (ONC) architecture. NETdisk provides a network-based booting mechanism for diskless workstations. *See also* ONC.

Net-IPC *See* IPC.

NetView IBM's products and services that provide network management functions in an SNA network. Part of the greater SystemView systems management line, NetView is composed of a series of modules, including Network Communications Control Facility (NCCF), Network Problem Determination Application (NPDA), NetView Logical Data Manager (NLDM), NetView Management Productivity Facility (NMPF), and optionally NetView/PC. *See also* NCCF, NetView PC, NLDM, NMPF, and NPDA.

NetView/PC A PC-based product that enables non-SNA devices to participate in the Network Management Architecture offered by NetView. *See also* NetView.

NetWare The network operating system used in file servers in Novell networks.

Network Layer   The third layer of the OSI Reference Model. Network Layer services find the best possible route for a message (or packet) to take through the network. *See also* OSI Reference Model.

Network Lock Manager   Part of Sun's Open Network Computing (ONC) architecture. The Network Lock Manager provides record and file locking in conjunction with Sun's Network File System (NFS). *See also* NFS and ONC.

NeWS   Network-extensible Windowing System. Sun's original Graphical User Interface (GUI) for the SunOS operating system. One unique aspect of NeWS is that it extended Adobe Systems' PostScript technology into the networking environment. And like many other Sun products, NeWS was licensed to other companies who ported the interface to other operating systems and environments. Sun has since moved on to use the Open Look GUI it co-developed with AT&T. *See also* GUI and Open Look.

NewWave   HP's architecture for a Graphical User Interface (GUI) that provides a common multiwindowed, graphical environment from which the end user can access applications residing on other systems. *See also* GUI.

NFAR   Network File Access Routines. DEC routines that can be used by programmers to integrate DECnet file access into their programs.

NFS   Network File System. A specification created by Sun Microsystems for a network-based file server that allows for record-level and file-level access in a LAN environment.

NFT   Network File Transfer. A DEC utility for file transfer via DECnet. Files can also be transferred from one system to another via the standard COPY command.

NIDL   Network Interface Definition Compiler. Part of HP/Apollo's Network Computing System (NCS) architecture. NIDL enables each participating program to declare the formats and types of data it will be sharing through NCS. *See also* NCS.

NIS.   Network Information Services. A module within Sun's Open Network Computer (ONC) architecture that maintains a common list of files in the NFS and who can access what files. Formerly called YP. *See also* ONC and NFS.

NJE   Network job entry. NJE provides a mechanism to distribute the processing of a job (or jobs) among multiple hosts.

NLDM   NetView Logical Data Manager. An IBM NetView module that monitors the information being collected from the network and looks for and reports any failures. *See also* NetView.

NMA   Network management architecture. A general term used to refer to a vendor's or product's approach to managing a network.

NMP   Network Management Protocol. A low-level protocol developed by AT&T that collects network failures and status data. *See also* Accumaster Integrator and UNMA.

NMPF   NetView Management Productivity Facility. An IBM NetView module that provides online assistance to the personnel monitoring the network. *See also* NetView.

node   An element of a LAN that has full routing capability. *See also* end node.

NonStop A Tandem Computers product line based on fault tolerance.

NPDA Network Problem Determination Application. An IBM NetView module that presents the current status of the network. *See also* NetView.

NRJE/3000 An HP 3000-based software product that provides SNA RJE access to an IBM mainframe using SNA SDLC communications. Also known as SNA NRJE and NRJE.

NRZ Non-return to zero. A line transmission scheme whereby multiple contiguous 1 bits are sent as opposing pulses, instead of two pulses with similar amplitude separated by a return to the zero (base) line. NRZ is frequently used by IBM equipment and infrequently used by other vendor's equipment.

NS/1000 and NS/3000 HP 1000 and HP 3000-based products that provide networking services in the HP AdvanceNet network.

O

ODA Office Document Architecture. An OSI upper-layer service that defines the format for complex documents containing text, data, graphics, voice, and video. Defined in ISO standard 8613.

OEM Original equipment manufacturer. The term OEM is used to describe companies that use equipment manufactured by another company as part of their product or solution. In most cases, the identity of the original manufacturer is concealed from the end user of the product. *See also* VAR.

OfficeVision IBM's integration of office automation and electronic mail products with the PC and PS/2 environment. OfficeVision can link PCs and PS/2s with AS/400 Office or PROFS. *See also* AS/400 Office and PROFS.

OLTP Online transaction processing. An approach to application processing that breaks up the various interactions between a user and application and enables them to be processed in small parts (transactions). Transaction processing environments have specific routing requirements, and the programs processing the transactions must be multithreaded.

ONC Open Network Computing. Sun's architecture for the interconnection of its computers and computer-related devices. This is equivalent to IBM's SNA, DEC's DNA, and HP's AdvanceNet.

Open Look AT&T's graphical user interface (GUI) for UNIX, developed jointly with Sun Microsystems. Open Look provides the user with a graphics-oriented, multiwindowed interface. *See also* GUI.

Oracle A relational data base product available on multiple computer systems developed and marketed by Oracle Corporation.

ORB Object Request Broker. A type of middleware that facilitates interoperability, and establishes a single platform on which objects request data and services on the client side or provides them from the server side.

OS/2   Operating System/2. A multitasking operating system for IBM-compatible computers that includes a graphical user interface called the Presentation Manager. OS/2 was originally developed jointly by Microsoft and IBM. Development is now solely the responsibility of IBM.

OS/SVS   Operating System/Single Virtual Storage. An IBM System/370 architecture operating system. Also known as OS/VS2 Release 1.

OS/VS1   Operation System/Virtual Storage 1. An IBM System/370 architecture operating system.

OS/VS2   Operating System/Virtual Storage 2. *See* OS/SVS for OS/VS2 Release 1, MVS for OS/VS2 Release 2.

OSF   Open Software Foundation. A group of computer-related companies that came together to define an industrywide standard for UNIX that is separate and distinct from AT&T's standard.

OSF/Motif   The graphical user interface (GUI) released by the Open Software Foundation for its version of UNIX. *See also* GUI.

OSI Reference Model   Open Systems Interconnection Reference Model. A layered architecture for the design and implementation of standards that relate to the interconnection of computer systems. The OSI Model is carved into seven layers. These seven layers, from top to bottom, are:

- *Layer 7.*   Application (end-user and programming services)
- *Layer 6.*   Presentation (data conversions and transformations)
- *Layer 5.*   Session (logical link set-up and management)
- *Layer 4.*   Transport (delivery and delivery acknowledgment)
- *Layer 3.*   Network (route management)
- *Layer 2.*   Data Link (data packaging and transmission)
- *Layer 1.*   Physical (physical transmission media)

P

PA   Precision Architecture. HP's name for its RISC architecture.

packet   A group of binary digits—including data, origination and destination information—that is switched as a whole. *See also* frame.

Packet switching   A networking technique in which multiple devices convert information into smaller packets and then send them on a common network. Within the network, packets can be routed or rerouted through many different nodes, as seen fit by the network. Packet-switching networks can be more cost effective than leased or dialable networks because charges are typically based on the volume of data instead of connect time or distance.

PAD   Packet assembly/disassembly. A device that converts between the X.25 packet protocol (normally LAP-B) and a nonpacket protocol (such as those used by asynchronous terminals) so that nonpacket devices can use a packet network. In addition to the protocol conversion, the PAD takes large blocks of information from the local device and breaks them into smaller packets for the network. Conversely, the PAD also takes the small packets from the network and assembles them into a large block of information for the local device.

PAM   Personal Applications Menu. An HP software program implemented in HP PCs in place of the standard COMMAND.COM program that comes with MS-DOS. PAM provides menu-driven services instead of COMMAND.COM's command line interpretation.

parallel   A data transmission method in which the bits in a character are sent at the same time on 8 channels rather than on a single channel. *See also* serial.

parity   The addition on a noninformation bit to a byte, making the number of ones in a byte either always odd or always even. This permits the detection of errors in bytes that have single-bit errors.

Pathworks   A collection of products that enables PCs, PS/2s and Macintosh computers to participate in a DECnet network. This includes storing files, sharing printers and emulating terminals.

PBX   Private branch exchange. A privately owned telephone routing system.

PC   Personal computer. Originally a term used to refer to the IBM Personal Computer based on the Intel 8088 processor as introduced in 1981. The term PC has, however, gone on to refer to a larger class of machines that run MS-DOS (or PC-DOS) and provide some degree of hardware compatibility with the IBM PC.

PC/AT   Personal Computer/Advanced Technology. IBM's first release of a Personal Computer using the Intel 80286 processor. The bus architecture of the PC/AT (two 8-bit PC-style slots and six 16-bit slots) went on to become popular in both 80286 and 80386 machines.

PC Convertible   IBM's early attempt at an laptop computer based on the Intel 8088 processor running the MS-DOS (PC-DOS) operating system.

PC-DOS   IBM's implementation of MS-DOS. *See also* MS-DOS.

PCjr   IBM's home computer based on its original PC design. The PCjr featured limited memory and expansion capabilities.

PCL   Printer Command Language. HP's generalized interface for its line of laser, ink-jet and dot-matrix printers. PCL uses scalable fonts and raster graphics but is not implemented in a high-level language. *See also* raster graphics.

PC LAN   IBM's PC networking product.

PCM   Plug compatible mainframe. Full-scale computer systems manufactured by companies other than IBM (such as Amdahl and Hitachi) that run IBM operating systems (for example, VM, and MVS).

PC-NFS   PC Network File System. Part of Sun's Open Network Computing (ONC) architecture. PC-NFS allows for PCs and PS/2s to access information stored in the Network File

System (NFS). PC-NFS also includes TCP/IP functions for terminal access and file transfer. *See also* ONC.

PC-NFS Lifeline Backup   An add-on to Sun's PC-NFS product. PC-NFS Lifeline Backup permits multiple PC disks on the network to be backed up to a single network disk or tape. *See also* PC-NFS.

PC-NFS Lifeline Mail   An add-on to Sun's PC-NFS product. PC-NFS Lifeline Mail permits a PC or PS/2 to participate in TCP/IP and UNIX electronic mail. *See also* PC-NFS.

PC-NFS Programmers Toolkit   An add-on to Sun's PC-NFS product. It implements Sun's RPC and XDR in the networked PC environment. *See also* PC-NFS.

PC-RT   Personal Computer Reduced instruction set Technique. *See* RT System.

PCSA   Personal Computer Systems Architecture, now called Pathworks. *See* Pathworks.

PC/XT   Personal Computer Extended Technology. The follow-up to the original PC (PC/AT), also based on the Intel 8088 processor.

PC/XT 286   A follow-up product to both the PC/XT and PC/AT that combined attributes of both machines into one system. The PC/XT 286 experienced limited success.

PDL   Page Description Language. The general term for a software-based printer interface that defines the page layout and contents. Examples of PDLs include GPI, PCL, and PostScript. *See also* GPI, PCL, and PostScript.

PDN   Public data network. A telephone company that offers data services to the public. A public data network does not have to use packet switching. *See also* PSN.

PDP   DEC's line of 16-bit technical computers. The PDP computers use DEC's Q-bus architecture and run several DEC operating systems.

Phases   In DEC terminology, the various revision levels of DECnet are termed phases. Since its first release in 1976, DECnet has had five major phases:

- *Phase I.*   Basic services for PDP-11 systems.
- *Phase II.*   Support for all DEC computers and operating systems.
- *Phase III.*   Support for network terminals and X.25.
- *Phase IV.*   Support for Ethernet.
- *Phase V.*   Support for OSI standards.

Physical Layer   The first (lowest) layer of the OSI Reference Model. The Physical Layer defines the physical interface for the network (for example, RS-232 for point-to-point networks, CCITT X.21 for interfacing to public data networks and 802.3/4/5 for LANs). *See also* OSI Reference Model.

physical unit   *See* PU.

Pick   An operating system developed by Pick Systems that features integrated multiuser and database support.

PIU Path information unit. The combination of the TH and BIU information from the IBM SNA data format. *See also* BLU.

pixel The smallest element of a screen display. Each pixel in a display can be manipulated in terms of color and intensity. In most cases, the higher the number of pixels, the higher the resolution of the display.

PM. Presentation Manager. The graphical user interface for OS/2. *See also* GUI.

PNCP Peripheral Node Control Point. A point in a PU 2.1 node that provides limited IBM SNA management functions to facilitate LU 6.2 peer-to-peer communications. The presence or absence of the PNCP facility differentiates between a PU 2.1 and PU 2 device.

Point-to-point A physical connection between only two terminals or computers.

polling A method by which a master device tracks the status of its attached devices. When the master device polls its attached devices, each device responds, indicating that it is present.

POP Post Office Protocol. An electronic mail protocol for UNIX systems developed by Berkeley Software Distribution.

POSIX Definition of an operating system easily ported from one computer to another. Developed by IEEE as standard 1003.

PostScript A print description language developed by Adobe Systems that provides multifont, high-resolution output. PostScript features scalable fonts and raster-based graphics. Because it is implemented as a high-level language, PostScript can be implemented on virtually any computer system. PostScript is also used for fonts and graphics displays (and called Display PostScript in that context). *See also* raster graphics.

POWER Priority Output Writers, Execution Processors and Input Readers. An IBM Job Entry Subsystem. POWER/VS is for the DOS/VS operating system, and VSE POWER is for the DOS/VSE operating system.

POWERserver An IBM line of servers for use in engineering workstation networks. The POWERservers use a RISC architecture and are part of the RS/6000 computer line. *See also* POWERstation and RS/6000.

POWERstation A line of IBM engineering workstations using a RISC architecture. The POWERstations are part of the RS/6000 computer line. *See also* POWERserver and RS/6000.

POWER/VS *See* POWER.

Presentation Layer The sixth layer of the OSI Reference Model. The Presentation Layer standards ensure that data is presented to each application in a format that can be understood. This includes ASCII/EBCDIC conversion, data compression/expansion and so forth. *See also* OSI Reference Model.

PRI Primary Rate Interface. The high-end interface in the Integrated Services Data Network (ISDN). The PRI offers 23 64-Kbps data/voice lines and a twenty-fourth 16 Kbps management line. *See also* BRI and ISDN.

PRISM   Parallel Reduced Instruction Set Multiprocessing. HP/Apollo's term for its approach to the RISC-architecture Domain computer.

Professional 300 A DEC product that implemented the basic PDP-11 computer architecture in a desktop model.

PROFS   Professional Office System. An IBM office automation and electronic mail product for the VM operating system (and therefore for IBM mainframes).

protocol   A set of rules by which two or more devices agree on information and code structures required for successful and error-free communications.

PS/1   Personal System/1. IBM's home computer introduced in 1990 and based on an 80286 processor. The PS/1 is an entry level system that does not use either the ISA or MCA bus standards. *See also* ISA, MCA, and PS/2.

PS/2   IBM's replacement to its original line of PCs. Most models in the PS/2 line feature IBM's MCA bus architecture. *See also* MCA.

PSDN   Packet-Switching Data Network. A data network offering packet-switching data services. *See also* PDN and PSN.

PSN Packet-switching network. Also packet-switching node. A packet-switching network routes small fragments of information (called packets) over a series of switched circuits. A packet-switching node is a device within the packet-switching network that can route a packet between several other packet-switching nodes. *See also* X.25.

PSPDN   Packet-switching public data network. A public data network offering packet-switching data services. *See also* PDN and PSN.

PU   Physical unit. In IBM terminology, a physical unit controls the attached links and resources (logical units) of a node. *See also* LU.

PU Type 1 (PU 1)   Workstations (for example, 3270).

PU Type 2 (PU 2)   Cluster controllers (for example, 3274) and mid-range processors (for example, System/3X).

PU Type 2.1 (PU 2.1)   Mid-range processors (for example, System/3X) that contain a PCNP. *See also* PCNP.

PU Type 4 (PU 4)   Communications controllers (for example, 3705).

PU Type 5 (PU 5)   Hosts that contain a SSCP. *See also* SSCP.

PW2   Personal Workstation Squared (the power of two). The Unisys line of PCs derived from the Sperry line of PCs.

Q

Q-Bus Internal and peripheral bus used in the DEC MicroVAX and PDP-11 Series computers.

R

RAID Redundant Array of Inexpensive Disks. A cluster of disks, viewed by the end user as a single device, that mirrors data to multiple drives. RAID provides fast throughput, fault tolerance, and error correction.

Rainbow DEC's original offering in the PC market. The Rainbow ran MS-DOS or CP/M, but was not hardware-compatible with the IBM PC.

RAM Random access memory. The high-speed but volatile memory used by computers of all sizes.

raster graphics A type of graphics handling in which the image is broken into a horizontal series of dots, with each line of dots called a raster. Using this approach, the higher the number of horizontal rows, the finer the resolution of the printed page. *See also* dpi.

RD Receive Data. A lead in the RS-232C interface, RD is used as the reception line for incoming information. In the full 25-pin RS-232C standard, RD is pin 3. In the abbreviated, 9-pin PC interface, RD is pin 2. *See also* RS-232C and TD.

ReGIS Remote Graphics Instruction Set. DEC's graphics interface to its VT family of graphics terminals.

RES Remote Entry Services. *See* JES.

REX Remote Execution. Part of Sun's Open Network Computing (ONC) architecture. Enables a user on one system to execute commands on another system. *See also* ONC.

RFI Radio frequency interference. Radio waves that can potentially interfere with the operation of electronic devices. The U.S. Federal Communications Commission (FCC) is responsible for regulating whether an electronic device (such as a computer) generates too much RFI or electromagnetic interference (EMI). *See also* EMI and FCC.

RH Request/Response Header. The part of the IBM SNA data format that defines the type of data in the RU. *See also* BLU.

RI Ring Indicator. A lead in the RS-232C interface, RI is used to tell the terminal or computer that the phone is ringing. Normally RI is used with dial-up modems, in which case the receiving device can decide whether it wants to answer the call or not. In the full 25-pin RS-232C standard, RI is pin 22. In the abbreviated, 9-pin PC interface, RI is pin 9. *See also* RS-232C.

ring topology A LAN topology that features a central ring on to which nodes are connected. *See also* bus topology, tree topology, and star topology.

RISC Reduced instruction set computer. An architecture for computers in which more functions are moved into software while relying on highly optimized hardware to obtain optimum efficiency. *See also* CISC.

RJE Remote job entry. The ability to submit jobs on a computer from an IBM RJE workstation (a combination of multiple devices, such as a card reader, card punch, printer and console) to a Job Entry Subsystem. RJE is often used as a general means for file transfer; in this situation, a computer emulates an RJE workstation when communicating with another computer running (or emulating) a Job Entry Subsystem (JES). *See also* JCL and JES.

RJE/1000 and RJE/3000   HP 1000- and HP 3000-based software products that provide RJE access to IBM mainframes using bisynchronous communications.

RLL   Run length limited. A disk encoding technique that results in 26 sectors per cylinder. RLL uses the ST-506 interface and is often used in place of MFM encoding on PCs because it is a denser storage technique (although it does require drives that are certified for RLL encoding). *See also* ESDI, MFM, SCSI, and ST-506.

RMON 2   A standard for remote monitoring. RMON 2 provides the means to proactively monitor an enterprise network, using an agent or probe to gather statistics and monitor for preset threshold levels.

RMS   Record Management Services. The part of DECnet that handles requests to access remote files. RMS interfaces with FAL via DAP. *See also* FAL and DAP.

ROM   Read only memory. A type of memory that can be read from but not written to. In contrast to RAM, ROM is low-speed, nonvolatile memory.

RPC   Remote procedure call. A set of routines that enables a program operating on one system to communicate with a program running on another system. This interaction might be for the simple purpose of program-to-program communications or can be used to implement a network-distributed application, whereby the individual tasks of the application are distributed across multiple systems and coordinated through RPCs. *See also* API, APPC, and IPC.

RPC API   RPC Application Program Interface. Part of Sun's Open Network Computing (ONC) architecture. A high-level interface that programmers can use to implement ONC RPC. *See also* RPC and ONC.

RPCGEN   RPC Generator. Part of Sun's Open Network Computing (ONC) architecture. A programming aid that automates parts of the RPC coding requirements. *See also* RPC and ONC.

RS-232C   An EIA standard for computer/terminal interfaces that defines the electrical and mechanical characteristics for the interconnection of data terminal equipment to data communications equipment for use at signaling rates up to 20,000 bps. RS-232C is frequently associated with a 25-pin connector. Often in a PC environment, only the following 9 of the full 25 leads are used: Carrier Detect (CD), Receive Data (RD), Transmit Data (TD), Data Terminal Ready (DTR), Signal Ground (SG), Data Set Ready (DSR), Request To Send (RTS), Clear To Send (CTS), and Ring Indicator (RI). *See also* CD, RD, TD, DTR, SG, DSR, RTS, CTS, and RI.

RS-422   An EIA standard for computer/terminal interfaces that defines the electrical and mechanical characteristics for the interconnection of data terminal equipment to data communications equipment for use at signaling rates up to 20,000 bps. RS-422 is frequently associated with a 5-pin connector.

RS-449   An EIA standard for computer/terminal interface that defines the electrical and mechanical characteristics for the interconnection of data terminal equipment to data communications equipment for use at signaling rates up to 2,000,000 bps. RS-449 is frequently associated with 37-pin and 9-pin connectors.

RS/6000 RISC System/6000. Introduced in 1990, the RS/6000 is IBM's line of RISC-based engineering workstations and servers. The RS/6000 line includes the POWERstation engineering workstations and POWERserver network servers.

RSCS Remote Spooling Communications Subsystem. The IBM Job Entry Subsystem for the VM operating system. RSCS does not, however, support attachment to SNA devices.

RSTS DEC's time-sharing operating system for the PDP/11 Series computers. *See also* CTS-300, DSM-11, and RSX.

RSX (RSX-11, RSC-11M, RSX-11M-PLUS) DEC's real-time and/or priority-driven multitasking operating systems for the PDP/11 Series computers. *See also* CTS-300, DSM-11, and RSTS.

RT System One of IBM's early engineering workstations. The RT System, originally called the PC RT, was based on IBM-proprietary RISC processors and had little in common with the rest of the PC line.

RTAM Remote Telecommunications Access Method. An IBM mainframe subsystem that handles application access and routing within the network. *See also* BTAM, TCAM, and VTAM.

RTE Real Time Executive. HP's operating system for the HP 1000 series computer.

RTS Request To Send. A lead in the RS-232C interface. RTS is raised by one side of the link when it wishes to transmit. If the other side is ready to receive, it responds by raising the Clear To Send (CTS) line. After transmission has begun, the Carrier Detect (CD) line is also raised. In the full 25-pin RS-232C standard, RTS is pin 4. In the abbreviated, 9-pin PC interface, RTS is pin 7. *See also* CD, CTS, and RS-232C.

RTS Reliable Transfer Service. In an X.400 electronic mail network, RTS works in concert with Message Transfer Agents (MTAs) to ensure that the best possible route for a message is taken. *See also* MTA and X.400.

RU Response Unit. The informational (data) portion of the IBM SNA data format. *See also* BLU.

S

SAA Systems Applications Architecture. A set of routines and transport mechanisms developed by IBM to isolate the development of applications from the specifics of the systems on which they will operate. Under SAA, a program can be implemented on one type of IBM system and then easily moved to another type of IBM system. An SAA-compliant application uses three SAA-defined interfaces: the common user interface, the common programming interface and the common communications support. *See also* common user interface, common programming interface, and common communications support.

SATAN Security Administrator Tool for Analyzing Networks. A free program that is used to detect vulnerabilities in networks. *See also* Gabriel.

SCSI Small Computer Systems Interface. SCSI is an intelligent, bus-oriented interface that enables a computer to transfer data between a disk, tape or other computer. A SCSI subsystem can support up to seven devices and each of these devices can communicate directly with one another. Thus, under SCSI, a computer can request the disk to back up to tape, and the disk will transfer directly to the tape without any further interaction from the computer. SCSI has become popular as a hard disk interface that offers storage of 26 or 36 sectors per track. One final advantage to SCSI as a disk interface is that it handles the relocation of bad disk areas on its own. SCSI is used in both PCs and mid-range systems. *See also* ESDI, MFM, RLL, and ST-506.

SDLC Synchronous Data Link Control. A bit-oriented protocol developed by IBM for use in SNA networks; SDLC is the de facto replacement for IBM bisynchronous communications protocols. IBM submitted SDLC to various standards organizations, and it has been adopted as ADCCP, HDLC, and LAP-B.

SecureRPC A part of Sun's Open Networking Computing (ONC) architecture. SecureRPC provides additional security to Sun's implementation of RPC. *See also* ONC and RPC.

serial A data transmission method in which the bits in a character are sent one after the other over a single channel. *See* parallel.

Session Layer The fifth layer of the OSI Reference Model. The Session Layer defines services that manage the administrative functions associated with moving information between two systems, such as requesting a logical link, maintaining the link and then tearing it down when the transfer is complete. *See also* OSI Reference Model.

SG Signal ground. A lead in the RS-232C interface. Signal ground provides a common reference ground between both sides of the data communications link. In the full 25-pin RS-232C standard, SG is pin 7. In the abbreviated, 9-pin PC interface, SG is pin 5. *See also* RS-232C.

Sixel DEC's graphics interface for printers. Sixel uses the lower six bits of a byte to correspond to six vertical printer dots. (In contrast, most Epson printers use all eight bits to correspond to eight vertical printer dots). The advantage to sixel is that the characters generated by using only the lower six bits stay within the realm of normal, displayable ASCII characters. Thus with sixel, graphics data can be sent to the printer over virtually any type of data communications link.

SLIP Serial Line Internet Protocol. A point-to-point link that can be used in a TCP/IP network to connect two TCP/IP devices together over a standard serial line.

SMP Symmetric multiprocessing. A multiprocessor implementation of a computer wherein an application can be broken (decomposed) into smaller tasks that can be distributed across the multiple processors and run in parallel.

SMTP Simple Mail Transfer Protocol. SMTP provides basic electronic mail functions in a TCP/IP network.

SNA   Systems Network Architecture. IBM's architecture for the interconnections of its computer and computer-related devices. This is equivalent to DEC's DNA, HP's AdvanceNet, and Sun's ONC.

SNADS   SNA Distributions Services. A distribution service for IBM computers operating in an SNA environment that allows for the transfer of files, documents, and electronic mail. *See also* DDM and DIA.

SNMP   Simple Network Management Protocol. A lower-level service that hunts through the network for failures. SNMP is often implemented within TCP/IP.

SPARC   Scalable Processor Architecture. Sun Microsystems' implementation of a RISC architecture computer.

SPARCserver   Sun Microsystems' line of file and network servers based on its SPARC design. The high end of the SPARCserver line pushes into the traditional mid-range market in terms of power and architecture.

SPARCstation   Sun Microsystems' line of engineering workstations based on its SPARC design.

Spectrum   The code name for the HP 3000 line of RISC computers.

SPX   Sequenced Packet Exchange. A Novell protocol that runs on top of Novell's older IPX protocol. Unlike IPX, SPX provides guaranteed delivery of network messages. In the OSI model, SPX is a transport layer protocol.

SQL   Structured Query Language. A standard that defines the language for extracting information from a database.

SSCP   System Service Control Point. A point in a host that provides SNA management functions. The presence of an SSCP enables a device to become an SNA PU 5.

SSP   System Support Program. The operating system for the IBM System/36.

ST-506   A disk interface commonly used in PCs. The ST-506 interface can use either MFM or RLL encoding. *See also* ESDI, MFM, RLL, and SCSI.

Star Cluster   A device that interfaces multiple DEC VAX systems (via CI links) to an HSC. This enables multiple VAX systems to access one or more sets of disk drives maintained by one or more HSCs. *See also* CI, HSC, and VAXcluster.

Star topology   A LAN topology that features a central hub to which nodes are connected. *See also* bus topology, tree topology, and ring topology.

StarLAN   A LAN implementation developed by AT&T that uses 1-Mbps cables in a star topology. HP used the original StarLAN implementation, then upgraded it to a 10-Mbps operating speed and changed the name to StarLAN-10.

Status Monitor   Part of Sun's Open Network Computing (ONC) architecture. The Status Monitor enables one system to determine whether another system has been restarted. *See also* ONC.

Sun   Sun Microsystems. A manufacturer of engineering workstations and the architect of NFS, ONC and SPARC. *See also* NFS, ONC, and SPARC.

Sun-3   Sun Microsystems' line of engineering workstations based on the Motorola MC68000 line of processors.

Sun-4   Sun Microsystems' line of engineering workstations based on its SPARC design. The Sun-4 term has been discontinued in favor of the SPARCserver and SPARCstation terms.

Sun386i   Sun Microsystems' line of engineering workstations based on the Intel 80386 line of processors.

SunLink   Sun's line of products for multivendor connectivity.

SunOS   Sun's operating system for its engineering workstations. SunOS is based on both AT&T and Berkeley versions of UNIX.

switched line   The line connection made as a result of dialing via the phone system (as opposed to a permanent leased line).

synchronous   A form of transmission in which the sender and receiver exchange timing information on separate channels to send a frame with no space or marking between characters. Because no start/stop bits are required, synchronous transmission is more efficient than asynchronous transmission for long messages. *See also* asynchronous.

System/3X   A general term used to refer to the IBM System/34, System/36 and System/38 lines of mid-range computers.

System/360   An IBM mainframe first released in 1964. Because of the way it handled multiple tasks and managed large amounts (at that time) of disk storage, the System/360 paved the way for the mainframe definition of today.

System/370   The System/370 was first released in 1970 as the follow-up to the IBM System/360 mainframe. The most important improvement in the System/370 was the introduction of virtual storage management. The System/370 remains the underlying architecture used in today's IBM mainframe products.

System/390   A system released by IBM in 1990 as a follow-up to the IBM System/370 mainframe. The performance of the System/390 has been greatly enhanced over that of the System/370 through the use of fiber-optic links and high-speed channel communications.

Systempro   Compaq Computer's mid-range computer offering featuring multiple Intel processors operating in conjunction with the Extended Industry Standard Architecture (EISA) bus.

T

T1   A standard definition for digital transmission in the Bell System T-carrier digital environment. T1 defines a path having 1.544 Mbps that can be broken into 24 channels of 64 Kbps service. Each of the individual channels is said to have a Digital Signal Level Zero (DS-0) rate and all 24 as a whole result in the Digital Signal Level One (DS1) rate. *See also* Fractional T1.

TCAM   TeleCommunications Access Method. An IBM mainframe subsystem that handles application access and routing within the network. *See also* BTAM, RTAM, and VTAM.

TCP/IP   Transmission Control Protocol/Internet Protocol. TCP/IP is a set of network services that provide interoperability between heterogeneous systems. The TCP portion is responsible for providing reliable and recoverable communications between two end points. The IP portions sets up the routing used by TCP to transmit. Joining TCP/IP are two other low-level services—User Datagram Protocol (UDP) and Internet Control Message Protocol (ICMP)—that are responsible for program-to-program communications and error reporting, respectively. Above TCP/IP are service applications to provide file transfer (FTP), terminal access (TELNET) and electronic mail (SMTP). TCP/IP was developed by the Defense Advanced Research Projects Agency (DARPA) and is commonly used as a transport mechanism in governmental, engineering and educational environments. *See also* FTP, ICMP, SMTP, TELNET, and UDP.

TD   Transmit Data. A lead in the RS-232C interface, TD is used to transmit information across the interface. In the full 25-pin RS- 232C standard, TD is pin 2. In the abbreviated, 9-pin PC interface, TD is pin 3. *See also* RS-232C and RD.

TELNET   TELNET is a TCP/IP application that enables a user to log on to a remote TCP/IP system.

terminal server   A product that connects terminals to a LAN, enabling the terminals to establish sessions on host nodes. *See also* DECserver, DTC, LAT, and TS8.

TH   Transmission header. The part of the SNA data format that defines the origin and destination of the message. *See also* BLU.

ThickLAN   An term used to define the standard baseband coaxial cable (10BASE5) used as the backbone in most IEEE 802.3 and Ethernet LANs.

ThinLAN   An term used to define the thin coaxial cable (10BASE2) used to interface PCs and office equipment in a LAN environment. ThinLAN segments can be interfaced to a ThickLAN backbone (or segment).

ThinWire   The DEC term corresponding to ThinLAN.

TN   Terminal Node. An IBM SNA term.

Token-passing discipline   A LAN discipline whereby a specific message, termed a token, is passed from device to device on the LAN. The device that possesses the token has the ability to transmit on the LAN and when the device is done transmitting, it releases the token to the next downstream device. Token passing and CSMA/CD are the two most prevalent LAN disciplines is use. *See also* CSMA/CD.

token-passing ring   *See* IEEE 802.5.

transceiver   The device that attaches nodes to a LAN. Digital's H4000 and H4005 are typical transceivers. Transceivers interface with transceiver cables that attach to the nodes. *See also* MAU and AUI.

transparent data Binary data transmitted with the recognition of control characters suppressed.

Transport Layer   The fourth layer of the OSI Reference Model. The Transport Layer standards ensure that information gets delivered to the intended destination and that it is delivered free of errors. *See also* OSI Reference Model.

tree topology   A LAN topology that features a linear backbone onto which nodes or other LAN segments are connected. The tree topology and bus topology are similar and, in fact, the two terms are often interchanged. *See also* bus topology, ring topology, and star topology.

TS8   Terminal Server 8-ports. An HP terminal server that enables terminals to access HP 9000 hosts over a LAN running TCP/IP.

TSO   Time Sharing Option. An IBM product that enables different users to use a mainframe by sharing the total available CPU on a percentage of time basis.

TTY   Teletype. Originally a specific keyboard/hardcopy device, the term TTY has gone on to become a general industry term describing a dumb terminal that is operated on a key-by-key or line-by-line basis.

TurboIMAGE   HP's proprietary relational database product.

Twinax   IBM's twinaxial cabling system for the 5250 family of workstations, as used with the IBM mid-range system line (for example, System/36, System/38, and AS/400). Twinaxial is similar to coaxial except, as the name implies, it uses two conducting cores. *See also* coaxial.

U

UA   User Agent. A software package that interfaces between a user and the X.400 electronic mail network. *See also* X.400.

UDP   User Datagram Protocol. UDP provides a means for two programs in a TCP/IP network to directly communicate with one another.

ULTRIX   DEC's implementation of UNIX for the VAX computer. *See also* VAXELN and VMS.

Unibus   An internal and peripheral bus used in Digital's VAX and PDP-11 Series computers.

Unisys   The company resulting from the merger of Burroughs and Sperry.

UNIX   A multiuser, multitasking operating system. UNIX was designed by AT&T (Bell Laboratories) to be a industrywide operating system that could be implemented on virtually any type of computer. In reality, however, several different vendors have implemented their own versions of UNIX with proprietary extensions that are largely incompatible with one another.

UNMA   Unified Network Management Architecture. AT&T's multivendor network management product.

V

V.3 CCITT international alphabet #5.

V.4 CCITT definition of structure for V.3 transmission over phone networks.

V.21 A CCITT standard for 300-bps modem operation over switched phone circuits.

V.22 A CCITT standard for 1,200-bps modem operation over switched and leased phone circuits.

V.22bis CCITT standard for 2,400-bps modem operation over switched and leased phone lines.

V.24 A CCITT standard for the interchange circuits between DCE and DTE. The V.24 standard is compatible with the RS-232C standard. *See also* DCE, DTE, and RS-232C.

V.25 A CCITT standard for automatic calling or answering equipment on switched networks.

V.26bis A CCITT standard for 1,200/2,400-bps modem operation over switched phone circuits.

V.27bis A CCITT standard for 2,400/4,800-bps modem operation over leased phone circuits.

V.27ter A CCITT standard for 2,400/4,800-bps modem operation over switched phone circuits.

V.28 CCITT definition of electrical characteristics for unbalanced circuits.

V.29 A CCITT standard for 9,600-bps modem operation over point-to-point leased phone circuits.

V.32 A CCITT standard regulating transmission up to 19.2 Kbps (asynchronous) or 1.2 Kbps (synchronous) over switched or leased phone lines.

V.33 CCITT standard for 12,200- and 14,400-bps modem operation over leased phone lines.

V.35 A widely used interface standard for data connections at rates up to 48 Kbps, defined by the CCITT. Note that despite the specification, the V.35 interface is frequently used to accommodate rates up to and including 64 Kbps.

V.42 CCITT error detection and correction scheme for modems.

V.42bis CCITT data-compression method for use with V.42.

VAN Value added network. A private network (normally over a wide area) offered on a commercial basis. DEC, HP and IBM all offer connectivity via their own proprietary networks. In the case of these three manufacturers, this network services its own locations, thus giving their customers local connection to the network at various locations across the country.

VAR. Value-added reseller. A company or organization that takes a product from one company, combines it with its own product (or service) and then resells the result to the end user. *See also* OEM.

VAX   Virtual Address eXtension. DEC's wide-ranging line of 32-bit mid-range and high-end processors. Capable of running either VMS or Ultrix, these systems are typically installed on a DECnet (Ethernet) network. The VAX line includes the 4000, 6000, 8000, and 9000 series of models.

VAXBI   The bus architecture used in the high end of the DEC VAX product line.

VAXcluster   A unique configuration of VAX systems that enable multiple VAX systems to share access to a large pool of disk storage. VAXclusters were implemented by DEC to provide systems with computing and storage capacity similar to that of IBM mainframes.

VAXELN   A real-time operating system for VAX computers. *See also* Ultrix and VMS.

VAXmate   A DEC 80286-based personal computer.

VAXstation   DEC's line of engineering workstations based on their proprietary VAX processor architecture.

Vectra   HP's line of Pentium-based PCs.

VINES   Virtual Network Software. PC network software by Banyan Systems. VINES is somewhat unique in that it can be implemented on top of existing network standards, like TCP, SNA or XNS.

virtual terminal   The capability to logically connect to one type of computer (or node) from a different computer (or node).

VLSI   Very large-scale integration. An approach to printed circuit-board design that uses the smallest possible number of individual components (chips), but with each component responsible for a broad set of functions. *See also* LSI.

VM   Virtual Machine. An IBM System/370-style operating system that can host other operating systems as resident processes.

VME   A general-purpose bus architecture. Frequently used in engineering workstations (such a Sun's) that use the Motorola MC68000 processor series.

VMS   Virtual Management System. A DEC operating system for VAX computers. *See also* VAXELN and Ultrix.

VS1   *See* OS/VS1.

VS2   *See* OS/VS2.

VSE   Virtual Storage Extended. An IBM System/370-style operating system.

VSE/POWER   *See* POWER.

VT50   An early DEC terminal type. The VT50 models (for example, VT52 and VT55) were not ANSI-compatible terminals. The VT50 family includes models that support both text and graphics.

VT100   DEC's follow-up to its VT50 family. The VT100 family (for example, VT101, VT102, VT125) included support for both VT50 operation and ANSI-compatible operation. The VT100 family includes models that support both text and graphics.

VT200   DEC's replacement family for the VT100. The VT200 family introduced the now familiar keyboard layout with separate cursor, editing and numeric keypads. The VT200 family includes models that support monochrome text (VT220), monochrome graphics, (VT240), and color graphics (VT241).

VT300   DEC's follow-up to their VT200 family. The VT300 includes performance and ergonomic improvements to the basic VT200 design. The VT300 family includes models that support monochrome text (VT320), monochrome graphics (VT330), and color graphics (VT340).

VT400   DEC's follow-up to the VT300 line. The VT400 features improved memory, screen fonts, and session capabilities.

VT1000   DEC's X Window terminal. The VT1000 includes graphics processors in support of the graphics-intensive X Window environment.

VTAM   Virtual Telecommunications Access Method. An IBM mainframe subsystem that handles application access and routing within the network. *See also* BTAM, RTAM, and TCAM.

VTS Virtual terminal services. An OSI upper-layer service to define a common terminal format that might be shared between open systems. Defined as ISO standard 9040.

W

WAN   Wide area network. A network composed of systems that are relatively far apart. A WAN can also encompass a series of LANs connected together over a wide area. *See also* MAN.

windows   An approach to the user interface that offers multiple applications to a user, with each application occupying a relatively small space (window) on the screen. The user can then select applications by window and zoom into or out of them. *See also* GUI. Also, the name of the Microsoft product that affords users this type of interface.

WPS-Plus DEC's word processing software for VMS systems. Also used as an integral part of ALL-IN-1. *See also* ALL-IN-1.

X

X.1 CCITT definition of service classes in public data networks.

X.2 CCITT definition of services and facilities in public data networks.

X.3 CCITT definition of packet assembly/disassembly (PAD) facilities in a packet-switching network.

X3.4 ANSI standard for a 7-bit information interchange code.

X3.15 ANSI specifications for bit sequencing of the X3.4 code in serial data streams.

X3.16 ANSI specifications for character and parity structure in X.34 transmissions.

X3.28 ANSI standard for the use of communication control characters.

X3.41 ANSI specifications for code extensions using the 7-bit V3.4 interchange code.

X3.66 ANSI definition of the Advanced Data Communication Control Procedures (ADCCP). *See also* ADCCP.

X.4 CCITT structure of V.3 transmission over public networks.

X.20 CCITT specification for interfacing devices using asynchronous transmission.

X.20bis A CCITT standard for interfacing terminals (DTE) and computers (DCE) over public data networks using asynchronous V-series modems.

X.21 CCITT specification for interfacing devices using synchronous transmission.

X.21bis A CCITT standard for interfacing terminals (DTE) and computers (DCE) over public data networks using synchronous V-series modems.

X.25 A CCITT standard for interfacing terminals (DTE) and computers (DCE) over a packet switching public data network (PSPDN). Because of its association with packet-switching data networks, X.25 has become almost synonymous with the term packet-switching network.

X.28 CCITT standard for start/stop device access to a packet assembly/disassembly unit (PAD). *See also* PAD.

X.29 CCITT exchange procedures for a PAD and a packet-mode DTE (normally a computer). X.29 is commonly used to facilitate terminal access over an X.25 network. *See also* PAD.

X.75 CCITT specifications for control and transfer between packet networks.

X.400 A standard for implementing electronic mail on diverse computer systems. X.400 has provisions for the exchange of messages, files and video information.

X.500 A standard for implementing common directory services on heterogeneous computer systems.

XDR External Data Representation. Part of Sun's Open Network Computing (ONC) architecture. XDR provides a common format for data being exchanged among heterogeneous systems. *See also* ONC.

XENIX An operating system marketed by Santa Cruz Operation (SCO) and based primary on UNIX, but offering some compatibility with MS-DOS.

XMI DEC's bus architecture used in the top-end VAX 6000 and 9000 systems.

XMODEM A public domain protocol designed to enable microcomputers to transfer files over telephone lines via modems.

XNS   Xerox Networking System. Xerox Corporation's networking services implemented over an Ethernet LAN.

XON/XOFF   A simple pacing mechanism implemented between sending and receiving units. Under this mechanism, the sender transmits until the receiver sends an XOFF character, signaling the transmitter to pause. When the receiver is ready for more data, is sends an XON character and the transmitter resumes sending. The XON and XOFF characters are normally the DC1 and DC3 control characters, respectively.

X Terminal   A graphics-based computer or terminal that supports the X Window protocol.

X Window   A specification developed at the Massachusetts Institute of Technology for a common graphical interface and set of protocols. X Window employs multiple windows to enable a user to concurrently access applications running on different systems.

Y

YP   Yellow Pages. *See* NIS.

Index

MACMILLAN COMPUTER PUBLISHING USA

A VIACOM COMPANY

Technical Support:

If you need assistance with the information in this book or with a CD/Disk accompanying the book, please access the Knowledge Base on our Web site at **http://www.superlibrary.com/general/support**. Our most Frequently Asked Questions are answered there. If you do not find the answer to your questions on our Web site, you may contact Macmillan Technical Support **(317) 581-3833** or e-mail us at **support@mcp.com**.

Complete and Return this Card
for a *FREE* Computer Book Catalog

Thank you for purchasing this book! You have purchased a superior computer book written expressly for your needs. To continue to provide the kind of up-to-date, pertinent coverage you've come to expect from us, we need to hear from you. Please take a minute to complete and return this self-addressed, postage-paid form. In return, we'll send you a free catalog of all our computer books on topics ranging from word processing to programming and the Internet.

☐   Mrs. ☐   Ms. ☐   Dr. ☐

me (first) ⬚⬚⬚⬚⬚⬚⬚⬚⬚⬚⬚⬚   (M.I.) ☐   (last) ⬚⬚⬚⬚⬚⬚⬚⬚⬚⬚⬚⬚⬚⬚⬚

dress ⬚⬚⬚⬚⬚⬚⬚⬚⬚⬚⬚⬚⬚⬚⬚⬚⬚⬚⬚⬚⬚⬚⬚⬚⬚⬚⬚⬚⬚⬚⬚

y ⬚⬚⬚⬚⬚⬚⬚⬚⬚⬚⬚⬚⬚   State ⬚⬚   Zip ⬚⬚⬚⬚⬚ ⬚⬚⬚⬚

one ⬚⬚⬚ ⬚⬚⬚ ⬚⬚⬚⬚   Fax ⬚⬚⬚ ⬚⬚⬚ ⬚⬚⬚⬚

mpany Name ⬚⬚⬚⬚⬚⬚⬚⬚⬚⬚⬚⬚⬚⬚⬚⬚⬚⬚⬚⬚⬚⬚⬚⬚

mail address ⬚⬚⬚⬚⬚⬚⬚⬚⬚⬚⬚⬚⬚⬚⬚⬚⬚⬚⬚⬚⬚⬚⬚⬚

Please check at least (3) influencing factors for purchasing this book.

ont or back cover information on book .... ☐
ecial approach to the content .... ☐
mpleteness of content.. ☐
uthor's reputation .... ☐
blisher's reputation .... ☐
ook cover design or layout .... ☐
dex or table of contents of book .... ☐
ice of book.. ☐
ecial effects, graphics, illustrations .... ☐
ther (Please specify): _____ ☐

How did you first learn about this book?

aw in Macmillan Computer Publishing catalog .... ☐
ecommended by store personnel .... ☐
aw the book on bookshelf at store .... ☐
ecommended by a friend .... ☐
eceived advertisement in the mail .... ☐
aw an advertisement in: _____ ☐
ead book review in: _____ ☐
ther (Please specify): _____ ☐

How many computer books have you purchased in the last six months?

his book only .... ☐   3 to 5 books..................... ☐
books .... ☐   More than 5 .... ☐

4. Where did you purchase this book?

Bookstore .... ☐
Computer Store .... ☐
Consumer Electronics Store .... ☐
Department Store .... ☐
Office Club .... ☐
Warehouse Club .... ☐
Mail Order .... ☐
Direct from Publisher .... ☐
Internet site .... ☐
Other (Please specify): _____ ☐

5. How long have you been using a computer?

☐ Less than 6 months   ☐ 6 months to a year
☐ 1 to 3 years   ☐ More than 3 years

6. What is your level of experience with personal computers and with the subject of this book?

	With PCs	With subject of book
New	☐	.... ☐
Casual	☐	.... ☐
Accomplished	☐	.... ☐
Expert	☐	.... ☐

Source Code ISBN: 0-7897-1179-6

7. Which of the following best describes your job title?

- Administrative Assistant .... ☐
- Coordinator .... ☐
- Manager/Supervisor .... ☐
- Director .... ☐
- Vice President .... ☐
- President/CEO/COO .... ☐
- Lawyer/Doctor/Medical Professional .... ☐
- Teacher/Educator/Trainer .... ☐
- Engineer/Technician .... ☐
- Consultant .... ☐
- Not employed/Student/Retired .... ☐
- Other (Please specify): _____ ☐

8. Which of the following best describes the area of the company your job title falls under?

- Accounting .... ☐
- Engineering .... ☐
- Manufacturing .... ☐
- Operations .... ☐
- Marketing .... ☐
- Sales .... ☐
- Other (Please specify): _____ ☐

9. What is your age?

- Under 20 ....
- 21-29 ....
- 30-39 ....
- 40-49 ....
- 50-59 ....
- 60-over ....

10. Are you:

- Male ....
- Female ....

11. Which computer publications do you read regularly? (Please list)

_____
_____
_____
_____
_____
_____
_____
_____
_____
_____
_____

Comments: _____
_____
_____

Fold here and scotch-tape to mail

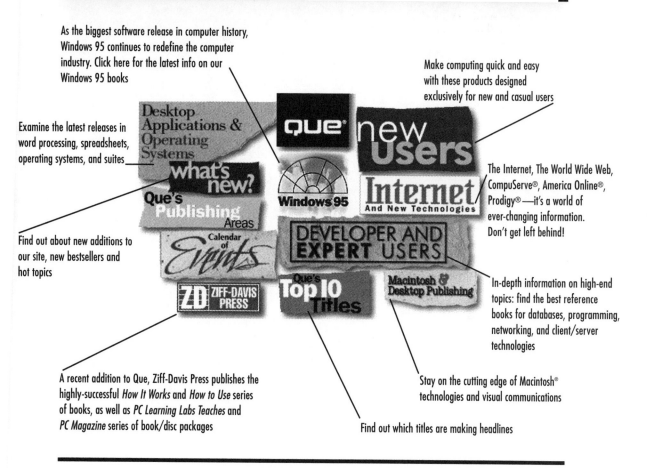

As the biggest software release in computer history, Windows 95 continues to redefine the computer industry. Click here for the latest info on our Windows 95 books

Make computing quick and easy with these products designed exclusively for new and casual users

Examine the latest releases in word processing, spreadsheets, operating systems, and suites

The Internet, The World Wide Web, CompuServe®, America Online®, Prodigy®—it's a world of ever-changing information. Don't get left behind!

Find out about new additions to our site, new bestsellers and hot topics

In-depth information on high-end topics: find the best reference books for databases, programming, networking, and client/server technologies

A recent addition to Que, Ziff-Davis Press publishes the highly-successful *How It Works* and *How to Use* series of books, as well as *PC Learning Labs Teaches* and *PC Magazine* series of book/disc packages

Stay on the cutting edge of Macintosh® technologies and visual communications

Find out which titles are making headlines

With 6 separate publishing groups, Que develops products for many specific market segments and areas of computer technology. Explore our Web Site and you'll find information on best-selling titles, newly published titles, upcoming products, authors, and much more.

- Stay informed on the latest industry trends and products available
- Visit our online bookstore for the latest information and editions
- Download software from Que's library of the best shareware and freeware

Copyright © 1997, Macmillan Computer Publishing-USA, A Viacom Company